During his remarkable career, David Hill has been chairman then managing director of the ABC, chairman of the Australian Football Association, chief executive of the New South Wales railways, chairman of Railways of Australia, director of Australian Airlines, a fellow of the University of Sydney Senate, president of the North Sydney Bears Rugby League Club, chairman of Sydney Water Corporation and chairman of CREATE, a national organisation responsible for representing the interests of young people and children in institutional care. He is the president of the International Association for the Reunification of the Parthenon Sculptures and the author of the bestsellers *The Forgotten Children* and *1788*. He lives in Sydney.

The GOLD RUSH

DAVID HILL

The fever that forever changed Australia

WILLIAM HEINEMANN: AUSTRALIA

A William Heinemann book
Published by Random House Australia Pty Ltd
Level 3, 100 Pacific Highway, North Sydney NSW 2060
www.randomhouse.com.au

First published by William Heinemann in 2010
This edition published in 2011

Addresses for companies within the Random House Group can be found at www.randomhouse.com.au/offices.

National Library of Australia
Cataloguing-in-Publication Entry

Hill, David, 1946–
The Gold Rush/David Hill.

ISBN 978 1 86471 130 1 (pbk).

Gold mines and mining – Australia – History.
Australia – Gold discoveries – Economic aspects.
Australia – Gold discoveries – Social aspects.
Australia – History – 1851–1891.

994.031

Cover design by Adam Yazxhi/MAXCO
Front-cover image: National Archives of Australia, 11423315
Back-cover image: State Library of Western Australia, 019039PD
Internal maps by James Mills-Hicks, www.icecoldpublishing.com
Internal design by Xou, Australia
Typeset in Sabon by Xou, Australia
Printed in Australia by Griffin Press, an accredited ISO AS/NZS 14001:2004 Environmental Management System printer

To Kerry and Ian 'Smiley' Bayliff

Contents

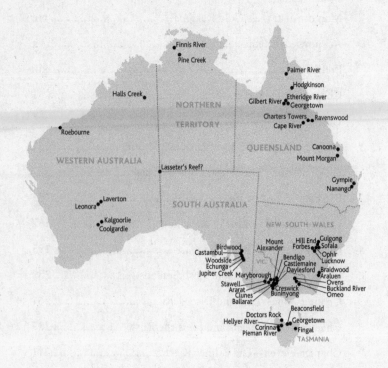

Australia's gold regions

Acknowledgements

It has been possible to tell much of the story of the Australian gold rushes from primary sources. From the mid-nineteenth century, when gold was discovered, there are hundreds of books, diaries, official reports and dispatches, parliamentary reports and inquiries, and scores of highly personal accounts.

I found the New South Wales Mitchell Library collection particularly useful but also discovered valuable material in the State Libraries of Victoria, Queensland, South Australia and Western Australia, the Powerhouse Museum in Sydney and the National Maritime Museum. The task of researching has become even more exciting with many libraries making more and more material available online, particularly the National Library of Australia and the Public Records Office of Victoria.

Also, a great deal of information comes from newspaper stories of the time. This includes not only the big-city papers but also the many newspapers from the goldfields, because practically every significant new goldfield soon had its own paper, even though many lasted only the year or so of the rush.

We are also indebted to the scores of local museums and historical societies around regional Australia – most of which survive with little funding and with only the support of dedicated local volunteers, and without which much of the priceless history of the gold era would be lost. Many of these local museums and historical societies have publications not easily accessed elsewhere. The list includes but is not limited to the following.

In Victoria, the Beechworth Chinese Cultural Centre, Castlemaine Art Gallery and Historical Museum, Chinese Museum (Melbourne), Clunes Museum, Golden Dragon Museum (Bendigo), Eureka Centre and Ballarat Art Gallery.

In New South Wales, the Braidwood and District Historical Society and Braidwood Museum, Gulgong Pioneer Museum, Lambing Flat Folk Museum and Orange Historical Society.

In Queensland, the Charters Towers and Dalrymple Research Group (Charters Towers Library), Gympie District Historical Society, Gympie Gold Mining and History Museum, Maryborough Wide Bay and Burnett Historical Society Museum and Ravenswood Court House Museum.

In South Australia, the Robe National Trust Museum, Old Customs House and Robe Information Centre.

In Western Australia, the Coolgardie Goldfields Exhibition Museum, Maritime Museum (Fremantle), Fremantle Historical Museum and Western Australia Kalgoorlie-Boulder Museum.

Again, I am indebted to my wife, Stergitsa, and my son, Damian, for their support, and my good friend Ian 'Smiley' Bayliff, who helped with much of the research.

I also need to thank a number of friends who helped gather material, including Wade Mahlo, Joe Rainbow, Des Mulcahy, Ted Fardell, Geoff Merrell from Newcrest Gold Mine, Peter Cassimaty, Richard Spencer and Emily Booker. Also, I am again grateful to everyone at Random House, including Kevin O'Brien, Nikki Christer, Alysha Farry and Jess Pearson, for their guidance, help and support.

Preface

In May 1851, the discovery of gold in western New South Wales by Edward Hargraves triggered one of the world's biggest gold rushes. Over the next half a century, gold fever spread from New South Wales to Victoria, New Zealand, Queensland, the Northern Territory, Tasmania and Western Australia. Only South Australia did not experience a major rush. For 50 years, from the mid-nineteenth to the beginning of the twentieth century, hardly a year passed when men were not scrambling to a newly discovered goldfield somewhere in Australia.

Hundreds of thousands hurried from overseas. In the first two years after news of the gold discovery reached Europe, more people arrived in Australia than had come in over 60 years since the First Fleet had arrived to establish the convict colony in 1788.

Gold was attractive because it was one of the few ways in which the overwhelming majority of men, who were poor and had little or no capital, could become rich – and often fabulously so.

The gold era brought sweeping and lasting changes. It produced great wealth and ensured the financial viability of the precarious Australian colonies. It stimulated a dramatic increase to Australia's population, put an end to convict transportation, challenged the British class system, laid the foundations of Australian egalitarianism and played a key role in the establishment of Australia as a nation.

Gold! is the story of the characters who chanced everything to cross great tracts of land and sea in the quest for great wealth. Some succeeded, but many failed. The dangers of the goldfields were legion, and the outcomes far from certain, yet nothing could stop the prospectors from coming in their thousands.

CHAPTER ONE

Hargraves

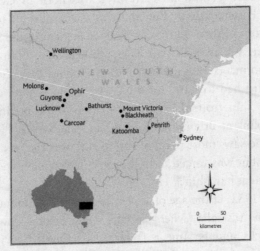

Western New South Wales

'This,' I exclaimed to my guide, 'is a memorable day in
the history of New South Wales. I shall be a baronet,
you will be knighted, and my old horse will be stuffed,
put in a glass case, and sent to the British Museum.'

On a fine summer morning on 12 February 1851, 34-year-old Edward Hargraves left his tiny hotel on horseback and headed north from Guyong along the Lewis Ponds Creek, where later in the day he would find a few specks of gold that would spark the rush that would forever change Australia.

Edward Hammond Hargraves was born in Gosport, near Portsmouth in England, on 7 October 1816, the youngest of three sons of an army lieutenant in the Sussex militia. Whereas his two older brothers were both found appointments with the East India Company Navy Service, Edward had to settle for a job as a cabin boy on a merchant ship from the age of 14, after some preliminary schooling at Brighton and Lewes in East Sussex. He later said he saw 'most parts of the world' over the next three years but was forced to 'toil incessantly' while experiencing 'great hardship'.[1]

In 1832, at the age of 17, Hargraves said he found himself in Australia, where he later bought some cows and bullocks and became a farmer. He recorded very little about his family other than to say that he married and first became a parent at 19, 'which was early enough . . . for a young man to marry, and have the cares and troubles of life crowd in upon him'.[2]

For the next 15 years, he worked as a publican and storekeeper but mainly as a farmer west of Bathurst, more than 200 kilometres from Sydney. The country had been opened up to farming after John Oxley had explored as far west as the Wellington Valley in 1817, which he had named in honour of the Duke of Wellington two years after the Battle of Waterloo.

By the late 1840s, now 33 years old, Hargraves had

little to show for his 15 years in Australia when news reached Sydney in December 1848 of the discovery of large quantities of gold in California.

Hargraves said that few believed the news at first, as 'the very existence of California'[3] was little known in Australia at that time, and there was no regular contact between San Francisco and Sydney. But this all changed when the ship *Colonial Times* arrived in Sydney with gold aboard in February 1849, and, within a month, ships crowded with passengers were leaving Port Jackson bound for California:[4]

> When, in due course, a vessel arrived with 1200 ounces of the precious metal aboard, the most incredulous were convinced. The immediate result was the outpouring of a tide of immigration, which, to compare small things with great, resembled the more recent 'exodus' from Ireland.[5]

In the first six months of 1849, 25 ships full of passengers left from Sydney for California, along with eight from Hobart, two from Adelaide and one from Melbourne.[6] Hargraves said that the discovery of gold in California had a bigger impact on Australia than it had on Britain:

> [If] the discovery of gold on the west coast of north America in the autumn of 1848 . . . at first so astounding . . . could disturb the quiet and the even tenor of the ways of the orderly, industrious and sober minded people of [Britain] . . . how much more must it have excited the inhabitants of Australia – men who for the most part have spent their whole lives in adventure . . . men who have been content, in search of a rude and often precarious

subsistence, to penetrate the dense forests, to make their way over trackless mountains, and locate themselves in far distant spots completely isolated from the haunts of men, except it be those of the native savages of the bush! To men so circumstanced, and so habituated to toilsome adventure, a simple voyage to an unknown and distant land was no impediment.[7]

Confessing that fortune had not smiled so favourably on him since he had first arrived in Australia, Hargraves became one of about 6000 who joined the rush to California[8] when he boarded the *Elizabeth Arden* bound for San Francisco in July 1849. Despite being hard up, he paid enough money to share one of the seven cabins on a ship that also carried 160 steerage passengers as well as cargo. Hargraves's cabin mate was Simpson Davison, who had also come to Australia from England but unlike Hargraves had been a successful farmer running sheep on the western plains of New South Wales.[9]

Davison was the son of a banker from Burlington in Yorkshire. Attracted by a desire for travel and the hope of some 'commercial adventure', he had come to Australia six years earlier. When he migrated, he admitted he knew very little about the place except that it was a successful wool producer, a convict colony and 'a great sandy desert'.[10]

When Davison brought his wool clip down to Sydney in 1849, everyone was talking about the Californian gold finds. After selling his wool, he admitted that he too had 'caught the contagion' and made plans to go to San Francisco as soon as possible:

As I approached Sydney, California was everywhere the

topic of conversation. There were 'California' coaches, and 'California' public houses, and 'California' drapers' shops, to arrest the eye in every thoroughfare. Five or six ships in harbour were laid on for California. Every unemployed man possessing the requisite passage-money was prepared to go to the land of gold.[11]

Cashed up from the sale of his wool, Davison asked a neighbour to care for his sheep and bought £300 of clothing and supplies, which he hoped to sell at a profit when he reached California. The *Elizabeth Arden* left Sydney in July 1849 and, favoured by a strong westerly, passed North Cape, New Zealand, a week later before heading north-east and reaching Pitcairn Island two weeks after that. During their two-day stop at the island, the passengers met the descendants of the *Bounty* mutineers, whose forebears had arrived there some 70 years earlier, including Isaac Christian, the third-generation descendant of Fletcher Christian. After being loaded with fresh water and food, which included pigs, fowls and goats,[12] the ship sailed on to California, arriving in San Francisco in October after a passage of 78 days.

Hargraves said that, as they entered San Francisco harbour, they saw more than 500 sailing ships 'presenting a complete forest of masts' and almost all of them stranded as their crews had fled to join the others in the rush to the goldfields.[13]

As soon as the *Elizabeth Arden* anchored, it too lost its crew, who rushed off to the goldfields leaving only one officer and four apprenticed boys to unload its cargo. Davison, Hargraves and the other passengers agreed to stay and help, which took three weeks, during which time they formed 'amongst us a party of eight, who agreed to join in an expedition to the gold fields'.[14]

At the end of October, after Davison had sold much of the merchandise he had bought in Sydney 'at a profit of 50%',[15] Hargraves and his partners left San Francisco to sail up the San Joaquin River, reaching the boom town of Stockton in three days. They then paid $500, or around £100, to hire a bullock dray of eight steers – with a driver who came from Ohio – to take them and their food and equipment the 113 kilometres to the goldfields.

During their journey, which was beset with bad weather, the men elected a committee, and Hargraves – who at six feet four inches (193 centimetres) tall and weighing 18 stone (114 kilograms) had a commanding presence – was appointed president. A Mr Potts was made secretary and a Mr Surgeon Jeston was made responsible for medical services. Davison was treasurer, because, he said, he owned a good gun. The gun also came in handy for shooting plenty of food along the way, including deer, antelopes, hares, rabbits, ground squirrels, geese, ducks and large Californian quails.

Upon reaching the goldfields, which were near York Town to the east of San Francisco, Hargraves and his colleagues threw themselves into mining – but quickly found that raw enthusiasm was not enough:

> Our first attempt . . . was a complete failure; eight of us worked hard the whole day, and returned to our tent at night, covered with mud from head to foot, with the scanty earnings of ten shillings, or eight pence each.[16]

Hargraves was to say later it was in the first few days of

digging in California that his thoughts were already on the possibility of finding gold in Australia, as the local countryside appeared similar to what he had seen in New South Wales:

> But far more important thoughts than those of present success or failures were, from the very first, growing in my mind, and gradually assuming a body and shape. My attention was naturally drawn to the form and geological structure of the surrounding country, and it soon struck me that I had, some eighteen years before, travelled through a country very similar to the one I was now in, in New South Wales. I said to myself, there are the same class of rocks, slates, quartz, granite, red soil, and everything else that appears necessary to constitute a gold field. So convinced did I become of the similarity of the two countries, that I mentioned my persuasion to my friend Davison, and expressed my belief that we should soon hear of a discovery of gold in that country, and my determination, if it was not discovered before my return to New South Wales, to prosecute a systematic search for it.[17]

When Hargraves shared his theory with his colleagues on the Californian goldfields, they laughed and thought him mad.

Hargraves did his best to make himself comfortable on the goldfields and fashioned a bed with a slate base covered with pine branches, boasting that he would not have 'envied a prince on his bed of down'.[18] But as winter gripped and many neighbouring miners froze to death in the bitter cold along the foothills of the Sierra Nevada mountains, he found 'it was scarcely possible to sleep from the intensity of the cold', and he often 'had to get up at night to shake the snow off the tent, for fear of its breaking through'.[19] He helped stave off the cold by first wrapping himself in a blanket, then two hemp flour sacks that had been wet so the flour had 'formed a sort of paste inside', which provided some additional insulation. He described how he would lower himself into one of the sacks and put the other over his head and shoulders, and this way 'managed pretty effectually to retain the natural warmth of the body' through the winter.

After working through the next five months and meeting with only moderate success, Hargraves returned to San Francisco, where he wrote on 5 March to a colleague in Sydney saying that he believed the country he knew in western New South Wales was likely to be gold-bearing:

> I am very forcibly impressed that I have been in a gold region in New South Wales, within 300 miles [480 kilometres] of Sydney; and unless you know how to find it you might live for a century in the region and know nothing of their existence.[20]

Hargraves was eager to return to Australia but did not do so straight away, later explaining, 'I was unwilling, after having taken so long a voyage in search of fortune, to return no richer than I came.'[21] Over the next five months, he went with his friend Davison to try the diggings in northern California, where they were only marginally more successful than they had been in the previous winter.

Towards the end of 1850, having now spent a year in California, Hargraves returned again to San Francisco and sailed for Sydney on the *Emma*, leaving on 23 November 1850 and arriving on 7 January 1851.

Hargraves was acutely aware that a reward for the discovery of 'payable' gold in New South Wales had remained unclaimed since 1849. The government of the struggling Australian colony had offered it in an attempt to stem the exodus of men to California. By the mid-nineteenth century, Australia was far from booming: 60 years after the establishment of the first British convict settlement, the total population of the country was still below 200,000. The reward was not fixed at a specified amount but would be paid 'in proportion to the value of the alleged discovery, when that was ascertained'.[22]

Hargraves wasted no time after returning to Sydney. Within a few weeks, he borrowed £105 from a friend, the solicitor James Norton,[23] and left alone on horseback to find the gold that he was convinced was in the hills where he had farmed years before:

> It was with an anxious heart, therefore, that I again landed in Sydney in the month of January 1851. On my passage thither and immediately on my arrival, I made known to my friends and companions my confident expectations on the subject; one and all, however, derided me, and treated my views and opinions as those of a madman. Still undaunted, on 5 February I set out from Sydney on horseback alone to cross the Blue Mountains.[24]

At the end of the first day, he reached Penrith, some 50 kilometres west of Sydney, and the following morning took the ferry across the Nepean River and began the climb over the mountains. Two days later, he had passed Mount Victoria and Hartley Vale and reached Bathurst, the major town 200 kilometres west of Sydney on the Macquarie River.

Hargraves had originally intended heading for Carcoar and carried with him a letter of introduction from the Sydney solicitor James Norton to Thomas Icely, who was an influential farmer of the local Coombing Park property. Icely was the son of a shipowner and merchant from Plympton in Devon who had come to make his fortune in Australia in 1820. On reaching Australia, he had become a successful merchant, magistrate, member of parliament and prominent pastoralist and miner in the Carcoar district, around 250 kilometres west of Sydney.

On the road to Carcoar, Hargraves met Icely, who was heading in the other direction towards Sydney. It seems that Icely had recently been offended by allegations made by Dr John Dunmore Lang and was hurrying to Sydney to initiate defamation proceedings. Dunmore Lang had accused Icely of swindling a fellow merchant of his ship and cargo. Hargraves decided to change course and, with the encouragement of Icely, headed for what he believed to be gold-bearing country further to the north:

> I then determined to visit Guyong, where I had been eighteen years before and the neighbourhood of which I believed to be auriferous.[25]

Cutting through the bush, he eventually found himself to the west of the Wellington Road rather than the north and was forced to spend another night camping rough. After reaching Fredericks Valley, which later would become famous as the Lucknow goldfield, he headed east and arrived at the tiny Wellington Inn at Guyong on the main western road from Sydney.

At the time, there were inns for travellers every 15 to

25 kilometres on the main roads from Sydney, but because of the hard economic times the innkeepers Hargraves met along the way were complaining that the squatters travelling to and from Sydney did not have the money for a hotel bed and more often were forced to camp in the bush.[26]

Hargraves stayed at the Wellington Inn for two nights, on 10 and 11 February. It was a good rest for his poor horse, which had carried the big man and his food and supplies for nearly 300 kilometres over the mountains in a little over six days.

By a remarkable coincidence, the owner of the Wellington Inn was someone Hargraves knew: Mrs Susan Lister. She was the widow of the sea captain who had commanded the *Wave*, which Hargraves had worked on as a cabin boy some 20 years before.

Hargraves was to learn that the Lister family had struggled since their arrival in Sydney in 1838. Captain John Lister's shipping agency had failed in its fifth year and Lister had lost all of his assets. He returned to seafaring, but the following year, 1844, his ship, the *Perseverance*, was wrecked off Stradbroke Island near Brisbane, and Captain Lister was again broke, as neither the ship nor its cargo was insured.

Lister then decided to find work in the country but, while travelling west across the mountains from Sydney, the family was robbed by highwaymen near Tarana, east of Bathurst, where they lost all of their money and belongings.

Luckily, when the family reached Bathurst, Lister was able to secure a job as the manager of a roadside hotel called the Robin Hood and Little John Inn in March 1846, at a spot called the Rocks, 20 kilometres west of Bathurst.

Things at last seemed to be going well for Lister when he later opened his own hotel, the Wellington Inn at Guyong, a further 20 kilometres west of the Rocks, but on 12 August 1850 he was killed when he was thrown from his cart on a business trip into Bathurst.

When Hargraves arrived at Guyong six months after Lister's death, the Wellington Inn was being run by Lister's widow and her 18-year-old son, John, who two days later would show Hargraves the way north along the Lewis Ponds Creek in the search for gold. Hargraves said that in addition to asking the Listers for help in providing a local guide, he also borrowed tools from them for prospecting:

> The landlady of the Guyong Inn [Wellington Inn], Mrs. Lister, had seen better days. I had known her during her husband's lifetime. She is now a widow. It occurred to me that I could not prosecute my plans efficiently without assistance . . . After dinner, therefore, I disclosed to her the object of my visit, and begged her to procure a black fellow as a guide to the spot I wished to visit first . . . She entered with a woman's heartiness into my views, and offered me the assistance of her son, a youth of eighteen years of age, who, she assured me, knew the country well.[27]

The next, fateful morning, 12 February, after two nights' rest at the inn, Hargraves rode off with John Lister north down the Lewis Ponds Creek – a tributary of the Summer Hill Creek, which, in turn, ran into the Macquarie River around 50 kilometres to the north.

The two men travelled 24 kilometres along the creek – as there were no established roads[28] – and, when they reached Yorkey's Corner (which was named after a shepherd named Yorkey who kept his hut there on the Lewis Ponds Creek above the junction with the Summer Hill Creek), Hargraves said he became overwhelmed by the occasion:

> I found myself in the country that I was so anxiously longing to behold. My recollection of it had not deceived me. The resemblance of its formation to that of California could not be mistaken. I felt myself surrounded by gold; and with tremendous anxiety panted for the moment of trial, when my magician's wand should transform this trackless wilderness into a region of countless wealth.[29]

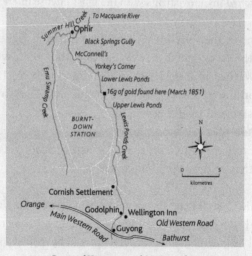

Route of Hargraves and Lister on their successful search for gold

At the time Hargraves and Lister reached Yorkey's Corner, the country was in the grip of a drought, and most of the Lewis Ponds Creek was dried up. When they found a small amount of water, they stopped to give the horses a drink, and they had a lunch of cold beef, damper and tea. Hargraves later said Lister was astonished when he announced that they were surrounded by gold:

> We now turned out our horses; and seated ourselves on the turf, as it was necessary to satisfy our cravings of hunger before I ventured on my grand experiment . . . My guide went for a drink of water, and, after making a hasty repast, I told him we were now in the goldfields, and the gold was under his feet as he went to fetch the water for our dinner. He stared with incredulous amazement, and, on my telling him that I would now find some gold, watched my movements with the most intense interest.[30]

Hargraves then used a pick to dig a ditch at right angles from the creek and a trowel to collect the earth, which he then washed in a gold pan in the watering hole. The first trial produced a speck of gold. In the next five, he found specks of gold in all but one.

While they were only tiny samples, it was enough for Hargraves to write later that 'no further proof was necessary' that gold was in abundance:

> 'This,' I exclaimed to my guide, 'is a memorable day in the history of New South Wales. I shall be a baronet, you will be knighted, and my old horse will be stuffed, put in a glass case, and sent to the British Museum.'[31]

Hargraves was able to dispense with any notion of modesty and declare, 'At that instant I felt myself to be a great man.' He returned that night to Mrs Lister's inn at Guyong, where he wrote a 'memorandum of the discovery', which he was later to give to the colonial secretary in Sydney as a 'memorial of the great event'.[32] He then set about trying to establish the scope of his find:

> More, however, was to be done before I could make public my discovery. It was necessary to ascertain over what extent of country in that district the same formation prevailed, in order to arrive at some notion of the probable extent of the goldfields.[33]

Over the next few weeks, with John Lister and one of Lister's friends, James Tom, Hargraves scoured the land for almost 50 kilometres to the Macquarie River. James Tom knew the country well. His family was part of a small village that was located a few kilometres north of the Wellington Inn called the 'Cornish Settlement', which included a number of families who had come to Australia to work as farmers and copper miners.

During their search along what was to become the extensive Bunandong diggings, Hargraves and his two young colleagues found no significant gold deposits, but Hargraves was later to claim that he was at least 'satisfied . . . of the auriferous character of the country'.[34] More than a week later, the three returned to Guyong, and after several days' rest James Tom left to take delivery of a herd of cattle from the Bogan River about 350 kilometres to the north-west, and his younger brother William took his place in the search for gold.[35] Hargraves then suggested that Lister and William Tom head north-east to the Turon River, while he went north again to explore the Macquarie River area and to visit the farm of a squatter named Cruickshank, who Hargraves said was an old friend.

Cruickshank and his wife were doubtful of Hargraves's claims that the area was rich with gold, so he took them outside the farmhouse to prove his point:

> [O]n my asserting that I felt sure we could find gold – fine, probably in small quantities – at their very door, we all three started to the river with a tin dish and spade; and, sure enough, the first pan of earth produced gold.[36]

Hargraves returned again to Guyong on 10 March having found only a tiny amount of gold but described the area as 'a good deal of promising country'.[37]

Hargraves admitted that by now he was anxious that someone else might claim the government reward before him, so he headed off to Sydney, arriving in late March, more than six weeks after having set out on his quest for gold.

Before leaving, he swore John Lister and William Tom to secrecy and showed them how to build and use a wooden cradle, which was capable of processing much more dirt than the pan. Hargraves had become familiar with the cradle in California, where it was also called the 'rocker'. It was a wooden box, less than a metre long and fitted with a series of trays of increasing lengths. Water was used to flush the soil cascading down through the trays, where the heavier gold particles were caught on the rim of each tray, or 'riffle'. A lever or handle protruding from the top of the box was used to shake, or rock, the trays of soil – hence the name 'cradle'. In California, it was usually operated by a team, with one man or more digging and shovelling soil into the box while another rocked the cradle and others fed water into it. While Hargraves was away, John Lister and William Tom went off with the cradle to look for more gold.

Arriving in Sydney after a four-day journey, Hargraves had to wait a week before being given an audience with Mr Edward Deas Thomson, the colonial secretary, because Thomson was committed to attending the Legislative Council of Parliament, which was still in session. On the morning of their meeting, Hargraves was caught in a torrential downpour and had to wait three hours in a wet coat before being ushered in to see the secretary.[38] When the two men finally met, Hargraves showed Thomson his specks of gold, which he later admitted were so small that they could be held 'on a three penny piece':

> Mr Thomson evidently doubted the truth of my story, and remarked that it was very strange the Government geologist had not found it, if it existed in natural deposit, as I represented. I told him I had come from California for the purpose of making the discovery, and there it was. I added that I believed the fields to be as rich as those of California; but that I expected to be rewarded for the discovery in a measure commensurate with its importance to the Government and the country at large.[39]

The following day, Hargraves was granted a longer meeting at which he was asked to put his claim in writing. According to Hargraves, Thomson told him that the discovery of gold would have a huge impact on the country:

> If this is a gold country, Mr. Hargraves, it will stop the Home Government from sending us any more convicts, and prevent emigration to California; but it comes on us

like a clap of thunder, and we are scarcely prepared to credit it.[40]

On 3 April 1851, Hargraves wrote to Thomson seeking £500 compensation for the expenses he had already incurred and a reward for having found payable gold. He wrote the letter from East Gosford, a town about 70 kilometres north of Sydney, where he was staying with his wife and daughters:[41]

> I would . . . leave it to the generosity of the Government, after the importance of my discoveries and disclosures have been ascertained to make me an additional reward commensurate with the benefit likely to accrue to the government and to the country.[42]

Hargraves had to wait almost two weeks with his family before he received a reply. In a letter dated 15 April, Thomson acknowledged Hargraves's claim and said that the size of the reward 'must entirely depend upon its nature and value when made known, and be left to the liberal consideration which the Government would be disposed to give it'.[43]

Now that Hargraves believed his claim for the reward was safe, he deliberately embarked on stirring up public interest and sparking a gold rush. He had, after all, still only been able to present a few specks of gold, and the size of any reward would be much higher if more gold was found in the region he had flagged to the government:

> I was anxious to draw public interest to my discovery, and induce as many persons as possible to set about digging

for the precious metal. To this end I proceeded at once to Bathurst, and everywhere, as I went along, I made known the fact of my discovery.[44]

To some extent, the cat was already out of the bag when, on 4 April, Hargraves's old friend Enoch Rudder wrote to the *Sydney Morning Herald* that 'a goldfield has been discovered extending over a tract of land of country about 300 miles [480 kilometres] in length'.

The Hargraves-generated publicity worked, and by the time he reached Bathurst several weeks later there were already hundreds of miners clambering to find their fortunes along the Lewis Ponds and Summer Hill Creeks.

On 2 May, the *Sydney Morning Herald* ran the first big story, giving credit to Hargraves:

THE GOLD DISCOVERY

It is no longer any secret that gold has been found in the earth in several places in the western country. The fact was first established on 12 February 1851, by Mr. E. H. Hargraves, a resident of Brisbane Water, who returned from California a few months since. While in California, Mr. Hargraves felt persuaded that from the similarity of geological formation there must be gold in several districts of this colony, and when he returned here his expectations were realized . . . The subject was brought under the consideration of the Government, who admitted Mr. Hargraves' claim for some consideration for the discovery, but of course could make no definite promise until the value of the gold field was ascertained. Mr. Stutchbury, the Geological Surveyor, is now in the district, and Mr. Hargraves has proceeded there to communicate with him, and in a few weeks we may expect definite information.

The government had instructed its only geologist, Samuel Stutchbury, to 'make a strict examination' of Hargraves's claim and report at the 'earliest convenience'.[45] The 52-year-old London-born Stutchbury had been appointed as the first government geologist in New South Wales and had arrived in Sydney only a few months earlier, in November 1850. His appointment had followed a letter from the colony's governor, Charles FitzRoy, to the colonial secretary, Earl Grey, in London the previous March suggesting an assessment be made of the 'mineral resources of Australia, since the colony was by now losing a large number of men to the Californian Gold Fields'.[46] Stutchbury was recommended for the job by the president of the Royal Geological Society, Sir Roderick Murchison.

Stutchbury was no stranger to Australia, as he had visited 25 years earlier as a geologist and marine botanist with the Pacific Pearl Fisheries and had written about a number of the country's native marine organisms. After returning to England, he had worked as a natural-history-museum curator in Bristol.

Hargraves was asked to provide Stutchbury with the exact locations of the gold finds, which Hargraves had delineated as 'Lewis Ponds and Summer Hill Creeks, Macquarie and Turon Rivers, in the Districts of Bathurst and Wellington'.[47]

While Hargraves had been in Sydney claiming his reward, John Lister and William Tom had continued mining in the same districts and had found a significant amount of gold, including a small nugget. When the young men and Hargraves met up again on 6 May, Hargraves agreed to formalise a partnership in a gold-mining company with Lister and Tom.

On 8 May, Hargraves organised a public meeting at the Carriers Arms Inn in Bathurst and told a packed audience about the gold in their region. At the time, Bathurst was a town of only about 2500 people living in 400 dwellings, most of which were small and built of timber. Both the *Sydney Morning Herald* and the *Bathurst Free Press* reported favourably on the speech.

A few days later, on 13 May, Edward Hargraves and Samuel Stutchbury finally reached the junction of Lewis Ponds and Summer Hill Creeks and encountered hundreds of miners already digging for gold.

Stutchbury's first report to the New South Wales governor, Sir Charles FitzRoy, about gold was guarded:

> I have the honour to inform you (hastily to save a post) that having been two to three hours at the gold diggings, I have seen sufficient to prove to me the existence of grain gold. Of course I cannot say more at the present moment, but will write again by the next mail.[48]

At the junction of the two creeks, the first rudimentary township of the gold rush had sprung up. It had already been given the name of Ophir, after the town in the Old Testament's Book of Kings that was a source of King Solomon's wealth. While Hargraves later claimed that he had named the town, it was more likely named by William Tom Snr, a local Wesleyan lay preacher and father of James and William.

On location, Hargraves was able to present Stutchbury

with 21 grains of fine gold in just three hours. Seeing this success, and the successes of Lister and Tom and many other miners now at the site, Stutchbury was satisfied. In another hastily written letter to Governor FitzRoy, he confirmed on 19 May that plenty of gold was being found. He also warned of signs of chaos, as desperate diggers descended on the goldfields:

> I have the honour to inform you, that since my last communication, gold has been obtained in considerable quality, many persons with merely a tin dish or other inefficient apparatus having obtained one to two ounces a day . . . The number of persons engaged at work and about the diggings (that is, occupying about one mile [1.6 kilometres] of the creek) cannot be less than 400, and of all classes . . . I fear, unless something is done quickly, that much confusion will arise in consequence of people setting up claims, &c; at present everything is quiet; many people are entirely without food, and stores are not to be got, although I hear some are on the road, which I hope will speedily arrive.
>
> . . . Excuse this written in pencil, as there is no ink yet in the city of Ophir.[49]

Such was the mad rush that the local copper mine at the Cornish Settlement south of Ophir was closed, as the miners abandoned it in favour of the gold diggings, leaving six drays loaded with copper ore with no one to move them.

The *Sydney Morning Herald* reported on 19 May that 'the business of the town [of Bathurst] was utterly paralyzed':

A complete mental madness appears to have seized every member of the community, and as a natural consequence there has been a universal rush to the diggings. Any attempt to describe the numberless scenes – grave, gay, and ludicrous – which have arisen out of this state of things, would require the graphic power of Dickens . . . we have heard of a great number who have started without any provision but a blanket and some rude implements to dig with. Such is the intensity of the excitement that people appear almost regardless of their present comfort, and think of nothing but gold. Of course all this must end in disappointment.

The next day, the *Herald* reported that the government was satisfied with Hargraves's claim, and on 3 June the government approved an initial payment of £500 and appointed him commissioner for Crown lands with the responsibility for finding more gold. For his job as commissioner, he was paid an annual salary of £250 and supplied with a covered wagon, two horses and an escort of two mounted policemen.

¤

Hargraves was not the only person with a legitimate claim to being the first to discover gold in Australia. Nor was he even the first to prospect for gold to the west of the Blue Mountains, and when he went looking in February 1851 it is highly probable that he was aware of some of the earlier finds.

The first known recorded discovery of gold in Australia had occurred a quarter of a century earlier, in 1823, when a government surveyor, James McBrien, surveying west of the Blue Mountains near Rylstone, found 'numerous particles of gold convenient to the river'.[50] In these early years of the convict colony, however, there was little official enthusiasm for gold, which was seen as a potentially destabilising threat to the settlement.

Three other men – John Lhotsky, Count Paul Edmund de Strzelecki and Reverend William Braithwaite Clarke – also claimed to have found gold in New South Wales, in 1834, 1839 and 1841 respectively. All of them encountered the same opposition from the authorities, who feared the prospect of gold could encourage an uprising among the majority convict population.

According to Reverend Clarke, he had gone with his discovery to the vice-regal country residence in Parramatta Park, about 20 kilometres west of Sydney, to meet the unwell governor Sir Charles Gipps, whose wife asked Clarke to stay and spend some time with her sick husband. When Clarke presented his gold samples, Sir Charles was unimpressed and dismissed the issue with the comment, 'Put it away Mr Clarke, before we all have our throats cut.'[51]

Clarke was one of a number of people to later assert that Hargraves would have been aware of these earlier discoveries before he embarked on his own search. He was partially successful in his complaints. In 1853, a select committee of the New South Wales Parliament recommended Clarke be paid a reward of £1000, and he was also to receive a £1000 reward from the Victorian Colonial Government.

Hargraves's old gold partner in California, Simpson Davison, was later to admit that his friend knew of the earlier gold finds in New South Wales before he began his search. He said that what attracted Hargraves to the area west of Bathurst was not, as Hargraves had suggested, the similarities of the terrain but his reading about the earlier discoveries some years earlier and then seeing gold samples from western New South Wales displayed in Sydney:

> That Mr. Hargraves did eventually make his first trials in the Western Districts is, I believe, entirely attributable to his seeing . . . in Sydney samples of the precious metal in the matrix of auriferous quartz veins, which had been already discovered in the districts beyond Bathurst.[52]

Another to come forward to challenge Hargraves and claim credit for having found gold earlier was the president of the Royal Geological Society, Sir Roderick Murchison – even though he had never been to Australia. Sir Roderick had initially based his assertions about the auriferous nature of eastern Australia on gold and ore specimens brought back to England by Count de Strzelecki in 1844, which Murchison compared with some ores from the Ural Mountains of Russia. In 1846, Murchison gave a lecture in Penzance, Cornwall, that urged local tin miners to migrate to 'New South Wales and there obtain gold from ancient alluvia'.[53]

Following the publication of his views, Murchison was sent more gold samples from Mr William Tipple Smith of Sydney, who said they were found on the western side of the Blue Mountains in New South Wales.

Smith was another claimant himself. On 24 January 1849, he took his gold to Deas Thomson and asked that his discoveries be shown to Sir Charles FitzRoy. He also asked whether he was entitled to a government reward for finding it. Deas Thomson wrote back to him in June 1850 using almost the exact words he would use in response to Hargraves a year later, saying that Smith must make known the location of his gold and that the size of the reward would depend on the size of the discovery.

Smith did not provide the location of the gold to the government, but he did record it in a memo addressed to John Korff, who was then the secretary to the Fitzroy Iron Works. It was precisely the spot where Hargraves would go in February the following year:

> Lewis Ponds Creek and Yorkey's Corner, these are very deep in which is the Quartz Rock which contains the Gold.[54]

After the announcement of Hargraves's success, Smith wrote again to Deas Thomson saying he was entitled to the reward. However, Thomson told Smith that he had not provided the exact location of the gold to the government and was 'clearly not entitled to any remuneration whatsoever'.[55]

Perhaps unsurprisingly, the most bitter and protracted opposition to Hargraves came from John Lister and the Tom brothers. The three young men disputed Hargraves immediately after his claim was recognised by the government, and together they would embark on a tireless campaign involving petitions and parliamentary inquiries that would last 40 years.

On 6 June 1851, only a matter of days after Hargraves was appointed commissioner for Crown lands, William Tom wrote to Colonial Secretary Deas Thomson claiming a share of his reward. Then, six months later, after failing to get a satisfactory reply, he wrote directly to Governor FitzRoy, claiming that he, his brother, James, and John Lister were Hargraves's partners and therefore entitled to a share in the government reward:

> [W]e are not altogether unwarranted in requesting some remuneration from the Government for the expense we of necessity incurred, in developing one of the richest pecuniary resources of the colony.[56]

Over the next year, their agitation against Hargraves resulted in the New South Wales Parliament agreeing to refer the question of who found the gold to a select committee for investigation.

By the end of 1852, the controversy had grown. In December, when Hargraves was being feted at an extravagant dinner in Melbourne, and two months before an equally grand banquet was scheduled in his honour in Sydney to commemorate the second anniversary of his gold discovery, he was the subject of some bitter criticism in the New South Wales Parliament.

The Legislative Council of New South Wales was Australia's first parliament. It was established in 1823 with a limited voting franchise, which meant its membership was dominated by owners of large farms and others from the propertied class. During a debate on the allocation of budget funds to the government's gold department, a number of parliamentarians said that no money should go to Hargraves.[57]

George Robert Nichols said that Hargraves's salary as commissioner for Crown lands should be terminated as he was at the time looking for goldfields for the Victorian Government and being celebrated in Melbourne. Nichols was supported by W. C. Wentworth, who dismissed Hargraves as a 'very shallow and impertinent person' who should not be paid a 'farthing'.

Deas Thomson attempted to defend Hargraves, saying that he was on approved leave in Melbourne and that to cut his pay would be 'very scurvy treatment'.

Mr William McLeay was not persuaded and responded to Thomson by calling Hargraves 'an imposter'.

The following year, the parliament decided to formally investigate Hargraves's claims after the tabling of a petition from John Lister and James and William Tom, which was presented to the parliament by James Bligh:

> A Petition from William Tom, junior, and James Tom, both of Springfield, near Bathurst, and John Lister, of Guyong, near Bathurst . . . representing their claim to be associated with Mr. Edward Hammond Hargraves, as the first discoverers of gold in Australia, and praying that their case may be taken into consideration.[58]

Three weeks later, on 29 June 1853, in the parliament building in Macquarie Street in Sydney, the inquiry first took evidence from Hargraves, who rejected the claim of Lister and the Tom brothers that they had found gold in the area before he arrived and alleged Lister had admitted to him 'he had never seen any gold in his life' before. He also rejected it was Lister's idea that they go looking for gold along the Lewis Ponds Creek.

Hargraves admitted he had not told Lister or the Toms that the reason he was going to Sydney was to claim the reward for discovering gold and said 'it was a matter they had no concern in'.

As to the critical question of whether they had a partnership agreement, Hargraves was emphatic:

No; the only arrangement made was, that they should have first diggings when the diggings were opened out.

Hargraves did, however, admit that he had at one stage described Lister and Tom as 'colleagues' in a letter, rather than 'guides', but 'might have used the word "colleague" improperly'.

The next day, William Tom gave his evidence. Tom said he had joined in a partnership with Hargraves when his brother, James, had left to take delivery of some cattle. He claimed that Hargraves had taken a quarter of the gold the young men had found when he was in Sydney as his 'share' in the partnership. He also claimed that Hargraves only paid for the gold later so he could describe it as a purchase and not an entitlement as a partner. In addition, Tom said that he, his brother and John Lister all believed Hargraves would include them – and their discoveries of gold – in the claim for a government reward.

A week after William Tom gave his evidence, it was John Lister's turn. On 6 July, Lister described to the committee how Hargraves had first arrived at the Wellington Inn at Guyong on 10 February 1851 and how, when he gave his name, Lister's widowed mother remembered him as the cabin boy who more than 20 years before had worked for her sea-captain husband.

Under questioning from Deas Thomson, Lister admitted it was Hargraves who chose the spot and washed the gold in the pan on the first day of its discovery, as Hargraves had claimed:

> Question: Who do you consider to be the discoverer of gold?
>
> Answer: We are duly indebted to Mr. Hargraves for the theory, but the Toms and myself are entitled to a portion of the reward for the discovery of a gold field worth working. Had Mr. Hargraves not joined me at the time he would most probably have gone to Wellington.
>
> Question: The discovery of gold was due to Mr. Hargraves?
>
> Answer: Yes.

Lister insisted, however, that while Hargraves may have been the first to find gold, it was he and the Tom brothers who found workable or 'payable' gold:

> Question: What is the merit of your claim? Is it the merit of having discovered gold in the first instance, or having discovered a workable goldfield in New South Wales?
>
> Answer: The merit of having discovered a workable goldfield.

At the end of its inquiry, the committee found something to support both sides. In their report to parliament in September 1853, they concluded that Hargraves was entitled to the full reward but also that the Toms and Lister be given a small reward – thus ensuring the controversy would continue:

> As regards the proposed gratuity of £5000 to Mr. Hargraves on the grounds that he was the first discoverer of

the auriferous wealth of the colony, your committee having taken a good deal of evidence, and among other witnesses have examined Mr. Hargraves himself, as well as Mr. John Lister, who with Messrs. William Tom junior, and Mr. James Tom, have presented a Petition to your Honourable House, setting forth their claim to the participation of this gratuity. The result of this evidence has been to satisfy your committee that Mr. Hargraves returned to the colony from California for the express purpose of searching for gold; that he showed the Petitioners the Californian method of obtaining gold by cradles; that while on the course of this instruction, and in the company of John Lister, he found some minute particles of gold; that shortly after John Lister and James Tom returned to a spot on the Ophir Creek, called FitzRoy Bar, and proved that gold in remunerating quantities could be procured there. Mr. Hargraves, it is clear, taught them how to find gold, which they eventually obtained. Your committee, therefore, approve of the proposed gratuity to him, though they think that Messrs. Lister and Tom are also entitled to a gratuity of £1000, which accordingly by recommendation should be accorded to them.[59]

When the report went to the parliament for approval, Deas Thomson recommended that Hargraves's reward of £5000 be increased to £10,000. Despite some opposition from those in the chamber who had already publicly attacked him, the motion was supported by a vote of 35 to 5.

Lister and the Tom brothers were far from satisfied, and over the ensuing decades they would become progressively more strident in their attacks on Hargraves. In 1871, frustrated that they had still been unable to discredit him, the three, now all in their 40s, published 'History of the Discovery of the First Payable Gold-field (Ophir) in Australia', in which they accused Hargraves of 'deception' and being an 'extraordinary failure'.

Hargraves was not totally without supporters and had friends as well as enemies in the New South Wales Parliament, who still believed he was entitled to a continued reward. In 1875, he was voted a life pension of £250 a year from the government, which was in addition to the £10,000 he had been granted more than 20 years earlier and the pay he had received as commissioner for Crown lands for two years in the 1850s.[60]

But Lister and the Tom brothers were not done yet. In 1890, nearly 40 years after the original argument, when the three were in their 60s and Hargraves was 74, they succeeded in persuading the New South Wales Parliament to have yet another inquiry. Hargraves was at the time incapacitated with a broken leg and fractured ribs, so the parliamentary committee traipsed from parliament to take his evidence in the house in which he was staying in the Sydney inner-city suburb of Forest Lodge.

On the day John Lister was scheduled to give evidence, 17 September 1890, he died. The parliamentary committee had to rely on the handwritten notes he had prepared for the hearings. Within eight days of Lister's death, his son, daughter and sister – who was married to his friend, William Tom – all died of the same influenza virus.

Two months later, on 17 December 1890, the committee tabled its findings, which were quite different from the earlier findings and at last gave some comfort to the Lister and Tom families:

(a) Although Mr. Hargraves is entitled to credit for teaching the Tom brothers and Lister how to use a dish and cradle and the proper methods of searching for gold; the Petitioners were undoubtedly the first discoverers of payable gold in Australia.

(b) Payable gold was unknown in the colony until April 1851 when the Petitioners found four ounces and handed it over to Mr. Hargraves who used it to gain his title and Government reward.

(c) Considering the trade stagnation prior to the gold discovery and the marked improvement that followed, the Committee consider that the Petitioners have not been rewarded sufficiently.

(d) Mr. Hargraves seems to have abandoned his search until the Petitioners advised him of their find while he was over 100 miles [160 kilometres] away. Mr. Hargraves acknowledges its receipt and that he took it to the Government, which no doubt caused the famous Proclamation to be issued by Governor FitzRoy. As a result, a new era and great strides in progress have followed ever since.

The following year, on 29 October 1891, Hargraves himself died. But, in another remarkable twist to the saga, only a week after his passing the full parliament found in his favour by rejecting the findings of the committee. According to a report, the 'House, as a whole, took little interest in the debate' and the committee was voted down by a vote of 39 to 23.[61]

Hargraves would die not knowing that his claim was,

after 40 years, still safe. He was buried in the Waverley Cemetery in Sydney, and his gravestone credits him for the discovery of gold:

EDWARD HAMMOND HARGRAVES
BORN ENG. 7/10/1816
DIED 29/10/1891
THE ORIGINAL DIGGER WHOSE
GOLD DISCOVERY STARTED THE
GREAT AUSTRALIAN GOLD RUSH IN 1851

CHAPTER TWO

Sydney: The First Rush

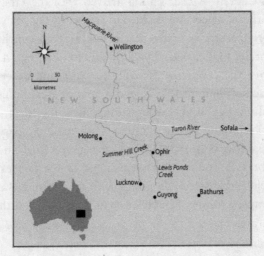

The first New South Wales diggings

No words can describe the excitement occasioned
in all classes of society by the announcement . . .
In less than a week the diminution of the street
population of Sydney was very visible . . .

Australia's first gold rush in May 1851 threw Sydney into turmoil as thousands of its citizens hurried over the Blue Mountains on the 250-kilometre trek to reach the goldfields around Ophir.

At the time, Sydney was a market town of around 60,000 people. It had been established 63 years before, when Captain Arthur Phillip arrived with the First Fleet of British convicts and decided to create the convict colony in Port Jackson in preference to Botany Bay, which is 12 kilometres to the south. By 1851, the city was the principal port for the export of the colony's wool and other farm products. It had also developed a host of local industries, including soap- and candle-making, distilling, sugar-refining, cloth manufacture, tanning, snuff-making, glass- and porcelain-working, salting and meat preserving, and iron and brass founding.[1] Although most of the houses were humble single-storey dwellings with no running water or sewerage, a guide to intended migrants described the city as attractive:

> [The town] now extends a length of two miles [3.2 kilometres] along the shores of the bay, presenting an elegant and uniform appearance that could scarcely be excelled by that of any English town of a similar size. Not only has it a number of beautiful buildings, but the long ranges of warehouses, factories and private stores, give the city an air of European civilization.[2]

By the time the first reports of Hargraves's discovery appeared in the *Sydney Morning Herald*, rumours of the gold finds had already been swirling throughout the city for some days, and the paper described the first gold specimens arriving in Sydney from Ophir on 15 May as causing 'a great sensation'.[3]

A week later, in the first of many dispatches sent about the gold to the colonial secretary in London, Sir Charles FitzRoy warned that the rush was already 'unhinging the minds of all classes of society'.[4]

The 55-year-old aristocrat FitzRoy had held a number of senior British Government positions before being appointed governor in Australia six years earlier but nothing in his long and distinguished career had prepared him for the turmoil of the gold rush that hit Sydney.

Born in 1796, the son of General Lord Charles FitzRoy, young Charles Augustus was sent to Harrow school at the age of nine before joining the Horse Guards when he was 16. At 20, he was promoted to captain, and at 25 lieutenant colonel before serving five years as the British deputy adjutant general in Cape Town. In 1831, at 35, he retired from the army and became the MP for Bury Saint Edmunds, a constituency controlled by his family. He then took appointments as lieutenant governor to the British possessions of the Leeward Islands in the West Indies and Prince Edward Island in Canada before being offered the more senior job of governor to New South Wales as the replacement for Sir George Gipps, who was being recalled.

FitzRoy and the local colonial authorities were powerless to control the events following the discovery of gold, other than to suggest it would be unwise to 'increase the excitement'.[5] The colony's deputy military chief, Colonel Godfrey Mundy, noted how Sydney's population rapidly began to empty as hundreds of eager gold seekers headed off to the diggings:

No words can describe the excitement occasioned in all classes of society by the announcement . . . In less than a week the diminution of the street population of Sydney was very visible, while Parramatta, previously half deserted, became dissipated.[6]

By late May, there were already between 500 and 600 people digging at the junction of the Lewis Ponds and Summer Hill Creeks, and a Sydney resident noted how the city shops quickly transformed their businesses to handle the demand for supplies and provisions for those wanting to join the rush to the gold:

Sydney assumed an entirely new aspect. The shop fronts put on new faces. Wares suited to the wants and tastes of general purchasers were thrust ignominiously out of sight, and outfits for gold mining only were displayed. Blue and red serge shirts, Californian hats, leather belts . . . mining boots, blankets, white and scarlet . . . The pavements were lumbered with picks, pans and pots, and the gold washing machine, or Virginian 'cradle', hitherto a stranger to our eyes, became in two days a familiar household utensil, for scores of them were paraded for purchase.[7]

It seems everyone was trying to capitalise on the gold frenzy. From late May 1851, advertisements appeared in the *Sydney Morning Herald* for everything from chocolate and cordial to finding prospecting teammates:

SHOVELS SHOVELS
50 DOZEN Lyndon's best diamond pointed Miners Shovels
On Sale at the Stores of

A, GRAVENY
320 Pitt-street
Sydney
Every description of tool required for a miners outfit,
which being manufactured on the premises, is warranted
to be of good quality –
Cradles, various kinds
Long Toms
Miners and common picks
Mauls and wedges
Crow bars, axes and tomahawks
Prospecting pans
Zinc and galvanized iron buckets
Balers, quartz and pints
Camp kettles, &c, &c

GOLD BOXES, FOR SHIPPERS

**A SUPERIOR DOUBLE-BARREL GUN,
ON A NEW PRINCIPLE**

LAVER AND CO's OPHIR CORDIAL
No one who values his health or comfort should proceed
to the Gold Field without a supply

CHOCOLATE
Every miner should provide himself with Peek & Co's
superior flake chocolate

GOLD MINES
Two strong, able young gentlemen are desirous of joining
some respectable parties in making up a proper number
for the Gold Field. They are prepared to contribute a
reasonable sum.

For the remainder of 1851, the rush to the goldfields was restricted to those already in Australia, as news of its discovery would not reach the outside world until September. It was not until the following year that the massive influx of prospectors from overseas began.

At the time, gold was worth more than £3 an ounce, when the annual wage for a labourer was between £20 and £30. Finding gold was one of the few ways that the overwhelming majority of people who had little or no access to capital could become rich.

Those on horseback took about five days to reach the goldfields, while most walked and took at least twice as long. Some of the walkers paid for their tools and supplies to be carried on a hired dray but most carried everything on their backs or in wheelbarrows. The cost of hiring a cart to take provisions to Ophir rose dramatically from four shillings and sixpence a ton at the beginning of the rush to 30 shillings a ton only three months later. The cost of food at the diggings also shot up. Flour, which could be bought at £25 a ton in Sydney, was costing more than double that near the goldfields.

Already, there was a roaring trade in the manufacture and sale of the wooden cradles in Sydney, which were being sold at around £1 each, and very soon a small army of carpenters was struggling to keep up with the demand to build them at the goldfields of Ophir.

The long line of prospectors looked similar in appearance to those who had left San Francisco for the Sierra Nevada Hills of California two years earlier. They wore the same hats, serge shirts and leather belts as the 'forty-niners' (named after the year 1849) and carried the same picks and pans. Many of the miners wore plaited-grass or cabbage-tree hats, or wide-awake felts, sometimes slouched in the later army fashion that allowed the rifle to be carried at the slope. They wore thick-soled boots and muddy trousers held up by red or green sashes instead of belts. Their red or blue shirts with rolled-up sleeves hung loosely outside their trousers.[8]

In another similarity with the California diggings, many of the Ophir diggers were armed. Guns would become a regular feature of the Australian gold rushes over the next five decades and would be used by the diggers to protect their nuggets and hunt for food. But, later, the guns would also be used increasingly for armed hold-ups and murders.

Colonel Godfrey Mundy was at the horse races west of Sydney a week after the rush began and saw the gold seekers pouring out of the city and heading for the goldfields in their droves:

> Driving on these two days to the races at Homebush – the Epsom of Sydney, ten miles [16 kilometres] from the city – I counted nearly sixty drays and carts, heavily laden, heading westward with tents, rockers, flour, tea, sugar, mining tools, etc – each accompanied by from four to eight men, half of whom bore firearms.[9]

During the same week, a *Sydney Morning Herald* reporter counted 30 drays waiting to pay at the first toll gate on the road out of Sydney and another 168 on the road beyond. Mundy was to contrast the 'strange jumble' of odd-looking carts overloaded with stores and unfamiliar equipment and 'escorted by parties of men . . . armed to the teeth' with the more orderly coach traffic he expected to see on an English highway. He was also concerned that many of the diggers:

> must have thrown all they possessed into the adventure; for most of their equipments were quite new – good stout horses, harness fresh out of the saddlers hands, gay coloured woollen shirts, and comforters, and Californian sombreros of every hue and shape.[10]

Mundy had already served in the British Army for more than 25 years when he had arrived in Sydney five years earlier, in 1846, as deputy adjutant general of the colony's military establishment. He described how all classes of people joined the rush, including 'builders, bookbinders, tailors and veterinarians', which was to create a chronic labour shortage for several years.

When Charlotte Godley arrived in Sydney in 1853 with her husband, John Robert Godley, who founded the Anglican settlement of Christchurch in New Zealand, she complained that the only reliable source of domestic help was the 'unsuccessful digger, whose health has suffered, or who has no luck at all', resulting in a somewhat dire situation for the ladies of the better houses:

> Hardly a man is to be found contented to remain where he is . . . you hear endless stories of ladies who have been used to large establishments, and giving parties now obliged to give up all thoughts of appearance, and open the doors even themselves . . . no servants are to be had, and many of the best and pleasant families literally driven out of the country by it . . . Almost all the best families there . . . are going home to England, and taking this opportunity of

getting out of the country; most of them hoping to return when things have returned into something like better order . . .[11]

It was calculated at the time the rush began that it would cost a party of four miners about £37 to be properly equipped with enough tools and supplies to reach the goldfields and begin mining. Of this, tools accounted for about £5, which included one cradle, six picks, a water lifter, two shovels, two zinc buckets, a crowbar, an axe, two pans and some 'nails, tacks, cord, tomahawk, etc'. A tarpaulin or tent cost about £6, and a camp oven, iron pot, kettle, 'pots, plates etc' another £2. A further £10 was required for food, which included 250 pounds of flour, 60 pounds of sugar, 7½ pounds of tea and 300 pounds of meat. Carriage and other expenses on the road would be £8, and £6 was needed for gold-mining licences.[12]

While this may have been the sensible budget, it was for many the equivalent to more than a year's wages, and most headed off to the goldfields short of many essentials.

In addition to the rush out of Sydney, the hopefuls came overland from other towns in New South Wales and even from as far away as Melbourne (Port Phillip Bay) and South Australia. In June, the *Sydney Morning Herald* also reported that 240 passengers arrived by ship from Melbourne, as well as from Adelaide and Hobart.[13]

The sight of hundreds of men, some with their wives and children, marching across country, often ill equipped and with insufficient food, sent fear into the local farmers.[14] Only two weeks after the rush had begun, Thomas Icely told the parliament he was frightened of the diggers coming overland past his property from Victoria and South Australia:

> I apprehend great danger to the residents in their own and the neighbouring districts from the great number of people who may be expected to pass through them from Port Phillip, South Australia, and the southern districts . . . I have removed my plate and my other valuables and do not intend to reside in my house. I fear that my own and all other stores along the line of road will be pillaged.[15]

By the end of May, a number of towns in New South Wales, including Goulburn and Maitland, were so alarmed at the loss of their labour force that local businesses offered rewards for the discovery of 'payable gold in their vicinity'. Local subscriptions raised £200 in Goulburn and £270 in Maitland.[16]

The news of gold decimated the population of Melbourne, more than 700 kilometres to the south. William H. Hall, who operated a general store in Melbourne's Elizabeth Street, described the exodus of people rushing to the north:[17]

> [T]he astounding news reached us of the discovery of gold in the Bathurst District . . . Our labourers left by ship-loads for the fields of Ophir and Sofala (a slightly later settlement), and it became difficult to carry on trade, labour became so scarce and valuable.[18]

A public meeting was held at which it was decided to raise a reward 'to any person or persons who shall disclose . . .

a gold mine, or deposit capable of being profitably worked, within 200 miles [322 kilometres] of Melbourne'.[19]

The Tasmanian Colonial Government got in on the act by starting a subscription for a reward for the discovery of gold with a first payment of £20. And across the Tasman Sea, Aucklanders petitioned the lieutenant governor to prohibit the exportation of food to New South Wales and to prevent anyone quitting the colony to join the gold rush unless they made provision for their families who would be left behind.[20]

Within weeks, a continuous line of men, women, children, carts, horses, drays and wheelbarrows had formed, stretching for 250 kilometres from Sydney to the goldfields at Ophir. As in California, and prefiguring what was to happen later in other Australian colonies, the crews of ships in Sydney Harbour and Newcastle Harbour deserted to join the rush, leaving their ships stranded. Spurred on by rewards offered by the ships' captains, a detachment of mounted police set off to comb the straggling line of gold seekers who were on the road to Ophir to bring back the sailors.[21]

On the way to the diggings, those who could afford it stayed at night in one of the roadside inns, but most camped on the side of the road. Those who did have the money for a hotel bed, including Colonel Mundy, complained of the low standard of service:

The inns were helpless . . . You were at liberty to ring the bells of parlour and chamber as much as you pleased, but there was no response – not even the too delusive 'Coming Sir' of the London waiter as he vanishes from your sight.[22]

Sir Thomas Mitchell, the famous surveyor, explorer and colonial road builder, joined the diggers in the early trek over the mountains from Sydney at the end of May. Mitchell had arrived in Australia as a 35-year-old in 1827 to become the colony's surveyor general and for the next 30 years was responsible for the layout of towns and the planning of roads both within and from Sydney. He was born in Scotland to a family of limited means but was able to acquire a decent education before joining the British Army as second lieutenant at 18. For several years, he fought in the Peninsular Wars against Napoleon, where he became an accomplished surveyor and mapmaker. Regarded as having a fiery temper, he was the last officer in the colony to be involved in a duel. He is said to have fired a bullet through his opponent's hat.

Mitchell was 59 years old when he left Sydney on Saturday 31 May 1851 on horseback to head for the gold-fields. The following afternoon, he reached Penrith, where the local ferry was working non-stop trying to carry more than a thousand people across the Nepean River each day. There were so many people lining up for the ferry – which could only take three carts or drays at a time – that Mitchell, his son and the rest of his team had to wait in line until after dark before they could cross.

That night, on the west of the river at the New Inn at Emu Plains, Mitchell wrote to the government in Sydney urging that a 'bridge of boats' be built over the Nepean to handle the heavy traffic for the goldfields until a proper bridge could be constructed.

The following morning, Mitchell began the climb over the Blue Mountains and overtook hundreds of diggers who were on foot heading for the goldfields. He said the road was 'tolerably good' but that water for the horses was scarce in the mountains and they were forced to pay sixpence a bucket from a pub where the publican said he had to cart in the water from more than six kilometres away.

On the Monday night, Mitchell and his team stayed at the Weatherboard Inn at the top of the mountains, where they met a number of returning diggers who had obviously done well enough to be able to stay at the pub. According to Mitchell, the diggers told them there was plenty of gold but they could not stand the cold at the mine site as the winter was approaching.

The following day, Mitchell and his party reached Blackheath, where they stayed the night, and the next day they went on to Mount Victoria then down to the western slopes. After two weeks surveying further west at Molong and Wellington, he arrived at Ophir and said he was surprised at how many people were already there:

> [We] soon came upon the road to 'the Diggings'. The road was deep in mud . . . Two drays with heavy trains and many men appeared in a steep slope in the road before us. We had fallen into a stream of population flowing to the Gold, and life seemed to go with it.[23]

By the beginning of June, there were already more than 2000 people at Ophir and about the same number stretching back over the mountains trying to get there.[24]

The first concentration of diggings was at the junction of Lewis Ponds Creek and Summer Hill Creek, where the township of Ophir was established at the base of a wooded, deep ravine below steep, craggy rocks. The road into the little township was steep and difficult for the horses. Within weeks, thousands of diggers had 'poured into the diggings from all directions . . . majors, magistrates, emigrants, and Norfolk Island expirees, all washing side by side'.[25]

Already by the beginning of June, only weeks after the rush began, a journalist noted how the beautiful woodlands of the area were being traduced by hard-working diggers moving whole hillsides:

> The point was occupied by about fifteen parties cutting straight into the hill, and as we looked down upon their busy movements, digging, carrying earth, and working the cradles at the edge of the water, with the noise of the pick, the sound of the voices, and the washing of the shingle in the iron boxes of the cradle, I could scarcely believe that barely two weeks ago, this was a quiet secluded gully in a far out cattle run.[26]

Three times a week, a heavy four-in-hand carriage made its slow and uncomfortable journey carrying passengers and supplies from Bathurst, nearly 50 kilometres to the east. Soon, a canvas church was erected and a timber police station and lock-up were built, followed by four hotels, a number of stores and a post office.

Sir Thomas Mitchell described the scene:

> Higher up and lower down the river, on the opposite bank . . . were numerous tents, as well as on the left bank of the river – and a bark home with placards about booking for mail, and about all kinds of stores sold there . . . At this place there was a perpetual thoroughfare, resembling people at a tryst or a fair.[27]

Among the 'numerous natives' around the mining site was an Aboriginal man called 'Tommy-Come-Last', who had accompanied Mitchell on an exploration further west in 1836. While there were still a number of Aboriginal people living around the gold district, the tribes had already been largely disenfranchised from their traditional lands by the squatters who had established farms across the west of the mountains in the previous two decades. Mitchell said that gold had no special significance to the local Aboriginal people:

> I ascertained that the aborigines have no name for gold – and that they had never known it, or seen it, until we shewed it to them. They accordingly call it 'Gold' from us.[28]

Mitchell selected the site for what would become the town, rather than just the township, of Ophir and planned the layout of its streets. He also met up with the government geologist, Samuel Stutchbury, and the gold commissioner, John Hardy, who had arrived on the goldfield on 2 June.[29]

As gold commissioner, Hardy was responsible for organising the local police, preserving the peace and issuing gold-mining licences to the diggers. On 20 May, the government had issued a proclamation that all gold was the property of the Crown. It could be mined provided the digger purchased a licence that cost 30 shillings a month.[30]

John Richard Hardy was 44 years old when he accepted the position of gold commissioner and headed off to Ophir to collect licence fees. He was born in Warburton in Sussex in 1807 and was educated at Charterhouse School and Cambridge, where he played cricket, before migrating to Australia as a 25-year-old in 1832. For most of the time before the discovery of gold, he was the police magistrate at Yass in country New South Wales and then at Parramatta in Sydney's west.

In his first official report to the government from the goldfield, Hardy said that Australia's first gold rush had got off to an orderly start:

> I am happy to say that I have not experienced the slightest trouble or annoyance from any person here; they refer all their disputes to me, without attempting to settle them by violence, and submit to my decision without a murmur. I have not sworn in any special constables; it is perfectly unnecessary, for every thing goes on in as orderly and quiet manner as in the quietest English town. There is no drinking or rioting going on.[31]

Most of Hardy's time in the early days was spent collecting money for licence fees. He said he collected 200 a day by walking from 'party to party' through the goldfield and working from 'nine in the morning until sunset' issuing licences, collecting money, registering names and measuring out the miners' allotted claim sites:

> I found that the width of the creek, the middle of the dry bed, the breadth of the flats, the nature of the banks and the ranges from which they are formed, made such different circumstances that any general rule is impossible. I have therefore marked out each person's ground as I gave the licence, never allotting more than forty feet [12 metres] frontage to the creek of any one person.[32]

Hardy reported in a letter to the colonial secretary that there was no shortage of basic food on the goldfields in those early days:

> My dray not having arrived, I am without provisions; but I supply my party from the ground at a moderate price, namely, meat (mutton) at 3 pence a pound, and flour at 7½ pence per pound, tea 2 shillings, and sugar 6 pence per pound . . . flour is the only scarce article, and this is little felt, from the great supply and cheapness of meat.[33]

The diet of the digger at Ophir was quickly established and would become the standard throughout the decades of the Australian gold rushes – flour, from which 'dampers' or bush bread was made, tea and sugar and, most importantly, mutton.

Australia is one of the few countries where meat was a prominent component of the basic diet – because it was easy to transport as it could be taken to the market 'on the hoof', slaughtered and sold on site. This was particularly the case with the first goldfields around Ophir, which were in the centre of hundreds of kilometres of established grazing country.

Colonel Godfrey Mundy described how he met a man on the goldfields who made more money from selling meat to the diggers than from mining for gold:

> [He] slaughters and sells his mutton which in flocks of fifty or a hundred are driven to his shambles from his relatives' pastures, each thus getting a handsome profit . . . The shop consists of an open shed, with bark roof, and a rank entire of fat sheep depending from the eves.

Twenty or thirty others were biding their time in a rude pen . . . Behind the shed the assistant was cutting innocent throats as fast as he could.[34]

The other regular food was the damper, which was already a staple part of the diet of the Australian bushman when it was adopted by the diggers. At its most basic, damper was made by mixing and kneading corn, barley or wheat flour with water and baking it on the embers of an open fire. It was usually flattened and cooked on either side until it sounded hollow when tapped. Alternatively, the dough could be wrapped around a stick and held over the fire while it toasted. For flavour, the diggers would add salt when it was available.

As both meat and damper could be cooked on an open fire, the digger did not need to carry any cooking utensils other than the 'billy' for boiling water for tea.

The standard accommodation of the digger was a canvas tent that he would share with his mates, or in some cases with his wife and children. As the historian William Glasson described it, over time, as the tents lost 'their pristine whiteness' and became worn and torn they were gradually replaced by 'gunyahs,[35] humpies and bark huts'.[36]

In addition to the diggers, there was an army of men engaged in the support industry, including carpenters employed in making rockers, shoemakers supplying and mending miners' boots and saddlers 'stitching dog shin bags for the gold dust'.[37]

Within a few weeks, stores and unlicensed or 'sly' grog shops began to spring up along the Summer Hill Creek towards the Turon River. Soon after that, the town of

Sofala, some 35 kilometres up the Summer Hill Creek and on the Turon River, came into being. By early July, there were an estimated thousand miners stretching 12 kilometres up the Turon River from Ophir:[38]

> The town of Sofala, with its church, was founded on the
> Turon soon after the diggings commenced; and at the end
> of the year two public houses had been licensed, one of
> which is said to have taken £500 on its opening day.[39]

The first-known big entertainment event occurred in the first month of the diggings on the night of 15 May 1851 when Queen Victoria's birthday was celebrated with a volley of 21 guns followed by the singing of 'God Save the Queen' and 'Rule Britannia' and a lot of drinking and singing into the night. The following month, on 18 June, there were celebrations of the anniversary of the Battle of Waterloo, which was still a major event on the calendar of the British Empire even though the victory over the French had occurred 36 years earlier. By the end of the year, there were regular concerts in Bathurst hotels or in hastily constructed wooden performance halls behind the pubs, as well as on the goldfields themselves.

Australia's first gold rush coincided with the onset of the southern-hemisphere winter, and a local paper noted that many people were still heading for the diggings who were not cut out for the harsh conditions:

> Many persons are now going to dig for gold who are
> wholly unfit for such work; men who would hesitate to
> walk the length of George Street in a shower of rain are
> going, at the beginning of winter, to a district where the

climate is almost English, and where they will not be able to get shelter in even the humblest hut.[40]

The *Sydney Morning Herald* tried unsuccessfully to warn people going to the diggings:

> The cold weather is beginning to cause sickness, and many persons were leaving the mining district from the inability to sustain the fatigue and hardship of gold digging. We expect to hear that two thirds of those on their way to Bathurst will be unable to work at the diggings until the warm weather returns which will not be for four months. We can only repeat the advice that we have repeatedly given to the laboring classes – remain steadily at your work and do not be seduced into going to the mines until the winter is over.[41]

As the temperature fell, the early winter rains were followed by snow. A journalist reported that in the morning the digger would come out of his tent and find the water in his pan frozen and the ground covered with 'hoar frost'.[42]

John Elphinstone Erskine, a 46-year-old sea captain, went to Ophir during that first winter while his ship, the *Havanna*, was in Sydney's Port Jackson. He arrived at Ophir on 30 July 1851, and his account was the first to be published in London when he returned there a few months later.

In Ophir, Erskine saw that large sections of ground had already been dug out and a number of shacks had been dismantled and moved on to new diggings:

> After breakfast, we walked down to the creek a few

hundred yards [around 275 metres] by the side of a dry gully, and came at once upon . . . the new township of Ophir . . . where about twenty huts and tents were standing, many having been removed. The whole of the sides of the creek, here eighty and ninety yards [73 and 82 metres] wide, with streams running through the bed . . . were dug and turned up to a depth of five or six feet [1.5 or 1.8 metres]. . . . In eight or ten holes parties were working, and their cradles rocking alongside . . . a very laborious occupation.[43]

Erskine noted that most of the diggers were still living in the tents they had brought with them, some with their families, which included 'some fine looking children'. Already, there were a few 'substantial huts', while others were being helped by the local Aboriginal people to build the temporary bark huts and others were still sleeping under their drays. The few solid wooden structures attracted a high price, and a wooden building of about ten square metres sold for £78 and was rented out for £2 a week.[44]

Two days later, Erskine went further up the Summer Hill Creek to the Turon River with the gold commissioner, John Hardy, who was collecting more gold licences. To catch those who tried to hide and avoid paying the fee, Hardy's assistant, Mr King, came from the opposite direction hoping to trap the evading diggers in the middle. However, Erskine noticed there was already widespread licence evasion, as many who said they were not mining recommenced work as soon as the commissioner and his assistant moved on.

When it came to the amounts of gold being found, Erskine said that 'we heard of nothing but great successes on the fields'. A typical success story involved a Mr Harvie, who had come with a team of diggers from Dapto, south of Sydney, and begun digging on the Turon near where the town of Sofala was being established on 30 June.

In the first fortnight, Harvie and his team met with little success, finding only a few tiny gold particles. On 17 July, they moved on to ground that had been abandoned by other diggers and found 43 ounces in three days. Then, after waiting two days for the river to subside after heavy rain, they started work again and in the next six days found another 154 ounces of gold.

Erskine jotted down a number of other success stories in his journal:

A party of three seamen . . . 1 nugget of 52 ounces, one of 40 ounces, besides smaller pieces.

Five men, £120 in one week.

Another party, £80.

Four boys, £280 in a month.

A party who occupied a deserted hole, £150 in one day. The following day, 2 pound of gold.

A Frenchman (Frederic) and his mate, £300 in a month.

Maccanch and party (six in number, 157 ounces in nine days, sold for £494 and ten pence. Mr. Hall's party, 3 to divide, five others hired men) 40 pounds, in a month, sold for about £18,000.

West of O'Connell's plains and party, 23 pounds, in three weeks, sold for £875.

Dawson's party, 200 ounces of which 9 pounds was procured in three days.

Whitehead's party, 135 ounces in five days.[45]

When Erskine returned to Sydney and then sailed for England, he took with him two small boxes containing samples of gold. He was carrying them for Governor Sir Charles FitzRoy to Colonial Secretary Earl Grey in London with the suggestion that they be given as a gift to Queen Victoria.[46]

Not all the diggers at Australia's first gold rush were successful, and soon an army of the failed were turning back. This would become a common sight on all of the Australian goldfields for the next 50 years. A journalist reported that the dejected miners made a sorry sight:

> The majority of them soon returned in wretched plight
> . . . Back they flocked with empty pockets, heavy hearts,
> and drooping heads, shunning all converse on the way.[47]

This started happening at around the same time that Colonel Godfrey Mundy set out himself to inspect Ophir in the middle of July. He said that he felt threatened by the hundreds of failed and desperate diggers trying to return to Sydney:

> Mortified, half starved, and crest fallen fellows . . . Some
> looked so gaunt, savage, ragged, and reckless, that my
> thoughts turned involuntarily to my pistols as they drew
> near . . . In my four days journey across the Cordorilla I
> met as I calculate, about three hundred men returning,
> disheartened and disgusted, towards the townships; many
> having sold for next to nothing the mining equipments,
> tents, carts, cradles, picks, spades, crows, and washing
> dishes, which had probably cost them all they possessed
> in the world three weeks before. They had nothing left

but 'possum rugs', and a suit of seedy clothes. A few had gold with them – 'no great thing' – they said. Some had drank and gambled away, or had been robbed of their earnings.[48]

On reaching the goldfield, he described the 'indiscriminate confusion' and said the winter had made life tougher as there was difficulty bringing in fresh supplies to the mine site:

> The weather at the mines had become bitterly cold, wet, and tempestuous; provisions were exorbitantly dear, owing to the difficulty of transport of stores across the mountains at this season. The Summer Hill Creek was flooded.[49]

Gold was now being discovered elsewhere in New South Wales, including in the farming district of Araluen Valley, 300 kilometres south of Ophir, near the town of Braidwood. The gold finds about ten kilometres further south at Majors Creek and another ten kilometres south from there at Araluen were reported in a number of colonial newspapers from mid-October 1851.[50]

In what is believed to have been the only time a woman discovered a new goldfield in Australia, a Mrs Baxter found gold near where she lived at Irish Corner near the current town of Reisdale about 20 kilometres south of Braidwood.[51]

The Braidwood diggings, which would flourish on and off for the next 25 years,[52] were in the mountainous region of the upper tributaries of the Shoalhaven River, and for much of the year the mining was made more difficult because of the cold. Richard Kennedy, who as a young man joined the diggings with his family the following year, described how the diggers had to empty their holes of freezing water during the winter:

> Many a morning when the frost would be severe and the ice thick, you would see the diggers break the ice and jump in up to their waists and commence bailing out with their buckets. This would sometimes take a couple of hours. Those men notwithstanding their arduous work were happy as princes, delighted, no doubt, with their pannikins being well filled with gold when evening came around.[53]

Kennedy and his family had reached the Braidwood diggings by walking for three months with a bullock dray carrying all their supplies and equipment the 280 kilometres from Sydney:

> There were no roads in those days, only bush tracks, and you had to get along as best you could. There were no bridges to span the rivers and creeks, if it was at all swollen by the rains, then you had to camp until the waters subsided.[54]

By the end of the year, thousands of diggers came to the site from Sydney and from the diggings around Ophir and Bathurst, prompted by enthusiastic newspaper reports such as the following from the *Maitland Mercury*:

> Several communications have reach [us] from the Araluen. One is from a Californian miner who states that it is his

opinion that the Braidwood diggings will prove as rich as the richest in California. There are from three to four hundred persons at work there and the generality of them are very successful.[55]

Meanwhile, back at Ophir, a growing scepticism by the middle of July about the magnitude of gold and its potential for the colony was quashed by the discovery of a huge 'one hundredweight' (40 kilogram) nugget by a local doctor, William J. Kerr. Until then, most of the gold found had been small flakes and the occasional tiny nugget, as larger pieces were usually embedded in quartz. Rumours of the discovery of such a large piece of gold were not widely believed until the nugget was brought into Bathurst by Dr Kerr's brother-in-law, the local member of parliament William Henry Suttor, on a horse-drawn carriage and put on public display. The news was reported by the *Bathurst Free Press*:

> The following day, however, set the matter to rest. About two o'clock in the afternoon two greys, in tandem, driven by W. H. Suttor, Esq., M. C., made their appearance at the bottom of William Street . . . Astonishment, wonder, incredulity, admiration and other kindred sentiments of the human heart were depicted on the features of all present . . . when a square tin box in the body of the vehicle was pointed out as the repository of the *hundredweight of gold* . . . which set the town and district in a whirl of excitement.[56]

'BATHURST IS MAD AGAIN' was the headline of the *Bathurst Free Press* on 16 July:

The delirium of golden fever had returned with increased intensity. Men meet together, stare stupidly at each other, talk incoherent nonsense, and wonder what will happen next . . . A hundredweight of gold is a phrase scarcely known in the English language. It is beyond the range of our ordinary ideas, a sort of physical incomprehensibility, but that it is a material existence our own eyes bore witness on Monday last.

The discovery of the Kerr nugget helped boost the rush, which would continue for many years along the creeks and tributaries of the Turon and Macquarie Rivers, which in turn led to the establishment of more gold centres, including Hill End and Hargraves.

On 18 July, the *Sydney Morning Herald*, which had hitherto been critical of the gold rush, now embraced it with the discovery of the Kerr nugget:

We have said the announcement of this fact startled the Colony; it will startle all Australia; it will startle England, Ireland and Scotland; it will startle even California; shall we exaggerate if we say? – it will startle the whole civilised world.

The *Herald* went on to predict that Kerr's nugget would astound Britain when news of it reached there:

When the mail arrives . . . when every newspaper . . . echoes and re-echoes the story of this MARVEL OF THE AGE – there can be no question that a sensation will be produced . . . From the monarch on the throne to the peasant at the plough, there will be astonishment, wonder and admiration. From the palace to the cottage, from the drawing room to the nursery, from the philosopher and statesman to the schoolboy, this LUMP OF GOLD, and the land which produced it, for a while will be the all absorbing topic.[57]

The *Herald* was confident that, as a result of the nugget, 'population and wealth will flow upon us' as ships would come 'in abundance . . . full of merchandise and passengers . . . The largest, the strongest and the swiftest steamers would come, railways would follow and the British capitalists would vie with each other to put their money into New South Wales.'

The *Herald* was right – but only partially. The gold discoveries in Australia would shake the world, and Australia would become rich. However, most of the action would be not in New South Wales but in the newly created, separate colony of Victoria, more than 700 kilometres to the south.

CHAPTER THREE

A Bigger Rush in Victoria

The big Victorian goldfields

Within the last three weeks the towns of Melbourne and
Geelong and their large suburbs . . . have been almost emptied
of many classes of their male inhabitants . . . Cottages are
deserted, houses to let, business is at a standstill, and even
schools are closed. In some of the suburbs, not a man is left.
The ships in the harbour are, in great measure, deserted.

Within weeks of the beginnings of the rush in New South Wales, a bigger gold discovery was made outside Melbourne in the Pyrenees hills of Victoria. The colony of Victoria had only recently been formally established as a separate territory from New South Wales[1] and its yields of gold would soon dwarf those of its northern neighbour. At the time, Victoria's population was less than 80,000,[2] and most of Melbourne's population of 23,000 lived in small one-roomed wooden houses. Only Bourke, Collins and Elizabeth Streets were paved; the rest were dirt lanes without footpaths that were covered either with dust or with deep mud after rain.

Within ten years of the gold finds, Victoria's population would exceed 500,000 and account for more than half of the country's total. The city of Melbourne would overtake Sydney to become Australia's largest city for the next 50 years.

Gold was discovered in Clunes in July 1851 and shortly after at Buninyong. Within weeks, bigger deposits were found north of Buninyong at Ballarat, and within months more discoveries followed over a wide area, including Daylesford, Creswick, Maryborough, Bendigo, McIvor (now Heathcote), Saint Arnaud, Ararat, Deep Lead, Pleasant Creek (Stawell), Castlemaine and Mount Alexander. Over the next three years, more diggings opened across a wide area north of Melbourne.

At the time of the gold discovery in Victoria, there had been very little development on the south coast of Australia. In 1800, James Grant surveyed the Victorian coast, but for the next 30 years European settlers were largely limited to those who made their living by catching whales near the shore and boiling them down for oil.[3] In

April 1803, an attempt was made to establish a convict settlement in Victoria when 467 people, including 299 convicts and some free settlers, landed on the southern end of Port Phillip Bay. However, the settlers encountered a shortage of fresh water and suitable timber and abandoned the mainland for Hobart in Van Diemen's Land[4] after only seven months.

From the mid-1830s, pastoralists from Van Diemen's Land began to ship cattle and sheep across the Bass Strait. John Batman established a grazing site that would later become Melbourne. By 1851, there were more than six million sheep on more than 1200 different stations or 'runs',[5] Port Phillip Bay had replaced Portland as the dominant port, and Melbourne and Geelong had become the principal towns. In 1850, Geelong rather than Melbourne was the heart of the farming district, a busier port and home to a number of metal foundries and small factories producing tallow, candles, soap, salt, flour, leather goods and felt hats.

During the early days, there were so few people it was felt there was no need for local government, until a police superintendent was sent from Sydney in 1835. In 1839, the police chief was replaced by Charles La Trobe, who was appointed from London as supervisor and would later become the first governor of Victoria.

At the time, the Port Phillip District was one of the smallest and remotest parts of the British Empire. When La Trobe arrived on 30 September 1839 with his wife and daughter, two servants and a prefabricated house, the settlement had a population of barely 5000. As Port Phillip was then still part of the colony of New South Wales, La Trobe was subordinate to its governor, Sir George Gipps, with whom he had an excellent relationship prior to Gipps's return to England in 1846.

Charles Joseph La Trobe had an unusual background for someone appointed as the head of a British colony, as he had no naval or army credentials, no management experience and practically no administrative training. He came from a Huguenot family that had escaped persecution in France by fleeing to England in 1688. His father had been a missionary who worked in southern Africa while young Charles was educated in Switzerland, where he stayed and worked as a tutor, became an accomplished mountaineer and wrote two books about his adventures.[6]

In 1832, as a tutor, he accompanied the younger Count Albert de Pourtales to the Americas and travelled across the western prairies and down the Mississippi River to New Orleans, which resulted in the publication of two more books.[7] In 1835, he married a Swiss girl, Sophie Mountmollin, before taking work with the British Government, which involved reporting on the future independence of the West Indies. In 1838, he was promoted to the rank of major, knighted and appointed as superintendent of Port Phillip.

At the time of La Trobe's appointment, the Port Phillip District was a free settlement – largely of farmers – and had resisted taking convicts as Sydney and Hobart had done. By 1851, the population of the Port Phillip District had grown to about 80,000, when it was given its own colonial status with the name Victoria and La Trobe was promoted to become its first governor.[8]

Despite the growth of its pastoral industry, Victoria was still a very small place. In the late 1840s, there was only a limited connection with Sydney via a weekly mail coach from Melbourne and Portland, or by an unscheduled, irregular sailing ship.[9] For the next 15 years, La Trobe lived relatively quietly with his family in what a visitor described as an elegantly furnished but modest home.[10]

When news of the discovery of gold broke in Victoria, it was to cause even greater disturbance than it had in Sydney a few months earlier. There had already been some letters published in the Melbourne newspapers at the end of May claiming the discovery of gold in Victoria.[11] On 4 June, the *Argus* reported 'a few specimens of gold' had been exhibited in a watchmaker's shop in Swanston Street that were said to have been found in the Pyrenees hills. The following day, the paper reported that 300 men were searching for gold in the Plenty Ranges and that some mounted police had been sent to maintain order. On Saturday 14 June, the paper ran its first headline story of the discovery of gold in Victoria:

GOLD DISCOVERY

The whole city was alive last evening with a report that a gold mine had at last been discovered . . . The location of the mines is not given, but it is said to be within 25 miles [40 kilometres] of Melbourne.

On 28 June, the *Argus* reported, 'At length we may safely venture to announce the absolute discovery of gold in Victoria.' On 7 July, the *Geelong Advertiser* ran the story that gold had been found at Warrandyte on the Yarra River only 25 kilometres from Melbourne:

The long sought TREASURE is at length FOUND! Victoria is a GOLD country, and from Geelong goes forth the first glad tidings of the discovery . . . We have been backward in publishing rumours of mineralogical discoveries, but we are satisfied now with the indubitable testimony before us. We announce that the existence of a goldfield in the Pyrenees is a great fact fraught with the greatest importance and a preface to a glorious run of prosperity to Victoria.

The following day, the *Argus* ran a headline 'GOLD AGAIN' and reported that 'a Mr. Esmond came into Geelong on Saturday last with several pieces of quartz, and some gold dust from the neighbourhood of the Pyrenees'.[12] Over the next few weeks, a succession of stories appeared in the Melbourne *Herald*, the *Argus* and the *Geelong Advertiser*, with a variety of headlines including 'GOLD', 'EUREKA', 'MANIA' and 'OFF TO THE DIGGINGS'.

It was not the first time the discovery of gold had been reported in the Victorian colonial papers. More than two years earlier, the *Argus* had reported it outside of Melbourne, but after some initial excitement the prospectors had abandoned the search.

The rush following the latest stories was immediate, and businesses of all kinds were forced to shut down when their entire staff deserted. Newspapers closed and banks were stripped of cash as depositors withdrew all their money to buy food and equipment. By early October, the Victorian newspapers were reporting that prices and wages were rising, there was no one to do the shearing and the harvesting, and that men were rushing to the goldfields oblivious to the high risks involved:

We have got an abundance of gold, and the evil effects of the discovery are following fast in the wake of it. Already wages are rising, the common necessities of life are rising, wood and water are rising. There is no appearance of . . . labour for our shearing and harvest being supplied . . . It is impossible to persuade [the men] that the whole matter is one of chance . . . Geelong and . . . Melbourne [are] being depopulated. The police force are handing in resignations daily; even the sergeants are leaving. The Customs house hands are off to the diggings, seamen are deserting their vessels, tradesmen and apprentices are gone, their masters are following them: contractors' men have bolted, and left large expensive jobs on their hands unfinished.[13]

While the discovery of gold in Victoria had the desired effect of stemming the outflow of people to New South Wales, it created an even more dramatic exodus from Melbourne to the new goldfields. William Hall, who had migrated to Australia in 1838 from England and opened a general store in Elizabeth Street in Melbourne, witnessed the rush:

I cannot describe the effect it had upon the sober, plodding, and industrious people of Melbourne . . . The excitement it created in Melbourne was so intense, so all absorbing, that men seemed bereft of their senses, magistrates and constables, parsons and priests, merchants and clerks, policemen and paupers, all hastened to Golden Point; the ships in the harbour were abandoned by many chief officers as well as by the seamen.[14]

By the end of September, there were already more than

a thousand diggers on the Victorian goldfields. A month later, there were more than 4000 at Golden Point goldfield at Ballarat alone, and already there were 25 horse-drawn carriages ferrying passengers to and from Melbourne each week.

At Golden Point, a township made of bark huts had sprung up in a vast sea of tents, and among the first outlets were 'a post office . . . two large general stores, an eating house, two lemonade establishments, a druggist, a barber, a greengrocer . . . and a doctor'.[15] To feed the hungry miners, as many as a thousand head of sheep and cattle were brought on the hoof each day, slaughtered and sold on the diggings.[16]

A journalist wrote that the goldfield, which had only weeks before been a combination of pristine wilderness and open grazing country, was already being traduced by thousands of diggers:

> It is now absolutely honeycombed with holes eight feet [2.4 metres] square, varying in depth from six to forty feet [1.8 to 12 metres]. The holes near the water are dangerous, as the earth falls in; one or two men have already been killed in this way, one or two have been murdered, and some robberies have taken place.[17]

Charles La Trobe had already written on 25 August to the colonial secretary in London, Earl Grey, to advise him of gold found on the upper Loden River, Buninyong, near Ballarat and Deep Creek, a tributary of the Yarra.[18] Six weeks later, he was to write to say that the gold was creating greater chaos than it had in Sydney:

It is quite impossible for me to describe to your Lordship the effect which these discoveries have upon the whole community . . . The discoveries earlier in the year in the Bathurst district of New South Wales unsettled the public mind of the laboring classes . . . The discoveries within our bounds . . . in comparative proximity to our towns, exercise a far wider influence upon our excitable population than did the discoveries in New South Wales.[19]

La Trobe complained that the 'mania' for gold resulted in men abandoning their jobs and families, towns being emptied and ships deserted:

Within the last three weeks the towns of Melbourne and Geelong and their large suburbs . . . have been almost emptied of many classes of their male inhabitants; the streets which . . . were crowded with drays . . . are now seemingly deserted . . . Shopmen, artisans and mechanics of every description [have] thrown up their employments . . . leaving their employers, wives and families to . . . run off to the workings . . . responsible farmers, clerks . . . and not a few of the superior classes have followed . . . Cottages are deserted, houses to let, business is at a standstill, and even schools are closed. In some of the suburbs, not a man is left. The ships in the harbour are, in great measure, deserted.

By November, only three months after the first gold rush in Victoria, Governor Sir Charles FitzRoy in Sydney also wrote to Colonial Secretary Earl Grey in London to say that Victoria was already overtaking New South Wales as Australia's major gold centre:

The richness and area of the gold fields which have been discovered in the neighbouring colony of Victoria already rival, if they do not exceed, in value the first discovered gold fields in New South Wales.[20]

Most of the diggers who first went to the goldfields came from Melbourne and Geelong and walked the most direct route, on which there were no established roads or tracks and only a number of rough stock paths. Most carried all of their food, clothes and tools on their backs, as it was too expensive to hire a cart:

[I]t being too great a luxury to place upon a dray or pack horse anything not absolutely necessary . . . This will easily be understood when it is known that carriers, during the winter, obtained £120 and sometimes £150 a ton for conveying goods to Bendigo (about one hundred miles [160 kilometres] from Melbourne).[21]

The easiest route from Melbourne was to the north through Seymour, but this involved paying the local publican £1 to cross the Goulburn River on his punt. Most avoided the fee and went the more difficult route. Others paid £1 for a ticket on the ferry from Melbourne to the port of Geelong on the western side of Port Phillip Bay and walked the shorter distance of 85 kilometres north-west through relatively flat, open country to Ballarat.

One of those who abandoned Melbourne was William Hall. Barely a month after news of the gold finds reached the city, he shut up his general store on Elizabeth Street and joined the rush:

Finding it impossible to carry on my business satisfactorily, I decided to sell all of my stock, and proceed to the mines. When this was effected, I made arrangements with three strong able-bodied young men – two of whom had been in my employ. I purchased a tent, provisions for three months, tools, cradle, and all the other [provisions] usually provided for the occasion, and, early in October 1851, started for Mount Alexander, leaving my wife and family in a neat little cottage a few miles from Melbourne.[22]

Hall confessed that he embarked on the quest for gold with mixed feelings and contrary to the wishes of his wife, as he had 'thrown up a good business and all the comforts of life'.[23]

Hall left Melbourne in spring and took five days to reach the goldfields:

[It] was excessively warm for the season ... so much annoyed by the flies, and the dust caused by the immense number of wagons and drays, equestrians and pedestrians, passing and re-passing to and from the diggings, that we were glad to tie our veils on our hats to avoid the annoyance.[24]

They travelled more than 30 kilometres through Flemington and Keilor before camping on the second night with hundreds of others on the side of the road. On the third day, they travelled 'a long dreary twelve miles' (19 kilometres) through the Black Forest before again forming a camp for the night with a large number of other prospective diggers.

On the morning of the fourth day, Hall said he shot a wild turkey, which 'made the whole party an excellent 'dinner' and allowed them to break the diggers' monotonous diet of mutton, damper and tea.

After passing through Kyneton, he arrived at the site, where he was surprised to see 'about 2000 tents and 10,000 diggers' in the immediate vicinity, 'all actively employed in removing surface soil, sinking holes with a pick, spade, and crow bar, or fossicking . . . with knives and trowels'. Already, the entire area was a honeycomb of holes dug so close together that Hall thought it 'utterly impossible' for the miners to dispose of the soil being dug out of their shafts.[25]

Pitching their tent 'not far from that of the Gold Commissioner', the inexperienced digger Hall decided to first understand how to mine for gold and left his mates to go around the mine site to see how it was done:

> I was resolved to gain all the information I possibly could
> before I set to work, and visited and examined every hole
> I could in order to see the system of working.[26]

One of the first people he met was a former customer named Johnson from 'upcountry' Victoria who was using his dray to earn money. Johnson told Hall that he earned £20 carting supplies to the diggings and would make at least another £20 carting passengers and luggage back to Melbourne.

Many were finding easy gold, and Hall described how he witnessed a 14-year-old boy and his 11-year-old brother find more than £4 of gold in less than a hour by reworking a pile of tailings.

At one hole, he found 'an old servant by the name of Jones' who had only recently arrived and found eight pounds of gold, which he said had 'earned as much in ten days as I should have done by harder work in two years'. At another hole, he saw two men pulling up a bucket that contained plenty of gold and asked if he would be allowed to see how they did it:

> I obtained permission to descend into it, being extremely anxious to see their system of working, and where the auriferous deposits were to be found. The hole was thirty-two feet [9.7 metres] deep . . . The surface-soil, a rich black mould, extended to the depth of two-feet, beneath which was a bed of gravel, about nine feet [2.7 metres] thick; then a bed of red mud, in which gold is generally found; immediately below which, and resting on the slate formation, was a stratum of blue clay, which contained gold in large quantities.[27]

At the bottom of the hole, he found a man scraping nuggets of gold from the sides of the shaft with a trowel, knife and shear-blade:

> In a few minutes, he pointed out a 'pocket', as he called it. On examining the spot, I found a rich deposit on the slate, between the interstices of which the nuggets were lying like so many grapes.[28]

The five men had been working the hole for 15 days. When they took Hall back to their tent, they showed him what they had found, which they kept hidden in a bucket under 'a coarse wrapper' and red mud. The gold weighed 27 pounds, five ounces and seven dwts,[29] which Hall calculated, 'after paying all expenses', would have yielded a profit of £1800.[30]

Hall returned to his party and the next day they began digging their own shaft. After several days, though, they had found little gold and were beginning to become despondent. None of the newcomers was accustomed to the hard physical work, and Hall complained that his 'hands soon blistered to such a degree, that the blood oozed from them down the handles of the tools'.[31] At the end of the first full day's work, he barely had the strength to eat:

> On returning to the tent I felt so prostrate and exhausted, that I thought that I should not be able to eat anything but after I had taken a glass of excellent sherry, the savoury smell of a homely meal . . . soon restored my appetite.[32]

The following day, they abandoned the hole and started another nearby. This time, after seven days, they reached the blue clay and were lucky to find several rich pockets of gold, which earned them more than £400.

Hall said that, with the discovery, the despondency among his mates vanished but finding so much gold made them greedy and deeply suspicious of everyone:

> They viewed everybody with distrust; and if any of my friends called, they watched them closely, as if they came to rob them. Their arms were . . . regularly at night-fall reloaded, and placed at hand ready for use. They became silent and meditative; all their purer and better feelings seemed absorbed in the prevailing passion . . . the acquisition of gold . . . The love of greed had obtained the ascendancy, and rendered them unpleasant associates.[33]

Hall decided to leave the syndicate, return home to his wife and family and then return to open a store on the diggings:

> I spent three happy days at home, and then proceeded to Melbourne, to purchase a tent suitable for the object I had in view, and stores; and in two days I started for Golden Point, with three dray loads of assorted goods, consisting principally of flour, tea, sugar, tobacco, butter, cheese, bacon, hams, wines, spirits, liqueurs, tools, and shop clothing; and pitched my tent at Forest Creek, paying a licence fee, the same as if I were digging, so that I might claim the protection of the police force.[34]

Hall's store was a success, and he later opened other successful shops at Friars Creek diggings and on the Goulburn River on the Melbourne–Sydney road.

The diggers who headed for the Victorian goldfields met with little resistance from the local Aboriginal people, whose lives had already been dislocated by white settlers who had taken their land for sheep farming in earlier decades. By the time gold was found in Victoria, the number of grazing sheep across the colony had increased and the local tribes had been almost totally alienated from the traditional lands that had sustained them for thousands of years.[35]

Since the arrival of the white man, the local Aboriginal people had also been decimated by alcohol, influenza, smallpox, measles, tuberculosis and venereal disease, which by the 1840s had afflicted more than 90 per cent of the Aboriginal women in Victoria's Loddon Valley.[36] In Australia as a whole, the Aboriginal population had fallen by almost half between white settlement in 1788 and the discovery of gold 60 years later.

Within a year of the first gold rushes, exposure to alcohol ravaged the Aboriginal population. In July 1852, a report by William Thomas, guardian of Aborigines for the Melbourne District, pointed to the imminent extinction of some local tribes, echoing the accounts of other officials:

> The present condition of the aborigines have in no way improved, but lamentably deteriorated. The discovery of gold has greatly affected their moral condition . . . [They,] generally speaking, appear to have become habitual drunkards, male and female . . . they no longer ply with their tomahawks to cut wood for the inhabitants, but prowl about the public houses and vile avenues, where they are encouraged by the improvident gold diggers into drinking . . . On various occasions they have been so drunk as to be found lying in the highways during the night . . . They have now been brought to an awful and dangerous state of degradation, so that the speedy extinction of Melbourne and Barrabool tribes are inevitable. Although the law is stringent upon those who supply blacks with liquor, it is now craftily evaded by them. Wherever a public house is, in town or in the bush, they will get a drink . . . The consequence is, that their frames are inverted in the absence of regular exercise, and their blood corrupted by continued dissipation.[37]

Back in Melbourne, towards the end of 1851, after several months of the gold rush, the shortage of labour caused by so many heading for the diggings was causing severe problems.

Governor La Trobe had been confident that, after some initial excitement, many would soon return to their old jobs, but a journalist noted that he was proved wrong when only three weeks later huge new discoveries were found 80 kilometres north of Ballarat at Mount Alexander:

> The Governor confidently expected . . . that many of the absentee adventurers . . . [would] . . . become disgusted with the severe toils, the hardship and the privations, and the precarious gains of the gold diggings. Another three weeks saw his predictions verified, and he was beginning to contemplate . . . the even flow of business again resuming . . . when the scarcely convalescent public suffered a most violent relapse of its old complaint. Mount Alexander, otherwise called Mount Byng, 70 Miles [113 kilometres] north west of Melbourne, had revealed its unparalleled treasures, and the temptation was irresistible.[38]

Word soon spread of spectacular discoveries, and it was reported that the gold at Mount Alexander was more plentiful and easier to extract than ever before:

> At Mount Alexander at the beginning of December [1851], a pound weight of gold was small remuneration for a party; many secured five or six; and there were instances of as much as fifty being the result of but a few hours labour.[39]

The same reporter claimed that the rush to Mount Alexander towards Christmas 1851 was even more dramatic than the earlier rush had been:

A wilder excitement than the first now took place, and a more multitudinous rush to the new diggings, where some 20,000 persons were soon congregated. The towns are again emptied of their male inhabitants; clerks, public servants, gaolers, and constables, caught in the infection and resigned their appointments.[40]

The depletion of labour became so great that the postmaster general reported he could not provide a reliable letter-delivery system, the superintendent of the prison said he had too few wardens and the colonial surgeon could not staff the lunatic asylum.[41]

To counter the problem, salaries for public servants were increased by between 50 and 100 per cent, but it did little to reduce the problem. Only female domestic servants, who were the least likely to run off and become gold miners, were still readily available.

By the end of the first year, prices of everything in Melbourne had jumped. A loaf of bread that earlier in the year had cost five pence increased fourfold to one shilling and eight pence by Christmas. Meat doubled in price, and bacon quadrupled from sixpence a pound to two shillings. House rents, hotel charges, cartage and boat hire had all risen by more than 50 per cent, while clothes, furniture and hardware had all more than doubled. It was now 'almost impossible to buy a saddle',[42] and the price of shoeing a horse had jumped fivefold to 25 shillings.

A local gentleman complained about the difficulties of trying to get by in Melbourne:

I cannot get a pair of boots made or mended in Melbourne if I were to give any money that might be asked. The baker will not undertake to supply me regularly, but will do the best he can. I pay 5 shillings a load of water, and 30 shillings for a single horse load of wood . . . I cannot at any price get a man to chop my wood and I think myself fortunate if I can prevail on the black gins (natives) to work for half an hour.[43]

A well-established pastoralist in Geelong complained that by November 1852 almost all of his servants were gone:

All of my people giving me notice . . . the cook left, though I offered her £40 a year to remain, and our domestic servants are reduced to little F— and J. M. —, who is still a mere child, a native black cook, and a native boy to wait at table.[44]

The size of the gold discoveries in Victoria brought hundreds of excited prospectors from the other colonies, including Tasmania, South Australia and New South Wales. The Tasmanians – or Vandemonians, as they were still then known – came in large numbers to the goldfields. As convict transportation had continued to Tasmania for longer than New South Wales and Victoria, many of those who came across the Bass Strait to try their luck were ex-convicts – and some were escapees still serving sentences. The Vandemonians were much despised and blamed for much of the crime and disorder on the mainland goldfields. They proved convenient scapegoats until the Chinese filled this role within a few short years.

The discovery of gold in Victoria was devastating for South Australia, as an estimated third of the adult male population headed for the diggings. An Adelaide school teacher, William Crawthorne, described how 'butchers, bakers, miners, hawkers, fishers, grocers, tailors, workmen, school teachers, clerks and officers' all left:

> Adelaide is in an awful state, everyone is leaving it – for the gold diggings . . . men are getting fortunes . . . in a few weeks . . . men are . . . going away leaving their wives and children behind – the Cads – work of all kinds is stopped.[45]

Within the first year of the rush, hundreds of people from South Australia were living in a city of tents on the banks of the Yarra River in a settlement named Little Adelaide. This tent city was populated by the large number of people who had walked overland to Victoria but had insufficient money to pay the high prices for accommodation in Melbourne.[46]

One of those who trekked overland to the Victorian diggings was Charles Rule, a miner who worked on the copper mines at Burra, 150 kilometres north of Adelaide. Rule was born in Cornwall and left Plymouth with his new bride, Emma, shortly after his 23rd birthday in September 1848 on the *Rajah* and arrived in Port Adelaide after 120 days' sailing in January 1849, which was still almost two years before Hargraves's claim to have found gold in New South Wales.[47]

On 2 February 1852, after three years at Burra, Charles Rule, his father-in-law, three other men and a ten-year-old boy embarked on an 800-kilometre trek to prospect on the Victorian goldfields. With horses and a bullock dray carrying all their equipment and food, they took a week to reach Adelaide, which Rule said he had not seen for three years, where they celebrated with a breakfast of 'bread, beefsteak, coffee and ginger beer'.[48]

Later on the same afternoon, they left Adelaide and headed off through Glen Osmond south-east towards Echunga and Macclesfield, which Rule described as good pastoral and agricultural country. After ten days, on 12 February, they caught the ferry across the 'splendid' 240-metre wide Murray River and found abundant fresh water. Rule said there were plenty of ducks and fish, which the Aboriginal people caught 'for a bite of tobacco or some white money'.

Two days after crossing the river, they encountered more travellers like themselves who were heading towards the gold, on a deteriorated sandy road. On Saturday night, 14 February, Rule complained that about 50 or 60 local Aboriginal people held a noisy corroboree that kept them awake. The following day being Sunday and the trekkers' rest day, they watched a battle fought between the local tribes:

We had the opportunity of seeing a fight between the Lake Albert tribe and the Grass Flat Blacks. They had two separate encounters, which lasted about half an hour each. I saw . . . one female speared in the breast, one man had a spear through his leg, another through the fleshy part of the thigh. There was a great deal of howling and hollering with them . . . I think some of them were wounded bad, as we were disturbed during the night by their howling and groans.[49]

A few days later, they were in very dry country that Rule described as the 'desert so much talked of', which was sand plain covered with 'low brushwood and prickly heath'. Eventually, they reached Lake Coorong, more than 500 kilometres from Adelaide.

When they came to some low, swampy country, they met a group of families heading for the goldfields who had lost their horses in the dense scrub and had become stranded hundreds of kilometres from any help. Rule said that none of the other parties could help them, so they were simply abandoned:

> We spoke to a party today who had lost 3 horses in it and were not able to proceed on their journey in consequence. Their case was one to be pitied, as they were more than 100 miles [160 kilometres] from any settlement and having women and children with them, were unable to proceed to the diggings without them and all the drays passing having enough to do to take themselves on.[50]

Towards the end of February, finding the days 'very hot', they reached the Border Inn and were told they were only 300 kilometres short of the Mount Alexander goldfields. By the beginning of March, they were seeing more sheep farms in western Victoria when they crossed the Wimmera River and came to Horsham, which was then only a small village of 'about 12 or 14 houses with a store and a public house'. When they reached Glenorchy, they were less than a hundred kilometres from Mount Alexander.

As they got nearer, they saw an increasing number of prospectors working the local creeks, and Rule said they knew they were close when he saw a billboard on a farm that offered hay for sale at 20 shillings a bushel and oats at 15 shillings a bushel.

After five weeks and one day, Charles Rule and his party finally reached the goldfields of Ballarat and worked their way through several kilometres of tents before they could find a site to start digging.

By early 1852, there were thousands of diggers on the Victorian fields – but news of the bonanza had reached the rest of the world several months earlier and tens of thousands more were already on their way from overseas.

CHAPTER FOUR

The World Joins the Rush

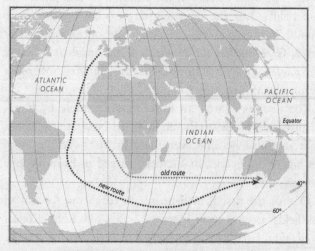

The Great Circle Route between England and Australia

My uncle gave me fifty pounds, saying, 'There, Myles, thou'rt little use here, lad; go to the "diggings", and see if thou canst be of any use there!' and with this unceremonial dismissal I took my departure.

The first news of the Australian gold finds appeared in Britain in *The Times* on 2 September 1851. 'The Gold Fever in Australia,' reported the paper, 'may yet put California to shame.' The story was picked up later the same day in the second edition of the *Liverpool Mercury*, which added that 'the country, from the mountain ranges to an indefinite extend in the interior, is one enormous gold field'. Over the next few days, other major papers around Britain ran with the story, including the *Belfast News*, *Glasgow Herald*, *Hampshire Telegraph and Sussex Chronicle*, *Ipswich Journal*, *Leeds Mercury*, *Morning Chronicle*, *Manchester Times* and *Preston Guardian*.

The articles caused an immediate scramble by hopeful prospectors for berths on ships to New South Wales. That scramble became even more intense when news of the bigger discoveries in Victoria arrived in Britain a few months later.

One of the first British people to reach the Australian goldfields from overseas was 22-year-old Lord Robert Cecil, who later, as the Marquess of Salisbury, was to be three times the prime minister of Great Britain.[1]

The young Lord Cecil caught wind of the New South Wales gold discoveries in Cape Town in July 1851, when the news was still on its way to London. Cecil had recently dropped out of his law studies at Oxford owing to ill health and had taken a long sea voyage on the recommendation of his doctor.

On hearing the news of the gold, Lord Cecil immediately changed his plans and, with a travelling companion, Sir Montague Chapman, boarded the *Amazon*, which was the next available ship heading from South Africa to Australia. After spending Christmas at sea in the

Great Southern Ocean, the two aristocrats landed at Port Adelaide on 30 January 1852.

In Cape Town, they had heard only about the New South Wales discoveries, but when their ship stopped off at Adelaide they were made aware of the later and bigger finds in Victoria. Cecil noted that the city of Adelaide was already being emptied of its population in the rush over-land to the goldfields of Ballarat and Mount Alexander, which were more than 600 kilometres away:

> We heard from the Port Master that gold had been discovered at Melbourne, and that Adelaide had been gradually drained of its population by the mania which the news had raised.[2]

Cecil said that when he and Sir Montague went into Adelaide after walking three kilometres over 'broiling hot' sand then driving 13 kilometres in a cart, the town was in desperate straits:

> In consequence of the emigration mania, excited by the discovery of the goldfields, the colonial revenue has for the time almost vanished. The customs, which used to produce £3,000 a week, have fallen to zero, land is unsaleable, property on which £1,500 has been spent has sold for £43.[3]

The departure of the *Amazon* on the next leg of its journey to Melbourne had to be delayed for two weeks because four of its crew deserted while the ship was in Adelaide. They had joined the other gold prospectors on the long walk to the Victorian goldfields. When the aristocratic

Lord Cecil finally reached Melbourne on 25 March, he was unimpressed with the colony, as he was with most of his stay in Australia:

> [It was] thronged with ephemeral plutocrats, generally illiterate, who were hurrying to exchange their gold nuggets for velvet gowns for their wives and unlimited whiskey for themselves, and who made the streets and hotels clamorous with drunken revels which now and again culminated in crimes of audacious violence.[4]

After 12 days staying at the Passmore Hotel on the corner of Lonsdale and Elizabeth Streets, Lord Cecil and Sir Montague Chapman took a carriage to have a look at the goldfields. Cecil was most unimpressed at having to share the 'spring cart' with the low calibre of his fellow travellers – something he would never be obliged to do as an aristocrat in England. According to Cecil, they included a young runaway merchant's son from Sydney, a man on his way to take up the job as postmaster at Mount Alexander and a man with his 'fashionably timid' wife, who shrieked loudly, and often, whenever the carriage lurched. However, their most frightening fellow passenger was a 'Yankee' and a veteran of the Californian goldfields who kept a pair of pistols in his belt:

> He was a coarse, hideous, dirty looking man, without an attempt to ornament or even neatness in his dress; yet he wore in his ears a pair of ear rings about the size and shape of a wedding ring.[5]

Cecil complained about the poor condition of the road and

of the incidence of highway robberies, which he said were occurring more frequently than the authorities were prepared to admit. They stopped at a number of wayside inns, which Cecil believed were unlicensed, or sly grog shops. At one, he described how he saw a roughly dressed digger arm in arm with a woman in 'exaggerated refinery, with a parasol of damask silk' that he thought would not have been out of place in Hyde Park in London. Lord Cecil was told she was a lady of notoriety from Adelaide named Lavinia, who would stay as the 'wife' of the successful digger for a few days in order to rob him of his savings. Such women were apparently common on the diggings and available for the 'modest charge' of one shilling and sixpence.

At 5.30 in the afternoon, the coach stopped for the night at the Bush Inn in Gisbourne, about 48 kilometres from Melbourne. Although the inn was full, Lord Cecil and Sir Montague – but not their travelling companions – were found beds and shown into a private room, 'on account of our black coats'.

The next morning, they were awoken at six o'clock but had to wait two hours before getting away. Annoyed by the delay, Lord Cecil criticised the drivers' 'characteristic Australian unpunctuality' for not having caught and harnessed the horses on time. Once on the move, he was to complain about the 'infamous road' and the 'fagged horses', and when driving through the Black Forest about 30 kilometres from their destination he said the road grew worse, the holes more numerous, the hills steeper and the dust 'absolutely unbearable':

> It hung like a dense cloud about the cart, getting into our
> eyes, ears, mouths, and nose, stopping respiration utterly

and clinging to hair, whiskers and beard as if it were flour.[6]

Later in the day, the driver came in for more criticism for 'having nearly finished a great bottle of brandy' and being too drunk to see a deep hole in which the coach became stuck. Eventually, by the 'incessant flogging' of the tired horses, they finally reached the diggings shortly before nightfall.

They had been warned not to attempt the eight-kilometre walk to the gold commissioner's tent but with a bright moon shining found the advice to be yet 'another Australian exaggeration'.

When they reached their destination, they were taken to the mess tent, where the officers were just finishing dinner. Lord Cecil and Sir Montague presented a letter to Commissioner Henry Wright from Governor La Trobe, which would ensure the upper-class Englishmen would receive special treatment on the goldfields.

After a late dinner, the newcomers met a number of people in the officers' mess, including a Roman Catholic priest of whom the young Lord Cecil was especially critical:

The same evening the Roman Vicar Apostolic Dr [Geoghegan] had arrived. He was a fat, droll, merry little Irish priest, very shallow and superficial, with a great deal of low cunning, and an evident desire to be 'all things to all men' by a display of liberality and a series of profane jokes.[7]

They slept in a tent, as there was no other accommodation

available, and the next day, a Sunday, ate a 'tolerable' breakfast, 'barring the absence of butter and milk', before being lent horses to go and look at the diggings with the police superintendent.

On the way, they saw two diggers carrying sacks of earth on their backs to a waterhole to wash for gold. However, being the Sabbath, mining was banned, and Lord Cecil described how the superintendent of police dismounted, gave his horse and whip to one of the offenders to hold, then scattered the contents of their sacks on the ground.

At first, Cecil said he was 'aghast' at what he thought to be the excessive, 'summary' justice but on reflection felt that there was too much turbulent behaviour and an 'evil temper of this evil age' that was coming from the middle classes as well as the lower classes and required firm action.[8] Shortly after this incident, the police rode off to break up a game of quoits, which was also forbidden on Sundays, and Cecil recorded it was one of a number of occasions he was jeered at by diggers for wearing the aristocratic clothing of a white hat and black coat.

The next day, they went with the police chief, Armstrong, to seize a sly grog shop. When they arrived, a number of police had already surrounded the tent, and Armstrong ordered those inside to be handcuffed before a search was made that revealed only half a keg of port. However, a police informer had told how he had witnessed grog being sold, so the tent was pulled down, the canvas was confiscated and the poles piled up and burned.

According to Cecil, the Ballarat gold commissioner had few resources for a big and dangerous job:

[He] rules a body of 100,000 men; exacts their licence fees, punishes their offenses, and guards their gold; For this latter purpose his only coffer is a tin paper box sealed by a sixpenny padlock; and his coercive force consists of three policemen, two carbines and a sword.[9]

At the end of Lord Cecil's long day in the goldfields, a tent was vacated for him and Sir Montague, and they were provided with a 'solid' dinner consisting of damper, mutton and potatoes, which was served in a widened pannikin 'something between a wash-hand-basin and a soup plate'. Lord Cecil was given the only chair, while Sir Montague sat himself down on the corner of the bed and the gold commissioner sat on an upturned bucket. The 'conventionality of a table cloth was, of course, not to be expected', and the commissioner, having given his only knives and forks to his guests, was obliged to eat his dinner using his penknife. After dinner, they drank brandy ('good fiery stuff'), while they sat around and smoked pipes.

The following day, they rode across to Golden Gully in Bendigo, which was then yielding rich gold finds. There were already so many holes that the area was honeycombed with shafts, to the extent that the narrow paths between them were undermined and unstable.

Lord Cecil described how he went down one of the holes to see a digger lying on his back picking out nuggets from the wall of the shaft with a penknife. The nuggets, he said, ranged in size from a 'pinhead to a flattened pea'.

Before leaving the goldfields, Cecil was to witness some unsavoury behaviour from the police. He was told how some of them would trick diggers who did not have licences by saying it was okay and that they could be issued with one on the spot. However, when the diggers climbed out of their holes to buy their licences, they would immediately be handcuffed and arrested.

Lord Cecil's observation that the heavy-handed practice tended 'to create more ill-will than tent burning or arbitrary fines' was prophetic because the savage policing of miners' licences would be a big factor in the riots and the killings at Eureka more than two and a half years later.

Finally, on the following Sunday, after barely a week on the Victorian goldfields, where he made no attempt to dig for any gold himself, Lord Cecil said goodbye to his companion, Sir Montague Chapman, and boarded the coach for Melbourne. On returning to the Passmore Hotel, he was to record another unpleasant encounter with the lower orders when at dinner some 'diggers took to abusing the waiter and throwing bread at each other; and I can confirm for my share of the pellets'.[10]

Two days later, he sailed on the *Mariposa* to Tasmania. He then returned to England and in 1853 became a member of the British Parliament but never visited Australia again. In 1868, he inherited the title of Marquesss of Salisbury and for the next 35 years held a number of posts, including secretary of state for India, foreign secretary and prime minister. Lord Robert later became the source of the expression 'Bob's your uncle', for handing out a number of plum government jobs to his nephew, Lord Balfour. Lord Cecil's small diary of his time on the Victorian goldfields only came to light 70 years later, after his death, when his daughter Lady Gwendolyn Cecil found it among her father's papers while writing his biography.

There was no shortage of advice in Britain for the

thousands of diggers who were readying themselves to sail to the far side of the world in search of gold. One of the first guidebooks, *The Emigrant's Guide to Australia*, hurriedly published and released in Britain in 1852, said there were great opportunities for the man who went with 'no capital but his labour, with stout arms and a stout heart'.

The guide, written by John Capper, began with a not-too-flattering picture of the Australian continent, with its large tracts of 'unprofitable . . . barren soil or rocky hills' and animals that were 'few and of little value', and its fruit that was 'very few and scarcely worth mention':[11]

> The most troublesome visitors to the settlement are mosquitoes and white ants; the bite of the former being painful to many persons, while the latter are destructive to clothing, and even furniture.[12]

However, the guide said there were plenty of jobs for the labouring classes and domestic servants:

> Should the intended emigrant be married so much the better, provided the wife be frugal and industrious; such a helper will not only be no expense, but she will often nearly earn as much as her husband.[13]

Children of ten and 11 years old could work as shepherds, and 14-year-olds could be 'quite as good as men' as stockmen or hut keepers, while the 'Australian peasant' could lead a happy life. 'The healthiest of climate, abundance of good food, freedom from all world cares' would transform the 'half starved . . . dyspeptic citizen into a ruddy, sleek and cheerful bushman'.[14]

The guide was pretty emphatic about those who should not go to the tough environment of Australia:

> Young unmarried women, unacquainted with any farm or agricultural occupation . . . the drawing room accomplishments of singing, dancing, painting and crochet, would stand no shadow of a chance against the highly prized virtues of churning, baking, preserving, cheese making, and small matters . . . Young men, accustomed to a feather bed existence, who have no idea of turning their hand to anything; or of roughing it in the bush, who imagining that something easy and lucrative will be sure to turn up . . . we warn against leaving their old fire side.[15]

The guide reassured its Church of England readers that their religious needs would be taken care of:

> Throughout all Australian colonies, the Church of England is recognized as the state religion, bishops for the various archdioceses have been appointed, with the usual establishments.

A large section of the guide titled, 'General Information to Emigrants of all Classes: the Outfit; the Passage; the Arrival', dealt with preparing for the voyage and getting to Australia. Prospective diggers were advised to pack hardy practical clothing and travel light, as once they reached Australia they would have to travel for up to 320 kilometres 'over rough tiresome country' to reach the goldfields, 'where every additional pound weight is additional burden':[16]

> Let men for instance avoid all sorts of fancy waistcoats, dandy boots, or costly cravats and ties: let women shun the idle vanities of silks and satins, of lace and ribbons, of many flounces and fashionable bonnets and . . . forget there are such things in the world as kid gloves, lavender water and toilet tables.[17]

Taking books was discouraged because of the extra weight, except of course for the Bible, 'which we should hope no immigrant family should be without'.[18]

For the voyage, emigrants were advised to wear old clothes, 'however shabby', and to keep their best for when they reached the colonies.

Aboard ship, they were informed that, as steerage passengers – which applied to around 90 per cent of the travellers – they would be allocated only 20 cubic feet (half a cubic metre) of space, which left only enough room for 'one box or bag' for each sleeping space, sufficiently large to hold one month's supply of clothing. At the end of the voyage, the passengers could retrieve the rest of their clothes from the hold of the ship.

Passengers were warned that, during a sea voyage that could last up to four months, they would be rationed to three quarts (just under three litres) of water a day, which would not be enough to wash clothes other than a 'very few small things'.[19]

Despite this, women were still expected to keep up appearances on board the ship. On the voyage, they were told they should take three cotton dresses, one pair of stays, four petticoats, 16 chemises, two flannel petticoats, 12 pairs of cotton stockings, four pairs of black stockings, six nightdresses and caps, six pocket handkerchiefs, four handkerchiefs for the neck, six caps, two bonnets, one cloak and shawl, one pair of boots, two pairs of shoes and eight towels.

To meet the increased demand for travel, London shipowners moved quickly to divert ships from Indian trade, and Liverpool shipowners bought and hired more transatlantic vessels from America.[20]

Gold diggers who were in a hurry to reach Australia were to benefit from a revolution in sea transport that was occurring at the time gold was discovered in New South Wales and Victoria: the rise of the clippers, or 'tall' ships. From the 1830s, the Americans had begun building a radically different sailing ship to the small, blunt-nosed vessels that had dominated shipping for several centuries. The clippers were bigger and had long, sleek, narrow hulls with extremely tall masts that carried huge amounts of square sail. They were also very fast. Before the clippers, 150 miles (240 kilometres) a day was considered a good speed for a sailing ship, but the newly designed ships could achieve more than 250 miles (400 kilometres) a day, and the best could cover more than 400 (645 kilometres).

The earliest clippers were used on the transatlantic route and also for the opium and tea trade with China. By the late 1840s, they were in high demand from diggers wanting to quickly reach the Californian goldfields.

The clippers also allowed a more adventurous and far quicker course to be sailed from Europe to Australia, called the Great Circle Route. Prior to 1850, the standard route from Britain to Australia followed a path laid down by the British Admiralty. It involved sailing easterly down the Atlantic coast before landing at the Cape of Good Hope. After leaving the Cape, the ships sailed at around 40 degrees south through the Great Southern Ocean.

The Great Circle Route allowed the bigger, faster and more seaworthy ships to sail in a huge arc across the Atlantic to about 20 degrees west then head well south of the Cape of Good Hope, avoiding the south-east trade winds off the west coast of Africa. In the Great Southern Ocean, the ships sailed at much higher latitudes, around 50 degrees south, where the westerly winds blew stronger. Ships travelling this way encountered snow, ice and ten-metre waves and would be unlikely to see land from the time they left Europe until they reached the south of Australia.

The first of the fast ships to reach Australia in dramatically reduced time caused a sensation. Before the clippers, the average sailing time between Europe and Australia was 120 days.[21] On 17 July 1850, still six months before Hargraves found gold at Ophir, the clipper *Constance* left Liverpool and reached Adelaide 76 days later. Early the following year, the *Runnymede* left Liverpool on 21 February and reached Adelaide 72 days later.

On 4 July 1852, the *Marco Polo* departed from Liverpool and, 'sailing on brave new winds', created a new record by arriving in Melbourne 68 days later. The *Marco Polo* had been built in New Brunswick in 1851 and initially used as a cargo ship across the Atlantic before it was bought in Liverpool in 1852 and converted for passengers to meet the demand for berths to the Australian goldfields. On its first voyage, it carried 990 passengers, most of whom were men. The single men were quartered at the front of the ship, the single women aft and the married in between. By sailing at latitudes of 55 degrees, the ship reached speeds of around 370 miles (595 kilometres) a day.

The progressive introduction of steam ships to replace sail to Australia would improve passenger comfort and further reduce journey times, but the change was slow and for most of the gold era sail was still dominant. By 1870, 20 years after the introduction of steam ships, sail still accounted for almost 60 per cent of international shipping tonnage. Combined steam and sail accounted for about 30 per cent and steam for about 12 per cent. It was not until the 1880s that steam accounted for the majority of international shipping tonnages.[22]

Conditions on board ships to the goldfields during the 1850s had improved considerably compared with earlier times, but they were still tough. Only the rich travelled in a cabin, and less than ten per cent paid for a first-class, second-class or intermediate-class cabin. The overwhelming majority wanted to reach the goldfields as quickly and as cheaply as possible, travelling steerage.

The price of a steerage ticket to Australia in 1851 was about £10, which was roughly equivalent to 40 weeks' wages for a farm labourer in England. Despite the dramatic increase in the supply of shipping, the industry was unable to keep up with demand, and the price of a steerage ticket rose to £26 in 1852 before easing slightly to £23 in 1854. The price of a first-class ticket was more than three times as much and by the end of 1851 had already reached £45.[23]

When the ships reached Australia, many lost their crews as soon as they weighed anchor, as the men deserted to join the gold rush. By the middle of the first year of overseas migration, there were 50 ships stranded in Port Phillip Bay and many more in other Australian ports without enough crew members for the journey home. The mail steamer *The Australian* had to be helped out of Sydney by volunteers, and when it was collecting mail in Melbourne and Adelaide police had to be 'stationed at her gangways' to prevent further desertion.[24]

Among the first to join the gold rush in the wake of the news reaching England was John Sherer, who said he went because he found himself 'a fortuneless young man without a trade':

> I left this country . . . apparently in every way unsuited to encounter the proclaimed difficulties of either a 'life in the bush' or at the 'diggings', but with ample stock of spirits and a natural love of adventure . . . My uncle gave me fifty pounds, saying, 'There, Myles, thou'rt little use here, lad; go to the "diggings", and see if thou canst be of any use there!' and with this unceremonial dismissal I took my departure.[25]

Sailing on the *Mary Ann*, Sherer met two other young men of similar social standing, John Brown and Thomas Binks. They decided to team up and go to the goldfields together once they reached Australia:

> On board ship I had formed an acquaintance with two young men who, like myself, had been of little use in their own country, and who, therefore, had decided to try their luck on the Australian diggings. They were resolute and good humoured, and belonging to the middle classes, consequently were possessed of such feelings and manners as I could associate with without experiencing any repugnancy.[26]

It was far from uncommon for people from the middle classes to go to the goldfields. Contrary to popular belief, the diggers from overseas were not overwhelmingly from the lowest or poorest classes, because the cost of sea passage was prohibitively high for most poor people, roughly equivalent to a year's pay for an unskilled labourer. The typical digger was a person from the middle, skilled or working classes who could somehow put together the cost of reaching Australia and still have enough money when he or she reached the diggings and started mining. Consequently, many of the arrivals had been educated, and the gold seekers who came to Australia from Britain in the 1850s tended to be more literate than the communities they left behind. Seventy-two per cent of the English and Welsh, 80 per cent of the Scottish and almost half of the Irish diggers could read and write.[27]

When Sherer and his colleagues arrived in Port Phillip Bay, the passengers from the *Mary Ann* were taken the final 13 kilometres in little boats up the Yarra River to Melbourne, which Sherer described as a small town of 15,000 to 20,000 people:

> It is built chiefly of brick, and consists of a series of wide streets running parallel to the course of the river. It contains many handsome public buildings and lines of shops, which, although they may not rival the first class of our metropolitan retail repositories of arts and manufactures, still may confidently be assigned a place behind the second.[28]

Sherer and his mates stayed only a couple of days in Melbourne before heading for the diggings, where they experienced mixed fortunes before striking it rich.

Another of those to arrive from England in the first year

of the overseas diggers was William Howitt, who reached Port Phillip Bay in September 1852 and calculated that 5000 to 6000 people were arriving in Melbourne every week.[29]

When Howitt arrived, he complained that passengers were charged exorbitant prices to be transferred from their ships in Port Phillip Bay to smaller barges for the remaining passage into Melbourne:

> The freight from London hither is £3 per ton; from the ship to the wharf, eight miles [13 kilometres], is just under half that sum, 30 shillings, and this, with the system prevailing at the wharves, and the enormous charges for the cartage thence in to town, the whole cost of transferring your effects to your lodgings is actually more than bringing them the previous 13,000 miles [20,920 kilometres], including the cost of conveying them from your house to the London Docks.[30]

Once he reached Melbourne, he was shocked by the price of renting accommodation and complained that 'two rooms, wretchedly furnished' cost between four and six shillings a week.

With more and more people pouring into Melbourne, whole new towns sprang up, and the land prices rapidly escalated:

> Just over the hill beyond the town, there meets you an extraordinary spectacle. It is an immense suburb stretching parallel with the town [of Melbourne] . . . covered all over with thousands of little tenements, chiefly of wood, and almost every one of them of only one storey high. These extend as far as the eye can command . . . the upper portion

being called Collingwood and the lower Richmond. These suburbs contain a population equal to that of Melbourne itself; and they have flung up from the vast influx of population, chiefly since the gold discovery.[31]

Howitt said that the local landscape had been completely flattened:

Every single tree has been levelled to the ground; it is one hard bare expanse, bare of all natural attractions; a wilderness of wooden huts of Lilliputian dimensions; and everywhere around them, timber and rubbish, delightfully interspersed with pigs, geese, hens, goats, and dogs innumerable . . . The streets . . . are not roads but quagmires, through which bullock drays drag fresh materials, with enormous labour ploughing the muddy soil up their very axles.[32]

Howitt also said that the diggers from overseas were forced to make a big adjustment for the heat and the dryness of the Australian bush, and found the insects difficult to handle:

The plague of flies in this shut up glen [on the Buckland River, Victoria] was something terrible. What do these vermin live on, where there is no living creature? Having here nobody but us to prey upon they assailed us with voracious fury. The little black-devil fly all day attacked our eyes, nose and mouth; and great blowflies in thousands blew our blankets, rugs and everything woollen, all over with their maggots, which were at once dried upon them by the sun.[33]

Women were something of a rarity on the goldfields in the early days. George Preshaw, who arrived from England in Victoria with his family, described the great excitement among the diggers when his sister visited him on the Mount Alexander goldfield:

> In December 1852, my father paid a flying visit and returned with my eldest sister, who was one of the first women on the Mount Alexander diggings. She drove up in a cart on top of some loading, and was five days on the road. As they rode through Forest Creek the cry ran along the lead, 'A woman! A woman!' Men shouted out to their mates below, who hurried to the top, and hundreds of eyes were fixed on her the whole way from Golden Point till she reached her future home at Campbell's Creek.[34]

As the goldfields became more established, the number of women and children who joined and worked alongside the males increased. In 1857, a census of the Victorian goldfields revealed that more than a quarter of the total of 160,000 people were females.[35] In 1861, the number of women had almost doubled, to almost a third of the total population.[36]

Among the women to go to the diggings in the early days was 22-year-old Emily Fillan, who went unmarried and unchaperoned by ship from Southampton in 1854 to meet her fiancé, who was already on the Victorian goldfields.

Emily Fillan was born in Saint Pancras, London, in 1832 and was the ninth of ten children. Her mother was Ruth Solomon, whose Jewish parents disowned their daughter when she married a gentile Scottish jeweller named William Fillan. As a girl, young Emily seemed to have a 'modestly secure' upbringing and was educated to be quite literate.[37] She was a fan of Charles Dickens, who wrote *Oliver Twist* and *Nicholas Nickleby* in nearby Doughty Street, and several references to Dickens can be found in the diary she kept of her journey to Australia and life in the goldfields.

It is not clear how she met her fiancé, William Elliot Skinner, who had left England to try his luck in the gold-fields the year before. William was the son of a farmer and gave his own occupation as blacksmith. He arrived in Sydney on the *Ganges* in June 1853 and headed for the goldfields at Ovens in northern Victoria.

Emily describes how she boarded the *Lady Jocelyn* on Sunday 4 June 1854, which was one of the early ships with both sail and steam engine to sail to Australia. After being rowed out to the ship, she found her berth, which 'was a nice one in an intermediate cabin' and remembers her brother Bill and family friends waving goodbye with handkerchiefs as the ship's little band played tunes. She was later in the voyage to note that the majority of passengers travelled steerage and had no cabin. They had paid 30 guineas and were 'shamefully treated', while 'the intermediate that pay 40 guineas have everything very comfortable indeed'.[38]

She was to share her cabin with three other women, two who were going to Australia to join their husbands and the third whose fiancé was on the same ship. One of the married women, a Mrs Thomas, was to take young Emily under her wing and would have appeared to the rest of the passengers as her chaperone. There were only 12 women on the ship and almost a hundred men.

On the first day, the ship left on a 'fair wind' and by evening Emily suffered seasickness and complained that those who had not experienced it had 'no idea' how awful it was.

Within two days, she was 'feeling quite strong and well and [able to] enjoy the sea air', thanks to the bottle of salts her fiancé, Will, had given her before he left England. But, as with so many others who made the journey to Australia, she was unimpressed with the quality of food and drink on the ship:

> Oh, what horrible coffee, so bitterly strong; no milk, nor sugar; almost black, and the biscuits have such a horrible taste . . . they are almost uneatable . . . Came down to dinner and found some very good soup and pudding, but the meat, black and uneatable.[39]

By the end of the first week at sea, as the days were already getting warmer, the passengers began to get into something of a routine. Emily said that they sat on the deck for most of the day, where she did 'a little' needlework but was forever being interrupted by other passengers wanting to stop and talk. Emily said she couldn't bear sitting below deck, even though the ship had a 'splendid saloon' that was 'beautiful throughout'. In the afternoon and the evenings, the band played and the passengers would sit up on deck till about ten o'clock before going down to their beds, which were 'very comfortable', even though some complained at having only horsehair mattresses.

After slightly more than a week at sea, they passed the Canary Islands, and life aboard the *Lady Jocelyn* began to become repetitive. Emily noted that while almost everyone around her kept a journal, she herself had little to say:

> Morning everyone busy writing journals. I hope they are all better hand at it than I am, or else they won't be worth reading – I fear – but there is such a sameness. There seems nothing to write about.[40]

Now it was getting hotter, and they looked forward to stopping at San Vicente, where they were promised oranges:

> They are so nice when one is thirsty. It is excessively hot now, we have scarcely any shadow at noon. I suppose we shall be getting to the Line [equator] soon and then we shall have it cold afterwards.[41]

The ship reached San Vicente in the Cape Verde islands off the north African coast on 16 June. As they passed an American ship at anchor, its band struck up 'God Save the Queen' and the British responded with the ship's band playing 'Yankee Doodle'. Having seen nothing but sea and sky for the previous few weeks, Emily said the land was enchanting and the port picturesque, and they enjoyed walking on firm land even though the ground was so hot that it seemed 'to scorch one's feet'.[42]

While in the harbour, the ship was surrounded by little boats carrying coal for the *Lady Jocelyn*'s steam engines.

Emily noted that many of the passengers and crew came back to the ship drunk on the local wine, 'which is so very bad stuff and soon takes effect'.[43]

After leaving San Vicente, they headed south and

crossed the equator on Sunday 25 June, which the sailors celebrated with the arrival on board of 'King Neptune' and a wild costume party that went well into the night.

By early July, they could see the Southern Cross, the constellation that can only be viewed in the southern hemisphere, and they experienced their first really rough weather. The ship was travelling at a fair 12 knots and rolling from side to side, nothing could be put on the table and passengers were being thrown out of their beds. The weather worsened and the temperature fell as they entered the heart of the southern-hemisphere winter, and Emily was to complain that she was doing less and less:

> It is now too cold to sit on deck for any length of time, even in the day, and the saloon is disagreeably crowded in the evenings. I generally lie in bed now till very late; the decks are so wet and uncomfortable, so I get some breakfast in bed and get up after that. I have quite got rid of the seasickness now, not having felt the least sick through all this rough weather. I enjoy the voyage very much, but am getting horribly lazy.[44]

Towards the end of July, there was a 'mutiny' among the sailors caused by the poor quality of their provisions, and the officers were obliged to provide better food:

> The captain says they shall be punished when they get to Melbourne. Poor fellows, the meat and biscuits they get are only fit for pigs.[45]

About halfway from the southern coast of Africa and the west coast of Australia, they encountered strong gales with hailstones, thunder and lightning, which made it too difficult to open the cabin door. In early August, the ship's doctor died. He had been ill for more than a month and had not been expected to recover. 'It was brought on by drinking hard – which seems to be a custom with most ships doctors'.[46] A gentleman chemist who was a passenger took his place, but they were fortunate that no one was seriously ill for the remainder of the voyage.

As the journey drew to its last weeks, Emily said that the ship's Scottish chief engineer 'sends for Mrs. Thomas and me every day'.[47] He had his own private cabin on the deck, and, while there was little good food still on board, they had dinner brought to his cabin, which included 'fowl and ham, tarts and puddings, and all manner of good things, and tea and toast in the evenings'.[48]

On 8 August, four days before they reached Melbourne, the wind died away and they steamed the rest of the way. They had only needed the steam engine on 18 of the 64 days of the voyage, and they reached Melbourne in a little over nine weeks.[49] The ship docked in Port Phillip Bay on the night of Saturday 12 August, and both Mrs Thomas's husband and Miss Fillan's fiancé came down to the wharf to meet them. After some difficulty, William Skinner managed to rent a dray to take their belongings to a friend's house in Collingwood, where they stayed before renting their own little flat for £1 a week until they headed off to the Ovens goldfields.

While England was to provide the largest number of diggers to the Australian gold rushes, the prospectors came from all over the world. Many came from Ireland in the aftermath of the potato famine, which had devastated the country from 1847, and also to escape what they saw as British oppression. The famine, which was estimated to have been responsible for more than a million deaths, was caused by a disease (*Phytophthora infestans*) that was believed to have come from South America and attacked the Irish potato crop. Potatoes were the staple diet of the Irish and more nutritious than the bread that formed the basis of the standard diet of the peasants of England and on the Continent. Many Irish lived almost exclusively on a diet of potato supplemented with a little buttermilk, salt, cabbage and occasionally fish.

Most of the predominantly Catholic Irish were already poor and living in squalid conditions on farms averaging only about ten acres (about four hectares) that were leased from typically aristocratic absentee British Protestant landlords.

By the late 1840s, about a hundred thousand poor and diseased people sailed in desperation from Ireland to Canada in cramped, unhygienic vessels that became known as the 'coffin ships'. Others made their way across the Irish Sea to the cities of Liverpool and Glasgow, where they were unwelcome and deported back to Ireland in large numbers.

The dire situation became worse from 1848 when financially indebted landlords evicted more impoverished potato-farming tenants. Thousands more died when those who could not afford the rent were evicted and could not find or afford food. Hordes of Irish people sailed for the United States, where they would account for more than 40 per cent of America's migrant population by 1850.

The news of the gold discovery in New South Wales and Victoria in 1851 resulted in more than a hundred thousand Irish migrants turning to Australia in the next decade and a further 300,000 by the end of the nineteenth century. The Irish would become a dominant influence on the cultural development of Australia.

One of the Irish who arrived in Australia during the first wave of migration from overseas in October 1852 was 25-year-old Peter Lalor, with his brother Richard. Peter was one of 11 brothers born to Patrick and Anne Lalor, who, until the potato famine, were relatively prosperous on a large leased farm of 700 acres (about 280 hectares). Peter was lucky to receive an education and studied as an engineer in Dublin. When he first arrived in Victoria, he found work on the construction of one of Australia's first railways, from Melbourne to Geelong. In 1854, after his brother Richard had returned to Ireland, where he would later become a member of the British Parliament and an advocate of Irish Home Rule, Peter Lalor headed off to the Ovens gold diggings. A few months later, he moved on to Ballarat, where he would become a major player in the bloody Eureka uprising later the same year.

After the British, the next biggest source of immigrant diggers was the Chinese. There were already several thousand Chinese workers in Australia before gold was discovered. They had come mainly from China's southern provinces to work on the sheep farms of New South Wales at a time when the decline in convicts to Australia was creating a labour shortage. Young Chinese were found work in various foreign countries in the 1840s and 1850s by local agents, who would promise them a better future and pay for the ship's passage, which would be repaid when they began earning money in their new land.[50]

When the Chinese returned home after typically one, two or three years, they would be replaced by new arrivals and would be a regular feature of almost all the major Australian diggings over the next 50 years. While no reliable figures exist, it is likely that a total of more than half a million came to Australia at some point during that time.[51]

Thousands of Chinese had gone to join the gold rush in California after the news had reached Hong Kong in 1848. Initially, the number of Chinese heading for Australia was quite low, and it would not pick up dramatically until 1854. It has been suggested that the reason for the lateness of the Chinese was that they feared the British and mistrusted British law, and it was only when mining for gold in California became more difficult and less fruitful that they turned towards Australia.[52]

The young Chinese men – there were practically no women – would toil for years in strange lands, sending as much money as they could back to their families before eventually returning home.

One of the first references to the Chinese being on the goldfields was made by the member of parliament Jas Macarthur in September 1852 and reported in the *Sydney Morning Herald* the following day.[53] Probably no more than about 500 new Chinese diggers reached the Australian goldfields that year, and more came in early 1853, as reported by the papers.[54] In 1854, they began to arrive in their thousands.[55] By the end of the 1850s, there were more than 40,000 on the Victorian goldfields and around 20,000 in New South Wales.

The Chinese migration to Australia and other parts of South East Asia and the Pacific came predominantly from Kwangtung Province in the south. In the nineteenth century, migration was an attractive proposition, given widespread corruption, political turmoil, dynastic decline, floods, crop failures, banditry and interclan rivalry.

Most of the Chinese destined for Australia would be ferried on coastal junks from Canton and elsewhere to Hong Kong, Cumsingmoon and Whampoa, where they would board bigger British- or American-owned ships for the voyage to Australia.

The ships' captains used a number of different sea routes from China to Australia, chosen according to wind or whim. If they were sailing for Australia around Cape Leeuwin, on the south-west, they might come first through the Makassar Strait and Lombok Strait, or alternatively through the Sunda Strait separating Java and Sumatra. If they were coming from Shanghai or Amoy, they might sail well east of New Britain and through the Coral Sea and down the east coast of Australia. The other east-coast routes from Hong Kong and Whampoa were via Singapore, then east through the Torres Strait and south along the east coast of Australia. Alternatively, they could sail via Manila and through the Ambon Strait to the Torres Strait.

The duration of the sea voyage varied greatly – from between 70 and 125 days – which made the journey times remarkably similar to those from England to Australia. The actual time depended on the type of ship, the time of year and the associated prevailing winds.

On the voyage out, the Chinese were forced to entertain themselves to overcome boredom, just as all of those who had embarked on the long voyage from Europe had done. They gambled and played dominoes, cards and chess. Some of the younger ones learned to smoke their first pipes of opium. Their musicians played fiddles, flutes, drums and cymbals.[56]

The ships from China met with their fair share of misfortune. In August 1854, the *Onyx* arrived in Port Phillip Bay from Hong Kong with news that 24 of its 214 passengers had died during the 123-day voyage. Within a few days, a further eight had died. According to Ha Foon, who was one of the surviving Chinese passengers, the ship had supplied rice, fish and vegetables but the fish was bad. Ha Foon said that he and his colleagues had avoided eating the fish, but many of the others, including the Chinese doctor on board, had eaten it and died. The coroner in Melbourne concluded they had all died of food poisoning.[57] There were also regular reports of ships arriving with their passengers suffering an outbreak of smallpox[58] or some other disease.[59]

On reaching Australia, the Chinese would have typically encountered the first insults and jeering as soon as they landed. Usually, for the first few days, they would camp on the outskirts of the town of their arrival, where they would buy mining equipment and other supplies from an established Chinese-owned store before heading off to the goldfields.

To reach the goldfields, they would load the heaviest equipment onto drays, for the trek could be several hundred kilometres. The Chinese men would travel on foot in single file, each carrying supplies in two baskets hanging from the ends of a long pole over their shoulders. Each man could carry up to 78 kilograms – more than their average body weight – in what has been described by the historian Eric Rolls as a strange slow jog:

> Their gait was not a true jog. It was a unique movement . . . halfway between a walk and a trot, smooth and fast.

Their thighs used to roll on their hips instead of moving backwards and forwards. When a European carries a load on a pole, it bobs up and down and bruises his shoulder. The Chinese carries loads of up to 78 kilograms balanced on the bamboo poles about 1.8 metres long that they brought with them. They carry them at an acute angle to the line of walk. Seen from the side, the pole kept a straight horizontal line as if the bearers had been on wheels.[60]

After the British and the Chinese, the next largest source of gold diggers on the Australian goldfields was Germany. By 1861, more than 20,000 Germans had been lured to Australia, and about half were on the goldfields around Bendigo in Victoria.[61]

One of the most successful of the German miners was Christopher Ballerstedt, who arrived with his son Theodore in 1852 before walking to the goldfields with their belongings in a wheelbarrow. Johann Gottfried Tobias Christopher Ballerstedt was born into a relatively comfortable middle-class family in Madgeberg in Germany in 1796. As a 19-year-old, he was drafted into the Prussian Army and fought at the Battle of Waterloo.

After marrying and then becoming widowed, Ballerstedt and one of his sons, the 21-year-old Theodore, headed in the late 1840s to the California diggings, where they were only moderately successful before hearing of the discovery of gold in Australia. Ballerstedt and his son joined several thousand other Germans on the fields around Bendigo at Diamond Hill, Victoria Hill, New Chum Gully and Iron Bark, and became spectacularly successful in quartz mining, which involved the crushing of hard, gold-bearing quartz rock from deeper beneath the surface.

Another to arrive from Continental Europe in the first year of the gold rush was the exiled Italian revolutionary Raffaello Carboni, who had read about the gold discoveries in the *Illustrated London News*. Carboni sailed from England on the *Prince Albert* in 1852 and would become a major player in the Eureka uprising.

Carboni was 35 years old when he arrived in Australia. He was born in Fioravanti in 1817 and studied in Rome, where he was first arrested for republican sympathies when he was 23. In 1848, he fought briefly in the failed republican uprising in Rome and was wounded in the leg, which was to trouble him through his later life. Forced along with other republicans into exile, Carboni went first to live in Hanover in Germany and later to London, where his command of French, German, Spanish and English, as well as his native Italian, allowed him to eke out a living as a linguist and language teacher.

After the Eureka rebellion, Carboni later returned to Italy and joined the successful Risorgimento, or unification of Italy, under the leadership of Giuseppe Garibaldi in the 1860s.

Among the French who came to the goldfields was Antoine Fauchery, an author and photographer who would provide some of the earliest photographs of diggers on the Victorian goldfields. Fauchery pointed out that most of the Continental Europeans who joined the gold rush to Australia sailed from British ports. He sailed from Gravesend on the *Emily* on 23 July 1852 and had enough money to pay for a cabin but still claimed it was a trying voyage:

[It was] midway between the Hotel Des Princes and the keg. For 625 francs, I had a weekly allocation of 3 lb biscuits, 2 lb salted beef, 1½ lb pork, ditto, ½ lb smoked fish, a little flour, rice, dried potatoes, butter, tea, brown sugar, salt and pepper . . . and a cabin smaller than those in which one undresses at the swimming baths, which I had to furnish at my own expense with a mattress and a water jug.[62]

Several thousand Americans also joined the rush to Australia, including 22-year-old George Francis Train, who came from Boston in early 1853 aboard the *Bavaria*. Train quickly established a very profitable import business by reselling goods at very high prices to a retail market hungry for luxury.

Also coming from America were many who had been on the forty-niners trail in California, including a number of returning Australians, such as Simpson Davison. Davison said that he had initially been sceptical when he heard about the claims of gold in Australia but was persuaded by a letter he received from a friend, Mr T. W. Bowden, who had been with him and Hargraves in California but was then back in Sydney. Bowden told Davison that his former companion Hargraves had been given a big reward and appointed gold commissioner, and that he too should hurry back:

You should lose no time in getting to Sydney or Port Phillip. I have seen Sydney newspapers by the last arrival, which contain astonishing accounts of the abundance of gold.[63]

As Davison and thousands of others tried to find a passage to the new goldfields, the shipping companies responded by providing additional ships for a regular service between America and the east coast of Australia. A typical advertisement was for the sailing of the *Isabella* from San Francisco to Sydney:

> For Australian gold mines, via Honolulu, the fine new Baltimore clipper, *Isabella*, will sail for the above ports on or before 5 February 1852, 400 tons burden. Master; Deane. Her accommodations are superior. Both cabin and steerage have been fitted up expressly for the comfort of passengers and supplied with new mattresses & etc throughout, which render it one of the best opportunities for parties wishing a speedy and pleasant voyage to the new gold regions. Early application is necessary, as only a limited number will be taken . . . apply on board, foot of Jackson Street . . .[64]

Similar advertisements appeared for ships sailing to the Australian goldfields from other American cities, including New York and Boston.

Davison left San Francisco on the American sailing ship the *Orpheus*, which had 50 cabin passengers and 150 in steerage. After an 'agreeable voyage' via Samoa and the Friendly Isles, he reached Sydney in September 1852. He said that he 'resolved to go direct to Sydney' but immediately after arriving was quickly persuaded to head to Victoria:

> We soon gathered the information that the goldfields of Victoria were the grand point of attraction . . . Gold, it

was said, was being dug out in Victoria in pounds, and not by ounces as in California.[65]

He stayed only long enough in Sydney to catch up with old friends and to write to Hargraves, who was now touring Victoria as gold commissioner. By the middle of 1852, everyone was trying to get to Victoria, and Davison had difficulty finding a ship to take him from Sydney to Melbourne but eventually found a berth on the *Shamrock*, which reached Melbourne in September 1852.

Davison felt that Hargraves should have acknowledged his involvement in the first discussions they had in California about the possible existence of gold in New South Wales. He was to later complain that he had sent his brother a letter of introduction to Hargraves from California but that their subsequent meeting went badly and Davison's brother never wanted to deal with Hargraves again. Davison also said that, after he returned to Australia, a number of letters he sent to Hargraves were returned undelivered.

Davison said of Melbourne, 'The bustle of the city was San Francisco all over again.'[66] He had great difficulty finding lodgings before leaving two days later for Bendigo, paying 'a shilling a pound' for the carriage of his mining tools and supplies.

On the way to Bendigo, he stopped to look at the Forest Creek diggings near Mount Alexander and met up with another of his old friends from California, a Mr Bourisquot, who was able to give him lots of local advice.[67]

Davison had teamed up with another colleague, and together they set up camp at a place called White Hill, which by the end of 1852 when they arrived had already been extensively mined for more than a year. Davison said the locals advised them that all the gold had already been found, but he was confident from his experience in California that he would be able to see gold where less experienced miners had not:

> We pitched our tent near the first White Hill, and I went out with a companion to prospect. The first man we met told us the usual tale, namely, that all the gold was dug out, and that we had arrived too late . . . However, on entering several shafts of deserted claims on the first hill, I was very well satisfied with the first examination. My experience in hill-digging and underground excavation here proved to be of great service to me. I saw with an experienced eye that many of the claims had been worked by inexperienced miners, and that therefore a great deal of virgin ground remained to be dug.[68]

Davison said that while he did not find any 'lead or line' of gold, he found irregular patches that made for the 'steadily remunerative and comfortable digging that could be desired'.[69]

In the first two years after the news of gold reached Europe, more people came to Australia than had come in the previous 60 years since the start of convict transportation. By the end of 1852, nearly 300,000 immigrants had arrived, and over the next twenty years the population of Australia would treble.[70]

CHAPTER FIVE

Life on the Goldfields

Destinations of daily stage-coach services to the goldfields,
Victoria, 1858

But night at the diggings is the characteristic time: murder here,
murder there – revolvers cracking – blunderbusses bombing
– rifles going off – balls whistling – one man groaning with
a broken leg, another shouting because he couldn't find the
way to his hole, and a third equally vociferous because he had
tumbled into one . . . Here is a man grumbling because he has
brought his wife with him, another ditto because he has left his
behind, or sold her for an ounce of gold or a bottle of rum.

Life on the goldfields was hazardous, with thousands of people – mostly men – spending months and even years living on poor diets, cramped together in tents or crude timber and bark huts, with little or no furniture, in heavily polluted country, where water was scarce and violence, crime, disease and death were rife.

The typical digger was a hardy, unshaven man who washed infrequently, lived and worked with a group of mates, and walked to the diggings carrying all his belongings or pushing them in a wheelbarrow. Ellen Clacy, who was one of the relatively few women in the early days to go to the goldfields from England, described how the typical digger carried all his swag:

> Most carried on their backs their individual property – blankets, provisions for the road, etc, rolled in a skin, and fastened over the shoulders by leather straps. This bundle goes by the name of 'swag', and is the digger's usual accompaniment . . . The weight of one of these 'swags' is far from light; the provender for the road is itself by no means trifling, though that is of course diminished by the way, and lightens the load a little. Still there are the blankets, the firearms, drinking and eating apparatus, clothing, chamois-leather for gold that has yet to be dug, and numberless other cumbersome articles necessary for the digger.[1]

Clacy was also struck by the spartan conditions of the typical digger's tent:

> The interior of the canvas habitation of the digger is desolate enough; a box on a block of wood form a table,

and this is the only furniture; many dispense with that. The bedding, which is laid on the ground, serves to sit upon. Diogenes in his tub would not have looked more comfortless than anyone else. Tin plates and pannikins, the same as are used for camping up, compose the breakfast, dinner and tea service, which meals usually consist of the same dishes – mutton, damper, and tea.[2]

Clacy came from a relatively well-to-do family in London, was literate and wrote a detailed account of the lives of men, women and children in the early days on the goldfields. She described how in London her brother Frank had become 'infected' with the gold contagion, and in less than three weeks they had 'packed, tinned and corded' their luggage and together taken the train from London to Gravesend, from where they set to sea for Melbourne in April 1852. Arriving in Port Phillip Bay in August, they found the harbour crowded with ships and almost all accommodation in Melbourne taken at extremely high rents.[3]

Clacy said that her brother Frank had teamed up with four other young men while on the ship to Australia, and together they hurriedly bought all the requisite supplies and equipment in Melbourne before hastening to the goldfields:

Still we would delay no longer, and the bustle of preparation began. Stores of flour, tea and sugar, tents and canvas, camp ovens, cooking utensils, tin plates and pannikins, opossum rugs and blankets, drays, carts and horses, cradles, etc, etc, had to be looked at, bought and paid for.[4]

The party had enough money to buy their own dray for £100 and 'two strong cart horses' for £90 and £100, along with a surplus amount of food from which they hoped to make an 'immense profit' when they sold it at the goldfields.

They left Melbourne destined for Forest Creek at six in the morning on 7 September with everyone walking beside the cart except for Ellen, who rode up on top. They had decided to 'camp out' during their 11-day trek 'to avoid the vicinity of the inns . . . on the way, which are frequently the lurking places of thieves and bushrangers'.[5]

On their way to the diggings, Ellen Clacy's party met up with three successful returning diggers who were camping near them:

> They were rather sociable, and gave us a good account of the diggings. They had themselves been very fortunate. On the very day that we had been idly resting on the borders of the Black Forest, they had succeeded in taking twenty three pounds weight out of their claim, and two days after, two hundred and six ounces more, making, in all, gold to the value (in England) of about eighteen hundred pounds.[6]

The happy diggers were on their way to Melbourne to have a good time and splash out before they returned to work again digging at Bendigo. When asked why they did not make better use of their hard-earned money, they simply replied, 'Plenty more to be got where this came from.'[7]

Finally, after ten days, Clacy's party reached Eagle Hawk Gully, where they established their camp and settled down to life on the diggings. For her party of six, Ellen Clacy was responsible for buying and cooking the food. They could only buy mutton at 'half a sheep at a time', which she roasted in the camp oven:

> We passed a butchers shop, or rather tent . . . The animals cut in halves or quarters, were hung around; no small joints there – half a sheep or none; heads, feet and skins were lying about for anyone to have for the trouble of picking them up . . . The mutton was baked in a large camp oven suspended from three iron bars, which were fixed in the ground in the form of a triangle, about a yard apart, and were joined together at the top, at which part the oven was hung over a wood fire. This grand cooking machine was, of course, outside the tent. Sometimes I have seen a joint of meat catch fire in one of these ovens, and it is difficult to extinguish it before the fat has burnt itself away, when the meat looks like a cinder.[8]

Clacy's party worked hard but fruitlessly for almost a month when, on 2 October, in 'a dark corner' of a shaft, they hit on a pocket that by nightfall had yielded five pounds of gold. Shortly before the discovery, one of the five young men in the party had left to return to Melbourne because, he said, he could 'no longer put up with such ungentlemanly work in so very unintellectual a neighbourhood, with bad living into the bargain'. He also complained that he could not continue to survive on the diet of tea, damper and mutton.[9]

Shortly after, amid talk that Eagle Hawk Gully was close to being mined out, Clacy, her brother and the three remaining partners decided to move on to Iron Bark, where stories were circulating of much easier and better mining.

At Iron Bark, they found many deserted holes among those still being worked and 'several women about', some of whom could be seen cradling an infant in their arms. Ellen Clacy said that the standard of living in the typical digger's tent or hut improved significantly with the arrival of women:

In some tents the soft influence of our sex is pleasingly apparent: the tins are as bright as silver, there are sheets as well as blankets on the beds, and perhaps a clean counterpane, with the addition of a dry sack or a piece of carpet on the ground; whilst a pet cockatoo, chained to a perch, makes noise enough to keep the 'missus' from feeling lonely when the good man is at work.[10]

In the first years of the rush, men outnumbered the women of Australia by a ratio of about four to one. Clacy warned women not to be carried away by the prospects of marrying a gold miner, however, because they would not make good husbands:

Much is said and written in England about the scarcity of females in Australia, and with a good many offers awaiting the acceptance of those who have the courage to travel so far, but the colonial bachelors, who are so ready to get married, and so very easy in their choice of wife, are generally those the least calculated, in spite of their wealth, to make a respectable girl happy.[11]

As they stayed longer on the diggings, the miners

increasingly built for themselves shacks from trees, bark and whatever materials they could find locally. William Howitt, who had arrived with his two sons at the Victorian goldfields in 1852, said the different influences of the American and Irish diggers could be seen in the design of their shacks:

> It is curious to see the various rude constructions of these huts and chimneys. Some huts are built of solid trunks of trees, laid horizontally, in fact, the log huts of America reconstructed here . . . Other huts are made of slabs. Placed upright and the roof often covered only with canvas. Others again are covered with bullock-hides. The chimneys are extraordinary pieces of architecture; some built horizontal, some of perpendicular timbers, up to the eves of the tent, and then tapering away to some height, covered with bark, or sheets of tin which have lined packages. Others, again, are covered with bullock-hides, and some with sheepskins, and not put on in any orderly style . . . You may generally distinguish the abodes of the natives of Ireland, by the picturesque resemblance to the cabins of the green Isle, being more remarkable for their defiance of symmetry than any others. They seem to be tossed up, rather than built, and are sure to have sundry black poles sticking out of the top, and pieces of sacking or old breaches hung up before them, here and there, to keep the wind from driving all the smoke down into the interior.[12]

The rapid expansion of the goldfields required an elaborate network to provide for the food and other needs of thousands of people. Commerce and enterprise quickly followed the diggers to the fields, and within weeks of the opening of any new diggings a variety of tent shops and stores would open up, selling a wide range of goods. For those who could afford it, shops on the diggings were soon selling sugar candy, potted anchovies, pickles from East India, Bass's pale ale, quality leather boots, baby cradles and clothing, cheese, butter, yellow soap, women's frocks, men's serge shirts and wide-awake hats, and tallow candles. William Howitt described the carts loaded with goods that arrived at the goldfields:

> The drays were laden with flour, corn, potatoes, sugar, tea spirits, bottled beer, and the like, as well as spades, buckets, & etc. On the roadsides were stores displaying plentiful assortments of wares of all sizes, hanging in front – tea kettles, bales of flannel, shoes, boots, readymade clothes, etc; in fact, all such things as diggers are in constant want of.[13]

Thirty-one-year-old William Diaper, who was born in Colchester in England and spent three years on the Australian goldfields in the early 1850s, described how he sold tobacco on the New South Wales Turon River diggings:

> As I was walking about Bathurst township, I follow'd a bell which an old man happened to be ringing. It was sale. Three hundred weight of Colonial tobacco was the first article: 6 pence per pound was bid. 7 pence was bid. 7½. 'No advance on 7½.' '8 pence,' I cried, and it was knocked down to me. I shoved it on a dray and took it out to the Turon. I hawked it about where drays and stores could not

get, at the back creeks, calling it the best 'American negro head'. I sorted it into two qualities – the best 10 shillings and the inferior 9 shillings a pound. Everybody preferred the best, and as soon as the best was all sold, I called the inferior 'best' too, and sold that at the same price. I realized a great sum in a very few weeks.[14]

Within a year, a range of manufacturing industries had sprung up on the goldfields, including cradle-makers, coffin-makers, iron-smiths, candle-makers, bootmakers and sad-dlers. At the same time, an increased range of imported goods, including fine cloth and clothing, fine furniture, silver, glassware and oil lamps, began to appear in the shops of the towns that had sprung up near the major diggings.

During the day, the goldfields were a hive of industry, but little work could be done at nightfall. After the evening meal, the diggers would sit around talking, drinking and smoking. In the age before cigarettes, tobacco was smoked in a pipe usually after the evening meal, when the pipe could be filled then lit from the campfire, as matches were still an expensive item to buy.

For the first few years, licences permitting the sale of alcohol were limited to public houses on the roads and strictly forbidden on the goldfields. However, sly grog shops were prevalent throughout all the goldfields and no amount of policing could rub them out. Ellen Clacy's gentility was offended by the 'abandoned and depraved characters' who sold the grog – particularly a woman who operated out of a nearby tent at the diggings:

Whilst her husband was at work farther down the gully, she kept a sort of sly grog shop, and passed the day in selling and drinking spirits, swearing, and smoking a short tobacco pipe at the door of her tent. She was the most repulsive looking object. A dirty gaudy-coloured dress hung about her shoulders, coarse black hair unbrushed, uncombed, dangling about her face, over which her evil habits had spread a genuine bacchanalian glow, while in a large masculine voice she uttered the most awful words that ever disgraced the mouth of a man.[15]

Ellen Clacy claimed the savage drinking on the goldfields produced wild behaviour, including violence, murder and even wife selling:

But night at the diggings is the characteristic time: murder here, murder there – revolvers cracking – blunderbusses bombing – rifles going off – balls whistling – one man groaning with a broken leg, another shouting because he couldn't find the way to his hole, and a third equally vociferous because he had tumbled into one . . . Here is a man grumbling because he has brought his wife with him, another ditto because he has left his behind, or sold her for an ounce of gold or a bottle of rum.[16]

Some of the grog shops managed to evade the law by not actually selling alcohol but proportionately upping the prices of other items sold at the store. The customer simply paid 'a shilling more for his fig tobacco, and his wife an extra 6d for suet' and the drink was provided free.[17]

John Chandler, who made a success of carting provisions to the diggings, after arriving on the goldfields as an 11-year-old with his father, explained how grog was smuggled in:

We loaded in Elizabeth Street, at a merchant's named Smithsons. Our loading was general stores and grog. The grog was in 5-gallon kegs, and addressed to different people, for there was no spirits allowed to be sold on the diggings. It was placed in the middle of the dray, and the sugar, tea, etc., packed all round it and over the top, so the troopers could not see that we had any grog on board.[18]

Chandler said that, despite the prohibition, grog selling was rampant:

All spirits found in any tent or store, were seized, and carried to the Commissioner's camp and destroyed. But there was a law so much evaded, for in nearly every instance, one tent in five was a sly grog shanty.[19]

By and large, the predominantly young diggers were fit and healthy, but this soon changed on practically all of the diggings due to a lack of sanitation and sewerage, and the pollution of the local water. Illness and disease were common, particularly typhoid and dysentery, and, as Ellen Clacy observed, there were few doctors with honest qualifications and their fees were very high:

It is no joke to get ill at the diggings; doctors make you pay for it. The fees are – for a consultation at their own tent, ten shillings; for a visit out, from one to ten pounds, according to the time and distance. Most are regular quacks, and they seem to flourish most.[20]

A journalist on the goldfields noted how profitable doctoring had become:

Doctoring must be a good trade at the diggings, if nowhere else in Australia. A man who some time ago left his native village in Suffolk, to try his fortune at the antipodes, writes home that he has earned £50 as a gold-digger in one month, but along with it the typhus fever, for the cure of which his doctor charged him £41.[21]

Injury and death were common on the goldfields, where there were no enforced safety standards other than the requirement that diggers hoist a scarf or flag above an open mineshaft. A large proportion of serious injuries and death occurred when men fell down deep shafts, when shafts collapsed or they were flash flooded with men still working in them. And many miners died at night, particularly after drinking, by falling into a mineshaft while trying to find their way back to their tents.

For children on the goldfields, there was no protection other than family. Ellen Clacy recounted a story of how she and her brother met a young ten-year-old girl named Jessie who lived on the diggings with her grandfather. Her mother had died, and Jessie made and sold candles and woven hats for the diggers because her grandfather had taken ill and was unable to continue mining. One morning, Clacy and her brother Frank found Jessie under a blanket on an old mattress alongside her grandfather, who was dead. Frank left a little money with the butcher and asked him to arrange for the burial of the old man. Together with his sister, Frank decided to take young Jessie, who had no known living relatives, with them when they decided to move on to Forest Creek.

After a short time at Forest Creek, near Mount Alexander, Ellen Clacy returned to Melbourne at the end of October 1852, taking young Jessie with her. There, she found foster parents to bring up the little girl. Clacy said she also established a fund for the young girl's upbringing from money donated to her by successful gold-mining colleagues. On 15 November 1852, after only four months in Australia, Ellen Clacy was farewelled at Williamstown on Port Phillip Bay by her brother Frank, young Jessie and her other friends, where she boarded a ship to return to England.

There were relatively few police on the goldfields to handle the inevitable crime that came with thousands of diggers competing with each other. The effectiveness of the police was further reduced by the disproportionate amount of time they spent checking miners' licences and hunting down sly grog operators. Most of the crimes against the diggers involved theft, which was often handled by the diggers themselves, either by summarily shooting the offender or banishing him or her from the goldfields into the bush, where, without any provisions, survival was difficult.

In the early years of the gold rush, the diggers would spend the Sabbath tidying their camp, going for walks and heading into the bush to hunt game, so as to provide a little variety to their diet. All over the camps on Sunday morning, there were church services, and by 1852 the Victorian Government was subsidising the four churches of 'England, Scotland, Rome and Wesleyan', so that preachers could go to the fields.[22]

In the early days of the discovery of gold, it had taken several days to reach the diggings – even for those on horseback or in a coach – but within only three years the journey from Melbourne to the goldfields had been reduced to a few hours and the price of the ride had been cut to make it more affordable to more diggers.

At the head of the revolution in coach travel was Cobb and Co., which was formed by four young enterprising Americans in 1854. All of the founders of the company – Freeman Cobb, from Massachusetts, John Peck, from New Hampshire, James Swanton, from New York, and John B. Lamber, from Kansas – had experience in California with Wells Fargo and Adams Express Co. before they arrived in Australia in 1853.

Cobb and Co. provided a fast, reliable service with comfortable coaches that travelled over virgin country at high speed and a competitive price. The company was the first to introduce to Australia the 'Concord' coach, which had first been built in Concord, New Haven, in America. The coach was vastly superior to the old English ones, which were too heavy, too slow and bounced uncomfortably on their steel springs. The secret to the Concord coaches was that, instead of being mounted on metal springs, the body of the coach was hung, or suspended, on long leather straps made of layers of thick bullock hide, which reduced the impact of jolts and gave the passengers a smoother ride. Cobb and Co. employed experienced American coach drivers and changed horses at intervals of 15 kilometres to increase the coach speed to over 20 kilometres an hour.

The Cobb and Co. coaches were painted vivid red and the company name inscribed in bright yellow on the side for their first service on 30 January 1854. This first service was a daily run that left the Criterion Hotel in Collins Street in Melbourne at 6 am bound for the Forest Creek and Bendigo diggings, plus a coach leaving from Forest Creek at the same time each day coming the other way. Soon, there were a number of coach companies in

Victoria, including Cobb and Co., The Royal Mail, Forest and Vinge's and the Estafete Line. In 1856, Estafete advertised a daily coach service from Ballarat to Melbourne that left at 8 am and arrived at four in the afternoon, with the horses being changed every 15 or 16 kilometres of the 150-kilometre journey. Alternatively, a daily coach ran from the goldfields to Geelong at 6 am, which then connected with the 1 pm ferry and reached Melbourne later the same night for a £12 ticket.

Freeman Cobb only stayed in Australia for a little more than three years, but the company he started in the Victorian goldfields became a legend and would grow into an enormous overland coach service that over the next three decades would operate on 98 separate routes throughout Australia, harnessing 6000 horses and covering 30,000 kilometres a day.

Cobb returned to America with one of his partners, John Lamber, in 1856. Another, James Swanton, went to New Zealand, and only one, John Peck, settled in Australia. Freeman Cobb became a senator in the Massachusetts legislature before going to start a new coach business in South Africa to service the diamond rush from Port Elizabeth to the Kimberley. He died in 1878 when he was only 47 years old.

It was not long after the start of the gold rushes that entertainers came to the diggings, and by the mid-1850s the best of British and European theatre troupes were touring and performing in hastily constructed concert halls near the goldfields.

One of the first concerts was at Bathurst in New South Wales in December 1851. It was a black-and-white minstrel show promoted as 'Nigga Concerts':

December the 1st, 2nd, and 3rd 1851
Howards' Ethiopian Entertainments
LAST WEEK OF THE
NIGGA CONCERTS
MESSRS C. V. AND G. B. HOWARD beg to announce
that they will present four of their amusing entertainments
at the
DANIEL O'CONNELL HOTEL[23]

In 1854, the Theatre Royal at Ballarat advertised:

Immense Attraction, for the first time the advanced
comedy, entitled Charles the Second, and the Roaring
Farce, by Mr. T. A. Hetherington, entitled the Stage
Struck Digger.
Wednesday 1 November 1854[24]

In 1856, Shakespeare was performed at the Theatre Royal
in Castlemaine:

THIS EVENING, FRIDAY, MARCH 2ND
In Shakespeare's Tragedy, in 5 Acts
MACBETH.
Which will be performed with all the original Music 'by
Locke', assisted by a powerful chorus.
Duncan, King of Scotland – Mr C. Walsh . . .
Lady Macbeth – Miss Herbert
To conclude with the very laughable farce of

THE LOAN OF A LOVER . . .
Prices of Admission – Stalls 8s, Pit 5s, Half-price to Stalls
only, at half past 9

Doors open at half-past 7. Curtain to rise at 8 o'clock precisely.[25]

The most sensational entertainer to come to the Australian goldfields was the exotic dancer Lola Montez, who arrived in 1855 and was already notorious throughout Europe and America for her salacious dancing, celebrated affairs and scandalous behaviour.

The most famous of her dances was the sensual 'Spider Dance', which, according to the advertisements for the show, was derived from the Spanish La Tarantula. It began with her wearing a spider mask, spinning a web across the stage, accompanied by eerie music, until she threw off the mask and became the spider's prey enmeshed in the web. As she struggled to free herself, she gradually became more immobilised until she collapsed. Then, the music would slowly rise in tempo and the dancer would become revived and begin searching for the spider in the folds of her petticoats. Lola would become more frenzied as the show reached its climax, when she ultimately found the spider, threw it to the ground and firmly stamped on it.

The dance was deliberately sensual and suggestive, and whenever it was performed the media would condemn it as immoral, which usually guaranteed the following concerts to sell out.

Lola was born in Ireland, the daughter of 18-year-old army ensign Edward Gilbert and his 14-year-old wife. Christened Maria Dolores Eliza Gilbert, she was taken as an infant to India, where her father soon contracted cholera and died. Shortly after, Lola's mother remarried a more senior officer, Major (and later General Sir John) Gragie. Young Eliza was sent off to school in Scotland under the care of her stepfather's family. After finishing school in Bath, the 16-year-old Eliza refused to wed an older man in a marriage arranged by her mother and instead married Lieutenant Thomas James.

She accompanied her new husband to his regimental posting in India, but, in 1841, when he ran off with the wife of a fellow officer, Eliza returned to London.

In 1843, having attempted an acting career, the 24-year-old Eliza made her debut as a dancer at London's Her Majesty's Theatre billed as 'Lola Montez, the Spanish Dancer', appearing between the acts of The Barber of Seville. The newspaper reviews were generally favourable. The Observer described Montez's performance as 'the novelty of the evening', the Evening Chronicle said she created a 'great impression', the Morning Herald said the act was 'extremely successful' and the Weekly Chronicle called it a 'triumphant' debut.

Over the next few years, Montez performed in a number of European capitals and was rumoured to have slept with various eminent figures, including Tsar Nicholas I of Russia and Franz Liszt. In 1846, she became the celebrated mistress of King Ludwig of Bavaria after performing in Munich. The monarch was besotted with the dancer, and, even though the affair was well known and unpopular, the king was unswayed by the feelings of his subjects.[26]

Returning to England on 5 January 1849, Lola signed for her luggage at customs in Dover as Marie, Countess of Landsfeldt, and settled in London. A few months later, with King Ludwig's blessing, she married George Heald, a junior officer in the Home Guards, but the marriage was immediately controversial when the press reported that she was a bigamist as she was still married to her first husband, Thomas James. She left London for Paris with her husband under the glare of the world's newspapers:

> Paris is in uproar . . . a terrible excitement. The famed Lola
> Montez, Countess of Landsfeldt, or Mrs. Heald, arrived on
> the 25th ultimo and took possession of the Hotel Beaujou
> . . . by seven o'clock PM Mr. Heald . . . arrived followed by
> a large number of servants and five carriages.[27]

The following year, George Heald was drowned in Spain, and Lola was reported by the *New York Times* to have begun a relationship with the wealthy newspaper proprietor Alexandre Djarier, who was subsequently killed in a duel.

In December 1851, Lola arrived in America. Her performances, first in New York and then in other cities, including Philadelphia, Boston, Baltimore, Cincinnati and Saint Louis, were usually to full houses and attracted favourable reviews.

In May 1853, Lola went to California, travelling with a newspaper editor, Patrick P. Hull, whom she married the following year. San Francisco was captivated:

> This distinguished wonder, this world-bewildering puzzle,
> Marie de Landsfeldt Heald, Countess of Landsfeldt, has
> actually come to San Francisco, and her coming has acted
> like the application of fire to the combustible matter that
> creates public curiosity, excitement or furor. Everybody
> is in a fever to catch a glimpse of the lioness, to come
> into contact with the power that has swayed hearts and
> potentates, and editors and public opinion and ill-natured
> criticism and what not![28]

Over the next year, Lola performed in San Francisco and other cities that had grown out of the gold rushes in California, including Nevada City, Sacramento and Grass Valley, to full houses and rave reviews.

On 2 July 1853, the 33-year-old Lola bigamously married the 27-year-old Patrick Hull, but within a month there were reports in the press that the two were arguing. The following month, Patrick Hull became another lover of Lola Montez's who died young, violently and mysteriously when, shortly after filing for a divorce and citing Lola's affair with a German doctor, he was found shot dead in the nearby hills.

In 1855, Montez was persuaded to tour Australia and sailed with Noel Folland from San Francisco on the *Fanny Major* via Honolulu and Tahiti on 6 June. From all accounts, it was a pleasant and uneventful voyage but for a report that Lola attempted to stab the ship's mate with a knife for having kicked her dog.[29]

Montez opened her Australian tour with a performance in Sydney on 23 August that was followed by seasons in Melbourne, Geelong and Adelaide. The Melbourne *Age* said she was 'applauded by a full house', and the *Adelaide Advertiser* reported 'a brilliant triumph'.[30]

But it was to be her tour of the goldfields in the theatres of Ballarat, Bendigo, Castlemaine and Forest Creek in February 1856 that caused the most sensation in Australia. Arriving at Ballarat, she was received like royalty as she toured the goldfields, christened mineshafts and mixed as easily with the diggers as she had in California. At a new mineshaft, a richly bedecked armchair had been rigged to a contraption that would allow her to be lowered in comfort down to the workings below. However, Lola spurned the offer of the chair and put her foot in the loop of the rope. With one hand holding the rope and another holding a glass of champagne, she is said to have given the order 'lower away'. The miners cheered and the story rapidly spread around the diggings.

After her first performances at the Victoria Theatre in Ballarat, which was at the back of the United States Hotel, hundreds of diggers jostled to buy a ticket for the sell-out shows. It was after one of her acts that she assaulted the editor of the *Ballarat Times*, Henry Seekamp, for a critical review that appeared in his newspaper. In the offending article in the *Ballarat Times* on 18 February 1856, Seekamp had said that Lola Montez 'has no claim to our respect, and whose notoriety is of an unenviable kind'.

According to press reports, Lola attacked the small editor with a whip, and Seekamp, who was known to have a fiery temper, fought back:

Yesterday evening Mr. Seekamp called at the United States Hotel, which adjoins the Victoria Theatre, and where this lady resides; hearing that Mr Seekamp was in the hotel she came down stairs with a whip which she had drawn as a prize at the Fancy Bazaar a few hours before, and laid it on with hearty goodwill. Mr. Seekamp retaliated with a riding whip which he had in his hand and ere long the combatants had each other literally by the hair. Some of the parties present interposed, and they were separated, not however, before 'neddies' and revolvers had been produced.[31]

Although the two were held apart, Henry Seekamp managed to break free and 'again made at his fair opponent, seizing her by the hair and dress; Madam on her part defending herself with great vigor'.[32] By now, a large crowd had gathered, which was reportedly sympathetic to Lola, and 'began to hoot and hiss Mr Seekamp and throw oranges, apples and other missiles at him'.[33]

At the end of the Australian tour, which had been as colourful and outrageous as any she had had in America or Europe, Lola sailed back to San Francisco on the *Jane E. Faulkenberg* from Newcastle on 18 May 1856. During the return voyage, Noel Folland mysteriously disappeared overboard on the night of 8 July, when the ship was passing Fiji. The *Golden Era* newspaper of San Francisco suggested it had been an accident. According to the paper, he and Lola had been celebrating Folland's birthday when he stepped on deck 'to empty a glass and being somewhat under the influence of champagne' a sudden lurch of the vessel pitched him overboard. So distraught was his widow that she 'no longer uses narcotics and stimulants [and] she has lost her taste for cigarettes and cobblers'.[34]

Back in America, Lola returned to the stage and was initially successful before her star began to wane. She never managed to reignite her career and, believed to have been suffering the tertiary stages of syphilis, died on 17 January 1861 aged 42. She is buried in the Brooklyn Greenwood Cemetery and has the simple inscription on her headstone, 'MRS ELIZA GILBERT – Born 1818 – died 1861'.

¤

Inevitably, the extraordinary things that were happening on the Australian goldfields had a major effect on the two towns of Sydney and Melbourne. Both were scenes of great extravagance and excess, as successful diggers went on spending sprees. As one witness recorded, many of the spectacularly rich diggers came to town with so much money that they were literally throwing it away:

> The gold diggers seem to act on the principle of 'lightly come, lightly go'. There are public houses in Melbourne where a man might be able to drink for a month at the expense of others . . . The other night a ballet girl who danced the highland fling (and very badly . . .) was rewarded with a shower – not of bouquets – but of sovereigns, half sovereigns, and silver . . . The men from the gold fields are rolling in gold, and so perfectly reckless of it that the anecdotes told of them are not only amusing but astonishing. One man put a £5 note between two pieces of bread and butter and ate it like a sandwich. Another rolled two £5 notes into a small ball and swallowed it as a pill.[35]

The combination of the gold-generated wealth and the surge in demand for housing sent the land prices skyrocketing. A recent arrival from England noted that by the mid-1850s up to three ships a day were arriving in Port Phillip Bay full of passengers, which was pushing the price of Melbourne housing to bizarre levels:

> We think 1,000 pounds or 2,000 pounds per acre near London high, but here it fetches from 4,000 pounds to 6,000 pounds. Houses are frequently pointed out to me in the outskirts, as having been sold, with a garden, for 10,000 or 12,000 pounds, which in the finest houses of London would not fetch above 2,000 pounds.[36]

French author and photographer Antoine Fauchery arrived in Victoria in 1852 and was amazed at how quickly Melbourne had grown by the time he finally left Australia in 1859. Fauchery spent much of his time on the goldfields, but he also opened a bar, the Café Estimanet Francois, in Little Bourke Street, catering for the growing number of French people and other French speakers from Switzerland, Canada, Italy, Jersey and Mauritius who had been attracted by the gold rush. He was impressed that Melbourne had become more sophisticated and 'offered people of all nationalities the mirage of their own homeland':

> The luxury of the carriages, of thoroughbred horses and of clubs, the vortex of trade in the big ports, the discussion of colonial interests undertaken in the three dailies, the public platform for meetings, scientific addresses, churches everywhere for all sects, public houses everywhere.[37]

In Sydney by the mid-1850s, the successful gold diggers could buy an incredible range of exotic food, including double Gloucester cheese, York and Westphalian hams, West Indian guava jelly, Indian curry powder, Turkey figs, Normandy pippins, Patras currants, Chesme raisins, Fry's chocolates, Rydeshaimer, Gesenhiemer, Hockheimer and Nirsteiner wines from Germany, Bordeaux and burgundies from France, Martell's brandy, Hun's, Graham's and Offley's port, Guinness, Dublin porter, English beers, rum shrub, French champagne and absinthe.[38]

At the Gold Diggers Arms Hotel in Sydney's Pitt Street in 1855, for two shillings and sixpence the menu included:

Ale or sherry . . .

Soups: Pascaline, Julienne and Hare.

Fish: Fried, and au gratin.

Hot Joints: Roast Beef and Boiled Mutton.

Entrées: Mutton cutlets, sauce piquant. Salami of Teal à la Bigarade. Sauté of Goose aux olives. Sweetbread of veal, sauce tomate. Tripe à la Lyonnais. Kidneys aux champagne. Sausages aux choux.

Cold Meats: Ham and Tongue. Potted Game. Partridge aux truffles, etc. Pate de foie gras. Mayonnaise of Lobster . . .

Vegetables: French beans, Cauliflowers. Artichokes. Peas and Potatoes.

Salad.

Cheese. Dessert.

The new wealth allowed for the import of exotic goods that had never been seen in Australia, including ice for cooling drinks, which was brought by the shipload from the north-east of America.[39] The blocks of ice, weighing up to 45 kilograms each, were stacked in the holds of ships and covered with hay, sawdust or wood shavings as insulation. About a third of the ice would melt on its way to Sydney and Melbourne, and a further half of what was left when it was taken up to be sold in the bars at the diggings. The arrival of a ship full of ice on a hot day in Sydney at the beginning of 1853 attracted large crowds:

Never did a vessel drop anchor in our harbor more opportunely than the good ship *Lowell*, which arrived at the beginning of last week, loaded with her luxurious freight. The intense scorching heat of Monday and Tuesday rendered her advent double welcome, and no sooner was the news of the nature of her freight bruited abroad than orders poured in from all directions for quantities varying from 1 cwt to five tons. We imagine Mr. Poehlman, of Café, George Street, to have been the largest speculator, if we may judge from the crowds that have lately thronged his salon to indulge in 'sherry cobblers', 'mint juleps' and every species of cooling and refreshing drink.[40]

Both Sydney and Melbourne were awash with alcohol. Nathaniel Pidgeon, a former cabinetmaker from County Wexford who came to Sydney and became an evangelist and temperance campaigner, noted that in one week in 1853, 90,000 gallons of beer, 70,000 dozen bottles of beer, 34,000 gallons of brandy, 2600 dozen bottles of brandy, 31,000 gallons of gin and 48,000 gallons of rum had landed in Sydney. 'By rough calculation', Pidgeon said it equated to a gallon of beer, a pint and a half of brandy, a pint and a quarter of gin and a quart of rum 'for every man, woman and child in the colony'. Most of the grog was adulterated by being watered down then mixed with tobacco juice or blue sulphate and copper to restore its flavour and pungency.[41]

The temperance movement began in Australia in the 1830s and flourished during the gold era, but it could do little to contain the diggers' consumption of alcohol. In July 1855, a petition by more than 7000 people called on the New South Wales Parliament to take steps to check the huge growth in drunkenness. In two years after the discovery of gold at Ophir, there had been a 50 per cent rise in the people being charged before Sydney's magistrates. In the police district of Sydney alone, there were more than 400 pubs – about one for every 112 inhabitants – including

29 on Sussex Street, 30 on Pitt Street and 90 on George Street. Following an inquiry, a parliamentary committee confirmed that the evils of excessive drinking were 'very forcibly exposed' but was unable to agree on any new measures to bring it under control.[42]

With so many men coming to town from the diggings, the number of brothels multiplied. In Sydney, they were scattered through all the major streets, including Castlereagh, Druitt, College, Riley and Victoria Streets, and through nearby Alexandria and Woolloomooloo. Sydney Police said there were more than 40 brothels in Woolloomooloo alone, chiefly occupied by juvenile prostitutes.[43]

According to an inquiry conducted by Police Inspector Detective Charles Harrison, about a third of the prostitutes in Sydney were young children, including boys as well as girls.[44] One case involved a 40-year-old woman who ran a brothel in a 'hovel . . . of one room about 12 feet [3.7 metres] square' with a 15-year-old boy. In another, three girls, the oldest being 11 years old, told how they earned money near Pyrmont Bridge 'from men and boys for going with them'. In yet another case, Harrison told how three common prostitutes in Sydney's Castlereagh Street were 'aged respectively 9, 11 and 12'. And Harrison recorded worse still:

Just before leaving Sydney in 1856, I was in Sussex-street about one o'clock in the morning; I found a little girl about 7 years of age standing at the entrance of one of the lanes. She told me she was waiting for another girl, her companion, who had gone into a house up the lane with a man; that she had no home, her father being dead and her mother in prison. I went to the hovel she pointed out, and on looking in between the openings of the boards, I saw a man, about 40 years old on a bed with a child. I burst open the door, rushed in, and struck the man a blow to the head, which severely wounded him, threw him down the steps to the rocks beneath. When I questioned the girl, she told me she was nine years old. I sent the children to the police station for protection, but as the man appeared to be seriously injured, I did not take him into custody.[45]

There was widespread social concern about the growth in prostitution. In November 1857, as reported by the *Argus* newspaper, one of a number of large public meetings was held in Melbourne, which resulted in a petition being presented to the governor calling on the government to introduce 'remedial measures', including the establishment of a female reformatory for prostitutes:

It is well known that many hundreds of abandoned females follow that infamous course in this city. Common prostitutes in large numbers parade the principal thoroughfares of the city after nightfall, and even by the day, whose conduct is frequently marked by the most shocking and outrageous indecency.[46]

An earlier suggestion in that newspaper canvassing the possibility of legalising and licensing prostitution had caused a predictable outcry, and the issue was never pursued by the government.[47]

Wealth had always been the protector of privilege, but the discovery of gold meant that even those from the lowest social classes could suddenly afford to pay for everything that had previously only been available to the upper classes. A journalist in Melbourne in 1852 described how the old social orders now meant nothing:

> What hope would agriculturalists and squatters have of procuring a sufficiency of hands for shearing and harvest time, when labouring men, staggering half drunk about the streets of Melbourne and Geelong, would accost without ceremony any well dressed gentleman they met and offer him three pounds a week if he would work for them at the diggings?[48]

The Melbourne storekeeper William Hall said there had never been such a sudden rise in wealthy people:

> The effect it had on society is strange and unprecedented in history; men, who, until this time, had never been masters of five pounds, are now worth thousands; a new aristocracy has sprung up.[49]

The same observations were being made in Sydney. Englishman Mr J. E. Pughe, who called in on Sydney on a visit to New Zealand in 1854, took a severe view of how women from the 'lower orders' of society in Sydney could afford to dress up as a result of the prosperity attained from the goldfields:

> This mania for dress is also carried out to an absurd degree amongst the house servants, and you are frequently amused on Sundays by seeing a dirty Trollope, who in the morning was up to her elbows in greasy water, a few hours afterwards transformed into (as she vainly imagines) a

fine lady. The external grounds for such a belief consisting in a pink or blue silk bonnet adorned with flowers of rainbow hues, a silk dress and mantilla to boot, gloves and parasol of course. In fact to such a ridiculous degree is this inordinate love of dress carried amongst the lower orders that it may be advisable for ladies in self defense to adopt the plainest costume they can assume.[50]

John Robert Godley said the emergence of affluence from the lower orders of society was 'galling to one's aristocratic pride':

> I can conceive no social state more disagreeable to live in than a community in which the labouring class is composed of gamblers (all gold diggers become gamblers in habit and character), and the aristocracy, that is, the richest and most powerful people, are the successful gamblers.[51]

Godley was born in Dublin, the son of an English landlord, and was educated at Harrow and Oxford. He had been to New Zealand to found the Church of England city of Christchurch in Canterbury. Stopping off at Sydney on his way back to England, he recorded the upheaval that gold was causing to society. On one occasion, he witnessed the wife of 'one of the highest functionaries of Government' in a Sydney shop deciding against buying a dress she thought too expensive. A 'common labourer' standing nearby told the shop assistant to give the woman the dress and that he had more than enough to pay for it. On another, he told the story of a ship's captain searching the usual haunts for sailors to replace his crew that had deserted to go to the diggings when a 'common seaman pulled out an immense roll of notes' and offered to buy the ship *and* the captain.

Godley did, however, note that the upper classes too were benefiting from the gold rush:

Most of the 'upper classes' have had a large share in the general prosperity. The banks have realized untold profits. All the merchants have done well; some have made large fortunes in the last two years. Even the stockholders [graziers] though they have had the hardest battles to fight, are probably better off than ever, the increase in the price of wool and meat having more than compensated for the increased cost of production. The only people who have suffered are those that live on fixed incomes, and perhaps some professional people, especially clergymen.[52]

But the gold rush did not benefit everyone in the cities, and there was widespread poverty, squalor and hardship due to the rapidly increased cost of living and a number of economic downturns that occurred in Australia during the decade of the 1850s.[53] J. E. Pughe, who had already criticised the social changes caused by gold, was aghast at the high cost of living in Sydney:

Imagine . . . milk . . . sold at the rate of 16 pence a quart . . . suspicious looking eggs, one third of which are possibly rotten, 4 pence to 6 pence each; bread 9 pence a 2 pound loaf; cabbage and cauliflowers 6 pence to a shilling each; fowls and ducks 5 to 7 shillings a pair; and beef and mutton in every respect inferior to Indian fed meat at 9 pence and 10 pence a pound . . . [and] servants £25 and £30 a year and their food . . . To keep a horse and gig with a groom could hardly I think be managed under £150 extra.[54]

According to William Jevons, who came to Sydney as a 19-year-old in 1854, the 'filth and vice' of the Rocks was worse than anything he had seen in London, Liverpool or Paris:

> As sewers and drains of proper construction are quite unknown here, as the streets are without any gutters except such as the drainage itself forms . . . the drainage of each house or hovel chiefly trickles down the hill, soon reaching . . . the front or the back of the next lower house. In many places filthy water is actually seen to accumulate against the walls of the dwellings, soaking the floors above which the family lives . . . Many houses . . . are built but a few yards from a wall of rock over which various spouts and drains as well as a privy or two continually discharge foul matter of the worst description.[55]

Jevons had arrived in Sydney to work in the new branch of the Royal Mint as an assayer for the next four years. He had attended London University and studied chemistry and was also interested in metallurgy, astronomy, sociology and photography. Later, he would become a famous economist. He noted how the gold boom had resulted in Sydney becoming hopelessly overcrowded and its main roads heavily congested:

> George Street, and a more disagreeable road it is impossible to conceive – dusty or muddy . . . It is crowded in the day time with herds of cattle and sheep, bullock teams, drays going up the country, mail coaches, omnibuses, diggers on horse-back etc.: in fact it is something like the roads must have been before the railways.[56]

The widespread poverty in Melbourne and Sydney gave rise to many children being homeless. At the end of 1859, a New South Wales parliamentary committee inquired into the 'conditions of the working classes'. The committee confirmed a 'considerable amount of destitution' and a 'festering mass of youth delinquency [and] vice of the most revolting manner' but concluded that 'all reforms must come from the people themselves'.[57]

Irish-born John Speering, who ran a pawnbroker's shop in lower George Street, told the inquiry he estimated that by the end of the 1850s there were about 2000 neglected children living around the Rocks district of Sydney. He said children of 12 and 14 years of age, both boys and girls, were earning a living as best they could. Some of the boys fished from the wharves to sell what they caught and slept in casks and old boilers along the quays.

Adding to the poor of the city was a large number of desperate men – some with families – who had spent all they had on the quest for gold but returned hungry and empty-handed. John Sherer, who returned to Melbourne with his mates in 1853 after striking it rich, saw many failed diggers, and many others heading for diggings that were sure to fail:

> Good God! A man shudders to think what will become of them! Many of them must starve or steal, and many of them perish by the innumerable means to which misfortune ever harries the weak and the wretched.[58]

Depending to a great extent on luck, the gold rushes had the power to improve a person's life beyond recognition or to completely destroy it.

CHAPTER SIX

The Eureka Rebellion

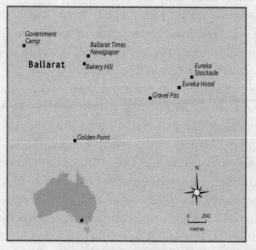

Eureka and surrounds, 1854

[W]e would have retreated, but it was then too late, as almost immediately the military poured in one or two volleys of musketry ... There were about seventy men possessing guns, twenty with pikes, and thirty with pistols, but many of those men with fire arms had no more than one or two rounds of ammunition.

From the start of the goldfields in both New South Wales and Victoria, there were tensions between the diggers and the governments over the licence fee. The levy in both colonies was set at 30 shillings a month per digger and entitled each miner to work a surface area of 64 square feet, or approximately six square metres. The licence was not transferable, had to be bought in advance and was only to be issued to men who 'had been properly discharged from employment or were not otherwise improperly absent from hired service'. It had to be carried at all times by the person who held it.

The official justification for the licence was that Australia, as a British colony, belonged to the Crown, and therefore any gold found in the land was owned by the Queen. As part of the British Empire, the Australian colonies were officiated by Queen Victoria's representative, the governor, who was appointed by the monarch on the recommendation of the Colonial Office in London.

Most of its subjects were loyal to Empire, and the structure of the local colonial society reflected that of England, from the largely hereditary ruling class down to the subservient lower orders. However, the discovery of gold would attract to Australia thousands of men and women from a host of other countries who felt no allegiance to the British Crown and little or no respect for British authority. This was particularly the case among many of the Americans, who, 70 years earlier, had won their War of Independence from the British, and the Irish, many of whom saw immigration to the Australian goldfields as liberation from British oppression at home. Added to the mix were thousands from various other countries of Europe that had experienced revolutions only a few years before, in 1848.

Many of the diggers who had struggled to reach the goldfields from the other side of the world found themselves in harsh and desolate conditions in the remote bush of Australia. Life on the goldfields was hard enough, with limited food, high prices, rough accommodation, lack of women and family, tedium, fatigue and loneliness, all of which contributed to the resentment of the diggers towards the licence tax and the heavy-handed ways of the police.

Even among many of the British loyalists who believed a licence fee was justified, there was a widespread view that the rate was too high, as it had to be paid before the diggers could start work and applied regardless of whether or not any gold was found.

The man responsible for the gold licence in Victoria was Sir Charles Joseph La Trobe, who had been appointed superintendent of the Port Phillip District in 1839 and had already served as the most senior official in the colony for more than 12 years before the discovery of gold.

La Trobe was promoted to become the first governor of the new, separate colony of Victoria in July 1851, only weeks before the gold rush began. Immediately, he authorised the introduction of Victoria's gold-mining licence fee, based on the one introduced in New South Wales the previous May.

The first protest meeting against the new 30 shilling a month licence in Victoria was organised at Buninyong near Ballarat on 25 August 1851. A sympathetic account of the meeting appeared in the *Geelong Advertiser* newspaper two days later:

Thirty shillings a month, for twenty six days work, payable in advance, is the impost demanded by our

Victorian Czar. Eighteen pounds sterling per annum, per head, is the merciless prospective exaction on an enterprise scarcely fourteen days old. It is a Juggernaut tax to crush the poor, and if attempted against the richer and more powerful parts of the community, would be fatal to the domination that is, and La Trobism in one twelvemonth would be spoken of in the past tense. Why should a lawful occupation, promising so much, be strangled at its birth? I say unhesitatingly, fearlessly, and conscientiously, that there has not been a more gross attempt at injustice since the days of Watt Tyler; it is an insult to common sense, and if passed by, by the journals of Port Phillip, without strict comment, it will be an indelible stain upon them. If such a thing as this tax be tolerated, it will be the first step to liberticide, for liberty cannot be where the foundation of all wealth is trammeled.[1]

One of the miners who spoke at the meeting was applauded when he said he was a 'free man, and a hard working man, willing to pay his fair share to the government, but he could not and would not pay thirty shillings a month for a licence'. Another said he had 'spent every halfpenny' he had outfitting and getting himself to the diggings 'and now I am to be taxed before I have been here a week, or had the opportunity of getting any of it back again'. Yet another said that he could not find enough gold to 'pay a shilling a day' to the commissioner. Another said they would all be 'driven to Bathurst', while another, who had been a gold miner in California, said 'the Yankees don't do it in this here fashion'.

The 50 or so men present carried what was to be the first of many resolutions that would be passed at numerous meetings leading up to the rebellion and massacre at nearby Eureka three years later. It described the licence fee as 'impolitic and illiberal', a threat to the viability of gold mining and too steep at 30 shillings. It also argued that many of the diggers had not yet been successful and should be given time to find gold before they were forced to pay a fee.

The first Victorian gold commissioner responsible for the collection of the gold-licence fee was 33-year-old Francis Doveton, who was appointed on 21 August 1851. The day after his arrival in Ballarat, he met a deputation of miners at his tent and made it clear that while he did not make the law he was determined to collect the licence tax. Many believe the first seeds of the Eureka uprising were sown by this confrontation between the uncompromising Doveton and the miners on 20 September 1851 – the day the government began collecting licences.[2]

Doveton was born in Northampton, the son of Reverend Frederick Doveton and his wife, Elizabeth, in 1817. He had already been in Australia for more than a decade before his appointment to the goldfields, having arrived in Sydney with the 51st Regiment of Foot in 1838 before serving in Tasmania as the police magistrate, where he reached the rank of lieutenant. Later, he would have one of the first six streets in the gold town of Ballarat named after him when the goldfield city was designed by William Swan Urquhart in late 1851.

In October 1851, with the rush only months old, Governor La Trobe made his first visit to the goldfields, where he formed the view that the diggers should be paying more for their licences. When he returned to Melbourne, he announced in December, without consulting his Executive Council, that the licence would be doubled to £3. However, an outcry ensued, and following the urging of his advisers he backed down, leaving the fee at 30 shillings a month.

More than three years later, and after the Eureka uprising, La Trobe would be criticised by a commission of inquiry for destabilising the licence system from the start:

> The Commission cannot but regard the whole procedure as pre-eminently inappropriate and unfortunate, illustrative as it must have been of haste, inexperience, or indecision and attended with effects on the mining population such as can only be too readily conceived to result from such unstable policy.[3]

The antipathy of many of the miners towards the authorities was made worse by the local police, who the diggers believed were corrupt and harassing. While there was plenty of crime to address, the police were preoccupied with the enforcement and collection of the licence tax. The intrusive treatment of the diggers by Doveton and his officers was despite the urging of the colonial secretary in Melbourne, William Lonsdale, to be discreet in the handling of the fee.

The calibre of the police was also a problem, as the government had trouble attracting good-quality men for its police force. Within the first six months of the goldfields, almost all the police force had left to join the diggings, and replacements were hard to come by, despite offering a 50 per cent increase in pay.[4]

Doveton's police superintendent, David Armstrong, was widely despised for his rough dealings with the diggers. Born in Dumfriesshire in Scotland in 1820, he worked as a blacksmith before becoming superintendent of police in Ballarat at 32 years of age. Armstrong was particularly savage in clamping down on small illegal grog sellers. Lord Robert Cecil, who had been an early arrival on the goldfields, went with Armstrong to see the seizing of a sly grog shop. When they arrived, police had already surrounded the tent and Armstrong ordered those inside to be handcuffed before the tent was pulled down, the canvas confiscated and the poles piled up and burned. According to Cecil, Armstrong told him 'he has had as many as nine bonfires blazing together at night in various parts'.[5]

Another witness to Armstrong's heavy-handed conduct was William Howitt. A Quaker and a highly moral man, Howitt was only moderately successful at gold mining but wrote a popular account of his time in Australia, which included a description of the behaviour of Armstrong and his men:

> The men employed by the police to hunt over licences were too often excessively ignorant and vulgar persons, who, never having before enjoyed the slightest shadow of power . . . exercise this now given, over men . . . with a coarse brutality which was intolerable to generous minds . . . Men who were found without licences on their persons, but who had them in their tents, were dragged off to the Government Camp, and . . . fined . . . if they remonstrated with the police, they would probably be instantly clamped into handcuffs.[6]

Howitt also described how Armstrong cracked down hard

on the small sly grog shops while taking bribes to let the big operators continue operating:

> [Armstrong][7] was originally a blacksmith, but he was appointed to the post of Inspector of Police . . . He was considered, for a long time, the most vigilant and efficient officer on all the gold fields. Why? Because he was continually hunting out and punishing the vendors of spirits. Nothing was so frequent in the newspapers and police reports as the exploits of [Armstrong], in discovering, fining, and burning down the tents of sly grog sellers . . . You would naturally suppose that all the sly grog shops, and sly grog sellers would soon cease to exist on the field . . . Nothing of the kind. On no field were more rum and brandy drunk . . . and thus . . . did not injure the Government revenue from the duty on spirits. . . . You will say, how did he manage this? By the simplest means in the world; and at once benefited the Government revenue, his own, and that of a select body of favoured tradesmen. [Armstrong's] system was to destroy relentlessly the small grog seller, and to allow and even protect the large one – for a consideration.[8]

Howitt complained that the corruption and the repression of diggers flourished because the Colonial Government of Victoria did nothing to stop it:

> No cries of outrage aroused it – no appeals to its justice were answered . . . and . . . official . . . peculation and bribery walked openly hand in hand.[9]

Raffaello Carboni, the Italian radical who arrived on the

goldfields in late 1852, described how, in January 1853, he was harassed by the police for his licence while digging for gold:

> I was hard at work . . . I hear a rattling noise among the brush. My faithful dog Bonaparte would not keep under my control. 'What's up?' 'Your licence, mate' was the peremptory question from a six foot [183 centimetre] fellow in blue shirt, thick boots, the face of a ruffian, armed with a carbine and a fixed bayonet.[10]

Carboni, who described the licence as 'a specimen of colonial brutedom', said that he sadly reflected when being yet again called on to produce a current licence that he had come '16,000 miles [25,750 kilometres] in vain to get away from the law of the sword'.

In May 1853, a big protest meeting of miners was held at Agitation Hill at Mount Alexander, and in June an Anti-Gold-Licence Association was formed at Bendigo, where more than 20,000 diggers from Ballarat, Bendigo, Castlemaine, Heathcote, Stawell and other diggings signed what became known as the Bendigo Petition, which detailed the miners' grievances. The 13-metre-long petition was bound in green silk and taken to Melbourne, where it was presented to Governor La Trobe on 1 August.[11] By the end of the year, thousands of miners were wearing red ribbons in their hats to mark their opposition to the licence fee.

A diggers' riot over the licence fee almost happened in New South Wales before it occurred at Eureka in Victoria. The diggers along the Turon River had first met to protest the fee at a mass meeting on 17 June 1851, but their request that the fee of 30 shillings a month be cut to seven shillings and sixpence was rejected. The diggers' agitation continued through the year, and by November, with a local politician championing their cause, the miners again protested the licence system, on similar grounds as their Victorian counterparts; it was exorbitant and inequitable, they said, in that it was imposed before the miner had begun work or found gold.

Tension on the Turon continued throughout the year, and in August another petition, which was drafted by one of Edward Hargraves's old California colleagues, Enoch Rudder, was sent to the government. The new petition included a number of additional demands, including the extension of the vote to miners and the abolition of the requirement that a candidate for parliament be a property owner.[12]

Then, in December 1852, rather than reducing the licence, the New South Wales Government introduced a new Gold Fields Management Act, which extended the licence to everyone on the goldfields, including storekeepers and tradesmen, even if they were not digging. Non-Britishers were to pay double the fee, and the penalties for licence evasion dramatically increased.

The diggers were incensed, describing the new measures as excessive, oppressive and unjust. Early in the new year, amid rising tensions, open warfare was only narrowly averted when several hundred armed diggers marched to fife and drum on 8 February into the township of Sofala but were dissuaded from violence as more troopers from the 11th Regiment arrived to reinforce the small garrison already there.

Shortly after, the situation was diffused when the

colonial secretary Deas Thomson signalled that the government was prepared to amend the Gold Fields Management Act 1852, and Governor Sir Charles FitzRoy duly asked the parliament to amend the law on 11 May 1853. On 1 October 1853, the licence fee was reduced by two-thirds to ten shillings a month, the alien tax was dropped and the fee reverted to apply only to those actually digging.

Back in Victoria, no such concessions to the miners were offered, and in 1854 the situation changed quite dramatically when a new governor was sent from England to replace Sir Charles La Trobe, who was returning to London.

La Trobe had wanted to return to England sooner and had submitted his resignation two years earlier, in December 1852. He was finally relieved on 6 May 1854, when he sailed from Melbourne on the *Golden Age*. His wife, Sophie, had been unwell for some years and returned to England while her husband was still waiting for his resignation to be accepted in London. She died in January 1854, before her husband sailed home, and La Trobe would later marry her sister Rose Isabella de Meuron in England.

La Trobe was not given any further government appointments but was awarded the Companion Order of Bath in 1858 and a pension in 1865. He died ten years later and is buried at Litlington, East Sussex. When he had arrived in 1839 at Port Phillip, the settlement had a population of barely 5000. By the time he left the colony of Victoria, its population had boomed to more than a quarter of a million.

His replacement as governor was the 48-year-old Sir Charles Hotham, who was a far more senior appointment than La Trobe had been 15 years earlier. Hotham was born in 1806 in Dennington, Suffolk, the son of a clergyman. At 12 years of age, he entered the navy and served initially in the Mediterranean before being promoted rapidly to the rank of lieutenant at 19 and post-captain at 27. In the early 1840s, he served in South America off Montevideo Bay, Uruguay. In the late 1840s, he was knighted and appointed British naval commodore for the west coast of Africa, and in 1852 he was the British head of mission in negotiating a treaty with Paraguay. Hotham was a reluctant appointment to Australia. At the outbreak of the Crimean War, he had sought command of a ship but was assigned the role of lieutenant governor of Victoria instead.

Shortly before taking up his new appointment on 10 December 1853, Hotham married Jane Sarah, daughter of Baron Bridport and grand-niece of Horatio Nelson, before boarding the *Queen of the South* for the voyage to Australia.

Hotham and Lady Sarah arrived in Melbourne on 22 June 1854, nearly seven weeks after the departure of Sir Charles La Trobe, and were greeted with great pomp and ceremony, which may have disguised some of the deep-rooted resentment of the diggers on the goldfields. As he crossed the Yarra River to enter the city under a giant banner with the words 'Victoria Welcomes Victoria's choice', Hotham said he was greeted by a cheering crowd of 60,000 people:

> Immediately in front of me a band of nearly 200 of the lowest orders forced their way into the procession and locked arm in arm, during the greater part of the road, sang 'Rule Britannia' and 'God Save the Queen'.[13]

Hotham first visited the goldfields with Lady Sarah three months later, when he travelled to Ballarat, Castlemaine and Bendigo. He said the gold would produce for the British Empire wealth and prosperity 'the world has never before seen'.[14]

In a report he sent to the colonial secretary in London, Sir John Bray Bart, he said the diggers were overwhelmingly loyal and obedient subjects. During the first stop at Ballarat, Hotham described that, when he and his wife were inspecting a mineshaft in Ballarat, 'thousands flocked to the hole' to meet them and the throng 'burst forth shouts of loyalty to Her Majesty, and cries of attachment to the old country'.[15]

After Ballarat, they went to Castlemaine and Mount Alexander, where they were overwhelmed by the enthusiasm and 'deafened by the shouts of loyalty', then on to Bendigo:

> But, extraordinary as this may seem, the manifestations at Bendigo far surpassed them. Not less than twenty thousand men assembled a league from the town to meet me – by force they took the horses from my carriage, yoking themselves instead, and dragged it into town. There were triumphant arches, flags, bands of music, vehicles gaily caparisoned, and a continued roar of cheering.[16]

The only note of dissent was at Bendigo, where Hotham recorded 'a slight show of disaffection' over the licence fee when he was given a petition calling for its abolition by some of the leaders of the miners.

He noted that he was at the 'place that the original agitation against the licence fee first commenced' and boasted that when he responded to the petition by telling the diggers that they must pay for 'liberty and order', he was 'loudly cheered' by the thousands present.

The Italian firebrand Raffaello Carboni, who witnessed the event, recorded a different impression. He said that when Hotham met the diggers, he told them how delighted he had been by the reception, thanked them for the petition and declared, 'I shall not neglect your interests and welfare.'[17]

Interestingly, in contrast to commands he would subsequently issue, Hotham also made the observation in his report to the colonial secretary that order on the goldfields could not be sustained by military force and that tact, management and reasoning were required:

> And now Sir, having endeavoured to inform you generally on the feelings of the digging population, I deem it my duty to state my conviction, that no amount of military force at the disposal of Her Majesty's Government, can coerce the diggers, as the gold fields may be likened to a network of rabbit burrows. For miles, the holes adjoin each other, each is a fortification . . . nowhere can four men move abreast, so that the soldier is powerless against the digger, who well armed, and sheltering himself by the earth thrown up about him, can easily pick off his opponent – by tact and management must these men be governed; amenable to reason, they are deaf to force . . .[18]

The best solution, according to Hotham, was women. He had been informed that there had been a big increase in the number of women on the goldfields and this had been responsible for the 'improvement in the manners and the state of feelings of the diggers':

It is through their influence that this restless population must be restrained; where the soldier will fail, the interest of the wife, and child, will prevail, and I would rather see an army of ten thousand arrive than an equal number of soldiers.[19]

While at the goldfields, Hotham and his wife met Robert Rede, who had been appointed gold commissioner to Ballarat only two months before. As the most senior government official on site, the gold commissioner was 'the Crown writ small' with the authority to punish minor crime, settle local disputes and commit serious crimes for trial.[20] Rede would become another significant figure in the events that unfolded over the next few months.

Back in Melbourne, a month after his trip to the goldfields, Hotham decided to clamp down on gold licences and ordered that, rather than occasional searches, there should be a systematic policing of the goldfields to find evaders twice every week. This decision was taken unilaterally, rather than through the regular meetings of the Executive Council that had been established by his predecessor, La Trobe. Already, the new governor was being regarded by many as secretive and obstinate.

The stringent police licence hunts – or 'traps', as they were known – inflamed the miners, and tensions were already running high by the first week of October 1854. Shortly after midnight on 7 October, the Scottish miner James Scobie and his mate Peter Martin stopped at the Eureka Hotel for a drink on the way back to their camp. Both were drunk. In an ensuing brawl with the publican, an ex-convict named James Bentley, Scobie was killed. After a hastily convened inquiry, the stipendiary magistrate, John D'Ewes, who was known to be a friend of the publican's, released Bentley and his colleagues, on the grounds of insufficient evidence.

Only three days after Scobie was killed, Johannes Gregorius, a disabled servant of the local Catholic priest, Father Smyth, was beaten and arrested for not having a mining licence. Emotions were running high – particularly among the Irish. A mass meeting was held at Bakery Hill at Ballarat on 15 October to protest the rough treatment of the servant by the police.

On 17 October, another mass meeting was held near the spot where James Scobie was killed, and a resolution was passed castigating the inquiry into his death:

> This meeting not being satisfied with the manner in which the proceedings connected with death of the late James Scobie, have been conducted either by the magistrate, or by the coroner, pledges itself to use every lawful means to have the case brought before other and more competent authorities.[21]

At the end of the meeting, a number of miners marched on the Eureka Hotel, and its owner James Bentley hurriedly rode off on horseback to the protection of the local police. An additional force of 30 armed police was sent to the demonstration but was unable to maintain order as the hotel was first stoned by the protesters and then set alight and quickly burned to the ground.

During the following week, more police reinforcements and a detachment of soldiers from the 40th Regiment arrived at Ballarat, as the authorities were growing increasingly concerned at developments on the goldfields.

On 21 October, Andrew McIntyre and Thomas Fletcher were arrested for the burning of the Eureka Hotel. A third suspect, Henry Westerby, was arrested later. The diggers reacted by calling another mass meeting, where it was resolved that bail would be collected to get their colleagues out of jail.

The next day, a large group of predominantly Irish Catholic diggers met to protest the treatment of Father Smyth's servant Johannes Gregorius, and the following day a deputation of the diggers approached Commissioner Rede seeking to have those responsible for the assault on the servant arrested and charged. On 25 October, the deputation, led by Timothy Hayes and John Manning, reported back on their meeting with Rede, and the mass meeting passed a stronger resolution calling for the sacking of the local police chief, James Johnston.

Realising the miners were becoming more militant and threatening, the Ballarat government camp developed a detailed plan for the upgrading of its defences on 27 October, and on the same day more military reinforcements arrived from Melbourne.

At the same time, Governor Hotham agreed to establish an inquiry into the death of James Scobie, but on 1 November a further seven men were charged with burning down the Eureka Hotel.

On 11 November, a mass meeting of miners at Bakery Hill decided to establish the Ballarat Reform League and elected a number of the diggers' leaders to draw up the charter for the league. The charter was radical for its time, although all of the principles it contained were ultimately adopted into the Australian political system. It called for universal suffrage, the abolition of property ownership as a requisite for becoming a member of parliament, payment for MPs, voting by ballot, and short-term parliaments. The diggers' charter also called for the abolition of gold licence fees, reform of the administration of the goldfields and an overhaul of the Crown lands laws. The *Ballarat Times* described the Ballarat Reform League as a major development in the history of Australia:

> This League is not more and not less than the germ of Australian Independence. No power on earth can restrain the united might and headlong strides for the freedom of the people of this country.[22]

November saw the emergence of a number of natural leaders among the diggers, including John Basson Humffray. Thirty-year-old Humffray was born in Newtown, Wales, in 1824. He was articled to a solicitor before he abandoned the law to try his luck on the Australian goldfields, arriving on the *Star of the East* on 19 September 1853. The handsome, well-built Welshman had been associated with the Chartists in north Wales and was to become one of the leaders of the Eureka rebellion. The Italian agitator Carboni said he was impressed with Humffray:

> [He] had an honest and benevolent heart, directed by a liberal mind . . . possessing . . . a fine forehead, denoting astuteness . . . a pair of eyes that mark the spell . . . A Grecian nose; of a mouth remarkable for the elasticity of the lips, that make him a model of pronunciation of English language.[23]

Humffray was elected secretary of the Ballarat Reform

League the following month and later, along with the radical Irishman Peter Lalor, would be the first parliamentary representative of the diggers when he was elected to the Victorian Legislative Assembly in 1855.

Well aware of the seriousness of the situation and acknowledging that the miners had been 'infuriated with rage' when they burned down the Eureka Hotel, Governor Charles Hotham quickly ordered a number of measures that he thought would stabilise the situation.

The board of inquiry set up by Hotham found that the judge who had first heard the evidence in the Scobie murder, D'Ewes, had taken bribes, as had the police officer Sergeant Major Milne. D'Ewes was sacked from the judiciary for subverting 'public confidence in the integrity, and impartiality, of the Bench' and Milne was to be prosecuted. At the same time, James Bentley and his accomplice, Thomas Farrell, were re-arrested to be tried for the murder of James Scobie.

Hotham was also determined to maintain order at Ballarat. Within four days, 450 extra soldiers and police were sent to the goldfields with orders 'to use force, whenever legally called upon to do so without regard to the consequences that might ensue'.[24]

Hotham mistakenly thought his package of initiatives had saved the day. In a dispatch to the colonial secretary, Sir George Gray Bart, on 18 November, the governor boasted that the miners' 'irritation had subsided', their riotous movement was 'now quelled' and the diggers had 'returned to their ordinary labour'.[25]

Within days, James Bentley, Thomas Farrell and William Hense were convicted and sentenced to three years' imprisonment for the manslaughter of James Scobie.

However, at the same time, the miners Henry Westerby, Thomas Fletcher and Andrew McIntyre were convicted and each sentenced to three years' hard labour for burning down the Eureka Hotel. On Saturday 25 November, Commissioner Rede reported he had been told that the government camp would be burned down if the convicted arsonists were not released.

On Sunday, a police inspector, Gordon Evans, advised his boss, Chief Commissioner Charles McMahan, that an imminent attack was being planned by the diggers on the government camp in an effort to release those convicted for the burning of the Eureka Hotel.[26] Also on the Sunday, a deputation of the Ballarat Reform League, consisting of Humffray, George Black and Thomas Kennedy, arrived in Melbourne for a meeting with Governor Hotham to be held the following morning, where they hoped they would be granted some concessions that would help diffuse the tensions at Ballarat.

The next morning, Monday 27 November, Governor Hotham received the deputation with courtesy and had a shorthand-taker present to ensure an accurate record was made of the meeting.[27] Things got off to a bad start when Hotham objected to the deputation referring to the diggers' 'demands', and after more than half an hour's discussion Hotham refused to consider releasing the men convicted of burning down the Eureka Hotel. He also said he was powerless to extend parliamentary representation to the diggers as the decision rested with London. The deputation left Melbourne to return to the goldfields empty-handed.

On Tuesday 28 November, a further detachment of the 12th Regiment arrived at Ballarat in time for another meeting of diggers called for the following day. The 'monster meeting' was widely publicised, including a poster printed on Henry Seekamp's *Ballarat Times* printing presses:

DOWN WITH THE LICENCE FEE
DOWN WITH DESPOTISM
WEDNESDAY NEXT ON BAKERY HILL

The meeting succeeded in attracting more than 10,000 angry miners.

The deputation of Humffray, George Black and Thomas Kennedy that had met with Hotham in Melbourne arrived back at Ballarat only an hour before the monster meeting, and when they reported that the prisoners charged with burning down the Eureka Hotel would not be released, the mood of the meeting turned sour. A large number of miners publicly burned their licences, and for the first time the Southern Cross flag was hoisted.[28] The meeting also unanimously passed a provocative resolution:

That this meeting, being convinced that the obnoxious licence fee is an imposition and an unjustifiable tax, pledges itself to take immediate steps to abolish same by at once burning all their licences. That in the event of any party being arrested for having no licence, that the united people will, under the circumstances, defend and protect them.[29]

The diggers had thrown down the gauntlet. There was no longer any reference to 'every lawful means' that had been part of the resolutions only a month before. The meeting was now threatening a fight if the authorities continued to police the gold-mining licences.

The meeting finished with a resolution that the men would meet again the following Sunday afternoon at the nearby Adelphi Theatre. The following day, Thursday 30 November, Rede ordered another licence hunt, but when the police reached the Gravel Pits they were stoned by the miners and had to retreat. Rede then read the Riot Act[30] and reinforced the police with soldiers, which resulted in several shots being fired by both sides. A police horse was reported to have been stabbed, a policeman wounded, a digger shot through the hand and eight miners arrested.

Rede then set the government on a collision course with the diggers, who had scheduled their next mass meeting for the following Sunday. He advised the colonial secretary of his intention to crack down on any further gatherings of the miners:

> The absolute necessity of putting down all meetings, public and private, I think must now be apparent for the abolition of the licence fee is merely a watchword. The whole affair is a strong democratic agitation by an armed mob. If the Government will hold this and other goldfields it must at once crush this movement.[31]

The Irishman Peter Lalor described how the situation rapidly deteriorated over the three days from Thursday 30 November till the attack on the Eureka stockade early on the following Sunday morning, 3 December.[32] The 28-year-old Lalor had only become prominent the day before, when he had spoken at the monster meeting of miners that resolved to meet the government with force if necessary. He said the miners had called a meeting, but none of the regular leaders were there to speak when the meeting started, so he found himself 'mounting the stump' to proclaim 'Liberty' for the miners and calling for volunteers.

Later, he claimed that it was on the Thursday afternoon during the licence hunt that the police had fired guns at unarmed diggers for the first time:

On Thursday morning the police and military came to look for licences; a digger, who, I presume, had no licence, was running away, when an officer of the police ordered his men to 'fire on him', to 'shoot him down' and he was fired at . . . I was working in a shaft at the Eureka, 140 feet [43 metres] deep . . . Suddenly the news was spread that the diggers were being fired on at the Gravel Pits. 'To Arms' was the cry, and all that could muster arms moved forward in great confusion towards the Gravel Pits.[33]

The following morning, Friday 1 December, Lalor said that the threat to the diggers the previous day resulted in more than 1500 miners turning out within two hours prepared to confront the police and the soldiers:

Great excitement now prevailed throughout the diggings, and early next (Friday) morning, some armed, began to assemble at Bakery Hill . . . and hoisted the Southern Cross . . . in about two hours, we numbered about 1500 . . . The rest of the day was spent in procuring arms, electing officers, and improving the organisation.[34]

The diggers organised themselves in a wooden stockade, which was a fencelike enclosure they had made of timber planks and old carts. Lalor, who found himself elected as one of the leaders even though he had no military experience, insisted that the enclosure was never intended as a fortress:

> On Saturday morning we commenced muster, at Eureka, about eight o'clock . . . it [was] found necessary that a distinct place should be marked off in which the men could muster together and be drilled, a piece of ground at Eureka was enclosed with slabs for that purpose . . . The Government have laid great stress on the erection of this enclosure, and have dignified it with the title of stockade, barricade, fortified entrenchment, and camp . . . but in plain truth it was nothing more than an enclosure to keep our men together, and was never erected with an eye to military defense.[35]

According to Lalor, there were still 1500 men at Eureka on Saturday evening 'ready and willing to use their arms in defense of their rights'. Lalor said they never intended waiting in the enclosure until they were attacked but had 'scouts and sentries' throughout the diggings and were prepared to send their sizable force anywhere in the diggings they might be needed.

Around midnight, after two false alarms, many of the diggers wandered off to their tents to sleep, so when the government attacked in the early hours of Sunday morning there were less than 150 men still in the enclosure. The government had many spies in and around Eureka and decided to mobilise more than 300 troops to strike at 1.30 in the morning when the miners' defences would be at their weakest.

Peter Lalor said they had no time to retreat:

On discovering the smallness of our numbers, we would have retreated, but it was then too late, as almost immediately the military poured in one or two volleys of musketry . . . There were about seventy men possessing guns, twenty with pikes, and thirty with pistols, but many of those men with fire arms had no more than one or two rounds of ammunition.[36]

The large force of police and soldiers surrounded and then attacked the stockade. After an exchange of heavy fire, the hopelessly outnumbered and outgunned miners were quickly overrun. During the fighting, 22 miners and seven soldiers were killed, scores more were injured and more than a hundred survivors were rounded up and jailed.

Charles Ferguson was one of a group of American diggers who joined the miners' resistance and was in the Eureka stockade at the time of the attack. He explained that a group of American miners had formed themselves into a company they called the 'California Rangers' after Peter Lalor had come to talk to them.

Ferguson was born in Cleveland, Ohio, and came to New South Wales to search for gold before heading south to Ballarat. According to him, many of the Americans who joined the California Rangers were experienced soldiers who had fought in the Mexican–American War of 1846–48 before joining the California gold rush of 1849. The California Rangers were some 300 strong and were commanded by Irish American James McGill.

Ferguson was one of only a handful of Americans inside the Eureka enclosure in the early hours of Sunday 3 December when the government forces attacked. He said he was returning after having been sent with a detachment of men in the early morning to fetch weapons from a nearby house when the attack took place:

> Just as I arrived . . . we saw a whole body of troops ascending the hill . . . we had barely arrived . . . when the pickets came running in with the information that the enemy were upon us. The alarm sounded. 'To Arms'. I had arrived not a minute too soon. Had I been a moment later I should have been shut out, for the stockade was in a brief time surrounded.[37]

Ferguson described how they could see the soldiers advancing 'just as the light of day was breaking in the east' and could hear their officer giving orders when one of the men in the stockade, Captain Burnette, 'stepped a little in front, elevated his rifle, took aim, and fired':

> This was the first shot in the Ballarat War. It was said by many that the soldiers fired the first shot, but that is not true, as is well known to many.[38]

Ferguson said that when it was clear the enclosure was going to be overrun, he tried unsuccessfully to escape:

> As I jumped the stockade I fell, and the soldiers who had demanded my surrender fired, and the ball passed through my hat. The fall resulted in making me a prisoner. I was not long, however, getting onto my feet, but found a party of troopers had headed me off in that direction. Turning, I jumped back in the stockade, but there was met by a number of soldiers. I attempted to rush through, but was seized upon by several and we had it rough and tumble for

a few brief seconds, and I finally got through and struck for another place to make my escape.[39]

Even though the diggers' resistance had ended, the police kept shooting. Peter Lalor claimed the 'unusual proportion of the killed to the wounded is owing to the butchery by the military and troopers after the surrender'.

However, Ferguson said it was only the police, not the soldiers, who kept shooting:

The soldiers had been told to cease firing, but the police kept it up. When they saw a poor fellow trying his best to get away, it had now become impossible for me to escape, as I again had been headed off, and seeing Captain Carter of the Police, I ran to him and surrendered.[40]

James Brown, an American colleague of Ferguson's, managed to evade his captors by sliding down a rope into a nearby diggers' hole, which was more than 30 metres deep. Despite being experienced with ropes, having worked on a man o'war sailing ship, he later said it took two hours to climb back out of the hole.

Ferguson said at the time of his arrest he saw the wife of another arrested digger, John Tye, 'running out in her night dress' begging for her husband to be released. The woman was 'pushed around roughly' by the soldiers before an officer rode up and ordered the release of her husband. Ferguson said that by eight o'clock in the morning it was all over:

While standing on the field with Captain Carter, I was able to observe the ghastly scene. The morning sun was just rising, and spreading its light over the forms of the dead and wounded men, who, but a few minutes before, were in fit health and manly vigour, but now many lay in their long, last sleep, and others moaning in their pain . . . Prisoners were frightened out of their senses, and asking the soldiers what would be done with them, the consoling answer was 'Why, hung of course'.[41]

Ferguson was one of the 114 prisoners who were taken and crammed into the wooden cell at the government camp, which was so tiny there was no room to sit or lie down:

I [was] in a painful condition, physically; my face had become greatly swollen from blows and bruises in the struggle with the soldiers . . . My clothes were torn and completely besmeared with blood.[42]

Later on the same Sunday morning, Henry Seekamp, the owner of the *Ballarat Times*, was arrested and jailed with the others. He was charged with 'seditious libel' for publishing four articles that it was felt had incited the diggers during November and early December.[43]

Seekamp had arrived on the Victorian goldfields from England as a 23-year-old to try his luck in 1852. He met with enough success as a gold miner to launch the *Ballarat Times* and the *Buninyong Creswick Advertiser* in March 1854. On the Sunday morning of the massacre, when he was arrested in his printing office, he was typesetting an editorial that was to finish with the words, 'This foul bloody murder calls for High Heaven for vengeance, terrible and immediate.' When the edition of the paper was finally issued on 3 December with the help of Seekamp's wife, Sara, it carried the late insertion, 'The Editor of the *Ballarat Times* has been arrested since the above was written.'

A government account of the destruction of the Eureka stockade was provided in a report by Captain J. W. Thomas, who was the commander of the Ballarat troops that attacked the miners:

The Major General has already been made aware of the fact that a large number of ill-disposed persons have for some days been openly organizing, drilling, and equipping themselves with the undisguised object of attacking Her Majesty's troops, and if possible, subverting government. Early on the 2nd ultimo, information reached me that the rebels were forming an entrenchment camp at the Eureka diggings, about a mile and a half from our camp, with the avowed intention of intercepting the force under the Major General's command en route from Melbourne. During the whole of that day [2 December] strong parties of insurgents were parading the diggings in every direction, many of them in sight of the camp, robbing stores, collecting arms, and forcing people to join their ranks. I did not consider it prudent to attack them, as they were not collected in one spot. I decided to attack their camp at daylight the next morning, for this purpose the troops . . . were ordered to assemble past 2 o'clock am. At 3 o'clock I left with this force . . . with perfect silence, the force arrived in about half an hour in front of the entrenchment and about 30 yards [27 metres] from under it. Under cover of a rise in the ground the detachments of the 12th and 40th regiments extended in skirmish order, each having its proper support . . . We then advanced quietly towards the entrenchment where the revolutionary flag was flying, at about 150 yards [137 metres] we were received by a rather sharp, and well directed fire from the rebels, without a word of challenge on their part. Then, and not until then, I ordered the bugle to sound the 'commence firing'. For about 10 minutes a heavy fire was kept up by the troops advancing, which was replied by the rebels: during this time I brought up the infantry supports and the foot police. The entrenchment was then carried, and I ordered the firing to cease. All persons found in the entrenchment were taken prisoners, and many of the fugitives were intercepted by the cavalry. The number of prisoners brought in was 125, a few of them however, I ordered to be released, as I was not satisfied they had been in the engagement. [The] number now in custody is 114.[44]

During the fighting at the stockade, a musket ball and two small bullets shattered Peter Lalor's left arm. Bleeding heavily, he was hidden under some wooden slabs and able to be secreted away after the fighting ended.[45] Lalor was then hidden by friends near Ballarat, where his shattered arm was amputated. He was taken to Geelong, where he was kept in hiding and cared for by his fiancée, Alicia Young. Word quickly spread that Lalor was alive, and Governor Hotham agreed to the posting of a reward for his capture:

WANTED

Person of the name of Lawler . . . height 5' 11" [156 centimetres], age 35, hair dark brown, whiskers dark brown and shaved under the chin, no moustache, long face, rather good looking and . . . well made man . . .

did use certain TREASONABLE AND SEDITIOUS LANGUAGE and incite Men to take up Arms, with a view to make war against Our Sovereign Lady the Queen.

Late on that Sunday morning, the hurried news of the attack on the Eureka stockade reached Melbourne, where Governor Hotham and most of the respectable members of Melbourne society were at church. After consulting with his colleagues, Hotham the next day declared martial law at Ballarat, and a strict curfew was imposed across the goldfields.

News of the attack on the diggers at Ballarat met with a mixed reception in Melbourne. Very quickly, there were a number of public declarations in support of Hotham and the action taken by the government. Hotham first received a letter from prominent squatters, which pledged 'support and our entire confidence at the prompt and energetic measures taken by the Lieutenant General for the preservation of order', and for having maintained 'law and the preservation of the community from social disorganisation'.[46]

The Melbourne Council wrote to Hotham with the 'desire to convey to your Excellency the assurance of our sympathy with your Excellency, in the position in which your Government has been placed by the recent distur-bances at Ballarat'.[47]

On 20 December, the Victorian Legislative Council passed a resolution 'That the Lieutenant Governor, having been placed in a painfully embarrassing position, since his arrival in Victoria, is entitled to the sympathy and support of this Council, and it pledges itself by every means in its power to aid him in restoring, and maintaining, law and order'.[48]

However, there was also widespread criticism of Hotham and the government's actions. Two days after the attack, the Melbourne *Age* newspaper published an editorial that questioned the decision to use force against the miners:

> When peace shall lie once more regained, and there shall be time for deliberate judgment, the citizens will reckon with the Government. Meantime, they will not pledge themselves to support it; and they will not organize themselves into bodies for the purpose of filling the place of that expensive military force, which should never have been sent out of Melbourne. [We] do not sympathise with revolt; but neither do [we] sympathise with injustice and coercion. [We] will not fight for the diggers nor will [we] fight for the Government.[49]

On 6 December, a public meeting was called outside Saint Paul's church on Flinders Street in Melbourne, which attracted a reported 6000 people and failed to pass the expected resolution of support for the governor. Five days later, Hotham attempted to diffuse the situation by establishing an inquiry into the events at Eureka, and the next day 13 of those who had been arrested at Ballarat were charged with high treason and taken overnight by coach to Melbourne to be tried.

If the immediate aftermath of Eureka was proving troublesome for the government and Sir Charles Hotham, the following year would prove even more difficult. On 10 January 1855, the commission Hotham had established to inquire into Eureka met with the governor and, even though their report was still two months off, tried to persuade him to grant a general amnesty to all those charged over the affair. Hotham would not hear of it and insisted that the trials of the 13 accused of high treason go ahead.

The first case was heard on 22 February, and the jury found John Joseph, a black American, not guilty. Joseph had been accused of firing the first shot, which had killed Captain Wise. According to newspaper reports, about 10,000 diggers turned up at the court to hear the jury's verdict, and when Joseph left he was carried around the streets of the city in triumph.[50]

The following Monday, 26 February, Irishman John Manning, a schoolteacher and journalist with the *Ballarat Times*, was acquitted. Manning was in the thick of it organising the stockade and was known to have written many of the inflammatory stories for the *Ballarat Times*.

Concerned with the acquittals, the government delayed the remaining trials for a month, which allowed for the swearing in of new juries. The result, however, was the same. A month later, on 19 March, Timothy Hayes, the chairman of the Ballarat Reform League and a mining partner of Peter Lalor's, who had migrated to Australia with his wife and children from Ireland in 1852, was found not guilty. Two days later, Raffaello Carboni was acquitted, even though the prosecution had eight eyewitnesses, including four police and four troopers from the 40th Regiment, who said they saw Raffaello inside the stockade fire a gun and attack them with a pike.

The Dutchman Jan Vennick was acquitted the next day, in a trial that lasted only a few hours, followed by Irishmen James Beattie and Michael Touchy the day after. The remaining six were all tried together and all acquitted on

27 March: Henry Reid, James McFie Campbell, William Malloy, Jacob Sorrenson, Peter Lalor's close friend John Phelan and Thomas Dignum, who was discharged at the start of his trial.

The commission of inquiry Hotham had set up delivered its report on the same day. It made a series of recommendations in favour of the diggers, including that the 'obnoxious' licence fee be abolished:

> It has been found unsuitable to the proverbially unequal fortunes of gold digging . . . The present system of a licence fee [should] be given up. The views of the Commission are that a revenue must not be derived mainly from a direct tax; this they propose to accomplish by a fairer and less obnoxious method, namely a moderate export duty.[51]

The commission was also highly critical of the way the licence fee had been collected, which, it said, led inevitably to violence:

> The licence fee has been undermined by widespread evasion, which has become a practiced and skillful art, and that its effective enforcement produced violent results . . . To carry out the law in its integrity . . . required a constant exercise of authority . . . scenes between the police and the miners, were a daily occurrence, where mutual irritation, abuse, and gross violence would ensue.[52]

The commission also made recommendations supporting two other demands of the diggers. It proposed extending the franchise to allow the diggers to be represented in parliament and suggested land be made available for miners to buy for the building of their own homes.

To further undermine the authority of the government, Peter Lalor was increasingly seen in public before the government backed down and revoked the reward it had offered for his capture. Later in the year, he stood unopposed as the member of parliament for Ballarat with John Basson Humffray, and they were elected as additional members of the Legislative Council when Victoria's new constitution came into force in 1856.

To add to Hotham's problems, on 3 April 1855, after the acquittal of all of the accused and the release of the report into the goldfields, the Melbourne *Age* published a damning editorial about the governor:

> In the short period of seven or eight months he has managed to alienate the sympathies of every class in the colony . . . earned a character for contemptible official treachery and evasion, and has brought the good faith of the Government into disrepute by a systematic breach of contract . . . and a disgraceful system of espionage.[53]

In June, the Goldfields Act 1855 was passed, which gave local courts the responsibility to hear matters previously decided by the dreaded gold commissioners. The Act also allowed for the election of members of the local courts, and in July the Italian revolutionary Raffaello Carboni was unanimously elected on Bakery Hill to the Ballarat Court.

Hotham continued as governor for the remainder of the year but in November sent his resignation to London. In the week before Christmas, and in declining health, he caught a chill while officially opening Melbourne's first gasworks. He died on New Year's Eve and is buried in the Melbourne Cemetery.

CHAPTER SEVEN

The Chinese

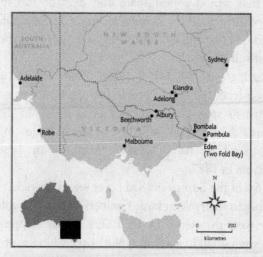

The Kiandra diggings

[A] race with whom we have little more in common than
with a race of baboons or a tribe of orang-utans.

No other group during the Australian gold era would suffer the same persecution, violence, murder and official discrimination as the Chinese.

They were attacked in public and in the press, and branded as barbarians, pagans and impure. The Melbourne *Argus* newspaper described them as 'a social evil' that would contaminate and degrade the superior European race.[1] The *Sydney Morning Herald* published allegations that the Chinese were guilty of infanticide and 'unnatural crimes'.[2]

Starting with Victoria in 1856, every colonial parliament introduced anti-Chinese-immigration laws in an attempt to stop the Chinese joining the gold diggings – South Australia in 1857, New South Wales in 1861, Queensland in 1877, Western Australia in 1886 and Tasmania in 1887.

Most of the Europeans had never seen a 'celestial' before they began to arrive in large numbers to hunt for gold, and many were threatened by their very different appearance. They were small in stature: typically the Chinese men were less than 150 centimetres tall, which was shorter than most European women. They shaved their hair from the temples across the front of the head and did not cut the back, which was gathered in a long ponytail that was usually tied towards the end with a ribbon. They dressed very differently from the European men, with loose, wide-sleeved tops and loose breeches, and wore soft slippers or sandals, or went about barefoot. They travelled in large groups of a hundred or more, wearing wide circular straw hats that peaked in the middle, and carried their possessions in two large baskets that were hung from the ends of a long pole resting over their shoulders. When moving, they took short, fast steps and appeared to be running very slowly.

A former London Missionary Society worker, Reverend William Young, who reported to the Victorian Parliament on the conditions of the Chinese during the first decade of the gold rush, said that most of the Chinese who came to Australia aspired eventually to return to their homeland but saw gold as a way of breaking the poverty cycle that enveloped them at home:

> They are great lovers of their country. The majority are looking forward with hope, to that happy consideration, the return to their fatherland; and are content to toil here, amid many difficulties and privations until they can lay by a sufficient sum wherein to carry out their heart's desire . . . Not only the home of the Chinese, but the tombs of their ancestors and their ancestral halls, act as powerful magnets to lure them back to the land of their births.[3]

The Chinese made no attempt to become part of the local community. As the local newspaper described, they built their own villages separate from the Europeans on the goldfields:

> The visitor to the gold field . . . cannot have failed to notice encampments of small uniformed size tents, huddled together and interspersed with sheep-herds, carpenter shops, and various similar establishments, denoting that a community with somewhat of an organization lives there . . . [There are] numerous beings, with umbrella-shaped coverings on their heads, who seem to have just stepped out of the china-ware whose grotesque figures were want to excite our youthful wonder.[4]

The Chinese came predominantly from the agricultural areas that stretched for about 240 kilometres south of the city of Canton and about the same distance west of Hong Kong. While they came from different districts, speaking different dialects, they 'managed to understand each other with tolerable ease'.[5] There were only a handful of women among them:

> Only a favoured few, who have ample pecuniary means, are in a position to bring their families here. There are not more than a dozen native women in the colony, and some of these are not wives but servants.[6]

According to Young, as many as 40 per cent of the men were already married and would eventually return to their villages and families.[7] Even though nearly all the men came without women, more than 80 per cent lived in a tent with a relative or friend and could rely on a network of support if they became ill or injured while working.[8] Examples of Chinese men who were neglected when they were sick were extremely rare. When they died and were buried, those who could afford it had arranged for their bones to be placed in a small wooden box or carpet bag so they could be returned to China to be interred alongside their ancestors.

When they arrived in Australia, the Chinese men would join an association or society that had been established to provide mutual protection and assistance. According to a local translator, the Chinese societies encouraged the principles of mutual caring: 'To love and help each other, the strong must not oppress the weak, and they must not injure the few.'[9] The rules of the society were enforced with fines and, in extreme cases, beatings with the rattan, or cane.

Reverend Young noted the industriousness of the Chinese diggers, who would typically work every day from sunrise until it was dark. Despite this hard graft, the Chinese also enjoyed a number of leisure pursuits, including gambling, drinking spirits and smoking opium with family or friends. Young said there were 50 Chinese gambling shops and 80 opium dens in Ballarat alone, and that four out of every ten Chinese men were addicted to opium. The opiate was not illegal and at the time was one of the biggest items sold into China by British traders. It was not until the 1880s that the Australian colonies attempted collectively to curtail its use, and it was not outlawed until 1908.

The Chinese brought most of their own opium to Australia, packing the 'black gummy substance' into small tins for the journey.[10] Far from trying to limit the trade, the Victorian Government saw it as a useful source of revenue, imposing a tax on it along with imported rice in 1855.

Young said that the addicts 'are not content with a fixed ratio, but desire and require accumulative doses'. He said the opium dens were evil and warned there was a risk the disease would contaminate the non-Chinese population – particularly women – unless they were closely watched:

> The opium shops which stud the Chinese camp so thickly are also dens of infamy and immorality. In these are found abandoned European women, some of whom have got into the habit of smoking the drug; and there is reason to fear that in the course of time the practice will spread among the European population. All these shops should be well watched, and kept under vigilant surveillance of the police.[11]

Much of Young's report dwelt on the health consequences of opium smoking and the high cost of maintaining a habit:

> The evils of opium smoking are: It ruins the constitution of those who are addicted; their bodies get decayed and weak, their skin becomes sallow, and their person emaciated. 90 Chinese out of 100 smoke opium. Out of 90, 30 are confirmed smokers. Wealthy Chinese smoke as much as £2–£3 worth of opium weekly, men in moderate circumstances over £1 weekly; men in poor circumstances 3 shillings to 4 shillings weekly.[12]

The Chinese gambled 'passionately, publicly and noisily', and there were Chinese gambling dens on practically every goldfield. Popular games included mah-jong, where the banging and rattling of the pieces on the table was a deliberate attempt to attract good spirits and chase away the bad ones. Fan-tan was also widely played, which is a game where the croupier empties a large number of small counters on the table from a steel bowl and removes them four at a time. The players bet on whether the last remaining amount of counters will be one, two, three or none. The Reverend Young was as offended by the gambling as he had been by the opium smoking:

> Evils of gambling. The gambler wins, he gives himself up to immorality, gambling, drinking and smoking . . . If the gambler loses, then he steals like a mouse, and pilfers like a dog.[13]

Young said that between 50 and 80 per cent of the

goldfield Chinese were regular gamblers and that gambling and opium constituted 'the two gigantic evils which have contributed to the impoverishment and demoralisation of the people to an extent which is truly lamentable and appalling'. He wrote that their plight was worsened because those unable to find gold could not find work, which in turn added to the rate of crime committed by their community.

That the Chinese were almost entirely men gave rise to the widely held view promoted in the newspapers that they were sexually depraved, and similarities were drawn with the earlier convict times in Australia when there were few women:

> It will be observed, that almost all the preceding objections to the Chinese refer chiefly to the absence of females; that all the vices which have been noticed are those which must be expected to flourish among a population composed wholly of males. The history of some of the Australian colonies, cursed with convictism, in which not the least evil was the disproportion of the sexes speaks eloquent of the social and moral plagues which such a state of things brings.[14]

The newspapers also reported on the pornography brought to the goldfields by the Chinese men:

> A large number of Chinese had arrived in the colony, many of whom had disgusting and filthy pictures, which they exposed to sell. Several of these men had been brought before the Police Court that day for this offence, and from them were taken forty or fifty pictures of a most disgusting nature.[15]

Many of the Europeans who had never witnessed any other worship than the Christian Church were confronted by the Chinese Taoists and Buddhists and their very different temples and ceremonies. In mid-1855, a move was made by a number of prominent Christians in Melbourne to promote conversion of the Chinese to the Christian faith:

> A public meeting was held yesterday evening, at the Mechanical Institution, for the purpose of forming an association for diffusing Evangelical Christianity among the Chinese in the colony of Victoria. The attendance was exceedingly numerous, there being upwards of three hundred persons present when the proceedings commenced. The Worshipful, the Mayor of Melbourne took the chair, supported by the Very Rev. the Dean of Melbourne, the Rev. Dr. Mackay, the Rev. Mr. Morrison, the Rev. Mr. Odel, the Rev. Mr. Darling, the Rev. Mr. Eggleston, and various other clergymen of other protestant denominations. There were also two Chinese Christians on the platform.[16]

Also in 1855, the first Methodist Church Mission aimed at Chinese conversion was established at Castlemaine in Victoria under the Reverend Thomas Ralston. In 1859, a Chinese Methodist church was built.[17]

The Reverend William Young noted that by the mid-1860s there were three Protestant missions to the Chinese on the Victorian goldfields, but the number that had converted to Christianity did 'not exceed 50'. He said there was also one Catholic mission but was unaware whether they had managed to baptise any Chinese people.

In 1861, Agnes Murray came to Ballarat from Ayrshire in Scotland and became a missionary and Bible reader. Over the next three decades, she built a number of mission halls at Golden Point and Little Bendigo. The Christians do not appear to have been overrun with converts, and by the 1880s the congregation of the Golden Point Chinese Mission Church numbered only about 70 people.[18]

Intermarriage between Chinese men and European women was uncommon, though not non-existent. In 1867, after well over a decade of Chinese immigration to the goldfields, Reverend Young reported that there were between 50 and 60 mixed marriages in the colony and about 130 children.[19]

Young noted that some of the Chinese took their European wives back to China and in some cases deserted them, 'leaving them to shift for themselves' in Macao or Hong Kong, but that the number of cases was 'rare'. Not so rare were the 'cases of European wives who desert their Chinese husbands'.[20]

The Europeans also believed the Chinese brought with them 'loathsome diseases' – a view reinforced whenever there were a number of sick Chinese arriving on ships that needed to be quarantined at Australian ports. There was also a fear among the European population that leprosy was widespread in the Chinese community, but by the mid-1860s Reverend Young reported there were only 27 known cases, which were concentrated around Bendigo.

There was widespread dislike of the Chinese even before they began to arrive looking for gold. From the late 1840s, a number of public meetings around the colony called on the parliament to stop the immigration of Chinese labourers to work on Australian farms.[21]

The Chinese did not begin to arrive in large numbers until more than two years after the first big rush of overseas migrants, but when they did the locals felt they were 'struck with the suddenness and the extent of the invasion'.[22] Within a year, violent assaults on Chinese miners became increasingly widespread, but most of the newspaper reports were more sympathetic to the Europeans who had carried out the assaults than to the Chinese victims:

> The serious evils that may any day arise from the presence of these strangers is plain from the perusal of the reports that reach us of their numbers in which they are already to be found at the different gold fields . . . we see . . . in the peculiarities of their language, dress, and habits of life, there is enough to unite the suspicions of other diggers.[23]

During an early anti-Chinese incident in 1854 on Meroo River, north of Ophir in New South Wales, a number of Chinese were shot. According to a local newspaper report, a few English diggers had been blocked by a large number of the Chinese from access to water for mining, so they went back to their camp at Tambaroora and returned with a large number of armed reinforcements:

> Several shots appear to have been fired, and three Chinese are missing – whether killed or not is impossible to say. Having driven them into the bush the diggers set fire to and destroyed several of their tents.[24]

The following month, a number of Chinese were assaulted and badly beaten at Iron Bark on the Forest Creek diggings in Victoria. They required hospitalisation. In the report of the incident, the newspaper sided with the assailants, suggesting the need for laws to keep the Chinese away:

> To speak the truth, there is a strong feeling against the Chinese population on the part of intelligent men, who question the usefulness of these foreigners as colonists and have strong objections to urge against them on the score of morality. The immigration of the Chinese is likely to be a subject which will call for the interference of the legislature.[25]

A catalyst for the Victorian Government to move against the Chinese came from the commission that inquired into the Eureka rebellion. In its report, only three months after Eureka, on 27 March 1855, the commission expressed surprise and concern at the number of Chinese on the Victorian goldfields and recommended that the government take steps to restrict further Chinese immigration:

> This number, although already almost incredible, yet appears to be still fast increasing, and is likely to increase still more upon the publication of the abolition of the licence fee . . . The question of the influx of such large numbers of a pagan and inferior race is a very serious one . . . and comprises an unpleasant possibility of the future, that a comparative handful of colonists may be buried in a countless throng of Chinamen.[26]

The commission also recommended that future ships from China be allowed only to land 'a certain limited number' and that above this they be forced to pay a fine of £10 for each Chinese man landed.

Over the next months and into the following year there was a clamour in Victoria for the government to take decisive action, with the newspapers stirring up fear and hatred of the Chinese:

> The presence among us of even 20,000 Chinese is a social evil of no ordinary magnitude. These men are aliens in language, customs and religion. They are regarded by the mass of the colonial population as inferiors.[27]

At the same time, there were rumours that many more ships were already in Chinese ports loading the hordes that would overrun Christian, white, Anglo-Saxon Australia.

On 12 April 1856, the government announced it was planning to present a bill to parliament to 'prevent the influx of the Chinese in the large numbers in which they now arrived'.[28] Three days later, at a big public meeting in the Mechanics Institute building in Melbourne, the Mayor of Melbourne and others called for the Chinese to be curbed. Melbourne had been panicked by the sudden emergence of a new tent suburb of more than 800 Chinese immigrants that had sprung up on waste ground on the left bank of the Yarra River.[29]

Meanwhile, violence on the goldfields was continuing, and the newspaper coverage remained sympathetic to the diggers, calling on the government to block the Chinese coming to the fields. On 17 April, the *Argus* reported that four British miners had been convicted in the Castlemaine Court for assaulting a number of Chinese and each fined five shillings:

> Some laws and provisions must promptly be brought in

to operation to avert the threatened evils, and effective restraint must be exercised on the hordes of unwelcome people.[30]

In early May, a Geelong newspaper correspondent warned that emotions were running high on the goldfields and 'a storm is brewing, which, if not averted by timely and prudent measures, will one day burst, and plunge Ballarat a second time into bloodshed'.[31]

By now, the government had become 'carried away in the whirl of public excitement'[32] and instructed the attorney general to draft legislation. On 23 May, the colonial secretary told the parliament that the government was soon to introduce laws to stop the Chinese by imposing a special tax on those wanting to come to the gold mines of Victoria:

> The question of the Chinese Immigration has become one of grave importance . . . Great alarm has been entertained by many as to the evils likely to arise from the influx of these people . . . It was undoubtedly necessary to frame certain rules, in order to prevent the evils which otherwise might arise . . . With that in view, the bill contemplated . . . the collection of certain rates on Chinese Immigrants.[33]

The Act to Make Provision for Certain Immigrants 1855 imposed a charge or poll tax on each Chinese person landing at a Victorian port and also limited the number a ship could bring into port to one for every ten tons of cargo. Initially, the tax was to be set at £5, but after nearly a month of argument in the Victorian Parliament it was raised to £10 per head.

Following its introduction, Governor Sir Charles Hotham wrote to the colonial secretary in London, Earl Grey, asking that the British Government also help stem the arrival of the Chinese:

> I hope that you will see fit to cause a circular to be sent to the consuls at the different ports in China, and Singapore, and Hong Kong, or other British ports, noting that it shall be imperative upon masters of vessels carrying Chinese to this colony to equalize the sexes, failing in which they will on arrival here, suffer a fine of £10 for each single male cabin passenger, and two pounds per head for the remaining single men. Without your interposition in this matter our youth on the goldfields will be trained in the vice and profligacy, and the moral growth of the colony blighted.[34]

However, the new tax, which was to be collected from the captain of each ship, resulted in one of the most ingenious tax-avoidance schemes and one of the most remarkable migration treks in history. To avoid paying the prohibitive £10 poll tax, the masters of the ships from China with men destined for the goldfields simply sailed past Port Phillip Bay, around the coast of Victoria and across the border to unload their human cargo in the colony of South Australia, where the tax was not levied.

Initially, the ships landed in Adelaide, leaving the Chinese with a walk of nearly 800 kilometres to the Victorian goldfields, where there were few tracks and no clear colonial borders. On 23 January 1856, the *Launceston* unloaded 240 Chinese people in Adelaide – 140 of whom held credit tickets organised by a wealthy

Chinese merchant. They created quite an impression on the locals when they arrived and quietly set up camp with their tents, started fires and boiled water for tea.

The first party to head overland to Ballarat in April 1856 hired a guide by the name of Lionel Edwards, who charged £2 for each of the Chinese. Edwards provided five two-horse drays for the heavier gear, but the Chinese carried most of their own supplies, tools and equipment on long poles over their shoulders.

More ships began to arrive in Adelaide, and on 3 March the little steamer the *Burra Burra*, which normally operated between Adelaide and Melbourne, began to ferry the Chinese from Adelaide 340 kilometres down the South Australian coast to the little settlement of Robe on Guichen Bay,[35] which reduced the overland walk to about 350 kilometres to Ararat, 450 kilometres to Ballarat and about 500 kilometres to Bendigo.

Adelaide, Robe and the Victorian goldfields

Over the next year, the tiny settlement of Robe in South Australia would become a thriving port as 20,000 Chinese men poured in to reach the Victorian goldfields while avoiding the colony's entry tax. At the time, Robe was one of the remotest spots in the British Empire, existing primarily for the export of wool from the farms of the hinterland and with a population of less than 200 people.

Thirty-two-year-old Henry Dudley Melville recorded how in 1857 'some forty-five' British-, American- and Dutch-owned ships 'came direct from Hong Kong to Port Robe landing about twenty thousand Celestials, exclusive of many hundreds landed by intercontinental steamer from Adelaide'.[36] Melville, who had joined the South Australian Police in 1845 and was the sub-collector of customs at Robe for 15 years from 1855, said the little township was shocked by the influx:

The Robe people were not prepared for the sudden invasion, and neither was I, the thing had been kept very quiet by the Hong Kong agents in order that the Victorian Government might not interfere with the wholesale smuggling.[37]

Thomas Smeaton was the newly arrived bank manager in Robe the day hundreds of Chinese appeared on the British ship the *Land of Cakes*:

Imagine yourself an inhabitant of Robe on Saturday 17 January 1857. No Banks, no electricity: no electric telegraph: everything on a mitigated scale: a sensation pervading the inhabitants that they were out of the world, in an intermediate state between existence and extinction

208

– when, those whose eyes happened to be open, perceived a ship! A ship actually coming into Guichen Bay!! And crowded with passengers!! Before many hours, the population of Robe had doubled.[38]

Smeaton said that most of the townsfolk had never seen an Asian person before:

It was well that all the passengers were alike and undistinguishable. All Chinese, all men, all with mooney faces, all with pig-tails. Had it been otherwise, had it been necessary for every resident of Robe to have stared at every individual Chinaman, Robe would never have recovered from the unwonted strain upon its rudely awakened faculties.[39]

On arrival in Guichen Bay, the Chinese had to make their own arrangements to reach the Robe shore, as the water under the town's little jetty was too shallow for the ships. According to Smeaton, the Chinese were forced by the owners of the local boats to pay exorbitant prices between five shillings and £1 each for the short trip, or to swim for the shore:

Arrived in the Bay. The next thing was to get ashore. The plan for anyone who had a boat was to go off, get the Chinese in anyhow, make them pay as much as they could, and even (it is said) take the money by force from someone Chinese, leaving him to settle with the remainder of the boat load, as best he could.[40]

Once ashore, the Chinese pitched hundreds of small tents

while preparing for the long trek overland to the Victorian goldfields, which included collecting, drying and eating the local seaweed.

Robe experienced a short economic boom catering for the large number of immigrants, but a local newspaper reported that the townspeople became anxious that the Chinese might react violently to being exploited by the locals, who were selling them food and supplies at exorbitant prices:

> We have three thousand Chinese camped around the town. Many of the locals are getting very apprehensive about their safety, in case of any outbreak among the Celestials, who have lately waxed somewhat indignant at the manifold impositions practiced upon them by the 'land sharks' here.[41]

Captains unfamiliar with Guichen Bay had difficulty navigating sailing ships into the cove. Customs Officer Melville recorded that three ships – the *Phaeton*, *Saltana* and *Konig Wilhelm I* – were all wrecked while sailing in or out of the bay during 1857. The *Phaeton* had been destined for Melbourne and was not covered by insurance when instead it had continued on to South Australia to avoid the Chinese poll tax.[42] Melville was particularly critical of the *Phaeton*'s captain for the loss of the ship:

> [He] sailed up the bay in grand style but went too far before putting his ship about, when he did he missed the stays and drifted onto the sand bank from which he never came off, no lives were lost but the vessel became a total wreck.[43]

The Chinese were expected to pay customs on all their belongings on arrival in Robe, and Henry Melville complained that on one occasion they broke into a locked shed to recover the opium that he had impounded until the import tax was paid.

On the overland trek to Victoria, the typical party of Chinese might number between a hundred and three hundred, but some groups totalled up to five or six hundred.[44] Each group could extend in a single-file line for several kilometres. They were described as being only 'four feet to four feet six inches' (120 to 140 centimetres) tall, yet carried more than their body weight in two baskets at the end of a pole over their shoulders, which contained bedding, cooking utensils, picks, spades, cradles, buckets and oil lamps.[45]

With the European guides riding on the leading carts and the Chinese jogging alongside, they were able to cover the distance to the Victorian goldfields in an average of about 25 days.[46]

The 'back door' of South Australia as a way into Victoria was closed at the end of 1857. Under pressure from Victoria (and local public opinion), South Australia introduced its own anti-Chinese legislation in June 1857, and by the end of the year no more ships were arriving at Robe.

Many of the Chinese from Robe settled at the Victoria goldfields around Ararat, where they were to suffer the same violence at the hands of resentful Europeans as had occurred on other diggings. On 8 June 1857, the local government official reported that about 20 European diggers had attacked the Chinese, burned down their camp and threw them off their claims:

I have the honour to inform you that a serious attack was last night made on the Chinese by the Europeans on the goldfield. The whole of one Chinese camp was burnt down and a considerable amount of property destroyed besides a number of Chinamen who were robbed during the row of large sums of money and gold.[47]

While most of the Chinese who came from South Australia avoided paying the Victorian levy, a number were jailed on their arrival. According to John Sadlier, a policeman in Hamilton in western Victoria, 'about one hundred' who had 'plodded patiently day after day' after crossing the border at Apsley were arrested by local police:

They were stopped and payment of the tax demanded, but the only answer was 'No savee', and they were brought before the magistrates. The sentence of two months in the Portland Gail did not seem to disturb them in the least. They camped in the police paddocks without guards to look after them, but they never thought of going out of bounds. Thence they were marched to Portland, where they camped in the reserve for public gardens . . . They never repined, never lost patience, nor did they give a moment's trouble; and when their sentence expired they walked away for their destination, placid and uncomplaining as if nothing wrong had been done to them.[48]

Meanwhile, the hostility towards the Chinese on the Victorian goldfields continued, and in July 1857 a riot occurred on the Buckland River near the Ovens diggings in northern Victoria. The trouble had begun when the Chinese miners moved onto diggings that had been abandoned by European miners. When the Chinese, who numbered about 2000, found gold there, a group of about 40 or 50 resentful former occupants decided to clear them away and resume digging themselves.

Armed with clubs, swords, knives and guns, the Europeans attacked the Chinese camp and burned down about 50 tents and a number of stores before chasing the fleeing Chinese down the river to nearby Sandy Point. By now, the mob had grown to several hundred, determined to rid the Chinese from the diggings entirely, which the lone policeman on the goldfield was powerless to stop. When they reached the Chinese camp at Lower Flat, many of the Chinese were bashed, wounded and robbed. Further on, as they tried to escape across the Buckland River, there was an exchange of gunfire, during which three diggers were wounded and a number drowned.

Two days later, police reinforcements began to arrive from Beechworth, and order was restored when a number of Europeans were arrested and charged. Only one of the offenders was subsequently convicted on the charge of causing a riot, while all the others were convicted of the lesser offence of unlawful assembly.

By the end of the 1850s, as a result of the poll tax and the decline in easily worked shallow alluvial deposits, the number of Chinese on the Victorian goldfields began to decline. According to a report to the Victorian Parliament, the Chinese population of the colony dropped by more than half between 1859 and 1867, from around 45,000 to barely 20,000.[49] Many of the Chinese returned to their homeland, and of those that stayed in Victoria many left gold mining to work on farms as shearers or to run their own market garden or other small business.[50]

But many joined the other diggers and began to spread north across the border to New South Wales, where a number of new fields were discovered in the late 1850s and early 1860s. By 1858, it was already estimated that almost a thousand Chinese were arriving in New South Wales each month, not only from China but also from Victoria.[51]

In New South Wales, the European diggers were equally hostile to the Chinese and had already been calling on parliament to restrict them on the goldfields as the Victorian Parliament had done. In 1858, diggers from Luisa Creek (Ophir), Rocky River, Meroo River, the Turon and Tambaroora had all put their petitions to either the local gold commissioner or the New South Wales Parliament.[52]

The Chinese were also on the receiving end of vitriolic attacks from the New South Wales goldfields newspapers, including the *Bathurst Free Press*, which described them as 'a race with whom we have little more in common than with a race of baboons or a tribe of orang-utans'.[53]

One of the fields that attracted the nomadic Chinese gold miners was the remote spot of Kiandra in New South Wales, which is one of the highest points in Australia. Gold was found at Kiandra high in the Snowy Mountains in the south-west of New South Wales in November 1859, and the rush that followed was in one of the remotest, coldest and most hazardous of all the Australian fields. Before the arrival of the white man, the Wolgal Aboriginal people used the area around Kiandra for summer hunting, as the harsh climate made it uninhabitable in winter. The Wolgal people lived most of the year in the surrounding lowlands around the headwaters of the Tumut, Murrumbidgee and Murray Rivers. An attempt had been made by white farmers to establish farming up at Kiandra in the late 1830s, but the venture had failed with the onset of winter, when most of the cattle perished.[54]

The Kiandra rush was spectacularly short and extremely rich. When an experienced miner from Yackandandah in Victoria came north to the diggings, he said he had never seen so much gold so close to the surface of the ground:

> One party of four men got 120 oz in a week, another party of three were getting 20 oz per day. Several large nuggets were found – 6 lb, 12 lb, 14 lb. Another party getting 1 lb weight of gold per diem.[55]

By March, there were more than 10,000 diggers on the field, and as winter was approaching more were on their way – even though Kiandra's first gold commissioner, P. L. Cloete, said that it could only be mined for four months of the year:

> The present diggings can only be worked from 1 December to the end of March; for the rest of the year the place is uninhabitable, and unapproachable, owing to the heavy snow drift.[56]

The lure of the gold not only kept the diggers there through the savage winter but also attracted more and more. During the winter, the *Sydney Morning Herald* correspondent wrote from Tumut to warn diggers against trying to reach Kiandra:

> I hasten to inform you that yesterday morning here the ice was four inches [10.2 centimetres] thick, and this morning

the wind blew very high from the south east, accompanied by snow. The snow has been drifting all night, and I am sure in some places it must be several feet in depth.[57]

The government had intended withdrawing its police from Kiandra with the first snowfalls but was forced to leave them there when the diggers, who were clearly not going away, protested to the colonial secretary on 23 March 1860 that increased lawlessness would be inevitable:

> Sir, we the undersigned, representing the commercial and mining interests resident on the Kiandra gold-field, having heard with extreme apprehension that instructions have been issued to the small police force stationed here to abandon the gold-fields on the first occasion of the fall of snow, respectfully beg to draw to the attention of the Government the evils which must result from the adoption of such a measure. The present population, is estimated at not less than 6,000 souls . . . who, in the absence of any legally recognized authority, would be subject to the marauding violence of that lawless class of characters invariably found on a new gold-field.[58]

Kiandra was also difficult to reach. The shortest route from Victoria through the mountains via Yackandandah and Lobb's Hole was still more than 500 kilometres from Melbourne and 225 kilometres from the northern Victorian goldfields of Beechworth. The way was rough, particularly towards the end, which was described as 'utterly impassable for wheels for the last 30 miles [48 kilometres], and very dangerous both for passengers and horses'.[59]

A longer but easier route from Victoria was taken to the

west of the mountains by Arthur Freeling, the surveyor general of South Australia, who was sent to report on the goldfield for the colonial government.[60] To reach Kiandra, Freeling first sailed more than a thousand kilometres from Adelaide to Melbourne and then travelled overland for more than 700 kilometres from Melbourne. His route took him from Melbourne via Beechworth to Albury on the Victoria–New South Wales border, then via Kiambla and Adelong.

On his way north through the Victorian goldfields, Freeling saw 'public houses rapidly springing up' to cater for the travelling diggers on the main road north out of Victoria, and at Albury he saw the first major bridge over the Murray River under construction. As he moved further up into the mountains, he found the terrain more challenging, and between Kiambla and Adelong the road became hilly and difficult for heavy carts. After Adelong, the road swung towards Kiandra across the Tumut River, which was 'wide, and runs with a rapid stream, and must be crossed with caution, if at all high'. Freeling said the melting of the snow made the river crossing more dangerous:

Goods are taken up the hill mostly on packhorses; still drays occasionally manage to get up. I witnessed one with a light load and sixteen bullocks struggling up, aided by a number of men, who with difficulty prevented the dray from capsizing. Finally, the last 30 miles [48 kilometres] is intersected by numerous boggy creeks, which, after the melting of the snows, or after continuous rains, would be impassable.[61]

When he finally reached Kiandra in April, a savage winter was already approaching, and most of the miners lacked any warm accommodation:

> The weather was extremely fluctuating; heavy fogs lay on the ground in the early morning, almost without exception. During two days, there was a great deal of rain, and during the night of the 22nd and 23 April, snow fell without intermission, covering the face of the country to a depth of three inches. This was the second fall of snow . . . Calico is the prevailing material of which huts are composed, and provides neither warmth from the severity of the weather, nor protection from the rain.[62]

Freeling was to urge South Australians against trying to reach Kiandra at that time of the year. Before leaving the goldfield in early May to report back to his government in Adelaide, he said that the journey would create 'hardship and privation' and that no one should try to survive the winter there. There was also the added risk, he said, of insufficient food. Indeed, the price of flour would climb to £1000 a ton, the highest on any Australian goldfield to date:[63]

> To brave the winter under a calico tent would be madness . . . the danger of attempting to winter in Kiandra this season will consist chiefly in the want of food. I was informed that, at the time I left there was not more than seven weeks' provisions remaining for the population.[64]

At the time that Freeling left to return to South Australia, a bank teller named George Preshaw was trying to reach

Kiandra, having been transferred there by his bank to work in the recently opened branch on the new goldfield.

Preshaw was to take a shorter route by sailing around the coast from Melbourne to the New South Wales south-coast port of Eden, on Two Fold Bay, then heading 250 kilometres north-west over the mountains.

Preshaw was born in Scotland and had migrated to Australia in 1852 with his father, mother, three sisters and a brother. He went to the Mount Alexander gold diggings when he was barely in his teens:

> I was a young digger, only thirteen year of age, but there were no schools on the diggings in those days, and all hands had to make themselves generally helpful.[65]

Shortly before Christmas 1854, after some moderate success, he said that when working deep in his hole in black soil about a metre from the bottom of the shaft he found it 'full of gold'.[66] Having completed what he described as his 'probation at the diggings', Preshaw decided to 'cast about for some occupation more congenial' to his tastes, when he had the good fortune to find a job in the Bank of New South Wales as a junior in the Castlemaine branch.[67] In 1855, he was transferred to New South Wales, and in 1860 to the bank's new branch at Kiandra. 'I did not relish the long journey,' he said. 'However, it had to be done.'[68]

Preshaw began his journey in Castlemaine on 9 May on a Cobb and Co. coach 'crammed with passengers' on 'exceedingly dusty' roads. On 17 May, he boarded the *City of Sydney* in Melbourne, and he arrived at the southern New South Wales port of Eden at three in the morning of 19 May.[69]

In Eden, he bought a horse for £20 and 'donned for the first time riding boots and breeches', which he found very uncomfortable, before heading off on the overland journey to Kiandra that would take eight days.[70]

At the end of the first day, the inexperienced horseman had only covered about 25 kilometres north along the coast to Pambula, and the following night a further 32 kilometres inland to Bombala. On the third day, he became lost in the rain and had to retrace his steps. He managed to find overnight shelter with a farmer who lived in a one-room bark hut with his wife and three children. The next morning, he paid for their hospitality by giving the oldest son his woollen coat. When Preshaw reached the Woolpack Inn at Woolway after four days, he met a man who had caught up with him after travelling only one and a half days from Eden.

On the last two days, the track became hilly and difficult to ride, and he had to twice cross the Snowy River, 'which was high, with a strong current running'. On the last day, he said the road was 'steep, bad and boggy'[71] and had to dismount and push his horse ahead.

When he finally reached Kiandra after dark on Sunday 27 May, the only available accommodation was sleeping on the crowded floor of the bar of Carmichaels Hotel: 'a most uncomfortable night I spent on the floor of the bar parlour ... cold and miserable'.[72]

From the following night, he found a bedroom of about two and a half by three metres in Kids Hotel that slept eight people. Preshaw thought he was lucky because he slept in the middle of the floor, so 'I was always sure of a fair share of the bed clothes'.[73]

He was to spend the next 14 months in the wilds of

Kiandra, where he said he 'saw more low life than I ever saw before, or have seen since'.

On his first day of work, he described the Kiandra branch of the bank, which was a tent with its floor under water from the melting snow outside:

> On the morning after my arrival at Kiandra the agent of the bank (Mr. Yates) . . . took me up to the bank, which I found to be a calico tent, built on the high side of the street . . . On entering I saw a young man behind the counter, and was introduced to him by Yates as his assistant (Mr. Swain). The young fellow was perched on a piece of bark which rested between two logs, a stream of water running under him; in fact, right through the building. I was puzzled to account for this, but on examination found it was caused by snow, which was a foot or two deep at the back of the tent, thawing. The floor was one mass of puddle. No fireplace, so of course, no fire; no door to the tent, but merely a piece of calico with a piece of sapling at the bottom, which was rolled up or down as the occasion required.[74]

The bank had no safe, and each morning Preshaw and his colleague Yates would walk 'three quarters of a mile' to the gold commissioner's camp with saddlebags and guns to collect notes and coins. In the evening, they would return with the bullion they had bought during the day, which was kept 'under one of the Commissioner's bunks'.[75]

During the first months, 'a motley collection of habitations of the very roughest and most primitive kind' sprang up, forming two streets at right angles to one another, on the slope of a hill.[76] By the middle of 1860, there were

72 businesses in Kiandra, comprising 25 stores, 13 bakers, 16 butchers, 14 pubs and four blacksmiths. There were a further 48 businesses spread through the nearby goldfield sites of Nine Mile diggings and Denison.[77]

Preshaw said the only place to be sure of a good hot meal in the early days was at Kitts Hotel, where the owner had built a restaurant to seat 60 or 70 but with only one door so diners could not leave without paying:

> [The] chance of a good meal, hot quickly served, and to be eaten with the assistance of knives, forks, and plates . . . the restaurant was crowded, Gold Commissioners, bankers, squatters, swell . . . burley diggers . . . shanty keepers, bullies, loafers, and niggers, all pierced with cold and impelled by hunger, that great leveller of distinctions, jostled and pressed eagerly to satisfy the cravings of their appetite.[78]

Preshaw said there was little entertainment available, but in September 1860 Carmichael's Empire Hotel opened a small dance hall with three dancing girls whose job it was to encourage the sale of grog:

> In a room 14 x 20 [feet, or four by six metres] I found some forty or fifty diggers standing about, smoking, chatting, and a few dancing. There were only three dance girls, and those who were fortunate enough to secure one as a dance partner must have found it hard work dancing on a floor fully an inch thick with mud . . . It struck me as a queer sight to see hairy faced men in pea jackets, and long boots, with pipes in their mouths, dancing together.[79]

It was in the middle of 1860, a little more than six months since the news of gold, that the Chinese began to arrive in Kiandra. The first group, of about 80, arrived on 4 June, and another 200 came from Beechworth in Victoria the following month. Over the next year, the total number would grow to around a thousand. While most of the Chinese came to mine gold, a few also established themselves as storekeepers, butchers, bakers, tailors and doctors.

At first, the Chinese camped close to the settlement of Kiandra, but, following complaints that they wasted water and had 'dirty habits', the gold commissioner forced them to establish a separate camp about two kilometres further east of the town.[80]

During the winter, the Chinese would be responsible for bringing much of the supplies to the town, where neither the horse-drawn carts nor bullock drays could handle the steep terrain and the deep snow. The *Sydney Morning Herald* reported that the Chinese also carried in heavy supplies for the construction of more solid buildings:

> This much abused race has lately proved itself invaluable to storekeepers and others by bringing in all kinds of goods from Russell's slung on their poles. Many are now carrying shingles and weatherboard. The loads these fellows will carry are tremendous. One brought in 140 lbs [63.5 kilograms] weight by himself in one day over a distance of more than twelve miles [19 kilometres].[81]

The Chinese also had a vital role to play in the establishment of the Kiandra newspaper, the *Alpine Pioneer*, started by the brothers John and Thomas Garret. John was a member of parliament and his brother the mayor of Wollongong and founder of the *Illawarra Mercury* newspaper. They were initially unable to transport the heavy printing press to Kiandra, which was 'twice locked in by snow' after the dray carrying the equipment had struggled 'sixteen days in getting six miles [9.5 kilometres]'.[82] The Chinese, however, managed to carry it on the final leg:

> Fifty Chinamen were engaged for this job, the drays were got at with considerable difficulty, and the entire loading weighing 4,400lbs, was carried a distance of fourteen miles [22.5 kilometres] through snow, and over very broken country in about ten hours.[83]

The Chinese may have rescued the printing press, but they were still despised, even by the newspaper they had saved. Shortly after it began publishing, the *Alpine Pioneer* ran an editorial attacking the Chinese and calling on the government to rid them from the goldfields:

> [The Chinese] pour in to the country in hordes, solely to dig and to carry away, rendering no return . . . they bring no women and do not care to settle . . . All that the Chinaman thinks of is his lump of gold . . . The Chinaman requires to be dealt with in a manner different from the other foreigner, and we do not think the export duty is the right mode of dealing with him.[84]

By the end of 1860, the easily dug gold was all gone, signalling the end of the rush after barely a year. A 'great exodus from Kiandra' began as the diggers, including the Chinese, drifted away to other fields.

Many joined thousands of others in the new rush to Lambing Flat, almost 240 kilometres directly to the north of Kiandra. Lambing Flat was the biggest new find for some years and possibly the biggest of all the New South Wales goldfields.[85] It would become notorious for the anti-Chinese riots that occurred over the following year.

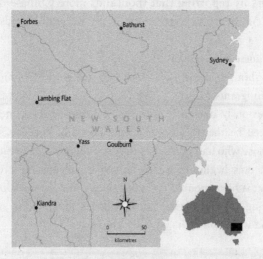

The Lambing Flat diggings

It is believed that gold had first been discovered at Lambing Flat in March 1860 by a black American named Alexander the Yankee, a cook for the local farmer James White, who had first squatted in the local area in the 1820s. Lambing Flat had been given its name for its proximity to Burrangong, which had been reserved for lambing ewes.

The first reports of gold appeared in newspapers in Sydney, Yass, Goulburn and Bathurst in July, when already there were between 100 and 150 men working along the Chance Gully diggings at Lambing Flat.

Some of the first white miners tested several grounds but, when they found the pickings slim, decided to move to other fields.[86] The Chinese then arrived, as they had done in so many other places, to rework the ground the Europeans had left, and they found plentiful gold. Already, the newspapers were adding to the fears of the European miners by reporting that thousands more Chinese diggers were on their way to the New South Wales goldfields:

Chinese in New South Wales

Within the last week a vessel freighted with 917 Chinese immigrants arrived in Sydney and but for a short time previously one with upwards of 1,000 of these moon-faced heathens anchored in the waters of Port Jackson. Those who had previously tolerated this class of intruders are now beginning to be alarmed at the constant stream that is being poured upon our shores, and the question is being eagerly asked, 'When will this immigration stop, and what will be its probable consequence?'[87]

By October, there were 500 Chinese and about 1200 Europeans at Lambing Flat. At the end of the year, the numbers had grown to more than 2000 Chinese and over 12,000 Europeans. The miners were living in about 600 tents or bark humpies along the Burrangong Creek, and the township that had sprung up already boasted a number of restaurants, several hotels that offered nightly dancing, a bowling alley, the Princess Theatre, a bank and dozens of general stores.

On 8 and 9 December 1860, a number of Chinese miners were driven off the diggings by the Europeans. On 12 December, the *Sydney Morning Herald* reported the 'Great Riot at Lambing Flat', during which it claimed two Chinese were killed, ten were seriously wounded and a number of their shanties were burned. Other papers claimed the Chinese had been 'scalped' of their pigtails or had their ears cut off.[88]

The end of 1860 saw the white miners claiming that the Chinese were wasting valuable water in the way they mined and were unhygienic in allowing polluted water to run back into the creeks rather than diverting it into 'settling ponds'.

On 25 January 1861, there was another riot, despite the presence of 80 mounted police, who were there to maintain order. On 27 January, about 1500 diggers held a mass meeting at which John Stewart, a former weaver from Paisley in Scotland, called for the 'pig tailed, moon faced barbarians' to be evicted from the goldfields.[89] The meeting ended with a band leading the stick-wielding miners to Blackguard Gully to drive off the 200 Chinese who were camped there. During the attack on the camp, many of the tents were burned and the Chinese men had their pigtails cut off.

On 31 January, the Miners Protection League was formed, and a few days later a deputation was sent to the local gold commissioner to protest that Lambing Flat was being 'swallowed up' by the Chinese.

Shortly after the police restored order, a number of the rioters were arrested and taken to the local lock-up. Hundreds of miners then marched on the courthouse demanding the release of their colleagues, who were consequently granted bail. The next morning, they appeared in the local court, were reprimanded and then set free.

In February, a petition signed by 3394 miners was

presented to the New South Wales Parliament calling on the government 'to relieve them of all Chinese' who were already at Lambing Flat or intending to go there.[90]

In an attempt to contain the problem, the local gold commissioner restricted the Chinese to a separate tract of land 'within boundaries of which they will have the privilege of digging, unmolested by Europeans'.[91] But, on 18 February, about 40 Europeans drove 200 Chinese from their allotted site and set fire to their homes and bedding.

The first commissioner appointed to the Lambing Flat diggings was David Dickson, who was already middle aged at the time of his appointment and had spent most of his adult life working behind the counter of a drapery store. Dickson set up his offices 20 kilometres away on the sheep farm of James Roberts, rather than close to the gold miners at Lambing Flat. Amid the rising tension, he rode the hundred kilometres to the larger town of Yass to seek reinforcements. A few days later, P. L. Cloete, who had previously been at Kiandra, arrived to take over the management of the troubled Lambing Flat. He was soon joined by a detachment of police of the Southern Mounted led by Captain Henry Zouch, who would play a leading role in the events that followed.

In Sydney, the government was well aware of the growing anti-Chinese sentiment, and an attempt was made to introduce a bill that would restrict their entry as both Victoria and South Australia had done. However, a complicated parliamentary procedure meant that the bill could not be approved, and it was not until the end of the year that a new anti-Chinese law was passed, by which time a lot more violence had been committed against the Chinese.

The telegraph had now been connected between Yass and Sydney, which meant that the government was quickly appraised of the problems at the diggings. On 25 February, a sizable force of almost 200 officers and soldiers, including artillery and mounted police, was sent to Lambing Flat. From Sydney, the force boarded the recently constructed railway line for the 50-kilometre trip south-west of the city to Campbelltown.[92] From there, they were loaded onto ten double-decker buses that were each drawn by four horses for the remaining 400-kilometre journey to Lambing Flat, which they reached on 11 March.

Shortly after the troops left Sydney, Charles Cowper, the 54-year-old premier of New South Wales, made a decision to personally go to the Lambing Flat diggings in an attempt to calm down the simmering tensions. Cowper, who had been nicknamed 'Slippery Charlie' by his parliamentary colleague Henry Parkes, was born in England in 1807 and brought to Australia as a two-year-old by his parents. After a private education, he embarked on a life on the land with a property granted to him near Goulburn. Over the next few years, he gradually acquired more properties before entering the New South Wales Parliament at 36 in 1843. In 1850, he resigned from parliament and spent several years working on what would become the first New South Wales railways. After re-entering parliament in 1853, he became premier in January 1861, less than two months before heading off to avert the crisis at Lambing Flat.

A week after the troops' departure, Cowper also caught the train to Campbelltown. Travelling on faster coaches, he overtook the military before Goulburn and arrived at

Lambing Flat on the evening of Saturday 2 March – more than a week before the army.

Cowper said that he wanted to 'investigate the alleged grievances of the diggers, and endeavour to prevent a collision'.[93] While at Lambing Flat, he made a number of speeches, culminating in mass meetings at Stoney Creek on 5 March and Spring Creek on 9 March, where he told thousands of miners that the Chinese were 'pests and nuisances' but made it clear their property could not be harmed and appealed to the diggers to obey the law. He also reminded them of a recent treaty between Britain and China that granted the citizens of both countries freedom in the other's territory.

When Cowper left to return to Sydney and the reinforcements arrived, there were more than 300 soldiers and police to keep order on the diggings. The press reported that, by the end of March, many of the Chinese who had left the diggings now felt safe to return, but that hostility towards them was growing:

> Telegrams from Lambing Flat state that many hundreds of Chinese had returned, and were returning, and are promised to resume, but isolated wholly from the Europeans. The latter, however, are still discontented, and clamour for the removal of the Chinese altogether.[94]

Any benefit of Premier Cowper's intervention did not last long, and the anti-Chinese incidents became more frequent. On 7 April, an estimated 6000 diggers 'armed with pick handles, revolvers, bowie knives etc' marched under brass banners into the settlement at Lambing Flat. The object of the demonstration was to threaten the storekeepers in the township and to fire their premises if they continued to sell supplies to the Chinese.[95]

However, by the end of May, with tensions appearing at last to be abating, the troop reinforcements that had arrived from Sydney and had been at Lambing Flat for more than two months began to be sent home. The more stable situation encouraged the previous Chinese to return to the diggings and new ones to arrive.

Within a month, though, the tensions returned, and on 30 June the worst riot occurred, resulting in more than a thousand Chinese diggers being driven out of Lambing Flat. During the assaults, many Chinese were seriously wounded, their camps were burned to the ground and their diggings destroyed.

An eyewitness account published in the *Sydney Morning Herald* and subsequently in a number of other newspapers ensured the event would forever be stamped in the annals of Australian history:

Another Outbreak at Lambing Flat
Expulsion of 1200 Chinese

By express to Yass on Saturday last it was pretty generally known that a roll-up would take place to-day against the Chinese. The immediate cause of it I cannot say. Some state that the diggers are determined to drive them off the fields, others that it is in consequence of their having struck a lead of gold at Buck Creek, and some assert that it is in retaliation for the Native Creek Dog Affair. Certain it is that it took place, and for destruction of property it exceeded any riot that has ever yet taken place on these fields. Between ten and eleven o'clock, at Tipperary Gully, the muster took place. Upwards of a thousand men, most of them armed with bludgeons or pick handles, headed by a band, and carrying several large flags, one inscribed with the words, 'Roll up – no Chinese!' formed into procession and marched into town.

On reaching the town several unfortunate Chinese were observed, and a general rush then took place. The Chinese took to their heels, but to no purpose, for they were caught, and several of them had their pigtails cut off, and were otherwise maltreated.

The mob, now between 2000 and 3000, crossed the main creek, and leaving the commissioner's camp on the right, ran for the camp of the Chinese, who were working inside the boundary set apart for them. The Chinese having taken flight, upwards of forty tents were burned down, and all property of every kind destroyed. They then proceeded to the ground where the Chinese were working, and destroyed all the windlasses and tools they could find, throwing them down the shafts. After proceeding about a quarter of a mile they again halted. Several shots were fired: it was then proposed they should proceed to Back Creek, a distance of six miles [9.6 kilometres], where several hundred Chinese were working, which was reached in about two hours. The Chinese had received information of their approach, and having packed up everything they possibly could to carry away, made a hasty retreat. Tents by score were set on fire; rice and stores of all kinds destroyed, butchers' shops filled with meat set on fire. For a distance of half a mile the burning tents showed the work of destruction. Not content with this, some men on horseback proceeded forward and overtook the Chinese – some 1200. They rounded them up the same as they would a mob of cattle, struck them with their bludgeons and whips, and made them leave all their swags. And now ensued a scene that defies description. Six or seven immense fires were made with clothing of all descriptions, stores, rice, blankets, boots, a large quantity of them quite new, being heaped together and set on fire, men with picks and axes destroying everything they could not burn. Having destroyed and burnt everything they could, they again formed into procession and returned to Lambing Flat, which was reached about half past 5 pm.[96]

In a later report, the *Sydney Morning Herald* said a number of the Chinese had been 'scalped':

I noticed one man who returned with eight pigtails attached to a flag, glorifying in the work that had been done. I also saw one tail, with part of the scalp the size of a man's hand attached, that had been literally cut from some unfortunate creature.[97]

A large number of the fleeing and wounded Chinese took refuge 20 kilometres away on the Currawong sheep farm owned by James Roberts and near to where the gold commissioner had established his headquarters:

After they were driven from Back Creek they made for Roberts station, distance of about twelve miles [20 kilometres] from this place, perfectly destitute. Mr. Roberts supplied them with flour, beef and what clothing he possibly could. Many were seriously injured; two lie there in a very dangerous state, and are not expected to recover. Some three or four are missing.[98]

There were at the time too few police at Lambing Flat, and a call for help brought Captain Zouch and a platoon of mounted troopers from Yass on 6 July. A week later, on Sunday 14 July, Zouch and his 67 men rounded up and arrested three men who were accused of being at the head of the riot.

By late afternoon on the day of arrests, the situation appeared calm, but by nightfall the threat of disorder returned with the arrival of a delegation of hundreds of diggers demanding the release of those who had been apprehended:

> Burrangong, Sunday, half past six pm – Three of the ringleaders of the late riots were arrested today. Great excitement prevails at the present time, and a 'roll-up' is coming from Tipperary Gully to release the prisoners. The whole of the force here are under arms; several of the stores in town are filled with men armed to protect them.[99]

The press reported later in the evening that the mob appointed a deputation to demand the release of the prisoners. They were told by Captain Zouch and an assistant gold commissioner, James Griffin, that the prisoners would be held against 'all hazards' and would be given a fair trial. He also assured the mob that the arrested men could be visited by their lawyers:

> Half past eleven pm – about 1,000 men crossed the creek and made for the camp. A deputation of four arrived, and requested to see the officer in command of the camp. Captain Zouch and Mr. Commissioner Griffin received

them. They asked what number had been arrested with respect to the late riot. They were informed that three were arrested; they then stated they were requested to demand their release. Both Captain Zouch and Mr. Griffin firmly, yet coolly, declined to release the prisoners, informing the deputation at the same time that the law must take its course – that the parties arrested would be brought before the court on Monday morning, exhorting them to return, impressed upon them the necessity of using their endeavours to disperse the mob.[100]

As the meeting ended, and Zouch and Griffin were turning to return to the camp, some of the men among the diggers fired off some guns, and Commissioner Griffin then went out and read the Riot Act:

Our Sovereign Lady the Queen chargeth and commandeth all persons being assembled, immediately to disperse themselves, and peaceably to depart to their habitations, or to their lawful business, upon the pains contained in the Act made in the first year of King George, for preventing tumultuous and riotous assemblies. God Save the Queen.[101]

The diggers were not mollified and continued to approach the camp. An order was given for the police to shoot over their heads, and the mounted police were brought to the front when the diggers fired again:

They had scarcely drawn up when a volley was fired, and two of the troopers' horses fell. The excitement now became intense; the troopers were now ordered to charge, but not to fire. Shots were fired in continual succession at them . . . The mob now closed in and approached the camp.[102]

Finally, the troopers were ordered to fire and the mounted police ordered to charge, and the diggers were driven back to the creek.[103]

After the crowd was dispersed, it was discovered that three of the troopers had been wounded by gunfire and four of the horses shot. Of the rioters, several were known to have been wounded and one killed from a bullet to the head. The *Sydney Morning Herald* reported the following day that the tension had not diminished:

Monday, ten pm – Since last night the excitement here is intense. The mob at Tipperary Gully are arming to a mass. The three men arrested were brought before the Bench today and committed for trial . . . The men committed have been admitted bail.[104]

At the same time, Captain Henry Zouch and Gold Commissioner Griffin consulted and agreed to evacuate Lambing Flat. They headed for the safety of Yass, taking the police force together with the local government officials, the *Sydney Morning Herald*'s correspondent and many of the town's merchants. As Zouch was to report, the odds were overwhelming and many more lives would have been lost:

Tuesday, eleven pm. The camp was attacked for the purpose of rescuing three prisoners for Chinese riots. We fought them for two hours and more. Attack commenced at a quarter to eight, and by ten o'clock we drove them off, killing and wounding many. Three, we know are dead, and we have heard of numbers wounded. My report will explain all. Seven special constables came to the camp – two only armed. There was no response made to the calls made to the respectable part of the community. Position I found untenable against the number that were prepared to revenge the defeat of Sunday night. Some 3,000, prepared and organized, were to attack, and have sworn to destroy the whole of us. I have brought away the whole force, wounded included . . . If I had remained lives would have been inevitably lost.[105]

The night they left, the police station and the courthouse were burned down. The following day, a deputation of miners headed to Sydney, where they wanted to present a petition to the governor, but they were denied an audience.

On hearing of the riot, the government again dispatched reinforcements to Lambing Flat, where seven men were arrested for their involvement. Six of them were acquitted when they were tried in Goulburn in August, while the seventh, Claremont Owen, was convicted and sentenced to two years in prison.

In the months that followed, a total of 1568 Chinese people made claims to the New South Wales Government for compensation totalling £40,000. The government recognised a little under half of the claims – 706 – and paid a total compensation of £4240. James Roberts, the sheep farmer and owner of Currawong, where many of the Chinese fled in search of sanctuary, was paid £2068 for the rations he provided to the refugees.

In November 1861, Premier Charles Cowper managed

to get two new laws through the New South Wales Parliament that were regarded as a victory for the diggers. The Goldfields Regulation Bill gave the government powers (that ironically it never subsequently used) to proclaim designated goldfields or parts of goldfields closed to aliens. The Immigration Bill imposed a poll tax on arriving Chinese miners similar to the earlier law introduced in Victoria. The New South Wales law went further in that it also denied the Chinese the right to become naturalised citizens.

In any case, in the early 1860s many of the alluvial goldfields in Victoria and New South Wales were being dug out, and a number of the Chinese began to go home to China, while others drifted onto the new fields, including in New Zealand, Tasmania and the Northern Territory. At the same time, large amounts of investment funds began flowing in from London and the other capital markets of the world for investment in the heavy machinery that would usher in a whole new type of gold mining.

CHAPTER EIGHT

The Gold Rush Spreads

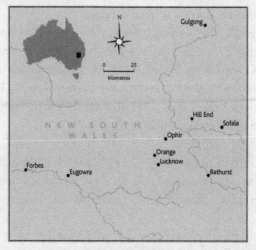

The Hill End and Gulgong diggings

. . . such was the case with almost all rushes. Men would try their luck for a month, or perhaps a fortnight, and if they failed, or did not meet success to satisfy them, would pack up their swags and would betake themselves elsewhere. In this way the population of the rush is very precarious, falling as quickly as it rises, receiving or losing a thousand in a few days, as the place gives or refuses to give its treasures.

In the late 1850s and early 1860s, big steam-powered stamping machines began arriving at the old goldfields to crush the quartz rock for its gold content. The diggers had taken all the gold they could from the soil, gravel and clay but could only extract a fraction of the gold that was embedded in the hard quartz. In almost every goldfield in Australia, mechanised, or 'reef', mining companies would progressively take over from the digger.

One of the earliest quartz-crushing companies to advertise a prospectus was the Fredericks Valley Gold Field Company in November 1851. The company sought to raise £30,000 for the purchase of Wentworth's land at Fredericks Valley, about 20 kilometres south of Ophir, and for the use of heavy machinery:

> Experience has shown that the Gold Fields in the locality cannot be worked on a large scale, and to the utmost advantage, without machinery to crush ore.[1]

The progressive takeover of gold mining by the big machines was seen by many as a threat to the diggers' livelihood, and on 7 February 1857 a meeting of about 1000 miners at Ballarat resolved to form the Peoples League to represent the interests of the individual diggers. However, no amount of concern was able to stop or even slow down the development of mechanised mining and the growth in diggers who switched to become paid wage earners of the big companies.

The rise of the mining companies created Australia's first class of rich industrial magnates. One of the first big steam stampers was brought onto the Ballarat goldfield in Victoria by the German miner Christopher Ballerstedt.

Ballerstedt struck it rich in 1854 when he bought a failed claim and sank a shaft to 90 metres, where he struck the rich quartz reef. Known as the 'father of quartz reefing', Ballerstedt built the original famous homestead Fortuna villa at Bendigo that was later enlarged by another mining mogul, George Lansell. Ballerstedt died in 1869 and is buried in Bendigo. His son, Theodore, returned to Madgeberg in Germany, where he died two years later.

By the beginning of the 1860s, there were more than 20 quartz-mining companies using over 70 quartz-crushing machines in the vicinity of Bendigo. By the early 1870s, Bendigo had more quartz mines employing miners than any other Australian goldfield, and the Bendigo companies were paying more than half of the dividends of all Victorian gold-mining companies.[2]

Another of the early successful moguls was the above-mentioned George Lansell, a 30-year-old soap- and candle-maker from Margate in Kent who was persuaded by his younger brother, who had worked as a seaman on a convict ship, to try his luck in Australia. Lansell landed in South Australia in 1853 and the following year walked with his two brothers, Wootten and William, from Adelaide to Ballarat, where they set up a butchery and a soap and candle shop. After several successful years, Lansell increasingly bought out old mines and dug deeper into the quartz, which he crushed with steam-driven stamping batteries. He was largely responsible for introducing the diamond drill to quartz mining in Australia and became director of 38 mines. Lansell was believed to have had some link with almost every mine in Bendigo and bought out the Ballerstedt mine when Theodore Ballerstedt went back to Germany.[3]

Lansell spent his last years in the rambling Fortuna mansion, which was built on four levels and included a spacious ballroom, music room, billiard room, dining room, private chapel, gymnasium and swimming pool. It was surrounded by vast gardens with an artificial lake, lily pond, trees and flowers from all of the continents. He gave liberal support to local charities and in gratitude the community raised a statue in Bendigo in his honour after he died.

Martin Laughlin was another successful investor on the Victorian goldfields. He was 22 years old when he sailed with his cousin Patrick Brennan in 1855 from Kilkenny in Ireland to Geelong and joined the search for gold at Pleasant Creek. As a working shareholder with Brennan, he reaped huge rewards from his investments in various gold companies. In the early 1860s, he was a well-known figure in Melbourne's Craig Hotel, regularly crossing the road to the 'corner' to speculate in shares.

Laughlin invested in the Melbourne Tramway company, owned a string of hotels and bought up large parcels of land. He was a keen sportsman, and two of his horses won the Melbourne and Caulfield cup double. He was also a spectacular punter and was known to bet thousands of pounds on a single race.

Unlike most of his business associates, he shunned public life. He was not a notable philanthropist but was generous to the Roman Catholic Church and its schools, and to the major Ballarat institutions, which included donating some valuable paintings to the Ballarat Art Gallery.

With the growth in gold companies came the proliferation of share exchanges in Australia's capital cities and major gold centres, including Ballarat, Bendigo and Bathurst, and later in Charters Towers in northern Queensland, Darwin and Perth. In many cases, the buying and selling of shares took place not in designated buildings but at any market established on a favourite street corner.

Ballarat's first major share trading took place outside the Unicorn Hotel on Sturt Street, which provided traders with shade, seating and a ready supply of alcohol and food. It was later replaced by the purpose-built Ballarat Mining Exchange, which was established on the site where the troopers had assembled in December 1854 before marching on the Eureka stockade. Officially opened in 1888, it became Australia's wealthiest exchange before closing in 1914, four years before the closure of Ballarat's last gold mine.

In Bendigo, the Sandhurst Mining Exchange occupied the Beehive building in Pall Mall, the city's main street. In the boom decade of the 1870s, up to six new companies were floated on this exchange every day. On the morning of 21 August 1871, the Beehive building, with the trading centre and all the brokers' offices, burned to the ground, but trading resumed almost immediately in the nearby Shamrock Hotel while a new trading centre was built.

Big-company reef mining also moved into the alluvial goldfields of New South Wales, including at Hill End. The coming of the big machines brought order to the process, and the frantic rush of the digger was replaced by a 'less feverish and more regular way' of gold mining.[4]

There had been alluvial mining around Hill End for almost 20 years following Edward Hargraves's original discovery at Ophir, some 20 kilometres to the south-west across the Macquarie and Turon Rivers. The first steam battery began operating at nearby Tambaroora in 1861,[5] and over the next decade the number of steam-operated mines at Hill End steadily increased. It peaked in 1872, when there were 225 companies operating hundreds of stampers with more than a thousand men working in the underground mines. By this time, Hill End had become a major gold town with a population of nearly 10,000 people, 28 pubs, an opium den, four fine stone churches and an oyster bar. The large number of people suddenly concentrated in a small area with inadequate water and sewerage led to high rates of disease and death, particularly among children.[6]

It was at Hill End that the world's biggest nugget was found. Known as the 'Holtermann and Beyer Specimen', or simply the 'Holtermann Nugget', it was discovered by the night shift working underground on the Star of Hope mine, in which the two major shareholders were Bernhardt Otto Holtermann and his Polish partner Ludwig Hugo Louis Beyer.

Holtermann was born in Hamburg, Germany, in 1838 and left as a 20-year-old to avoid military service. He planned to meet up with his brother, who was already in Australia.[7] Travelling steerage on the *Salem*, he arrived in Melbourne on 12 August 1858 but was unable to find his brother, who had 'gone to the diggings'. Hampered by a lack of English, Holtermann took a job as a steward on the ship *Rebecca*. After sailing to New Caledonia and other Pacific islands, he arrived back in Australia in January 1859.

After he and Beyer met in Sydney, the two men walked with their swags to Tambaroora near Hill End, where they had agreed to form a mining partnership. At first, they were unsuccessful, and Holtermann was forced over the next couple of years to work in a number of other jobs, including being a ferryman and running a hotel. In February 1868, Holtermann and Beyer married the sisters Harriet and Mary Emmett, who were from a well-known local family from nearby White Rock, near Bathurst.[8]

From 1868, Holtermann and Beyer worked for 'small rewards' on their Star of Hope mine and were forced to take in new partners to raise more working capital.[9] It was four years later, at 11 pm on 10 October 1872, that the night shift at the mine made the spectacular discovery of the huge nugget, which was 150 by 66 centimetres, weighed 286 kilograms and contained more than 3000 ounces of gold.[10] Holtermann, who was the mine manager, was called, and he was careful to have the gold specimen photographed in one piece before it was moved and later broken up.

The famous image of the Holtermann nugget was taken by the photographer Beaufoy Merlin, who, with Charles Bayliss, operated the American and Australasian Photographic Company, which they had opened as a store in Hill End in 1872. Holtermann commissioned the company to take a marvellous set of photographs that were later taken on international tours and became known as the Holtermann collection.[11] The set of large plates traces life on the goldfields – particularly Hill End – and in early Melbourne and Sydney.

Holtermann left the goldfields to build a huge mansion at Lavender Bay on the north side of Sydney Harbour, which later became part of the Shore private boys' school. Holtermann was an early advocate for building a bridge across Sydney Harbour and argued for more migration to Australia. For a short time, he was a member of the New

South Wales Parliament, after succeeding on his third attempt to be elected. He died on his 47th birthday on 29 April 1885 after 18 months of treatment for stomach cancer, cirrhosis of the liver and dropsy.[12]

One of the last of the alluvial gold rushes in New South Wales occurred at Gulgong, less than 70 kilometres north of Hill End, in April 1870, when a local farmer, Tom Saunders, found gold sticking out of the ground at what was to become the centre of a new town.

The famous English novelist Anthony Trollope visited Gulgong the year after gold was discovered as part of a trip to Australia with his wife to see their son, who was sheep farming near Grenfell in New South Wales. They sailed on the *Great Britain* from Liverpool on 14 May 1871, arriving in Melbourne on 27 July. During the ten-week voyage, Trollope finished writing the novel *Lady Anna*. While in Australia, he travelled extensively by coastal steamer to Victoria and Queensland, where he visited the goldfields at Gympie, and to New South Wales. He also went to Tasmania, 'the little known territory' of Western Australia and to New Zealand, which provided him with the material for his book *Australia and New Zealand*.

Trollope said he was fascinated by the idea of visiting Gulgong, which was 'the rush of the day', and where until only very recently there had been no town and no streets:

> The great attraction proposed to one visiting a rush seemed to consist in the sight of a congregation together of a great deal of men, without the comforts of life . . . There were 12,000 people at Gulgong, all of whom had collected themselves thither within a few months. The place had begun to be a place about a month since.[13]

To reach Gulgong, Trollope travelled by coach with the local gold commissioner past the town of Sofala, near Ophir, which had now shrunk to only a fraction of its former size:

> On our route we passed the little town of Sofala, which was in point of time the second established gold-field in New South Wales, Ophir having been the first. Sofala is now a poor little town, containing 644 inhabitants, of whom a considerable proportion is Chinese . . . 'fossicking' amidst the dirt of the river, which had already been washed by the first gold seekers.

During the three days it took to reach the new goldfield, they passed hundreds of diggers walking towards Gulgong:

> As we went we saw parties of men, generally ten or twelve in number, either leisurely tramping along the road with their swags on their backs, or taking a mid-day siesta under the gum trees. The man who travels on foot in Australia . . . always carries his swag with him – which consists of his personal properties wrapped up in a blanket. The blanket is an essential necessity, because the man sleeps out in the bush, beside a fire. And he carries a pannikin and a 'billy'. The latter is an open pot in which he boils his water and makes his tea – for a bushman will always have a bag of tea in his swag. The 'billy' is as essential as the blankets.[14]

After 20 years of gold rushes, Trollope was surprised at how unhurried the men seemed in making their way to the most recent find:

And these men were making a rush! They seemed to me to rush very leisurely . . . They have probably done it before, and know, if not the tale of the hare and the tortoise, at any rate the moral of the story.[15]

At Gulgong, the principal diggings were in the centre of the town on a knoll that was named Red Hill. There were only two streets, 'at right angles' to each other, and already hundreds of shacks and tents that appeared to Trollope to have been constructed within one or two days:

Everything needful, however, seemed to be at hand. There were bakers, butchers, grocers, and dealers in soft goods. There were public houses and banks in abundance.[16]

Trollope was able to find a small hotel 'made only of slabs' but was grateful to have been given a room to himself. The surrounding country he said was of 'ugly masses of upturned clay which always marks the gold-seekers' presence'. He described how, on a tour of the mines, he was invited to lower himself with his foot in the noose of a rope 45 metres down a shaft, where he found 'six or seven' men working at the bottom.

While he was at Gulgong, Trollope noticed that alluvial mining was in decline and the population was already falling. Many of those who stayed switched to work for the companies that had brought in the big steam-operated batteries, while others moved on, as they had for many years, to continue the search for the big find on any new field they had heard about:

Backs were turned to Gulgong as well as faces towards

it. Then I learned that such was the case with almost all rushes. Men would try their luck for a month, or perhaps a fortnight, and if they failed, or did not meet success to satisfy them, would pack up their swags and would betake themselves elsewhere. In this way the population of the rush is very precarious, falling as quickly as it rises, receiving or losing a thousand in a few days, as the place gives or refuses to give its treasures.[17]

While Trollope was at Gulgong, four-year-old Henry Lawson was living with his family in a tent on the north-eastern edge of town, where his father tried – with little success – mining for gold.[18]

Lawson, who would later become one of Australia's greatest writers, was born on the goldfields in 1867. His Norwegian father, Niels Herzberg Larsen, was a sailor who jumped ship in Australia in 1855 to join the gold rush. Larsen married Louisa Albury in 1866 and together they had three children. With the anglicised name of Lawson, the children did not enjoy a stable childhood as their father was often away and their schooling regularly disrupted.

Many of Lawson's classic Australian bush characters – typifying the underprivileged, the itinerant, the social out-cast, the persevering, the humanist, the sad and the laconic – were shaped by his experiences on the goldfields as a boy. 'In the first fifteen years of my life,' he said, 'I saw the last of the Roaring Days on Gulgong Goldfields – I remember the rush as a young boy would his first pantomime.'[19]

Many of the independent diggers also headed to New Zealand, after news of a big gold find in the South Island got out. The big rush occurred when a 35-year-old Australian, Gabriel Read, found gold in Central Otago, at what became known as Gabriel's Gully, near Dunedin, in May 1861.

Gold had been found earlier in New Zealand, but it did not produce the same clamour as Read's discovery. In 1842, visiting whalers had found it on the Coromandel Peninsula on the North Island, which caused a brief rush that soon petered out. In 1856, gold was found again on the Aorere River on the north of the South Island near the town of Collingwood, which attracted several thousand diggers and boosted the development of the area around Nelson. However, it was Gabriel Read's find in Otago that would double New Zealand's population over the next decade.

The province of Otago is at the southernmost point of New Zealand's South Island and stretches about 200 kilometres from south to north and about the same distance from west to east. At the time gold was discovered, its small, largely farming population was around 20,000, which was similar to the populations of both Melbourne and San Francisco at the time of their first rushes.

Thomas Gabriel Read was born into a reasonably well-off family in Tasmania in 1826. His mother was a milliner's daughter and his father a merchant and a banker, and young Gabriel was given a decent education. In 1849, he went to the Californian goldfields but met with little success. The following year, he returned to Australia and to the new gold diggings in Victoria but was not successful there either and decided to go home to Tasmania.

In 1860, he heard gold had been found on the Mataura River in New Zealand and sailed on the *San Pedro II* for Dunedin, arriving at Port Chalmers in February 1861. After finding the amount of gold on the Mataura limited,

Read decided to prospect further upcountry, where, in May 1861, after shovelling some gravel, he said he 'saw the gold shining like stars in Orion on a dark frosty night'.[20]

The New Zealand goldfields

By the end of the year, 14,000 hopefuls had already reached Otago. The diggers came from all over New Zealand, including from Auckland and Wellington, where the local paper complained that the 'temptation has been too great', and 'ship load after ship load' left for Dunedin.[21] When news reached Australia, many more were 'smitten with the New Zealand mania'[22] and rushed to book a passage. By the end of the year, thousands were heading for New Zealand from Europe,[23] and the local Dunedin newspaper was carried away by the rush:

The diggings are not only of great extent and richness
. . . but immediately surpasses either the Victorian and
Californian diggings of the present day.[24]

The New Zealand boom was given another boost when a
second major discovery was made the following year close
to the modern town of Cromwell, and for a short time
Dunedin became the biggest city in the country.

In 1864, there was another new rush when gold was
found on the Wakamarina River in the province of
Marlborough towards the north of the South Island,
which attracted more than 6000 workers to the diggings.[25]

Then, in 1865, a bigger find at Okarito near what was
to become Charleston on the west coast of the South Island
brought many more from the Victorian goldfields, including many New Zealanders who had decided to return
home. The west-coast gold was discovered by a 41-year-
old Irishman, William Fox, who was a former seaman
and veteran of the goldfields of California, Australia and
Topeka, in the Arrow district of Otago. Two years later,
Fox made another, larger discovery even closer to the town
of Charleston, which prompted the last gold rush of New
Zealand's west coast and boosted the local population to
35,000 by the mid-1870s.

In 1868, gold was again found on the North Island, at
Thames, in a short-lived rush that caused the population
to peak at more than 18,000, making it for a short period
the third-largest town in New Zealand after Dunedin and
Auckland.

By the 1870s, the gold was in decline, and the number of
European miners began to fall before their departure was partially offset by the arrival of more Chinese who came in large

numbers to work on the diggings as they had in Australia. In New Zealand, the Chinese met the same hostility and discrimination they had encountered across the Tasman. The New Zealand Government eventually copied the Australian colonies and introduced the Chinese Immigration Act 1881, which imposed a £10 tax on each arriving Chinese person. In 1896, the tax was increased to £100.

Tasmania, too, was not without its own rush. Only four months after the original announcement of Hargraves's first discovery at Ophir, news of gold there was reported in the *Hobart Colonial Times*:

> Gold in Tasmania. Shortly we expect the discovery of a goldfield will be revealed to the excited inhabitants of Van Diemen's Land. We know of one individual who has for several days been exhibiting a specimen of the precious metal on the wharf. The discoverer intends to pursue his explorations in order to ascertain the probable location of the gold field, and to make it known to the committee and claim the [government] reward. That there is gold in the colony cannot be doubted.[26]

There were more reports before the end of the year, which included the claim that one gold discoverer 'has about half a bushel of this auriferous metal in his possession'[27] and another that said gold had also been discovered 'on one of the islands of the Bass Straits' that separate Tasmania and the mainland.[28]

From the first rush in early 1852, several hundred diggers worked around Fingal in the north-east of the colony, and the first steam battery began operations there in 1859. Over the next two decades, there were a number of new discoveries in Tasmania's west and north-west that prompted rushes by eager prospectors, but none were big enough to attract large numbers from the goldfields on the Australian mainland.

In the 1860s, gold was found on the Pieman River, but access by ship to Macquarie Harbour on the colony's west coast was hazardous and the goldfields difficult to reach. By the 1870s, gold was discovered across a wide area including Doctors Rock near Wynyard and along the Savage and Whyte Rivers. Further east at Brandy Creek, William Dally and his brother David found gold in 1877 at what was renamed Beaconsfield after Benjamin Disraeli, the British prime minister who was raised to the peerage of Earl of Beaconsfield in 1876. In the late 1870s, several hundred Chinese came from Victoria to work at the Hellyer River and other sites in Tasmania's north-east until, in 1887, the Tasmanian Government followed the other Australian colonies and introduced legislation to keep out the Chinese.

The biggest gold discoveries in Tasmania occurred in the 1880s and included the profitable Lefroy mine near Georgetown in 1882 and the Golden Ridge mine in 1883. Also in 1883, Tasmania's biggest single nugget, weighing 243 ounces, was found at Corinna in the north-west. By the end of the 1890s, Tasmania's alluvial mining dropped sharply, and by the end of the century there were very few prospectors still on the diggings.

The gold rushes also spread to Australia's Northern Territory in 1871. There had been a number of earlier indications of gold in the territory, starting with explorer John McDougal Stuart, who reported a probability of gold when he had surveyed the region in 1862.

Three years later, H. F. 'Fred' Litchfield found gold on the south side of the Finniss River, about 100 kilometres south of Darwin, when he was a member of the Boyle Finniss exploration team in the territory. In 1836, Boyle Finniss had been one of the earliest settlers of South Australia. In 1855, he became the first premier of South Australia and in 1864 the government resident in the Northern Territory, where he led a major surveying expedition of the top end.

However, the first big rush in the territory came with the discovery of gold at Pine Creek about 225 kilometres south of Darwin in 1871 by men digging post holes as part of the construction of the overland telegraph from Adelaide to Darwin. Within months, the story was extensively reported in the southern newspapers, suggesting there was good 'reason to believe [gold] exists in considerable quantities'.[29] Official confirmation of the discovery came in August 1871 with a report of the South Australian surveyor George MacLachlan, who wrote that he had found good samples of gold in all the areas he tested:

> This sample . . . will be proof that there is a payable gold field in the Northern Territory and, in my opinion, it only requires a few prospecting parties, well equipped for 12 months or so, to establish it. There is not a doubt that there are large deposits of gold in the Territory.[30]

Reaching the Northern Territory goldfields and surviving on them was to be a major challenge for those who joined the rush. In 1871, Edward Bagot and John Chambers formed a company in Adelaide and arranged for a party of experienced men to go there. Sailing in a small two-masted brigantine named *Alexandra*, the nine men took four months to travel the 4000 kilometres from Adelaide to Darwin, clockwise around Australia. They were caught in a hurricane off the north-western Australian coast that severely damaged the ship, tearing its sails and wrecking its rudder.

After reaching Darwin in March, they made rafts from casks to float their supplies up the Blackmore River, which runs south from Darwin Harbour, before loading everything onto ten horses and a bullock dray for the balance of the 225 kilometres to the field.[31] The alternative routes, sailing around the east coast of Australia or walking overland from Queensland or the south, were equally hazardous.

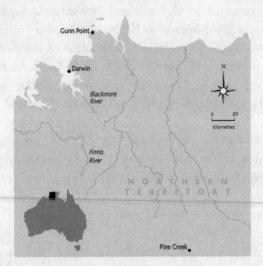

The Northern Territory

More than a year later, the situation had not improved. When 38-year-old G. A. Norman arrived to take up the

job as manager of the Northern Territory Gold Prospecting Company in May 1873, he described the 'bungling', 'muddle' and 'misconduct' that confronted him in Darwin after a 19-day voyage from the south on the *Gothenberg*. Norman, who had 20 years' experience as a mine engineer in Victoria, said there were six ships in the harbour trying to unload but no wharves, so they were forced to lower everything into small boats to be rowed about 25 kilometres to Southport. He said that most who had come to work for the new gold companies were unsuitable:

Many of the men were totally unacquainted with mining of any kind, and unfitted for the duty they were sent to perform. Some of these men never proceeded further than Palmerstone; some advanced 40 miles [64 kilometres] into the interior, to Stapleton Creek; many never lost sight of the telegraph posts; others planted themselves on the banks of some creek, on a picturesque spot, and quietly received their advanced pay in Adelaide, until the whole grog and provisions were consumed, when they struck their camp and pronounced it a 'duffer'.[32]

Thousands of diggers found their way to the territory, but within a few years the alluvial gold was dug out and the steam reef-mining machines were taking over. By the end of the 1870s, most of the European diggers had drifted away, but there were still thousands of Chinese working the field.

The Chinese population of Darwin had been very small prior to 1874, when it had suddenly trebled with the arrival of 187 Chinese men who had been contracted in Singapore to work for two years under the control of the Colonial Government of South Australia, which was then responsible for the territory.[33] They had come as part of a scheme to offset a shortage of labour needed for the development of the north but instead drifted towards the goldfields to rework the alluvial diggings, as the Chinese had done in the earlier goldfields of Australia. By the start of the 1880s, when the alluvial gold was declining, there were more than 2000 Chinese, who constituted more than 90 per cent of the miners around Pine Creek. In the 1890s, there were still 27 stamp batteries operating around 15 Pine Creek mines, which employed many of the Chinese, but by the end of the century the output of gold had fallen to only a fraction of the rush days.

The only Australian state that did not experience a big gold rush was South Australia. Gold had been found at the Montacute copper mine at Castambul, about 25 kilometres north-east of Adelaide, in 1846, from which a brooch was made and presented to Queen Victoria. However, the initial excitement turned to disappointment when the mine produced little gold. In 1851, more gold was discovered at Echunga, and there were a number of other small local finds between 1852 and 1858. Over the next 30 years, there were other, smaller rushes, including Jupiter Creek (1868), Para Willi (1869), Birdwood and Ulooloo (1870), Waukaringa (1873) and Woodside (1879), the Algebuckina and Neales Rivers (1880), and Teetulpa (1886).

The presence of abundant gold in the other colonies – particularly in neighbouring Victoria – was devastating for South Australia. An estimated third of the colony's men left for the eastern goldfields in the early 1850s. By the end of 1851, a desperate colonial administration was trying to attract some of the benefits of the eastern gold discoveries to South Australia.

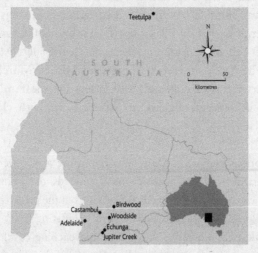

South Australia's goldfields

The exodus to Victoria had created a serious shortage of coinage in the colony, as prospectors had taken as much as they could to grub stake their gold mining. In January the next year, the colonial government passed the Bullion Act 1852 and paid three pounds 11 shillings an ounce for bullion, which it minted into new coinage. This was a much higher price than the two pounds 15 shillings being paid for it in Melbourne, and it resulted in nearly 3000 ounces of gold being deposited in the South Australian Assay Office in February 1852.

To make the Victorian goldfields closer, the South Australian Government built a shorter road for the gold escorts. Until then, the usual route followed the coast to the south-east of Adelaide via Mount Gambier and Portland and was more than 800 kilometres. On 28 January 1852, the colony's deputy surveyor general was sent with a team of workers to build a more direct track that was suitable for drays and carts. Digging wells along the way, they produced a route of less than 600 kilometres. On 10 February, Captain Alexander Tolmer left Adelaide with the first gold escort. He returned on 20 March with a quarter ton of gold and 400 letters for the families of South Australian diggers, to streets lined with cheering crowds:

> Glorious News . . . Many an anxious eye was yesterday averted from the noontide meal towards the point at which the Great Eastern Road issues from the picturesque Mount Lofty Ranges, and many a palpitating heart was gladdened, when the sight of an approaching cavalcade gave assurance that the gallant Captain Tolmer had not only accomplished, but even anticipated the time of his promised event.[34]

Throughout all of Australia's gold rushes, a pattern repeated itself whereby the diggers would exhaust a gold-field of its alluvial supplies before the big steam stampers took over to mine the rest. This meant that the miners were always keen to hear of new surface finds, so they could migrate to fresh diggings and easy pickings. And the country's supply of gold was suitably bountiful that the rushes went on and on, spreading gold fever and its attendant abandon and disorder from colony to colony.

CHAPTER NINE

Law and Disorder

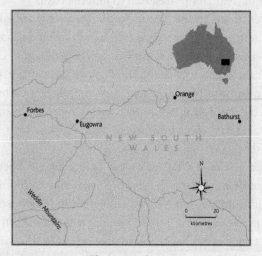

The Eugowra diggings

Gardiner was armed – he had a double barrelled shot gun
slung over his horse and two revolvers on his person . . .
When I declined to go with him, Gardiner put his hand on his
revolver, and said, 'I've come for you and you must come.'

There was a dramatic rise in crime and lawlessness as a consequence of the gold rushes. The sudden generation of great wealth, the emergence of entirely new towns and thousands of immigrants pouring in to the diggings from overseas were too much for the relatively small colonial police forces, which had already been decimated when many of their troops deserted to join the rush.

Even though most groups of diggers were armed, they were still prey to the gangs of bandits that infested the bush along the roads to and from the goldfields. On the diggings, order was maintained more as a result of the administration of rough justice by the diggers themselves than by the police, who were anyway preoccupied with enforcing and collecting licence fees and breaking up sly grog shops.

One of the earliest and most spectacular robberies of the gold era involved the theft of more than 8000 ounces of gold from the ship *Nelson* while it sat in Melbourne harbour ready to sail for London on the night of 1 April 1852. The story was widely reported around the world, with the *New York Times* saying of the daring raid, it 'almost surpasses belief, from the magnitude of the spoil carried off, and the coolness with which the job was undertaken'.[1]

The 600-ton *Nelson* had arrived from England at Port Phillip Bay on 18 November 1851, only months after the start of the gold rush, but was unable to make the return voyage for more than four months because most of the crew had deserted to join the diggings.

Early in the new year, the ship was towed to Geelong at the western end of Port Phillip Bay, where it was loaded with wool before returning to Melbourne to find a crew for the voyage to England. On the afternoon of 1 April, with the ship prepared for departure, a heavily armed police guard rowed out to the *Nelson* and signed over a large consignment of gold for London, which was then put in the ship's strongroom. In addition to the cargo, the ship was to carry about 30 passengers – most of whom were enjoying their last night ashore before the ship sailed. Captain Wright was also ashore, leaving the ship in the hands of the first mate, Henry Draper, the second mate, Carr Dudley, and several other crew members. There were also two women passengers in their cabins. No satisfactory explanation was ever given for why a ship with such valuable cargo was left with so little security.

Sometime between midnight and 1 am, between ten and 20 men rowed quietly out to the ship in two whaling boats with cloth in the rollocks to prevent any noise. All hands had retired at about 11 pm, leaving the second mate on watch on the deck. He said that he saw a boat rowing from the shore but had no suspicion of its crew's intention until it was alongside.

The thieves were armed and quickly climbed aboard, overpowered the guard and took the 23 boxes of gold that were stored below deck. During the raid, which woke all those on board who had been asleep, only one shot was fired, which wounded the first mate, Henry Draper.

Even though the alarm was quickly called, the thieves managed to lower all the gold boxes into the rowing boats and make a successful getaway. The two deserted rowing boats were found on the beach at Williamstown and Saint Kilda, along with the broken boxes, a little gold dust and a few tiny nuggets.

Over the next days and weeks, the hunt was on for the thieves, and the Victorian Government offered a reward of

£250 – or a conditional pardon – for information leading to the arrest of the robbers:

> It having been represented to the Government that during the night of the 1st instant, or on the morning of the 2nd instant, a robbery was perpetrated on board the ship 'NELSON' (now lying in the Port of Melbourne) and a large amount of gold taken there from . . . a Reward of Two Hundred and Fifty Pounds will be paid to any Person or Persons who may give information as will lead to the apprehension and conviction of the perpetrators of the said robbery.[2]

On Monday 5 April, two men were arrested in Geelong at a bank trying to send money on to Sydney. Later that same day, four of their colleagues were also caught, and three more over the next few days. Five of them were tried and convicted. James Duncan, James Morgan, John James and Stephen Fox were all given long prison sentences, and the fifth, John Roberts, was subsequently released when he managed to establish an alibi. Some of the money was found on the men when they were arrested, but the bulk of the gold has never been recovered, leading to suspicions that the robbery was masterminded by a well-known and disreputable Saint Kilda publican who 'fenced' the gold and paid off the robbers very soon after the heist.

During the gold era, many of the biggest robberies involved the holding up of the escorts, which were the coaches carrying loads of gold that were escorted by an armed guard of police and troopers.

From the start of the gold rushes, the digger had the choice of selling his gold at the diggings, for perhaps a shilling an ounce less than he would be paid for it in the city. Most did this, because by taking the gold back themselves they risked being held up and robbed on the way.

At first, the gold bought at the diggings was carried on the mail coach, but this soon became too dangerous. The first government service with armed troopers and police began in September 1851, from Ballarat to Melbourne. In addition to the government-run service, a number of private escorts started offering guaranteed security and faster delivery from 1852.

The biggest and most dramatic robbery of the gold period took place about 300 kilometres west of Sydney near Eugowra in western New South Wales. Nearly 3000 ounces of gold and £4000 in banknotes and coins was stolen from the gold escort on its way from Forbes to Sydney.

Alluvial gold was found at Forbes – named after the New South Wales chief justice Sir Francis Forbes – on the Lachlan River in June 1861. Within six months, there were nearly 30,000 on the diggings, and by the end of the first year more than 7000 ounces of gold had been found. The gold boom at Forbes did not last long, however, and within two more years the population had dwindled to barely 3500.

The escort had left Forbes around midday on Sunday 15 June 1862 and was headed to Sydney carrying the gold and the money for the Orient Bank, the Bank of New South Wales and the Commercial Bank.[3] The police officer in charge of the escort, Sergeant James Condell, was sitting with his gun up next to the experienced driver John Fegan, who was well known on the western line, and sitting inside the coach with the gold in iron boxes were Senior Constable Henry Moran and three other constables.[4]

Despite the large amounts of gold and money being carried, there was no mounted guard riding alongside, which at that time was not unusual. Only the week before, the escort had carried more than twice as much gold and coinage with the same level of protection.

Over the next few hours of the journey, nothing happened to alarm the escort as they passed Hanbury Clements's farm about 45 kilometres from Forbes and, at about three in the afternoon, approached the Eugowra Rocks, which were large volcanic stones that peppered the neighbourhood. Ahead, there were three bullock drays drawn up and blocking much of the road. There was nothing exceptional about bullock drays being on the road, but when the coach slowed down to pass through the narrow gap, the path in front was completely blocked.

Suddenly, several armed men in red serge shirts and with blackened faces came out from behind the rocks, surrounded the coach and opened fire. One shot hit Sergeant Condell in the thigh, knocking him off his seat, and another went through the hat of the driver, John Fegan. Inside the coach, the police were attempting to return fire when a shot from the ambushers hit Constable Henry Moran in the groin.

As the first gunmen quickly fell back to reload their guns, some of their colleagues moved forward and fired again at the coach. Both Sergeant Condell and the driver Fegan were now on the ground. The horses, frightened by the gunfire, began to pull free of the coach, attempting to bolt, and the coach capsized. Realising they were outnumbered and outgunned, the police ran off into the bush, leaving the treasure to the robbers.

Meanwhile, the local farmer, Hanbury Clements, who

had heard the gunfire, headed on horseback towards the escort and came across the coach driver Fegan, who was trying to get as far away from the scene as possible. Clements pressed on, expecting to find the bodies of the police who Fegan had told him had been shot. However, as he neared the rocks, he first saw Sergeant Condell limping towards him and, behind, the other police who had managed to escape the scene. Clements then offered the police the sanctuary of his farm and hurriedly rode off to Forbes to alert the recently promoted inspector of police for the western district of New South Wales, Sir Frederick Pottinger, of the hold-up.

Sir Frederick William Pottinger had been born in India in 1831, the second-youngest son of Lieutenant General Sir Henry Pottinger of the East India Company, before being educated privately, then at Eton. In 1850, he purchased a commission in the Grenadier Guards, where he is said to have gambled away a large part of his inheritance before migrating to Australia to try his luck at gold mining. In 1856, not having made his fortune, he joined the police and spent the next few years on the gold escorts in southern New South Wales.

The team of bandits had by now made good their escape with the iron boxes of gold and cash and reached their camp, which was about three kilometres away across rough country and behind a high ridge. On arriving, they gave some grog to the owners of the bullock drays they had captured earlier, then forced them to lie face down on the ground while the outlaws made their getaway.

As soon as Clements arrived in Forbes with the news of the hold-up, Police Chief Pottinger hastily put together a force of 11 troopers, two Aboriginal trackers and a number of local volunteers, and hurried off in search of the bushrangers. The police reached Clements's farm a little after two the following morning. With the help of the trackers, they picked up the trail of the gang and reached their campsite a little after daylight, barely 12 hours after the robbery had taken place.

At the camp, the embers of the fire were still burning and the remnants of the gang's clothes were at its edges – the robbers had burned them to prevent their being used as evidence against them. Also at the camp were the broken iron boxes that had contained the gold and money, plus a number of posted letters scattered across the ground. The tracks leaving the camp suggested the gang was heading south, in the direction of the Weddin Mountains, which were about 60 kilometres away.

Within days, newspapers around Australia were full of accounts of the daring raid, and everyone took it for granted that Frank Gardiner was the gang's leader, even though the police did not yet have any firm evidence that he was involved.

Gardiner was born in Scotland and was christened Frank Christie, the son of Charles Christie and his wife, Jane, who immigrated to Australia in 1834 with their five children when young Frank was five. The family settled in Boro near Goulburn in New South Wales, and by 20 years of age Frank had branched out from farming to become a horse thief. In 1850, he was jailed for five years in Victoria for stealing horses but escaped from Melbourne's Pentridge Prison after serving only one year of his sentence. Three years later, in 1858, he was again caught and jailed, under the name of Frank Clarke, for stealing horses in Goulburn. In 1859, he was paroled and went to western New South

Wales, where he operated a butcher's shop on the Lambing Flat goldfields at the time of the anti-Chinese riots there. By 1861, he was known to have become a bushranger and was wanted for shooting and wounding two policemen, Middleton and Hosie, near Oberon. By 1862, he was the leader of a gang of highwaymen based in the Weddin Mountains.

On 18 June, only three days after the robbery, the government in Sydney posted a reward in the *New South Wales Police Gazette*:

MAIL AND ESCORT ROBBERY
£1000 REWARD AND PARDON TO AN ACCOMPLICE
Whereas it has been represented to the Government that on the afternoon of the 15th instant the Gold Escort from the Lachlan was attacked on the road between Forbes and Orange by a band of armed men, said to be ten in number, and described as dressed in red shirts, red caps, with their faces blackened, who fired on and wounded the police forming the guard, opened the Mail Bags and Letters and carried off a large amount of Gold Dust and Money: Notice is hereby given that a reward will be paid by the Government for such information as shall lead to the Apprehension and Conviction, within six months of this date of each of the guilty parties; and a pardon will also be granted to any accomplice in the above outrage who shall first give such information.
CHARLES COWPER
Colonial Secretary's Office, Sydney, 17 June 1862

Meanwhile, back at Eugowra, Police Chief Pottinger continued to follow the tracks of the thieves, which were becoming harder to follow after the fall of some heavy rain. He split the search party into two groups, giving 33-year-old Sergeant Charles Sanderson four troopers and an Aboriginal tracker while keeping two policemen and the civilian volunteers in his own group. Sanderson was to head in a direction slightly west of south towards the Weddin Mountains and Pottinger in a more direct route to the south.

After camping the night, Sergeant Sanderson's party searched for about 30 kilometres along the Lachlan River before deciding to cross and head for the Weddin Mountains.

Early on Thursday 19 June, Sanderson's tracker saw a rider ahead who immediately turned and headed into the bush. Following the tracks, Sanderson's men soon came across a hastily abandoned campsite with the fire still smouldering, tea in the billy and some bread and meat set out ready for cooking. There were also some blankets and mail strewn on the ground.

Picking up the tracks of five horses, the pursuers quickened their pace and eventually caught up with a riderless horse that turned out to be the heavily laden and slowest-moving packhorse of the bushrangers. It was carrying more than 1200 ounces of gold in four bags lashed to its saddle.

Sanderson's team continued to follow the tracks of the other horses but was unable to keep up. The bushrangers had taken a lot of trouble to equip themselves with first-class horses, while the police were issued with fairly standard mounts that were well below the calibre of those they were following. Calling off the search on the western side of the Weddin Mountains, Sanderson and his team headed back to Forbes, where they handed over the gold they had recovered to the local authorities.

Meanwhile, Pottinger and the other search party had not heard of Sanderson's success and were following the more southerly route to the east of the Weddin Mountains towards the Riverina region of southern New South Wales. When they reached Narrandera, about 240 kilometres south of Forbes, a number of the volunteers who had gone to help capture the robbers, including Hanbury Clements, turned for home, leaving Pottinger with only two men to continue the hunt.

Shortly afterwards, Pottinger was given a lead when some passengers on a recent journey on a Cobb and Co. coach in southern New South Wales said they had seen from the coach five or six heavily armed riders leading a heavily loaded packhorse.

According to newspaper reports at the time, Pottinger believed he was chasing not Gardiner but a group of Victorian bushrangers who had come north for the robbery and were now heading home:

Sir Frederick Pottinger has traced six of the party who robbed the escort to Point, in Hay District, 100 miles [161 kilometres] from Deniliquin. They are evidently making for Victoria and it is hoped they will be captured at one of the crossing places. Pottinger believes that Gardiner had nothing to do with it, but rather that it was a party of Victorian bushrangers.[5]

A week later, Pottinger and his two colleagues, Lyons and Mitchell, came across three riders, who had with them a fourth horse, near the town of Hay. When questioning the men, the one leading the packhorse raced off into the bush, while Pottinger and his men drew their guns and held the other two, Charles Gilbert and Henry Manns. The one that got away was Charles Gilbert's brother John.

When questioned, Charles Gilbert and Henry Manns told Pottinger they had left the goldfields at Lambing Flat three days before, but when searched they were found to be carrying more than £150 in Commercial Bank notes and more than 213 ounces of gold.

Convinced he had caught two of the Eugowra gold-escort robbers, Pottinger telegraphed his news to Deniliquin, Wagga Wagga and Sydney before starting the 240-kilometre trek with his two manacled prisoners back to Forbes.

At around one o'clock the following afternoon, they were suddenly jumped by three armed men with blackened faces, who included John Gilbert and the gang leader, Frank Gardiner.

The ambushers first fired on Detective Lyons, who was leading the prisoners, shooting his horse in the neck and causing the terrified beast to bolt off into the bush, carrying the banknotes they had taken from the prisoners. Lyons, who had dropped his revolver when he was thrown from his horse, also ran off into the trees.

Suddenly, four other men appeared from the side and began shooting at Pottinger and Mitchell, who, after exchanging fire, were forced to retreat, leaving the bushrangers to free their colleagues and reclaim some of the money.

Pottinger was concerned that the bushrangers would pursue him for the gold that he still held, but, after securing the help of nine troopers and two Aboriginal trackers supplied by Captain Battye of Lambing Flat,[6] managed to safely reach Forbes the following morning.

Over the next few weeks, Pottinger and his police managed to arrest a number of men in the western district who were involved in the hold-up. On 9 July, Pottinger went very close to capturing Gardiner himself near Wheogo, and would have shot the gang leader but for the failure of his gun to fire at the critical moment.

Pottinger said that, late at night, he and a party of police had surrounded the house of a Catherine Brown because they had become aware that Frank Gardiner was 'enamoured of Mrs. Brown' and was taking advantage of her husband's absence:

As we were concealed at a distance of 150 yards [137 metres] . . . I observed a man mounted on a white horse approaching Brown's house at a quiet pace . . . suddenly the noise of the horses hoofs sounded nearer and nearer; when I saw Gardiner cantering leisurely along; I waited until he came within five yards [4.5 metres] of me, and levelled my carbine at him across his horses shoulder (the weapon, I swear, being about three yards [2.7 metres] from his body). I called upon him to stand; I cannot be mistaken, and on my oath I declare that the man was Frank Gardiner; deeming it not advisable to lose a chance, I prepared to shoot him, but the cap of my piece missed fire; Gardiner's horse then began to rear and plunge, and before I had time to adjust my gun, he had bolted into the bush; as Gardiner was riding away on the back of the frightened animal Sergeant Sanderson fired at him, as also did Holster; I called out to those who could hear me to 'shoot the wretch'. Gardiner, however, made his escape; we then proceeded to Mrs.

Brown's house, and having seen her she frankly admitted that Gardiner had been at her place.[7]

(Pottinger's account of nearly capturing Gardiner was later contradicted in a story in the *Miner* newspaper, which was republished in a number of other papers a few months later. According to an unnamed member of Pottinger's team, the police chief had staked out Brown's house but was too far away and 'his chance of shooting Gardiner, even by moonlight, was one in a thousand'.[8])

One of the arrested men, 24-year-old Daniel Charters, was granted bail. He then approached Sergeant Sanderson to tell him he had been forced to participate in the Eugowra robbery and was prepared to name the others if given immunity from prosecution. Charters, who would become the key witness in the subsequent trial, identified the other men involved, including some who were already in jail and others who were subsequently rounded up and charged.

However, on 24 August, Ben Hall, William Hall, John Brown, John Walsh and Patrick O'Meally were discharged from the Forbes Court due to lack of evidence.[9] (Most of them would return to a life of crime. Ben Hall would later become one of Australia's most famous bushrangers, before he was shot dead by police three years later near Forbes on 4 May 1865. Ironically, one of the police involved in the shooting of Ben Hall was James Condell, the senior police officer in charge of the Eugowra gold escort.)

In October, the four men still in custody were taken from the Forbes lock-up to Bathurst, where three of them – John McGuire, Alex Fordyce and John Bow – were committed for trial. The prosecution decided it did not have enough evidence against 24-year-old John O'Meally, and he was released. (O'Meally also resumed a life of crime and was shot dead during an attempted robbery at the end of the following year.)

Then, on 2 December, Pottinger and his men arrested Henry Manns on the Wombat gold diggings near Young, and Manns would join McGuire, Fordyce and Bow in the upcoming Eugowra robbery trial.

It was not until 24 January 1863 that the four accused men were handcuffed in pairs, put in leg irons and transported in a well-guarded coach surrounded by 18 armed troopers from Bathurst for trial in Sydney. Three days later, a huge crowd turned up at Sydney's Criminal Court to catch a glimpse of the prisoners when they arrived and had to be kept at bay by more than 50 mounted troopers.

The trial began on 3 February, but Henry Manns was excused on a technicality, which left only McGuire, Fordyce and Bow as the defendants. The first prosecution witnesses included Sir Frederick Pottinger, Sergeant Sanderson and the coach driver John Fegan. However, everyone was waiting for the star prosecution witness Daniel Charters, who began by explaining how he worked on a farm on the Lachlan valley when one day Frank Gardiner rode up and forced him to join the gang:

> Gardiner rode up to me about fifteen yards [14 metres] in advance of the others . . . he wanted me to go with him for a few days. I said I could not . . . He said I must go as he wanted me to show him the road to some place he did not name. Gardiner was armed – he had a double barrelled shot gun slung over his horse and two revolvers on his

person . . . When I declined to go with him, Gardiner put his hand on his revolver, and said, 'I've come for you and you must come.'[10]

Charters said that he went reluctantly with Gardiner's gang and they camped outside Forbes while Gilbert went into town to buy six more shotguns and some supplies, including a tomahawk. According to Charters, Gilbert arrived back at their camp at around three in the morning with three other men. On the following Saturday night, they camped near Eugowra, where the next day they planned the hold-up of the escort that was due to leave Forbes around midday. Charters said Gardiner let him go back to mind the gang's horses that would be needed for the getaway, so he was not involved in the subsequent shooting:

> We crossed the creek, and went on to Eugowra Mountain . . . We tied our horses up by the direction of Gardiner; we each had a gun then. We then went to the large rocks overlooking the road. We remained for a short time. Gardiner went down to the road, stepped the distance, returned and said, 'That will do.' . . . It was then suggested that someone should go back and look to the horses we left tied up. I proposed to go back and after Gardiner studied for a while, he said, 'Very well, you go; you're bloody frightened of your life, and you're the best to go.'[11]

Charters then explained how, after the robbery, the gang headed south, Gardiner started to divide the booty and they were forced to abandon their camp as the police neared. Finally, Charters said Gardiner let him go, giving him only £50 after a packhorse carrying much of the gold was lost to Sergeant Sanderson.

During the long cross-examination, Charters was confronted by what the defence counsel suggested were discrepancies in his evidence and spent much of his remaining time in the witness box denying he was at the robbery voluntarily or that he received his share of the loot.

The jury retired at 4.35 pm on Thursday 5 February and at 10 pm told the judge they were unlikely to agree on a verdict. After being locked up for the night, the jury returned at 9.30 the following morning and said that reaching agreement would not be possible. They were duly discharged and a new trial was started two weeks later.

The second trial now included Henry Manns, who had been excused from the first trial, and with four defendants it otherwise ran much the same as the first. This time, when the jury retired on the evening of 26 February, the judge made it clear he wanted a decision: 'It is a quarter to 8 o'clock. I shall return to this court at half past 9 to receive your verdict.'[12]

At 9.45 pm, the jury returned to say that they had agreed to acquit John McGuire but found the other three, Alex Fordyce, Henry Manns and John Bow, guilty.

In passing the death sentence on the three, Chief Justice Stevens decried the public's sympathy for the criminals and its disregard for their law-abiding victims:

It is my painful duty to pass on you the sentence of death . . . It is too much the habit to lavish pity on the criminals, in forgetfulness of the outrages and misery of which they have been the authors. Some consideration is due to the police, who expose their lives in the discharge of their duty, to the interests of the community, in the security of the produce from the gold fields, where there are some ruffians, no doubt, but also many hardworking, honest, industrious men, having women and children dependent on them. See to what a state of things this lawlessness has reduced us. Here is the proprietor of cattle, who joined a band of ruffians to rob, to wound the innocent – to kill them, unless merciful Providence intervened. There is a nest of ruffians about the Weddin Mountains; and there seems to be scarcely one about the place who is not willing to join the robbers in their crime.[13]

Shortly after the trial, the Executive Council of the colony agreed to commute the death sentence of 42-year-old Alex Fordyce to life imprisonment with hard labour.[14] Fordyce, a stockman and sometime barman, was reprieved because, it was argued, his gun failed to fire and as a result he did not actually shoot anyone.

The Executive Council refused to budge on the death sentences of John Bow and Henry Manns, which resulted in a deluge of petitions to the governor, Sir John Young, who finally agreed to reprieve Bow, a 20-year-old stockman from Penrith. The last-minute appeals on behalf of Henry Manns were not enough to persuade the governor, who told the petitioners on 25 March that he would face the gallows the following day:

I need scarcely assure you that I have given the subject of your petitions the most careful and anxious consideration and that I deeply feel the heavy responsibility of the occasion . . . It is with pain, therefore, that I have to inform you that I have arrived at the conclusion that the case of the prisoner Henry Manns is not one which would justify my exercising the Royal prerogative in his favour on my own individual responsibility.[15]

The 24-year-old Manns became the only member of the armed gang to be executed. He was hanged the next morning at the rear of Darlinghurst Gaol in Sydney in a botched execution that was reported in graphic and awful detail by the *Sydney Morning Herald* the following day:

When at length . . . the bolt was drawn, there ensued one of the most appalling spectacles ever witnessed at an execution. The noose of the rope, instead of passing tightly round the neck, the knot coming round in front of the face, while the whole weight of the criminal's body was sustained by the thick muscles of the poll [head].The rope in short, went round the middle of the head and the work of the hangman proved a most terrible bungle. The suffering and the struggles of the wretched being were heartrending to behold. His body, swayed about, and writhed, evidently in the most intense agony. The arms repeatedly rose and fell, and finally, with one of his hands, the unfortunate man gripped the rope, as if to tear the pressure from his head, a loud guttural noise meanwhile proceeding from his throat and lungs, while blood gushed from his nostrils, and stained the cap with which his face was covered. This awful scene lasted for more than ten minutes, when stillness ensued and it was hoped that death had terminated the culprit's sufferings. Shocking to relate however, the vital spark was not yet extinguished, and to the horror of all present, the convulsive writhings were renewed – the tenacity to life being remarkable, and a repetition of the sickening scene was only at last terminated at the insistence of Dr. West, by the aid of four confines, who were made to hold the dying malefactor up in their arms while the executioner readjusted the rope, when the body was let fall with a jerk, and another minute sufficed to end the agonies of death . . . The body was lowered into a shelf shortly before ten o'clock, and it was with deep regret and indignation that some of the spectators saw the hangman attempt to remove a pair of new boots from the feet of the corpse. This revolting act was, however, instantly prevented, and the body, which was decently attired, in a white shirt, moleskins and blouse, was removed to the dead house, where it remained untouched until the arrival of a hearse, procured by the relatives of the criminal, to whom the authorities had decided to it turn over for internment.[16]

Manns's mother had requested that the body of her son be handed over so he could be buried at the cemetery in Campbelltown, 50 kilometres south-west of Sydney. After it was taken down from the gallows, it was quickly taken in a cart to the Haymarket in Sydney, where it was transferred to a coffin provided by the family before being taken through a large crowd to the train for the journey to Campbelltown.

Much of the stolen gold from the robbery was never accounted for, and Frank Gardiner, the gang's leader, had vanished, along with the woman he had spent time with in the west of New South Wales, Catherine Brown.

Then, 18 months after the execution of Manns, the police received information that a man fitting Gardiner's description was running a pub somewhere on the Apis

Road near the new goldfields outside of Rockhampton in central Queensland. It is believed that Catherine Brown had written to her sister, who was living in the Murrumbidgee region of New South Wales, whose husband talked about it locally and the police heard the story.

Sailing on the *Balclutha*, Police Detectives Pye and McGlone and trooper Wells reached the port of Rockhampton on 11 February 1864, where, with the help of local police chief Lieutenant Brown and his Aboriginal troopers, they found and arrested Gardiner, Catherine Brown and Gardiner's partner, Craig, a month later in the pub. When McGlone jumped Gardiner, the other police had to draw their weapons to hold back a number of diggers at gunpoint who had leapt to Gardiner's aid.

Gardiner and Catherine Brown had escaped the police net around the Lachlan nine months earlier and headed the 1300 kilometres overland on back roads via the New England ranges and the Darling Downs to Rockhampton, in Queensland.[17] The couple did not stay long on the coast but left for the Peak Down goldfields. When passing through Yamba, they fell in with a Mr Craig, who agreed to partner them in opening a pub.

Gardiner was taken to Rockhampton, where, 'heavily ironed', he was charged with having 'committed various highway robberies in New South Wales'.[18] Catherine Brown was charged with 'concealing and assisting a bushranger' and Craig with harbouring a criminal, although both would later be acquitted.

The police took Gardiner to Brisbane, where he was held in the city lock-up before sailing on to Sydney on the steamer *Telegraph*. They left in the nick of·time, as a local lawyer for Gardiner arrived at the prison with a writ of habeas corpus from the Brisbane court.

There was great excitement in Sydney when Gardiner was taken to a cell in Darlinghurst Gaol. The colonial authorities and some of the newspapers were frustrated at the romantic popularity of the bushrangers. These outlaws terrorised the countryside, robbed gold escorts, bailed up travellers and stole all their belongings, shot and sometimes murdered the police and innocent members of the public, and cost the public thousands of pounds in policing. Yet, to many of the public, they were heroes, and their deeds were surrounded by great mystery and bold adventure.

While everyone knew that Gardiner was the leader of the celebrated Eugowra escort robbery, the police could not persuade Daniel Charters to again be the key prosecution witness, so Gardiner was charged over an earlier incident where the prosecution was more confident of its case and its witnesses.

Gardiner stood trial for the shooting with intent to kill of John Middleton and William Hosie at Fish River, almost a year before the Eugowra escort robbery, on 16 July 1861. In three days, the case was over, and when the jury came back at 6.25 pm with a verdict of not guilty the courtroom broke out into an uproar that the judge had difficulty quietening. The prosecution then told the judge that there were other charges against Gardiner, and His Honour thought it prudent to first clear the overwhelmingly pro-Gardiner public gallery before ordering him back to the cells.

It was two months later that Gardiner was brought again into the court, where he was charged with the lesser offences of robbing, 'while under arms', Messrs

Horsington and Hewitt, to which he surprised everyone by pleading guilty. He was also found guilty of wounding with intent to do grievous bodily harm, and the judge made the most of the conviction by imposing a heavy sentence: 32 years in prison.

Within a year of Gardiner starting his long sentence, Sir Frederick Pottinger, the man who had successfully chased and captured most of the Gardiner gang, was dead. In February 1865, he was sacked from the police force following a series of incidents involving threatening behaviour, drinking on duty and the breach of police regulations.[19] Then, on 5 March 1865, he accidentally shot himself in the stomach while reboarding a coach in the Blue Mountains on his way to Sydney[20] and died several weeks later. He is buried in Saint Jude's cemetery in the Sydney suburb of Randwick, and his tombstone reads:

Sacred to the Memory of
Sir Frederick William Pottinger Baronet.
Formerly of the Grenadier Guards
and for many years a zealous and active officer of the
police in New South Wales,
Born 27 April 1831. Died 9 April 1865.
This monument is erected by his friends in the colony.

Meanwhile, back in Sydney, as Gardiner began serving his long sentence, a concerted campaign was started by Gardiner's family and friends for his release that would continue unabated for several years. At the centre of the campaign were Gardiner's two sisters, who petitioned the governor, Sir Hercules Robinson, for the release of their errant brother:

> Your petitioners humbly implore your Excellency's merciful
> considerations of their unfortunate brother's case, towards
> remission of his terrible sentence, on the following grounds
> ... Previous to his apprehension he was obtaining his living
> as a storekeeper in Queensland for nearly two years having
> abandoned his former career of wickedness, and had left
> the colony fully determined to lead a life of honest industry
> ... that if your Excellency be pleased to grant him a pardon,
> he will be thus afforded the opportunity of redeeming the
> past ...

Over the next few years, the army of petitioners grew in
size and stature to include a number of members of parliament and the colonial secretary, William Foster, who said
he 'had much pleasure in testifying to the fact of Christie's
[Gardiner's] good character during the entire period of his
incarceration' and urged the government to give Gardiner
'favourable consideration'. A local medical practitioner, Dr
Moffit, also claimed that Gardiner had 'completely recovered from his evil ways, and that it would be perfectly safe
to permit him to go at large'.[21]

Eventually, the then colonial secretary, Henry Parkes,
called for a report from the sheriff and Gardiner's jailer,
who said on 12 September 1872 that a reduction in the
prison sentence would be acceptable, particularly if it
involved Gardiner's being exiled to another country on his
release.

On 20 July 1874, amid political and public outcry,
Gardiner was released from prison. He immediately sailed
for California, where he opened a bar in San Francisco's
red-light district of the Barbary Coast. Over the next
25 years, there were occasional newspaper reports in

Australia about him, including that he was drinking too much, had fallen on hard times and was sleeping in the streets. In another, it was claimed that he was involved in the robbery in Utah of a wagon train of immigrants heading for California.

Gardiner was reported to have died in Colorado in 1903 aged 73, and with him went the secret of what happened to the bulk of the unrecovered gold from the Eugowra gold-escort robbery nearly 40 years earlier.

Or did it?

There were a number of stories suggesting that the gold was later recovered. In one account, Gardiner was said to have given detailed instructions as to where the gold was buried to an Irish friend in San Francisco who went to Australia, dug it up and took it back to America.[22] It was also said that Gardiner had a daughter while in California, who, with her Australian husband, was given a map showing where the gold was buried. They were rumoured to have returned to America with 'thousands of Australian sovereigns'.[23]

However, none of the rumours were ever confirmed, and it seems more likely that much of the unrecovered gold from the escort robbery remains buried somewhere south of the Eugowra Rocks. The entire haul of bullion and gold coins taken during the hold-up would have been too heavy even for good packhorses to carry over a long distance while being chased by police, and it is probable that Gardiner would have hidden much of it before making his escape.

CHAPTER TEN

Queensland Joins the Rush

The Gympie diggings

In the following month, the town of Brisbane resembled a hive of
bees at swarming time, pushing and shoving. Lawyers, parsons,
doctors, shopmen, shopkeepers, and everyone else who could walk,
could be seen swaggering up with blankets, making their way across
the hills and treacherous track via Durundur for the new diggings.

The big gold rush at Gympie in 1867 came in the nick of time for the fledgling Queensland colony. With a tiny population of 23,000 settlers, Queensland had gained independence from New South Wales only eight years earlier and was in the depths of a severe economic depression. The Bank of Queensland closed its doors, there was little money in the colonial treasury, the public works, including the construction of the first railway line from Brisbane to Ipswich, had been abandoned and the unemployed were protesting in the streets of the capital.

The huge gold find by the semi-literate loner James Nash some 160 kilometres north of Brisbane in October 1867 is widely believed to have been the 'golden gleam shot across the midnight sky of the colony's adversity'[1] that prevented Queensland's collapse.

James Nash was born in Beanacre, Wiltshire, in England, one of five sons of a farm labourer. At nine years of age, he joined his father working on farms. At 23, with practically no education, he followed two of his brothers to Australia and spent the next ten years as an itinerant farm labourer and prospector, walking thousands of kilometres around the various goldfields.[2] In 1863, having met with little good luck, he moved to Queensland. He wandered for several years on the diggings near Gladstone in central Queensland and then at Nanango north-west of Brisbane before he found gold at Gympie.

Queensland was a penal settlement for more intractable convicts from 1825 to 1839, when convict shipments ended and free settlers began farming across the Darling Downs in the colony's south-west. Local agitation for independent status began in the early 1850s, and Queensland became a separate colony, named after Queen Victoria, with its own government in June 1859.

Gold had previously been found at a number of places in Queensland, but none of the earlier finds were to generate the same excitement as James Nash's at Gympie.[3] A decade earlier, gold was found at Canoona station, about 50 kilometres upstream on the Fitzroy River from the tiny central Queensland settlement of Rockhampton that had been established three years before by pioneer farmers in the region.

Three months after the Canoona discovery, several hundred diggers who had already reached the site were joined by about 1500 others who had sailed up from Sydney after reading of the discoveries in the newspapers.[4] But, by the time the men from the south arrived, there was little ground worth pegging, as the field covered only a few acres, which had already been scratched down to the bare rock. Many of the prospectors who had travelled thousands of kilometres from the south stayed only a few disappointing hours before deciding to turn back – only to meet other hopefuls still on their way there.

From boom to bust, the rush at Canoona had lasted only 66 days, and over the next few years the diggers spread out along the tributary creeks scratching for new finds. Gold was found at one of these tributaries, Crocodile Creek, in June 1866, and by August about 3000 people were on the site, around a thousand of whom were Chinese.

On Sunday 6 January 1867, a gang of European diggers attacked the Chinese armed with picks, shovels and axes, and drove them off their claims. The fleeing Chinese sent a messenger on horseback for help, who arrived at Rockhampton on Monday night. The gold commissioner, 66-year-old Scot John Jardine, immediately sent a mounted force of police who arrived early next morning and, with the help of a local European builder, identified and arrested ten diggers.

The accused were taken back to Rockhampton and denied bail. Subsequently, four of the men were released because of insufficient evidence and the others charged with riotous behaviour. In March, and after two months in the lock-up, the remaining six were tried. Two were acquitted, and the other four were convicted and each sentenced to nine months' jail. While not severe punishment, it was one of the rare instances where violence against the Chinese was dealt with properly by the justice system.

Before James Nash discovered the gold bonanza at Gympie, he had been mining at Calliope, about 150 kilometres south of Canoona, close to the central Queensland port of Gladstone. Calliope was named after the ship that brought the New South Wales governor Sir Charles FitzRoy on a visit to the area in 1854, and gold had been found there in 1862.

Early in 1867, Nash had left the limited pickings of Calliope to join about 400 other diggers who had gone to Nanango, where some gold had been discovered about 180 kilometres north-west of Brisbane. The rush to Nanango had started when Zachariah Skyring, a well-known Brisbane cattle and sheep dealer, came back to Brisbane and stirred up the public's interest in selling some gold he had found to a local jeweller.[5] However, the gold at Nanango proved to be limited, and after only a few months most of the diggers began to drift away – including, as an eyewitness recalled, James Nash:

There was a man on the field more remarkable than the rest. He lived by himself alone on a solitary hill, and never associated with anybody. One fine morning . . . it was noticed the man from Calliope had cleared out, no one knew where or cared.[6]

Years later, Nash recounted to the *Gympie Times* newspaper why he decided to leave Nanango to walk more than a thousand kilometres north back to Calliope by himself following the 'postman's tracks':

About the middle of August, 1867, I left Nanango for Gladstone. I had been working some time in Nanango; there was nothing there worth staying for, so I thought of going to Gladstone, trying all the likely places on the way. I had nothing but my dish, pick, and dog with me.[7]

About 170 kilometres north of Brisbane, at Bella Creek, he fossicked for a few days and found a few ounces of gold before his pick handle broke off. He then headed 100 kilometres north to the port town of Maryborough on the Mary River to cash in his gold and buy some new mining tools. Nash said that he was at first unable to sell his gold:

I went to Maryborough where I tried two banks and several stores but could not sell the gold. (Times were so bad that they hardly knew what gold was like.) At last I tried Mr. Southernden a second time, and he allowed me three pounds for it, £1 in money, the rest in tools and rations.[8]

After walking back to where he had found the gold, Nash decided to work further up the creek than previously and over the next six days found 75 ounces of gold. Again, he walked back to Maryborough, where he caught 'the first steamer for Brisbane' to sell his gold. An eyewitness said he created great excitement among the locals when he displayed his wares:

> We got the shock of our lives at ten o'clock in the morning when we decided to stroll down Queens Street. To our astonishment we saw a black crowd of men gathered around Flavelle Bros jeweller's shop. On looking into the window we saw two silver dishes heaped up with gold; to us they seemed as big as cricket balls. Some pieces we were told weighed 19 ounces.[9]

Nash said he was aware all eyes were on him when he went into the shop and was deliberately vague about where he had found the gold:

> The Honourable William Henry Walsh [member of parliament for Maryborough] was in the shop as I came in, and watched me sell the gold, and there was a man watching from the street, whom I knew was a digger. Mr. Walsh asked me where I had got it, and I said, 'Oh, up north.'[10]

People anxious to learn where the gold had been found were told by the jeweller that Nash was staying at the nearby Saint Patrick's Tavern. They staked out the hotel where Nash had booked his room for a few nights, only to discover that he had slipped away from Brisbane at 10 pm that night on the steamer *Yarra Yarra*, bound for Maryborough.

Nash said he was eager to get back to his goldfield and stayed only long enough in Brisbane to buy himself a horse and cart, fresh supplies and more mining gear before returning to his camp, where he planned to meet up with his brother John:

> I bought a horse from Mr. Redhead (farmer), and a dray from Kent's saleyard, and a cradle made at the old Pimblico shop. I took a steamer back to Maryborough . . . Went to Travis's store for tarpaulin, rations, corn and chaff; then started for my camp.[11]

On 16 October 1867, Nash went in to the Maryborough police station to report his discovery and officially claim the site, which meant the whole world became aware of the location of his discovery. The following day, the *Brisbane Courier* newspaper ran a story from Maryborough that said the two Nash brothers had the previous day registered their claim and brought to town 75 ounces of gold they found 'on the Mary River near Widges Crossing'.[12]

Now that Nash's destination was known, hundreds immediately followed him in the hope he would lead them to the goldfield. Very soon, 'every town in Queensland caught the contagion' and joined the rush.

By the end of October, several thousand diggers were already at Gympie and, as the *Maryborough Chronicle* reported, many had rushed there totally ill equipped and without enough money to buy food:

> There are 2,000 to 2,500 men on the ground. Some exceedingly rich quartz has been got by some, whilst at the same time numbers of men are said to be starving. There

is danger of stores being rushed and plundered. Many have arrived without a shilling in their pockets and have done no good since their arrival. The great complaint is of the number of people on the field who are not diggers, and who are without ways and means of living.[13]

Most of the prospectors journeyed from Brisbane to Gympie by one of two routes. One was by taking a steamer about 300 kilometres north along the Queensland coast then a further 40 kilometres up the Mary River to Maryborough, followed by an overland trek 100 kilometres to the south to Gympie. Alternatively, as a prospector recorded, it was possible to walk the 170 kilometres from Brisbane, which was more difficult but favoured by many because it was cheaper:

In the following month, the town of Brisbane resembled a hive of bees at swarming time, pushing and shoving. Lawyers, parsons, doctors, shopmen, shopkeepers, and everyone else who could walk, could be seen swaggering up with blankets, making their way across the hills and treacherous track via Durundur for the new diggings.[14]

Very soon, the news reached further and the rush was on from the southern colonies:

When the news reached Sydney, it turned that city into something resembling a madhouse cut loose. Steamers and sailing vessels were filled up almost before they could get ready to start for Moreton Bay, and after arrival the ships had to look after themselves. Captains and crews were as eager to start in the hunt for gold as their passengers.[15]

By November 1867, only a month after Nash had returned to the goldfield, there were already 25,000 people on the site, which was initially known as Nashville but the following year changed to the Aboriginal name of a local tree called Gympie.

One of the earliest on the new diggings was 23-year-old Edward B. Kennedy, who with his mates had decided to try his luck there.[16] Kennedy had first arrived in Queensland in 1864 and worked on a number of cattle stations. Later, he was an officer in the Queensland mounted police force, which was largely made up of Aboriginal men and white officers.[17] Kennedy said he was unimpressed by the poor quality of immigrants who were attracted to Queensland's goldfields:

Emigrants still poured in with every ship . . . Chiefly the refuse and scum of London and the manufacturing towns, who landed on Queensland shores totally devoid of both capital and character. I think I saw the biggest lot of roughs landed in a port north of Brisbane that I had ever seen in my life trooping out of a ship.[18]

The township of Gympie quickly grew. The tents soon gave way to slab huts and then stout timber buildings along the 1.6-kilometre long and 12-metre wide Mary Street.[19] Kennedy said he was 'astonished with what rapidity the bakers, butchers and storekeepers flock to the diggings',[20] and within a year there were hundreds of stores in Gympie and the surrounding gullies. The *Nashville Times* reported that by February 1868 there were already 560 registered businesses and more than 1500 mining licences issued in Gympie, only four months after Nash's gold discovery. On the town's main street there were dozens of pubs, including the Royal Prince of Wales, Fulton's Melbourne Hotel, Sinclair's Horse and Jockey, the Maryborough, Farley's, The Freemason Hotel and Croakers Northumberland.

Kennedy said there was heavy drinking every night, particularly Saturday, when a range of entertainment was available:

> The night par-excellence was Saturday night; the whole length of the street was so full of diggers that we could hardly move at all, and what with singing, swearing, fighting and drinking, bargaining for loaves, beef, sausages for Sunday dinner, the noise was tremendous, while every public house was crammed with men discussing their various finds . . . We entered a music hall shortly afterwards (one shilling entrance), heard some good songs and recitations, witnessed some fair boxing, and the best step dancer that we had ever before seen performing to the lively tune of two fiddlers.[21]

The hopefuls continued to flock in throughout 1868, which was to be the bonanza year for the alluvial miners at Gympie, producing about 150,000 ounces of gold.

A few Chinese had been at Gympie from the beginning, but it was not until the following year that they began to arrive in larger numbers. At first, there was little hostility towards them, with the *Maryborough Gazette* saying in May 1868 that they were no trouble:

> The Mongolians [Chinese] have lately been arriving in gangs. Their favourite place seems to be the flat end

of Nash's Gully. They are orderly and harmless and we presume there can be no objection to them.[22]

The gestures of goodwill did not last, however. Following their usual custom, the Chinese moved in and reworked sites that had been abandoned by the less patient Europeans. But when the Chinese successfully re-dug thousands of pounds' worth of gold, the resentful diggers jumped their claim and drove them from the goldfields as they had already done further north in Queensland and in the southern goldfields of Victoria and New South Wales. Edward Kennedy noted that many Chinese had their pigtails torn out by the roots:

> All the Chinese diggers were chased off by the Europeans during our stay – they numbered six hundred . . . 'Roll up, roll up', we heard roared all through the camp, and at once Celestials were flying helter-skelter, taking flying leaps over claims, sometimes into them, when they would be dragged out by their pigtails and cuffed on again. At first they started laden with buckets, pots, bedding and other gear; gradually this was cast aside as they whirled away with an incessant jabbering which was only equalled by the oaths and shouts of the pursuing party. Those who had coiled up their pigtails got off the easiest, but when that appendage was flying behind, the owner sometimes came to grief, as the waggling tail was too tempting.[23]

One of those who went to the goldfields from Brisbane was young Catherine Murphy, who would meet then marry the discoverer of Gympie gold, James Nash, in July the following year. Years later, she wrote an account of how the gold saved her family and many others from the depression that had hit Queensland:

> My father had a business in Fortitude Valley, and found it very hard to make a living for a family of ten. Money was scarce. A great Depression hung over the colony. The Queensland bank had failed; their £1 notes sold for ten shillings and less, there were hosts of unemployed, immigrants, navvies from up the line Ipswich way. Hundreds of them were loafing around the city vowing vengeance against the authorities if they did not find them work or food. There was no money in the Treasury, and therefore no public works in progress.[24]

Catherine said the discovery of gold came in the nick of time, as 'revolution was in the air', but the disaffected instead hurried off on the 'inaccessible track' north of Brisbane in search of the 'wonderful richness' of gold at Gympie:

> I had a splendid view of the road via [Fortitude] Valley to Gympie, of the different styles of conveyance – drays and spring carts, and horses, packed from head to tail with tin dishes, picks and shovels and blankets, and billy cans, all rattling and noisy, filling the air with their sound as they all rumbled along. The men would be talking and laughing as if they were on their way to a race meeting, instead of facing they knew not what privations and difficulties.[25]

Catherine's younger brother had earlier left school and joined the rush with a number of his schoolmates. When the family had heard nothing, Catherine's mother had teamed up with some other women who were going to join their husbands and headed for Gympie to search for her son. When she had reached Gympie and found him fit and well and successful at the diggings, Catherine's mother had decided to open a store on the goldfields and sent for the rest of the family to join her from Brisbane.

After selling up the family home and small shop in Fortitude Valley, Catherine, her brothers, sisters and father, who had been crippled years earlier in a riding accident, sailed on the paddle-wheel steamer the *Lady Bowen* from Brisbane to Maryborough:

> When we arrived at Maryborough, I got a letter from mother advising me to come to Gympie by coach, and to leave my father and the children, to come on by team. I preferred to stay with the rest of the family and take care of them. We started on a bright morning in June seated on our mattresses etc., piled up on the wagon.[26]

Catherine travelled to Gympie in June when the climate was mild and dry. Gympie's annual rainfall is around 112 centimetres a year, with about half falling in the four summer months of December to March when the daily temperature usually exceeds 30 degrees Celsius:

> Towards sundown the driver would unyoke his horses near the creek and make a fire at a big log, boil a big billy of tea and sweeten it with a big pannikin of sugar. We then spread a cloth on the grass and had tea . . . The creeks were bad to cross and most of the load had to be taken off and reloaded on the other side.[27]

Arriving at Gympie, Catherine said she was surprised to see the large township that had sprung up in only a few months:

> When we got to Gympie up on the hill over one long street, we were amazed at the grotesque looking township of very primitive buildings and tents dotted all over the place, and hundreds of men filling the spaces and making it hum like a huge fair.[28]

A large crowd of men came to see the rare sight of a woman on the goldfields, which made Catherine feel nervous:

> The first night of my arrival I went to the front of the house to arrange a lamp. I noticed a multitude of men blocking the street before our place. I asked a person near me what they were there for. He said, 'They've come to see the new girl.' I simply fled to the back room. But they were not at all a bad lot. They had no intension of intruding.[29]

During the day, Catherine described how everyone worked hard 'digging and fossicking', except for 'a lot of parasites' who did not work but seemed to be having a good time taking the honest diggers' money by 'card cheating and other dishonest means'.

Many of the diggers were enjoying success, including finding nuggets only a metre or so from the surface in a number of rich gullies. The hillsides around Gympie were full of tents and red flags that miners were obliged to hoist as a safety warning next to each of the hundreds of open shafts.

At night, Catherine and her family stayed in their little home, while most of the men were outside:

While we were enjoying ourselves . . . indoors, outside
in the street crowds of men were shouting, laughing and
singing, and playing violins, accordions, cornets, and
even Jew's harps, and others were fighting.[30]

There was no shortage of food, as beef and sheep farmers
had settled the fertile surrounding country about 20 years
before gold was found and regularly brought stock to the
goldfields for the hungry miners. Catherine Murphy said
that the Chinese provided food too but were not appreci-
ated for it:

Soon the Chinamen grew plenty of vegetables for which
they never charged a very high price. The rich scrub land
so near proved a veritable gold mine to the industrious
Celestials, who are so very useful on a diggings and yet so
thoroughly disliked by the miners.[31]

Among the thousands who came later to the boom town
of Gympie was Andrew Fisher, who would make the town
his political base before becoming three-times prime minister of Australia. Fisher was born in Ayrshire in Scotland
in 1862 and at the age of 11 followed his father into the
Scottish coal mines. At 17, he was elected as secretary of
the local miners' union but was sacked and blacklisted following miners' strikes in the early 1880s. At 22, he and his
younger brother James migrated to Brisbane, arriving on
the *New Guinea* in August 1885. After two years of working in coal mines, Fisher and his brother went to Gympie
to look for gold.

Fisher became a prominent member of the Gympie
community and active in local church, union and political

affairs. Tall, well built, with sandy hair and dark moustache, he is said to have kept his strong Scottish accent throughout his adult life.

He was first elected to the Queensland Legislative Assembly in 1893 and, after Gympie voted strongly in favour of Queensland joining the federal nation of Australia in 1899, he was elected as one of a number of Labor members of the first national parliament in 1901. At the end of the year, at 37, he married Margaret Jane Irvine, the daughter of his Gympie landlady. In keeping with his British working-class background, Fisher would be on the radical left of the Labor Party and would become prime minister in 1908, 1910 and 1914.

The discoverer of gold, James Nash, is said to have initially become rich, earning more than £10,000 in the first year with his brother, but he lost much of his fortune by investing in a number of mining ventures that subsequently failed.

By the end of September 1868, most of the easily dug alluvial gold was gone and there were only a few new finds. Most new gold was now reef gold, embedded in hard quartz, and the digger was progressively taken over by the big steam stampers that crushed the gold-bearing quartz.

The first quartz-crushing machine to arrive at Gympie was named the 'Pioneer' and was erected upstream from Nash's Gully in March 1868. (James Nash himself had never been part of the mechanised method of mining.) It was relatively small, with two batteries of five stamping heads each and driven by a 12-horsepower steam engine. From 1869, practically all the future gold mining at Gympie was by machines.[32] In April 1868, James Nash wrote to the Queensland Government to claim the £3000 reward they had offered for the discovery of payable gold. In his letter of application, he emphasised the benefits of his discovery to the fledgling colony of Queensland:

[Gympie] is producing more gold in proportion than any other Gold Field as yet discovered in the Australian Colonies and which at the present time offers such inducement to Capitalists as may be seen from the number at present anxious to invest in further developing the resources of the district.[33]

Unfortunately, Nash's discovery, while of unarguable benefit to the colony, did not strictly comply with the conditions of the reward, which stipulated that the gold had to be discovered within 90 miles, or 145 kilometres, from Brisbane. Gympie is a little over 160 kilometres from Brisbane. Eventually, Nash received £1000 – a fraction of the value of the gold he had found. In 1885, aged 51, he was given the job of keeper of the government explosives store at £100 a year and spent the rest of his years around Gympie, where he was a popular figure. He died in 1913 aged 79 and is buried in the town cemetery.

The year after Nash made his big discoveries in Gympie, new goldfields opened up almost a thousand kilometres further north, following the discoveries on the Cape River by 35-year-old surveyor Richard Daintree.

Daintree was born in Huntingdon, England, the son of a farmer, and after studying at Cambridge for a year he headed to the Victorian gold rush in 1852. After a return visit to England in 1856, he went back to Australia, where he worked as a surveyor and pursued his hobbies of photography and prospecting. In 1864, he became a pastoralist partner in north Queensland with William Hann, who would later lead the expedition that found the first gold on the Palmer River in Far North Tropical Queensland.

Over the next three years following Daintree's finds, prospectors spread out across more than 500 kilometres of the forbidding country of north Queensland on far-flung gold sites from Ravenswood to Charters Towers, Georgetown, the Gilbert and the Etheridge Rivers.[34]

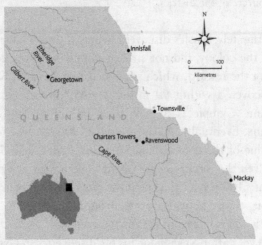

The North Queensland goldfields

Many of the gold rushes across north Queensland were relatively short-lived because most of the gold there was embedded in hard rock that needed to be crushed with heavy steam-powered stamping batteries. The first steam-powered crushing machine arrived at Ravenswood towards the end of 1869 and began operating in early 1870. Most of the local miners then had to make a choice as to whether to become labourers on the mechanised diggings or drift off to try their luck on other alluvial fields.

The biggest of the early fields was at Ravenswood, about 100 kilometres to the east of Cape River, which by May 1868 had more than 4000 people and a township with more than 50 pubs.

One of those who found his way to Ravenswood and ended up running a pub on the diggings was a 28-year-old Danish carpenter named Thorvald Weitemeyer, who had come to Australia from Germany to seek his fortune seven years earlier in 1861.

Weitemeyer had initially left the family home in Copenhagen and gone to Hamburg to work in a furniture factory rather than follow his father into the building trade. Living in a boarding house, barely able to understand German and working from six in the morning till eight o'clock each night, the young Dane complained that his life in Hamburg 'did not suit my idea of liberty'.[35]

One Sunday evening, while walking the streets of Hamburg, he saw in a shop window a large placard on which was printed in red letters 'Free Emigration to Queensland, Australia'.[36]

At the time, Queensland was one of a number of Australian colonies looking to promote development and boost its population by offering assisted migration. Weitemeyer knew very little about Australia other than remembering being taught at school that nature was reversed there: how leaves hung downwards from trees instead of upwards, how rivers ran inland away from the sea, how the inland seemed to be a vast lake of salt water and how the swans were black, not white:

I am certain I had never heard of the name Queensland before, and my impression of Australia was that it was the place to which criminals were sent . . . I had also read something about gold diggings in Australia . . . and I did not believe it.[37]

After a few days of pondering, he joined 600 other Germans, Danes, Swedes, Norwegians, Finns and Russians who spoke and understood no English but shared the 'same spirit of recklessness and poverty' and boarded a ship to Australia.

After a 'tedious' voyage, where they saw no land from the Canary Islands off the coast of Spain until Tasmania and the food was 'wretched and insufficient', they reached Queensland four months later. Weitemeyer found employment as a carpenter and for the next two years worked up and down the Queensland coast.

Having saved up more than £100, Weitemeyer said he had 'no particular idea where I should go', and decided to try his luck on the nearest goldfield, which was Ravenswood, about 180 kilometres inland from Townsville.[38] Packing his only horse with a swag containing a blanket, clothes and tea, sugar and flour, because it 'is a custom in Queensland on all occasions to be independent as possible',[39] he spent the next few days travelling to Ravenswood:

At last I was on the gold-field. What a magic spell there seemed to me in the words. All the old fallacious ideas connected with the word crowded into my mind. Runaway nuns dressed in men's clothes, princes working like labourers and labourers living like princes.[40]

Along the main street of Ravenswood were timber and tent hotels, boarding houses and stores, and behind it a vast number of tents where the miners lived. Weitemeyer was critical of the anti-Chinese feelings he encountered, which he believed to be hypocritical:

> All over Australia, but especially in Queensland, there is a bitter feeling against the Chinese. People say they ought to be forbidden from coming to the country, because they work too hard and too cheaply, and eat too little at the same time . . . [but] a white man is always praised if he is hard working and frugal.[41]

After unsuccessfully working for gold at Ravenswood, Weitemeyer heard of another gold find about 50 kilometres away near Charters Towers and immediately joined in, saying that in the excitement 'we ran rather than walked'.

Here, he was unlucky again, but he noticed that yet again a shanty store had been hurriedly set up and was doing a roaring trade for the newly arriving diggers, so decided to set up his own store:

> The hut I put up was very primitive. Just one room about fourteen by twelve feet [4 by 3.5 metres], made of saplings, packing cases, bark, or anything I could get at all suitable.[42]

Soon, he was making a fortune. Every morning, he would ride into town to gather supplies and bring them back to his little store:

> Long before daylight I was up and got my four horses together . . . in a racing gallop, I had to tear into the

butcher's, baker's and grocer's. My goods would stand ready for me when I came. I would just fling the stuff on the horses, leave my order for the next day, and be back in time to sell bread and meat for breakfast.[43]

After breakfast each day, Weitemeyer carried water from the creek to brew and cask hop beer, cleaned up the shop, served the people with grog, fed the horses, made himself breakfast and ejected a 'loafer or two':

> In the afternoon I had sometimes to send a man for more rations. And from five o'clock to ten, to eleven, twelve, and sometimes all night, there would be a lot of fellows drinking outside the shanty.[44]

Weitemeyer complained that the work was never ending and full of trouble, particularly from the men who became drunk:

> Fellows would get drunk and grow quarrelsome every day; if they were not very big I would not mind so much . . . [but] I would sometimes even have to keep two retainers in free grog to assist me in the 'chucking out' business.[45]

Watering down grog was a feature of most of the grog shops on the goldfields, and Weitemeyer admitted doing it too. He said that the storekeeper he bought the grog from showed him how to use only two-thirds of the rum and still keep it over proofed by mixing it with water and tobacco. The same happened with all the spirits, which resulted in 'all sorts of vile poison and most disgusting stuff'. He added that he believed practically no pubs ever sold pure spirits.

The little pub was very profitable, but Weitemeyer became increasingly worried about where to hide his money, as there was no bank close by and no local police. For a while, he hid all the takings in a bucket that he kept in a hole underneath a big cask in which he made beer, until he got drunk one Saturday night and blurted out where the money was hidden:

> One Saturday night, or more correctly Sunday morning, when a lot of men were drinking outside my hut under the sunshade, and when I myself had imbibed more than was good for me, I began . . . to boast of my money . . . The party appeared as if they did not believe me, on which I called them all into the hut. There I asked them to look under the cask while I tilted it over . . . A bucket was buried in the ground nearly filled with silver . . .[46]

Weitemeyer lamented that, after that, his recollections were not clear and he slept on the bar counter. When he woke, the money of course was gone:

> I was so disgusted with myself and the whole business that I told [the men] I would not be a shanty-keeper again for all the gold in Queensland.[47]

Weitemeyer then joined a fellow Dane, Thorkill, and headed north looking for gold. He found all the gold-fields deserted, though, as the word had arrived of a major gold discovery almost 1000 kilometres away at the Palmer River in the far north of Queensland. According to Weitemeyer, he resolved to go there himself later.

As the gold mining spread further north, the diggers

encountered more violent objection from the local Aboriginal people than had been the case in the more heavily European-populated areas of New South Wales and Victoria. Since the spread of farming in north Queensland from the early 1860s, the white settlers had with impunity killed and driven the blacks from lands where they were considered a nuisance for helping themselves to sheep, cattle and even horses.[48] But in many parts of the north and far north of Queensland, the Aboriginal tribes resisted the intruder, and a number of gold-mining sites were abandoned following hostile attacks from the local peoples.

Gold was discovered on the Gilbert River more than 500 kilometres north-west of Charters Towers in 1869, and it attracted more than 3000 diggers. The local Jana tribe was hostile to the newcomers from the start, and there were early reports of Chinese miners missing, believed murdered. Over the next three years, there were increasing reports of isolated European diggers being murdered, and in 1873 the hundred remaining people in the little township of Gilberton abandoned the settlement when the local Aboriginal people 'systematically attacked' it and killed two of the people in the town.[49]

The numbers of diggers on the fields of north Queensland were already dwindling by the early 1870s, as everywhere the easily available alluvial gold was being mined out and operations were being taken over by the big steam-operated quartz crushers. Then, in 1873, news spread down through Queensland of a spectacular gold discovery on the Palmer River, more than 700 kilometres north of Charters Towers and 2000 kilometres north of Brisbane, which caused yet another stampede.

CHAPTER ELEVEN

The Palmer River

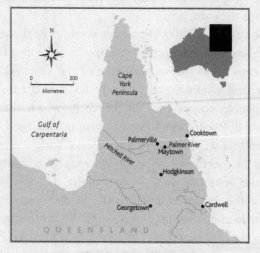

The Palmer River diggings

In every camp along the beach for two miles was unmistakable
evidence of wholesale cannibalism; heaps of human bones
and skulls were found besides the fires at which they had
been cooked. Lumps of half eaten human flesh was found
in the gins' dilly bags . . . They are of the most ferocious
expression of countenance, and are large and powerful men.

The Palmer River gold rush was one of the wildest, most lawless and most dangerous gold rushes the world had ever seen. It was characterised by mountainous terrain, hundreds of kilometres of jungle track, violent Aboriginal people, alleged cannibalism, a dry season in which a man could die of thirst and a wet season that would wash away entire settlements to leave stranded men to starve to death.

The Palmer is 2000 kilometres north of Brisbane, deep in the heart of the tropics on Cape York Peninsula. The river runs from the western side of the Great Dividing Range and winds for 200 kilometres through the most inhospitable country to the Mitchell, which flows for another 200 kilometres before opening into the Gulf of Carpentaria on the western side of Cape York.

The far north-east coast of Queensland is Australia's, and one of the world's, wettest places. On the western side of the mountains, where the Palmer flows, almost the entire annual rainfall of around 180 centimetres falls during the four-month wet season of high summer. For the rest of the year, the rivers and streams dry up and there is little running water.

As well as extreme environmental conditions, the Palmer also brought together the most volatile mixture of peoples yet seen on the Australian goldfields, including desperate Europeans hardened from years of gold hunting in the south of Australia, hostile Aboriginal tribes and the Chinese, who for the first time would become the majority on an Australian goldfield.

The opening of the Palmer River fields came as the direct result of the Queensland Government's efforts to find more gold, which had already pulled the colony back from the brink of bankruptcy and set it on a course of prosperity.

A number of explorers had already been to Far North Queensland when, in 1872, the government commissioned a search for gold in the remote far north of the colony.[1] The man chosen to lead the search was William Hann, an experienced explorer, pastoralist and farmer who, with his brother Frank, had come from Victoria to run a cattle station near the Burdekin River, which was then one of the most northerly settlements in Queensland, about a thousand kilometres north of Brisbane. Hann was asked by the government to explore 'as far north as the 14th parallel of latitude, the character of the country and its mineral resources with a view to future settlement and occupation'.[2]

Hann's team of explorers included a geologist, Norman Taylor, a botanist, Dr Thomas Tate, a surveyor, Frederick Warner, a couple of hands and a local Aboriginal guide named Jerry. They also took 25 horses and provisions for five months, which included 20 sheep 'on the hoof' for food.

They left Fossilbrook, an outstation of Mount Surprise, in central north Queensland, on horseback on 26 June 1872 and headed north towards Cape York Peninsula, where they crossed the Lynd and Tate Rivers before reaching the Mitchell, which they followed upstream. In early August, they found another river running into the Mitchell that Hann named the Palmer after the then Queensland premier, Arthur Palmer.[3]

On one occasion, they were attacked by a local Aboriginal tribe, which they warded off with gunfire. This was the first of many hostile incidents between the local inhabitants and the intruders on the Palmer that would become increasingly violent over the coming years.

Late on the afternoon of 5 August, the surveyor Frederick Warner found a small quantity of gold embedded in a piece of granite while prospecting down on the banks of the Palmer River. Hann said he had offered a small reward as an incentive to the first man to find it:

> [I] had offered a reward of half a pound of tobacco to any person who would find gold; early in the day Mr. Warner returned from a prospecting walk . . . [and] claimed the 'weed' at the same time, showing me the gold in the dish.[4]

The explorers were not overly excited about the discovery, and, after another ten days of looking for more, Hann said they abandoned the search.[5] After leaving the Palmer River, they headed north-east through swampy and mosquito-infested territory, reaching the mouth of the Endeavour River on 21 September.

Along the way, Hann had recorded another incident when they used their guns to shoot the local Aboriginal men, who they thought were threatening them:

> We saw them coming from all directions in front of us, and all with bundles of spears, but, how many natives there were we could not say . . . As they kept advancing in great numbers, it was now time to show them we were not to be trifled with; so two of the party fired upon them at a long distance, to endeavour to check their advance.[6]

After leaving the Endeavour River, the party turned south and began their journey home, which was more difficult as their rations were diminishing every day and water becoming scarce, as it was nearing the end of the eight-month dry season. They arrived back at Saint George on 12 November after being away for nearly five months.

The explorers did not claim the gold they found was worth much. The botanist Tate recorded in his diary that 'the prospects we obtained were certainly not payable and did not average more than two grains to the dish'.[7] In his report to the government in early 1873, Hann was guarded about the gold discovery and said he would 'caution any but experienced, well provided bushmen against coming there to prospect'.

Back on the goldfields on the Etheridge River, 700 kilometres to the south of the Palmer, where the pickings from gold mining were becoming slimmer, the suggestion of a new untouched gold prospect was too much for some. Within a couple of months, a 35-year-old gold-mining veteran, Irishman James Venture Mulligan, had organised with five mates to leave Georgetown and head north to check out the Palmer.[8]

Mulligan had arrived in Australia from Ireland in 1860 and worked in the Victorian goldfields before moving north to Armidale in New South Wales. There, he opened a butcher's shop and mined for gold in the nearby Peel River.[9] He went to Queensland to join the rush at Gympie in 1867, then to Gilberton in 1871, before moving on to the Etheridge.

Mulligan and his team left Georgetown on 3 June 1873 and began by retracing Hann's tracks northwards through 'desert country of the roughest and poorest description'[10] to the Tate River and Walsh River, where they headed north, taking a short cut directly towards the Palmer.

When they crossed the Walsh River, they were followed

by hundreds of Aboriginal tribesmen, and Mulligan recorded the first of many of his encounters with the locals:

> The first night the blacks tried to burn us out . . . Some of our party were fishing, the rest of us were pitching tents, when a few darkies showed themselves on the opposite side of the river, stretching their necks up out of the long grass like wild fowl, once in a while, to scrutinize our camp. Soon after the grass was set on fire a few yards above the camp on our side. Simultaneously it was fired on from the opposite side . . . they brandished their spears, threw big stones down the hill at us, cooeying and gesticulating in the most excited manner. We took precautions and burned the grass around our camp, looked after our horses and examined our firearms. After this we kept night watch.[11]

On reaching the Palmer, Mulligan and his mates started to find alluvial gold in their pans almost immediately.[12] Over the next week, they collected about six ounces of gold before Peter Abelsen made a cradle from the local softwood and soon they were finding plenty more.

Mulligan recorded that, by 24 August, their supplies were nearly exhausted.[13] Carrying more than a hundred ounces of gold, which they had collected along 64 kilometres of the river, they decided to return to Georgetown, report their find and then come back to continue mining.

Back in Georgetown, Mulligan's return after three months away created great excitement, particularly when the local gold warden, Howard Saint George, inspected the gold and posted a sign on the outside of his bark office that read 'J. V. Mulligan reports the discovery of payable gold on the Palmer River. Those interested may inspect at this office the 102 ounces he has brought back.'[14]

By the time news of the finds had arrived in Brisbane from Cardwell, which was then the most northerly port in the state, all of Queensland was abuzz and gold miners in the south were already packing their bags and heading as fast as they could for the Palmer.

Mulligan tried to alert the diggers to the special dangers of gold mining in the Tropical North, and in what was to be a prophetic letter he wrote to the *Queenslander* newspaper to warn about the risks of being stranded in the wet season:

> Already exaggerated accounts and too much excitement exist here. If people rush the place without rations they will perish, for there is no getting back in the wet season across the rivers that lie between.[15]

But the lure of the gold was too much, and hundreds of desperate miners, fearing that the bounty would be taken before they reached the Palmer, were soon on their way. As Mulligan left Etheridge on 15 September to rejoin his mates on the Palmer, he was followed by a large crowd of about a hundred, including some women and children, with 300 horses, who were determined to use him as their guide to the gold.

Three days later, nearly all 400 people in Georgetown 'have left, or are about to leave for Palmer',[16] and the recently established gold town of Charters Towers and the port of Townsville were almost emptied of their populations.[17]

On 20 October, the police sub-inspector of Georgetown

reported that already a crisis was developing as there was no food at the Palmer and the road was unsuitable for transporting supplies:

> There are 600 men on the Palmer and a good deal more en route to the diggings. No rations whatsoever are to be bought, and there is only eight tons of flour in transit by horse teams. The road is impassable for bullock drays on account of there being seventy miles [113 kilometres] of broken, slaty country. A first class horse team was six days travelling seventeen miles [27 kilometres]. Supplies for the police have been on the road now for five weeks and barely half way there yet.[18]

Those who could afford them took packhorses or hired carts, but most took only what they could carry on their backs. A typical digger carried a swag of 70 to 90 pounds, which included a blanket, some clothes, a pick, a pan and some flour, tea and sugar. Few heeded the warnings that nothing could be bought on the Palmer and trusted to fate that they would be able to find food as they went.

As had been the case in the earlier goldfields in the south, most of the Europeans carried guns for hunting and also for their own security – but here they would be used more for the killing of the Aboriginal natives, the Chinese and each other.

Meat was again the cheapest and most readily available food, which could be brought into the goldfields on the hoof. However, the demand from the growing number of hungry miners who had brought too little food quickly pushed the price of the limited available cattle from £7 to £10 and finally to £30.[19]

Some tried hunting for food, but, as Mulligan was to complain, 'the fish will not bite . . . and the birds are scarce and . . . hard to kill'.[20] The miners were also reluctant to move too far away from their camp for risk of encountering hostile local natives.

The natives also aggravated the food shortage by setting alight bush fires to burn the grass that was needed as fodder for the bullock drays that were trying to bring in supplies.

These local Aboriginal tribes were less nomadic than the tribes from the south and resented the intrusion and disruption caused by the newcomers. They tended to make permanent camps on high ground but near reliable sources of water. James Mulligan said that they built huts in the shape of marquees covered with tea-tree bark and straw rope, which were designed to protect them from mosquitoes:

> They do not like being put off their fishing grounds on the river . . . and they determined to keep possession of the back grounds, so they have cleared the gullies of diggers two or three times. One lad got speared in the foot, and a horse was speared in three places. He was still living and some of the spear broken in him.[21]

Yet, despite all the hardships, the diggers kept coming, and many found large amounts of alluvial gold. Within a few weeks, the tent township began spreading down the banks of the Palmer River and up the tributary creeks, which were given such names as Oaky, McLeod's, Greasy Bill's, Stony, McGann's, White Horse and Sweeny's.[22]

The first little township, Palmerville, that sprang up

on the banks of the river soon had a one-room pub and a store in the middle, which had a dirt floor and was made of a rough timber frame with walls and roof of bark. The first substantial building was a log lock-up, built by an Aboriginal police detachment under the supervision of a sergeant sent up from Etheridge.

From the start of the rush to the Far North, the Queensland Government was aware of the need to supply the growing number of diggers and began looking to establish a port on the Far North coast that would be more accessible than the overland route from the south. In September 1873, it appointed 49-year-old George Elphinstone Dalrymple, who had already led a number of northern exploration parties, to head up an expedition to find the site for a suitable port. Dalrymple was asked to survey 'all rivers, inlets etc between Cardwell and the Endeavour River, and ascertain how the . . . rivers are navigable for small craft'.[23]

Pastoralist, experienced navigator, explorer, politician and adventurer George Augustus Frederick Elphinstone Dalrymple was the tenth son of Lieutenant Colonel Robert Dalrymple of Aberdeen. In his 20s, young George had left Scotland to become a tea planter in Ceylon before moving on to Australia in 1857, where he became a pastoralist in the Darling Downs in southern Queensland. For many years, he actively promoted the exploration and opening up of the north and in 1859 had published 'Proposals for the Establishment of a New Pastoral Settlement in Northern Australia'. In the 1860s, he was the state's colonial secretary and a member of the Queensland Legislative Council.

Sailing with two chartered cutters, the *Coquette* and the *Flying Fish*, Dalrymple took over a month exploring the coast before they reached the Endeavour River. On 20 October, when they landed at Trinity Bay, which is north of current-day Cairns, Dalrymple made an early claim of cannibalism by the local tribes, which would be made more frequently later by gold miners on the Palmer River. He described how the local Aboriginal people blocked his landing party and were 'poised' to throw their spears when the order was given to shoot them. After the explorers had scared the locals away, they examined their camps:

> In every camp along the beach for two miles [3.2 kilo-metres] was unmistakable evidence of wholesale cannibalism; heaps of human bones and skulls were found besides the fires at which they had been cooked. Lumps of half eaten human flesh was found in the gins' dilly bags . . . They are of the most ferocious expression of countenance, and are large and powerful men.[24]

They reached the Endeavour River on 24 October, but the next morning, before they could conduct a study of the site, the Australasian Steam Navigation Company's *Leichhardt* steamed into the river and unloaded more than a hundred eager prospectors from Bowen, Townsville and Cardwell who were in a hurry to get to the Palmer. The *Leichhardt* was the first of hundreds of ships that would come, and so, before the government could make a decision, the settlement of Cooktown was established.[25] Dalrymple described how the previously tranquil spot was hurriedly transformed:

> On the day before [Friday] we had sailed into a silent,

lonely, distant river mouth with thoughts going back a century to the arrival of the brave navigator, its discoverer, its people, in knee breeches, three cornered hats, and small swords, pigtails and silver shoe buckles. On Saturday we were in the middle of a phase of enterprise peculiarly characteristic of the present day – of a young digging township – men hurrying to and fro, tents rising in all directions, horses grazing and neighing for their mates, all around us – the shouts of sailors and labourers landing more horses and cargo, combined with the rattling of a donkey-engine, cranes and chains.[26]

The first major party of 108 prospectors left Cooktown for the Palmer on 28 October 1873. Most did not have horses and carried their 70- to 90-pound swags of tools and supplies on their backs.[27] They were followed by about 20 Chinese, who were not allowed to join the party but kept close and brought up the rear.

Although the trek to the Palmer was much shorter from Cooktown than from Georgetown in the south, it was still a difficult and dangerous journey, particularly with the coming of the wet season and a number of rivers to cross. Sixty kilometres from Cooktown, the eager diggers crossed the Normanby River and, after another 60 kilometres, the Laura River before reaching a steep rocky pass – which earned the name 'Hell's Gate' – that led down to the Palmer River.

Early in the morning of 5 November, the prospectors' camp west of the Normanby River and on the way to the Palmer River was surrounded and attacked by more than 200 Aboriginal people. Two miners had been chased back to the camp and had given the alarm, which allowed for the hasty erection of barricades shortly before the onslaught. In the first wave of the assault, about 20 of the natives were wounded or killed by the guns of the white men, while the spears lobbed over the barricades managed to inflict only a few injuries. The encounter, which gave the place the name of Battle Camp, was the first of many violent run-ins on the track between Cooktown and the Palmer.

Mulligan said that, very soon, 'the whole of the Palmer River had . . . become a living mass of men scattered all over the country',[28] and already the diggings were regarded as the richest and most extensive ever found in Queensland.[29]

By November, the wet season was about to arrive, and the new warden at the Palmer, Howard Saint George, reported that food was already short and no more miners should try to reach the goldfield until the end of the rains:

No one should on any account attempt to come here before April next year. Rains will come on by Christmas when all travelling must cease. Many now here must clear before the rain because they will find it impossible to get rations. Besides, the gold now being found is all in the bed of the river and all the work there must cease with the first rain.[30]

Few of the miners who came up from the south had any notion of the power and the devastation of the wet season, which totally transformed the Palmer. When the rain came, it swept over the region like a blanket, blotting out the hills and hammering down in a blinding torrent that turned everything to mud. Within minutes, dry riverbeds were flooded by raging torrents and mining sites were suddenly swept away by the rising river.

Most of the estimated 200 men who tried to return to Cooktown with the onset of the rains had practically no food left. James Venture Mulligan, who had made the original gold finds, was now back with his mates and described the desperate situation facing many of the diggers:

> When we started from the Palmer there were about 200 leaving, and most of the others were waiting for the last moment, trying to get all they could before the wet. As soon as the rain sets in they will have to leave the river and try the gullies and terraces, as the Palmer has every indication of being a large river. It is nearly 200 yards [183 metres] wide, and high water mark is [4.5 metres]. Of the 200 leaving, many have not a pound of flour; in fact, I do not know how they will get down. There are three large rivers to cross and, if caught by the rain, they can neither go forward nor back. Rations and supplies are almost exhausted.[31]

Many of the diggers arrived back in Cooktown with no food or money and needed the Queensland Government to subsidise the shipping to get them back to the south.

Back at the Palmer, where gold was being found in good quantity, many stayed in the field, even though their rations were depleted and the onset of the wet would make it impossible to get out or to get any fresh supplies in.

During the first wet, men guarded their supplies with guns, and hungry miners ate horses, snakes and even pet dogs. Dysentery and typhoid attacked and killed many, both at the Palmer and on the road out towards Cooktown.

As the first of the rains arrived, more than 40 cartloads of supplies coming overland from the south 'of every sort and size'[32] were unable to cross the flooding Mitchell, and on the south bank of the river a village of the stranded emerged with men, women and even small children having to wait till the end of the wet. At the same time, there were an estimated thousand people stranded on the road from Cooktown to the Palmer, unable to go forward or back.[33]

One of those was Thorvald Weitemeyer, the Danish grog-store owner from Ravenswood who was robbed of all his takings before heading for the Palmer River. When he had begun his journey about a thousand kilometres to the south in Townsville, he said he had heard that getting to the Palmer would be difficult:

> To go to the Palmer at that time was easier said than done. The Palmer goldfields lay somewhere in a totally unexplored country, and none had been known to reach the Palmer from the Cape after the commencement of the wet season. Many unsuccessful attempts had been made, and the returning parties spoke loudly of the 'impossibilities' on the road, such as the swollen rivers, swamps, marshes, mountains, blacks, and what not besides, and what seemed to me to be the worst, no supplies of any kind were to be found on the field.[34]

At the time, there were so many desperate to go to the Palmer that there were not enough steam ships available to take them, but Weitemeyer was able to find a passage on an overcrowded schooner by paying the inflated price of £5 for each of his horses and two pounds ten shillings for himself. He described how, after leaving Townsville, the passengers found themselves sailing into a hurricane, which was common in the wet season:

> There was accommodation below decks for about forty horses . . . On the deck was accommodation for as many passengers as could find standing room . . . A strong wind was blowing . . . until at last it blew a perfect hurricane . . . The horses of course suffered. At one time they would stand nearly on their heads . . . their masters were, for the most part, lying in a hopeless condition up on the deck . . . The horses began to die . . . and to haul the poor dead brutes up and throw them overboard took us all our time, seeing that very few of us were capable of such work.[35]

Weitemeyer said that during the storm they saw another ship, the *Lord Ashley*, trying to reach Cooktown, bashed and flying a distress signal:

> [The] heavy deck cargo caused the ship to rock that it looked as if it were capsizing every time it lurched over. Two of her masts were already overboard . . . the people were engaged in throwing the horses overboard alive . . . we . . . could give no assistance.[36]

Only 16 of the 40 horses on Weitemeyer's ship were alive when it reached Cooktown, which he described as wild:

> There were some thousands of people all camped in tents. Those who intended to start businesses in Cooktown had pegged out plots of ground in the main street and run up large tents or corrugated iron structures in which all sorts of merchandise was sold cheap enough . . . All the loafers,

pickpockets, and card sharpers seemed to have trooped in from Brisbane, Sydney, and Melbourne . . . and the robbing of tents seemed to be a daily occurrence . . . [There were] many destitute and good for nothing people . . . there was also a great deal of sickness, especially dysentery, and the doctors required cash down. It was a common sight to see men lying helpless, writhing in pain on the ground, some of them bellowing out for pity or mercy . . . Men would pass such a poor object with the greatest of apathy.[37]

Weitemeyer then ignored all the advice to wait for the dry season, and he set off with hundreds of others:

At the eight mile [13 kilometre] there was a large camp of diggers, who said they could get no further nor get back to Cooktown. I should have remained there; but as I saw next morning some preparing to go a little further, I started with them.[38]

The journey proved hugely difficult from the start, and early on he was forced to destroy a horse that had become bogged in the mud:

The whole road so far, almost ever since I left Cooktown, was strewn with clothes, boots, saddles, rations, in such quantities that would have made enough to have opened a good store . . . I met scores of men, who, having thrown everything away, were struggling to reach Cooktown again on foot.[39]

At the first major river, the Normanby, which is only 60 kilometres from Cooktown and only a quarter of the way to the Palmer River, the rising water level made it impossible to cross, and Weitemeyer was forced to camp there till it subsided. On the other side of the river, there was a camp of returning diggers who were ill and starving:

> On the banks of the Normanby River, there was at the time a sight . . . I doubt if fiction could invent anything more strange . . . Several hundred men were camped on the north side of the river waiting for the flood to subside so they might get over. We had rations in any quantity . . . On the other side of the river was an equally large camp. The men there were the diggers who, when the first news of the Palmer broke out, had, before the wet season set in, gathered to the 'rush' from the Etheridge, Gilbert, Charters Towers, Cape and other outlying places, and who, having eaten their rations and gathered their gold, were now trying to reach Cooktown to purchase supplies. A perfect famine was raging over there.[40]

Weitemeyer said that the two sides looked helplessly at each other, one with plenty of food and the other with no food but plenty to pay for it:

> There we were, looking across at one another – they shaking their gold-purses at us, and we showing them the flour bags.[41]

In desperation, two hungry men stripped off their rags of clothes and strapped them to horses before forcing the horses into the raging current, which dragged them downstream. 'Getting hold of the tail with one hand and swimming with the other', they somehow both managed to cross, 'but it looked so desperate an undertaking that the others did not venture'.[42]

Weitemeyer said the two miners brought the first reliable news from the Palmer for some months, and among all the news of great gold finds there was also personal tragedy:

Among the tales of suffering . . . was that of one of my shipmates who, while looking for gold in one of the tributaries of the Palmer, had been cut off from the main camp by the river rising so that he could not cross to get away . . . His dead body was found in his tent . . . He had died of hunger, yet under his head was a bag with eighteen pounds' weight of gold found in it.[43]

Weitemeyer said that they passed their time stranded on the riverbank as best they could. Among them was a band of musicians, and Weitemeyer joined them with his flute, which he always carried with him:

It really seemed strange, in the heart of the wilderness, to hear strains of Strauss or Offenbach.[44]

In the hot, wet weather, the campers suffered from mosquitoes at night and flies during the day. When the rains eventually eased and the river levels began to fall, the prospectors crossed the Normanby and resumed their trek to the Palmer – except Weitemeyer, who said he had seen enough:

When the weather settled and people began to cross the river I had a good look at the poor emaciated fellows who came across, some of them with very little gold, and all of them more or less broken in health. Then I began to ask myself whether the game was worth the candle . . . [so] instead of going on towards the Palmer I sold my rations for a good piece and returned to Cooktown.[45]

Back on the coast, Cooktown was swelling with newcomers still anxious to get to the goldfields. By February 1874, only four or five months since Mulligan's find had become known, there were already more than 3000 people either in Cooktown or struggling to reach the Palmer.

Cooktown was booming and would soon become Queensland's second busiest port, after Brisbane. It had now been officially chosen by the Queensland Government as a base for its administration of the Palmer goldfields, and more and more ships laden with gold miners were arriving from the southern ports of Australia and from overseas.

By the end of 1874, the town had 300 permanent residents, and galvanised iron and weatherboard shacks were already replacing many of the tents that made up the township. Amid the buildings was a new weatherboard brothel owned by 'Palmer Kate', who had with her about a dozen young prostitutes from the south.[46]

Within only a couple of months of the new year, hundreds of buildings had sprung up along the three-kilometre-long Charlotte Street, which ran from the wharves to the beginning of the Palmer Road. During the dry season, the town was hot and dusty, and during the wet its streets became deep in mud.

On a visit to Cooktown, Mulligan said he was 'surprised to see the magnitude of it', a town of thousands of

people and 'in full swing'.[47] The township had more than
63 hotels and 20 eating houses, 32 stores, six butchers, five
bakers, three tinsmiths, four tent-makers, six hairdress-
ers, seven blacksmiths and a number of doctors, chemists,
boot-makers and saddlers. It also had a customs house,
banks and a post office. At night, the main street lit up
from end to end with the kerosene lamps that burned in
the pubs, dance halls, gambling dens and brothels.[48]

Not everyone was enjoying success in Cooktown,
which was also the last refuge of the failed diggers who
had survived the return from the Palmer with no gold, no
money and nowhere to go. Many of the impoverished that
could not find work were reduced to moving around the
tents begging for food.[49] As the *Queenslander* newspaper
recorded, the town was also full of illness, disease and
death:

> Impure drinking-water coupled with warm, though
> not excessively hot, weather and a badly chosen site for
> settlement, are the chief causes of this unpleasant result.
> Charlotte Street . . . skirts the mangrove-margined slimy
> river bank for more than half a mile. The humid air
> hereabouts is very oppressive, and would seem sufficient
> to account for a great deal more sickness than Cooktown
> has ever yet experienced.[50]

At the end of 1875, dysentery reached epidemic propor-
tions, and in the absence of a hospital the police station
was filled with the sick and the dying.[51]

It was early in the new year of 1875 that the first
shipload of Chinese miners arrived from China on the
Victoria. A small number of Chinese who were already in

Australia had been on the first ship from Townsville the previous October, but by Christmas an estimated 2000 Chinese were either on the Palmer or on their way there.

Now that news of the gold had reached China, thousands more would come over the next two years, so that the Palmer would become the first goldfield in Australia where the Chinese would outnumber the Europeans. By the end of 1875, the gold warden on the Palmer, Sellheim, reported that the Chinese already outnumbered the Europeans by a ratio of more than three to one,[52] and Mulligan would complain that by the end of the decade the lower Palmer 'was literally swarming with Chinese . . . [for] . . . a distance of about 150 miles [241 kilometres]'.[53]

To reach the goldfields, the Chinese carried everything themselves, and, unlike the Europeans, only a few carried guns:

> They trudged jauntily along in Indian file with their giant cane hats up to three feet [nearly one metre] in diameter, their scant habiliments, and bare occasioned feet, carrying on their bamboos ponderous loads of provisions and tools and household goods sufficient to crush into the earth the most sturdy of our own countrymen.[54]

The Chinese shared out their loads, with each specialising in what he would carry. The responsibility of each member to the rest of the group allowed for few if any personal effects:

> One, perhaps, would be freighted with rice only – 100 or 150 pounds of it – while another carried some half

a dozen iron buckets and a cradle at one end of his bamboo balanced with a dozen sheet iron metal plates and a gun that might have seen service in the American revolutionary war at the other end. Others again groaned under perfect donkey-loads of picks and shovels and dishes and tents and utensils of all kinds together with innumerable sundries packed in their own neatly constructed wickerwork baskets and fixed to their long bamboos in every conceivable fashion in order to arrive at a just equilibrium.[55]

Once they reached the Palmer, the Chinese demonstrated the same efficiency they had shown on the southern gold-fields. They lived frugally and survived on fewer provisions than the Europeans. They worked hard and were happy to take over abandoned claims and rework the soil more thoroughly to find the gold missed the first time around. The hard work paid off, and it is estimated that in each of the boom years of 1876 and 1877 more than 50,000 ounces of gold was officially sent back to China, while even more was smuggled out to evade customs duty.[56]

Despite the successes, many of the Chinese experienced the same hardships and failures as every other digger – and, according to reports from the Palmer, they were dying at a much higher rate than the Europeans from typhoid, dysentery, scurvy and leprosy.[57] This led the newly established *Cooktown Herald* to report in early 1876 that large numbers of the Chinese were starving and unable to find gold:

A gentleman who arrived in town yesterday from the Palmer informs us that the district is overrun with destitute

Chinese in a state of starvation, wandering here and there, unable to obtain the necessities of life, and that they are committing wholesale robberies for bare subsistence.[58]

The *Queenslander* reported that the sick Chinese were being brought into the nearest settlement on the Palmer River and abandoned by their colleagues, 'leaving them to their fate'.[59] And, in 1878, the paper reported that many of the Chinese had been reduced to eating grass for want of food.[60]

There were also reports that the Chinese were especially susceptible to cannibalism by the local Aboriginal people. James Mulligan said that many of the Chinese were caught by the Merkin tribes at the rocky entrance to the Palmer called Hell's Gate, where 'the Blacks carried away the Chinese wholesale and ate them'.[61]

The Chinese in Far North Queensland would experience the same persecution and violence from white diggers that had occurred in the southern Australian goldfields. When gold was discovered at the junction of Sandy Creek and Oaky Creek, a sign was nailed to a tree that read, 'Any Chinaman found further up this creek will be instantly seized and hanged until he is dead'.[62]

The Chinese were also despised by many local government officials. In 1876, William R. Hill, who was the gold warden at the township of Bryerstown, which had sprung up on the Palmer, described how he would arrest more than a hundred at a time for evading paying their mining-licence fee:

The wily Chinkey tried to use every dodge to evade payment . . . I had on several occasions to round up and arrest mobs of them, from one hundred and one hundred and fifty, escort them miles to my camp . . . retaining their swags until they found the ten shillings . . . I carried a long light chain on a pack horse with seventy five pairs of handcuffs attached, so I had 'accommodation' for one hundred and fifty, and on camping we opened one part of the chain and secure the lot round a tree.[63]

Soon, there were public meetings in Cooktown passing resolutions calling on the government to 'consider the desirability of preventing the influx of Chinese on the northern goldfields'.[64]

On 25 April 1875, the *Cooktown Herald* reflected the prevailing paranoia:

This immigration has many features which distinguish it from any previous Mongolian rush in colonial history. Cooktown is situated so near the great ports that empty out their surplus coolies into neighbouring countries, the facilities for reaching the gold diggings are so unusual, the expense is so comparatively slight that, apart from other considerations, it is a small wonder that John Chinaman is hurrying here, with his stick and his baskets filled with pots and pans, as fast as he can.

By the following year, in May 1876, the campaign against the Chinese had become even more emotive when the *Cooktown Herald* forecast widespread violence unless measures were taken to rid the Far North of the Chinese:

It is no longer a question of repelling a coming invasion, so much as to defend, not alone our hearths and homes, but our very lives against the invaders who swarm around us. The danger is imminent and deadly, and unless the most strenuous measures be at once taken, it may ere too long, one of the most disastrous and bloody chapters in Australian history will have to be recorded.[65]

With the news that another 800 Chinese had arrived on the *Singapore* and the *Adria*, James Venture Mulligan, the man who started the Palmer rush, moved a resolution at a public meeting in Cooktown calling for a stop to the arrival of any more:

> that this meeting views with apprehension the anticipated arrival of large numbers of Chinese on our northern goldfields and the imminent danger of serious collisions, and is of the opinion that it is desirable to bring the matter under the notice of the Government.[66]

The local businessman F. W. J. Beardsmore, who had rented the Cooktown wharves from the government, introduced his own poll tax on the newly arriving Chinese. Every newly arrived man from China was roped in on the wharf and not allowed to land without paying the £1-per-head tax. The Chinese of course protested, and few had the money to pay the tax anyway, but their provisions were confiscated until local Chinese businesses under protest paid the levy. No one questioned Beardsmore's right to impose and collect the tax.[67]

By the end of March 1875, there were already 5000 Chinese on the Palmer or on their way from Cooktown. The following year, in response to growing hostility towards the Chinese, the Queensland Parliament passed a law similar to those passed in earlier decades in Victoria and New South Wales, to restrict Chinese migrants coming to the goldfields.

During the parliamentary debates, Member of Parliament Mr P. McLean, who had spent several years mining in the goldfields, told the parliament of the feelings of bitterness towards the Chinese:

> Whenever a Chinaman appeared upon a gold field, every chance of a European making a livelihood was lost forever . . . Whenever a number of Chinamen put in an appearance on a gold field, all of the water was at once taken up, and in a short time it was not only rendered unfit for cooking, but also for Europeans' gold-washing. Therefore, in defense of themselves, the Europeans had to chase the Chinese away . . . Something must be done with the Chinese in this colony. They did not consume the same articles as the Europeans, nor contribute the same amount of taxation to the revenue, and it was only reasonable that by some means or other they should be made to pay their fair share.[68]

Parliament passed The Chinese Immigrants Regulation Act 1877 in August, which provided for a poll tax – to be collected by the masters of the ships – for each of the disembarking Chinese. When the measures did not seem severe enough to be stopping the inflow of migrants, the Act was later amended so that ships could only bring in one Chinese migrant for every 50 tons of the vessel.[69] At the same time, the poll tax was increased to £30 per head.

As had happened more than 20 years earlier in Victoria, an attempt was made to evade the tax, and many Chinese were unloaded from their ships at other ports than Cooktown. Some were taken up the Bloomfield River, some 50 kilometres south of Cooktown, to walk the 240 kilometres to 'China Camp' at Bryerstown on the Palmer. Others were landed at Cape Tribulation, about 95 kilometres south of Cooktown, which left a trek of a little over 300 kilometres to the Palmer River.[70]

By the end of the year, the mining warden at the Palmer River, P. F. Sellheim, reported that 'the provision of the new legislation regulating Chinese immigration have considerably diminished the number'.[71] But for many shopkeepers and traders, it seemed that the only problem greater than having too many Chinese was having too few, and it was quickly noticed that the falling numbers were hurting the local economy. By early 1878, European storekeepers at Maytown on the Palmer were petitioning the government to complain that the mining-licence tax, which also had to be paid by the Chinese, was contributing to the decline in their numbers and should be reduced.

But by now, the Palmer was already in decline anyway. The roaring days had been in 1875 and 1876, and by the end of the 1870s most of the alluvial gold had been worked out. What helped extend the life of the gold boom in the Far North for a short time was the discovery of the new field at Hodgkinson. Having witnessed the boost that the Palmer River goldfields had given to the Far North, the Queensland Government decided in 1875 to sponsor another expedition to find gold.

To head the expedition, they selected James Venture Mulligan. With £500 of government money, Mulligan and his team, which included Frederick Warner, who had originally found gold on the Hann expedition to the Palmer

338

three years earlier, left Cooktown at the end of April 1875 and headed south-west. When they reached the Mitchell River, they spent the next few weeks going upstream and 'passed through land where no white man had passed through, and wherein no white man dwelt'.[72]

While travelling along the Lynd River, they saw the charred remains of humans, but Mulligan did not say if they were the result of some burial ritual or the victims of cannibalism:

> We came on a black's camp, and saw some mummies; some were smelling offensively. We saw where some human skulls had been burnt, but could not tell if they were of blacks or whites.[73]

After exploring for five months, they returned to Cooktown on 23 October, having found no significant gold.

Mulligan had hoped the government would provide more money, but when it would not he set out again in February 1876 'at his private expense'.[74] This time, on the junction of the Mitchell and Hodgkinson Rivers, he found what he described as 'payable gold for reefing'. The site of the new field was about a hundred kilometres south-east of the Palmer and about a hundred kilometres from the coast, and roughly the same distance from the ports of Cairns and Port Douglas.

When the explorers returned to Cooktown with their news, Mulligan warned in his report that the gold was only prevalent in reefs, and that alluvial gold was so limited it was 'only fit for Chinese'. Nevertheless, some diggers claimed that Mulligan had privately suggested there was plenty of gold for all, and yet another mad rush was under way.

In April 1876, the *Brisbane Courier* tried in vain to warn the prospectors of the dangers of mining the Hodgkinson:

> Let it be repeated to all those who have their eyes fixed in this direction, that the Hodgkinson country is almost waterless except in the main water channel, during eight months of the year . . . and water for gold washing will only be found at wide distances apart . . . No man should come who has not the means to prospect on his own account for months without reward, who is not willing to endure considerable privation and to pay exorbitant prices for everything he gets; to work patiently and uncomplainingly for but scanty returns.[75]

When Mulligan left Cooktown to return to his claim on the Hodgkinson, he was again followed by hundreds of excited prospectors hoping to be led straight to the gold. There were also hundreds waiting to follow him at Bryerstown on the Palmer River on the way there.[76]

Within hours of Mulligan's departure, the *Blackbird* arrived at the port of Cooktown to unload another 125 diggers and 45 horses. The diggers had intended to go to the Palmer but changed their plans to follow Mulligan. In the first weeks of April, more than 1200 new hopefuls with 300 horses landed at Cooktown and headed after the others to the Hodgkinson.

Arriving on the banks of the Mitchell at the end of the wet season, Mulligan wanted to wait till the flooded river subsided, but, as the *Queenslander* newspaper recorded, the mob would not hear of it:

> The great crowd forced the passage of the Mitchell in the face of no inconsiderable peril to life and limb and property, the scene . . . was indescribably exciting and ludicrous, and in all its details perhaps unparalleled in Queensland history. Imagine a confused multitude of men, mostly in a state of nudity, of horses and mules, and here and there a headgear of a woman. The atmosphere was charged with lusty vociferations in choice terms of the bullock drivers' vocabularies, with gesticulating, yelling, and whip cracking to urge through the current the poor, heavily packed animals. Others crawled their uncertain way over logs and rocks in imminent danger of their lives, had hairbreadth escapes, and lost swags innumerable.[77]

News of Mulligan's find at the Hodgkinson had also reached the Palmer, and many of the diggers who felt the gold there was becoming exhausted joined those coming down from Cooktown. Altogether, more than 2000 miners went to the Hodgkinson, which in turn stimulated the establishment of the ports of Cairns in 1876 and Port Douglas in 1877.[78]

Most of those who went in the hope of finding gold were disappointed, because, as the *Queenslander* reported in June, 'as a payable alluvial field the Hodgkinson . . . has proved an unmistakable failure', and only reef mining survived for any length of time.[79] Of those who returned to the Palmer, many found their claims had already been taken over and worked by the Chinese.

Back in Cooktown, angry diggers wanted Mulligan lynched, as they held him responsible for exaggerating the

Hodgkinson's bounty. Mulligan said he only escaped by raising his rifle at the ringleaders and threatening to shoot his way out:

> The storm gathered in the mob as they drew up towards me . . . They began to lecture me, and used all kinds of threats as to what they were going to do – lynch, hang and what not . . . On their approach to my horse I warned them not to touch his bridle. As the man that did so would get a shot through the arm, and the man that laid hands on myself would get shot through the heart.[80]

The Palmer River gold rush lasted less than ten years. Reef mining would last a few more years at both the Palmer and the Hodgkinson but was never as big as alluvial mining and accounted for only about five per cent of the total gold mined in Far North Queensland.[81]

By the early 1880s, the Palmer was finished and the diggers drifted away. A few went even further north up the Cape York Peninsula to mine for gold at Normanton, at Coen and on the Winlock River. Some went to Mount Morgan, which opened in 1882, or over to Papua New Guinea. Many drifted back to where they had come from.

The Chinese drifted away as well. The poll tax and the restriction on them working the goldfields had stemmed the inflow, but it was the exhaustion of the alluvial gold deposits that finally drove them from the Palmer. Many went home but many stayed, too, to open up stores or to become farmers.

Cooktown also dwindled to become almost a ghost town. By the 1880s, the two newspapers that had opened had closed: the *Cooktown Herald* in 1878 and the

Cooktown Courier in 1879. A railway from Cooktown to the Palmer had been started in 1884, and the first 45 kilometres of track had been laid by the end of the following year. In 1891, a railway bridge over the Laura River had been finished, but with the decline in Palmer River gold the project was abandoned and never completed.

James Venture Mulligan, who is widely regarded as starting it all, moved on and continued prospecting for many years. In 1903, at 66 years old, he married a 47-year-old widow, Fanny Maria Bulls, but was killed four years later during a brawl in Forsyth's pub in Mount Molloy.

By the end of the 1880s, Cooktown's streets were largely deserted, buildings were left in ruins and lean goats roamed Charlotte Street feeding on what scraps they could find. Most of the diggers went back to where they had come from. However, a number went across to Western Australia to follow the gold finds from the Kimberley range in the north-west then down to the Pilbara, some thousand kilometres to the south, and eventually to the last great Australian gold rush in the 1890s, in the desert regions of Coolgardie and Kalgoorlie.

CHAPTER TWELVE

The Wild West

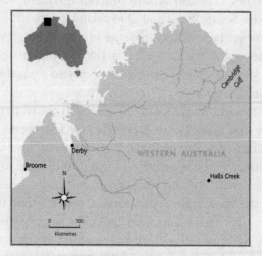

The Halls Creek diggings

The difficulties of hospital work were almost insurmountable
for lack of water . . . and in despair, when the water
supply ran out, nurses often tried to cool burning
bodies by damping the sponge in whisky or brandy; two
liquids of which Coolgardie never ran short . . .

Western Australia's first gold rush started in July 1885 when Charles Hall and a party of six prospectors found eight ounces of gold from the narrow bed of a dry river in the Kimberley[1] range, more than 500 kilometres inland from the tiny port of Derby on Australia's remote north-west coast.

Charles Hall had already worked for many years on the New South Wales and Queensland goldfields. He and his partner Jack Slattery, plus five of their mates, had gone prospecting in the Kimberley in 1885 following a government survey two years earlier that reported a possibility of gold in the region.[2]

In November, Hall, Slattery and their party arrived in Derby and headed with packhorses for four weeks along the largely dry Fitzroy River. They followed the tracks of the earlier Forest expedition to a spot they were to name Hall's Creek.[3] By Christmas, they began to find gold, but early the following year and with most of the team ill with scurvy they decided to head the 550 kilometres back to Derby to register their claim and replenish their supplies.

Hall and Slattery then sailed 2000 kilometres south to Perth to claim a reward of £500, which the Western Australian Government had offered for the discovery of payable gold in the colony back in 1872.

The news of the find resulted in hundreds and then thousands hurrying for the new El Dorado, even though the newspapers were again warning the inexperienced of the hazards of trying to reach, then survive, the region during the long, hot dry season:

No ambitious digger should attempt to reach the fields unless provided with capital and possessing a stout and manly heart to bear and overcome the difficulties. In a few weeks, almost at present, it would be inadvisable to go at all, unless with horses and provisions . . . Most of the . . . diggers are . . . strongly advised not to go until the wet season is near, as when they left they had to come five miles [eight kilometres] to get water, and that it must be fully 20 miles [32 kilometres] from where the gold is found to where there is water . . . It would be much better for those who can wait in the other colonies to do so till the next wet season.[4]

More than 10,000 people – largely men – would head for the Kimberley over the next two years, even though many were hopelessly ill-equipped for the venture. There is no reliable record of the number who died in the harsh conditions trying to cross the waterless desert or in crocodile-infested coastal waters, or who reached the goldfields only to fall foul of dysentery, scurvy, sunstroke, hunger and thirst.

At the time, the Kimberley had two small ports, Broome and Derby – neither of which was connected to the telegraph – and a scattering of sheep and cattle stations over millions of square kilometres. In the summer, the temperature exceeds 45 degrees Celsius, and in the wet season from December to March more than 500 centimetres of rain renders the rivers and creeks impassable. For the remainder of the year, the creeks and rivers dry up and there is a serious shortage of water.

By April 1886, the initial trickle of gold seekers had become a flood when the government resident in Derby, Dr Thomas Henry Lovegrove, wrote enthusiastically to the governor in Perth, Sir Frederick Napier:

I have very great pleasure in informing Your Excellency that most favourable reports have reached Derby from the goldfields. Five parties are down, all bringing alluvial gold, some more, some less; there are now something over four hundred ounces in the town. The professional diggers speak highly of the field and predict one of the largest rushes that have been seen for years.[5]

Almost as soon as the story of the great gold discovery at Halls Creek appeared in newspapers around Australia, diggers began heading there from Queensland and the Northern Territory.[6] A number of the newspapers also published a map of the Kimberley showing the 560-kilometre track to Halls Creek and what was officially named the 'Kimberley Goldfields' in 1886.

Tensions between the diggers and the local Aboriginal people soon erupted into violence, and the first fatal clash is believed to have followed the abduction of an Aboriginal woman by one of the diggers.

In June 1886, Fred Marriott was killed when he was speared through the heart. The Europeans retaliated by riding after the Aboriginal people and shooting about 40, although no rigorous inquiry was ever undertaken to assess the exact number. Police Sergeant Troy, who had gone to investigate reports that some Aboriginal people had been killed at Mary River, returned to Derby to provide one of the early reports on the state of the diggings. He said it had taken 21 days to reach the diggings and 17 to return, and he counted 268 men, 100 packhorses, 21 horse-drawn drays, seven bullock drays, 15 handcarts and 16 wheelbarrows heading for the goldfields.

From early in 1886, the first ships had begun to arrive

at Derby, and the little township began to quickly grow:

> During the past year great changes have taken place in
> this district. The population has increased, the township
> has gone ahead to a wonderful extent, and now has two
> good hotels, five stores, a blacksmith and a wheelwright
> shop, and a boot makers establishment. The new jetty is
> nearly completed.[7]

With loaded drays, it took up to five weeks to reach
Halls Creek, and already the track was littered with dead
horses, broken drays and abandoned equipment. The local
Aboriginal tribes were also making the journey more hazardous by poisoning the grass that provided feed for the
horses and bullocks.

Within a few months, an alternative route was found,
which significantly cut the overland trek to Halls Creek.
On 6 June, the *Afghan* became the first ship to pass Derby
and enter the Cambridge Gulf, near what would become
the town of Wyndham on the mouth of the Ord and
Durack Rivers. The road from Cambridge Gulf 'was hor-
ribly rough' and almost waterless in the dry season, but it
stretched for only 360 kilometres to Halls Creek compared
with 560 from Derby.

There was no food to be bought en route, and the local
flora and fauna offered little by way of sustenance, as the
Europeans were still ignorant of the bush tucker that sustained the local Aboriginal population. The situation was
partially alleviated by the fledgling farming industry in the
region, which meant there was about 12,000 head of cattle
spread through the Ord Valley.

The Halls Creek gold rush had more than its share of

misery and hardship but it also had stories of luck and hero-
ism. One involved 'Russian Jack', who abandoned his gold
mining to save an injured digger. John (Ivan) Fredericks was
born in Russia in 1864 and as a teenager arrived in New
South Wales. He wandered a number of goldfields before
heading for Halls Creek, where he pushed all of his worldly
possessions around in a wheelbarrow. In Halls Creek, there
is a statue to him inscribed with the words:

> This monument [is] to honour all the pioneers of the
> Kimberley region. 'Russian Jack' once carried a sick friend
> more than 300 kilometres in a bush made wheelbarrow
> seeking medical attention over track that exists in name
> only. His feat symbolizes the mateship and endurance of
> the pioneers of the region then lacking the communities
> of civilization. Died 1904 Perth. Impoverished. Fremantle
> Cemetery.

It is believed that by the beginning of 1887 up to 100,000
ounces of alluvial gold had been taken out of the
Kimberley goldfields before the diggings began to decline.
As more and more emaciated diggers returned to Derby
empty-handed, the positive press reports began to be
replaced with less-enthusiastic accounts:

> Most discouraging accounts still come to hand from the
> Kimberley Goldfields, in fact it is pronounced an unmitigated
> duffer, a huge failure, and it is feared that hundreds of men
> who were led there will have a bad time of it.[8]

The rush was over early in the year, and the small mud-
brick ghost town of Halls Creek, with its post office, shops

and a few houses, is all that remains. Many of the diggers went back to the southern colonies of New South Wales and Victoria, and others went to try their luck looking for gold a thousand kilometres to the south in the Pilbara ranges, about 160 kilometres east of Roebourne. Gold had been discovered there in 1888. Within a few short years, Halls Creek would be almost forgotten, with the discovery of what would be the biggest and the longest of all the Australian goldfields, almost 3000 kilometres further south in Western Australia around Coolgardie and Kalgoorlie.

The rush began when 22-year-old Arthur Bayley and his 40-year-old partner William Ford were prospecting in the remote parts of the east of the state when, on a Sunday afternoon in June 1892, Ford struck a rock with a tomahawk and found gold at what would become known as Coolgardie.

The Eastern Goldfields of Western Australia

Gold had been found elsewhere in Western Australia after Halls Creek and was being mined in small quantities in Yilgarn, north-east of Perth, when the finds of Arthur Bayley and William Ford 500 kilometres to the east sparked the rush of 1892.

When Bayley rode on horseback nearly 200 kilometres into the tiny township of Southern Cross carrying 554 ounces of gold, he would have little idea that it would be the start of gold-mining operations that would last into the modern era.[9] Within a month, John M. Finnery, the gold commissioner at Southern Cross, went with Bayley to confirm the discovery and reported that 150 prospectors had already reached Coolgardie and another 170 were on the road trying to get there.

Both Arthur Bayley and William Ford were born in Victoria. As a 16-year-old, Bayley had gone to Charters Towers in Queensland in 1881 looking for gold and then on to the Gulf of Carpentaria, where he met and teamed up with Ford.[10] In 1887, they went to Western Australia and prospected around Southern Cross but with little success.

There had been some remarkable advances in technology in the 40 years between Edward Hargraves finding gold at Ophir in 1851 and Bayley and Ford's discovery in Western Australia. Sailing ships had by now almost totally been replaced by steam, most countries had built extensive railway networks, the telegraph reduced communication time around the world from many months to a few minutes and industry, including mining, was now largely mechanised. Increasingly, modern urban households were connected with electricity, water and gas, and the first underground railways were being built.

But for all the progress elsewhere in the world, the remoteness and dryness of the goldfields of the Western Australian desert made the terrain tougher and more hazardous to reach and then mine than that of the eastern states 40 years earlier.

It has less than three centimetres of rain a year. There are no running rivers and the desert country supports very little vegetation or wildlife. More than 20 years before the discovery of gold, the explorer John Forrest, who would later become the premier of Western Australia, claimed the land had little value and was 'worthless' even for pasture.

It is unlikely that there has ever been a situation where so many people lived for so long with so little fresh water as occurred during the last decade of the nineteenth century on the Western Australian goldfields.

Coolgardie was an extremely difficult place to reach. It is more than 500 waterless kilometres from the west coast and more than 400 kilometres from the south coast of Western Australia. At the time, the railway reached only as far as Northam, less than a hundred kilometres from Perth, and beyond that there were no established roads.

Nine months after Bayley and Ford's discoveries had sparked the rush, an Irish prospector, Paddy Hannan, found even more gold 40 kilometres further east, at what was to become Kalgoorlie, which proved to be an even bigger source of gold than Coolgardie.

Hannan's find would spark a rush from the east coast of Australia and from around the world, and over the next few years gold would be discovered in a wide arc covering hundreds of kilometres to the north and east of Coolgardie and Kalgoorlie.

Among the first to join the rush were two English

aristocrats, 22-year-old David Carnegie and 24-year-old Lord Percy Douglas. Percy was the son and heir to the Marquess of Queensberry, and at the time of his arrival in Australia his younger brother Lord Alfred 'Bosie' Douglas was involved in a celebrated homosexual relationship with Oscar Wilde in London. Their father, who is credited with developing the modern rules of boxing, was outraged by his son's sexual preferences and was largely responsible for setting off the legal process that resulted in the famous prosecution, conviction and imprisonment of Oscar Wilde. Percy's travelling companion, David Carnegie, was born in London, the son of the Earl of Southesk, and educated at Charterhouse school and the Royal Engineering College before working for a short time on a tea plantation in Ceylon, where he was said to have been unhappy.

Lord Douglas and David Carnegie had planned to search for gold in the east of Australia, but when their ship arrived in the port of Albany in the south of Western Australia in September 1892 they heard the news that Bayley and Ford had discovered gold at Coolgardie only a couple of months earlier. Abandoning their earlier plans, they left the ship and headed for Perth, with the intention of joining the rush to Coolgardie.

After the 400-kilometre journey to Perth, they were unable to gather much information about the recent gold find other than being told that the long trek to the east was nearly impossible and they would 'never get there'.[11]

Carnegie said they were grateful that they at least had the money to buy horses, as most of the prospectors were walking the 550 kilometres to the diggings:

We started with one riding and one pack horse each. These

and the contents of our kitbags represented our worldly possessions, but in all this we might count ourselves lucky, for many hundreds had to carry their belongings on their backs – 'humping their bluey' as the expression is.[12]

They first made for Northam, about a hundred kilometres to the east of Perth, before following the recently completed telegraph line to York and on to the town of Southern Cross, which was 360 kilometres from Perth. Gold had been found near Southern Cross in 1888 but it had not been enough to generate the rush that was now occurring. The tiny township had been established only two years earlier, but after Bayley's discovery of gold at Coolgardie nearly 200 kilometres further to the east it soon became the 'last outpost of civilisation' and the gateway to what became known as the Eastern Goldfields of Western Australia.[13]

There was too little water for all the men and their animals heading to the goldfields, and fights were breaking out at the few watering holes along the road:

What scenes of bitter quarrels these watering places have witnessed. The selfish striving, each to help himself, the awful suffering of man and beast, horses and camels mad with thirst, and men cursing the country and themselves, for wasting their lives and strength in it.[14]

A few months after Carnegie and Lord Douglas headed out, a 34-year-old Scot, John Marshall, followed them on the road from Perth. Marshall had gone to America as a 19-year-old and fought in the Indian Wars. He later prospected in the Rocky Mountains for three years before arriving on the east coast of Australia in 1883. In 1891, after the failure of his newspaper business in Cobar, in New South Wales, he ended up in Bunbury, Western Australia.

Marshall said that when he started on his trek at the Northam railhead, there were already 2000 prospectors camped around the railway station waiting for the drought to break and for the road to be opened to Coolgardie.

With his colleagues, Marshall walked as far as Southern Cross, where they needed a police permit to go further because the limited available water on the route to Coolgardie had to be rationed. For the remaining 200 kilometres, they were only permitted to take the barest essentials:

> It was stated that we would have to obtain a passport from the warden to get water on the road between the Cross and Coolgardie. A certain number of teams were permitted to go out from Southern Cross each day, loaded with provisions. No grog, building materials, or unnecessary provisions were permitted to be carried.[15]

On the way, Marshall's party met a number of returning diggers dejected with failure, whom he described as 'living epistles of hardships and troubles . . . many of them pinched and wan, with hair prematurely grey'.[16]

The seven-day trek was made easier for Marshall because he and his mates managed to meet up and travel with an Australian who was returning to the goldfields with horses and a cart. On the way, Marshall described how most of the available water was needed for the horses and only the barest amount was left for the men to drink.

Using water for washing was out of the question, and the men were taught a new way to bathe:

> At an accommodation house on the road, where we stopped for dinner, the landlady apologised for not being able to find us water in which to wash our faces, and informed us it was usual for travellers to knock the dust off each other with a handkerchief, and wipe their faces with a hat.[17]

Marshall said the only water they were allowed with their meal at the hotel was for a cup of tea, as it all had to be carried in from more than 60 kilometres away.

Meanwhile, Carnegie and Lord Douglas reached Coolgardie. It was destined to quickly become a thriving miners' town with a population of more than 15,000, but at this time it was still only 'an open forest of eucalyptus dotted here and there with the white tents of the camps of the diggers'.[18]

The shortage of water meant that the diggers had to resort to dry-blowing to separate the gold from the alluvial soil. Dry-blowing involved using the pan in much the same way as the water-assisted method, as in moving it from side to side to cause the dust and gravel to fall or be blown over the edges, leaving the heavier gold in the grooves on the edge of the pan. Carnegie said the work was made harder by the heat:

> . . . with the thermometer at 100 degrees in the shade, with the 'dishes' so hot that they had often to be put aside to cool, with clouds of choking dust, a burning throat, and water selling at a shilling or half a crown a gallon . . .[19]

The nearest reliable source of water was carted in by horse trains or camel caravans from a well almost 60 kilometres away. Carnegie said that the water brought in could not keep up with the growing army of gold diggers arriving at the site:

> Water at this time was carted by horse-teams in wagons with large tanks on board, or by camel caravans, from a distance of thirty-six miles, drawn from a well near a large granite rock. The supply was daily failing, and washing was out of the question; enough to drink was all one thought of; two lines of men on either side of the track could daily be seen waiting for the water carts. What wild rush ensued when they were sighted. In a moment they were surrounded and taken by storm, men swarming on them like an army of ants.[20]

Towards the end of the first year, as the summer temperatures rose and the water crisis worsened, many of the desperate diggers tried to return to Southern Cross only to die of thirst on the way. Back in Coolgardie, the surviving miners were abandoning their horses through lack of water:

> It was a cruel sight in those thirsty days to see the poor horses wandering about, mere walking skeletons, deserted by their owners, for strangers were both unable to give them water, and afraid to put them out of their misery lest damages should be claimed against them.[21]

Conditions were so severe that the government's gold commissioner closed the road to and from Coolgardie.

Shortly before Christmas, not having found any gold, Lord Percy Douglas left the goldfields to try to arrange the finances 'by which our coffers might be replenished'. Carnegie stayed on, teaming up with 'an old artillery man' named Richardson, to continue digging. Richardson had appeared at Carnegie's campsite 'in a pitiable state . . . half dead from dysentery' and emaciated after being unable to keep up with his horses, which had wandered off looking for water. Carnegie and his new partner heard of a small 'soak', or well, about 20 kilometres from Coolgardie and, seeing no likelihood of rain and finding no gold, decided to take their only remaining horse and provisions into the 'silent bush'.[22]

Carnegie and Richardson were to spend Christmas in the scorching desert, where they could only escape the heat of the sun by crawling on their hands and knees into the small hut they had built out of tree branches. For Christmas dinner, which Richardson described as his worst ever, they 'swept the floor clean of ants and other homely insects' and ate a meal of dried apples and weak tea.

Carnegie continued to dig for nearly six months with no significant success, and in June the following year he returned to Coolgardie to buy more supplies, only to find the town almost totally deserted. News of Paddy Hannan's discovery of big nuggets of gold some 40 kilometres to the north-east had arrived at Coolgardie, where the finds of gold had been steadily decreasing, and almost the entire population had left on the same afternoon for Kalgoorlie. Carnegie, who was still down on his luck, decided to follow the townspeople with his new partner:

> The 'rush to Hannan's' had depopulated Coolgardie and the next day saw [us] amongst an eager train of travellers bound for a new site of fortune . . . It was now midwinter and the nights were often bitterly cold. Without tent or fly, and with hardly a blanket between us, we used to be shivering at night.[23]

While men around them found their fortune, Carnegie and his mates had no luck and after a few weeks were forced by declining supplies to abandon their search and return to Coolgardie, where some of the gang decided to split and go their separate ways.

It was while Carnegie was back at Coolgardie that the tragic gold rush to 'Siberia' occurred, in October 1893. Four men had arrived back in Coolgardie – Bob Bonner, Alec Cellis, Alec Nesbitt and Bill Frost – with more than 50 ounces of gold that they had found more than 120 kilometres north-north-west at a site that, because of its harsh and barren landscape, would become known as Siberia.

The area was not properly mapped, and the successful miners warned that there was absolutely no water. The caution was unheeded, and several hundred desperate gold seekers packed their swags and hurried off, as they did whenever a report of a big goldfield arrived in town.

The rush was to have disastrous consequences. Within weeks, failed prospectors were staggering half-dead back to town with reports of others who had already perished. On hearing that men had already died and others were struggling to return, the local gold warden John Finnery ordered a party of men with camels loaded with water to head out to rescue the stricken miners. However, when the superintendent of water, Fred Renou, reached about

600 miners camped on the road to Siberia at Moorowig, he reported that most ignored his urging to abandon the quest and return to Coolgardie. At the site itself, many of the 200 diggers already there wanted to leave but were scared they would die of thirst on the way back.

Meanwhile, back at Coolgardie, Carnegie had just about completely run out of luck and had nothing more to show for nearly a year in the desert than a few specks of gold:

> Dame fortune was good to some, but not to us, like many others, she turned a deaf ear, and after many weeks' toil we had to give up the battle, for neither food, money, nor gold had we. All I possessed was the pony, and from that old friend I could not part. The fruits of my labours, or should I say my share in them, I sent home in a letter, and a few pin's-heads of gold so sent did not necessitate any extra postage. Weary and toilworn we returned to Coolgardie.[24]

It was then that Carnegie was excited to hear that his old friend Lord Percy Douglas had returned from England to Perth, having 'come out to all appearances on top' in his battle in the financial world. He had raised the investment funds so that Carnegie could renew their gold prospecting, from which they expected 'great things'.[25]

Supported by new capital, Carnegie spent the next year with a number of different partners travelling thousands of kilometres to the north and further east, returning periodically to Coolgardie to replenish supplies.

During the months they were out in the desert, there was no water for washing or shaving, and Carnegie said that his party's only drinking water came from boiling the muddy water dug from below the hard crust of the dry lakes in a condenser:

> I joined the crowd of fortune hunters; and a queer looking crowd they were too, for every third or fourth swagman carried a small portable condenser, the boiler hanging behind him and the cooler in front; every party, whether with horses, carts or camels, carried condensers of one shape or another.[26]

Carnegie said he started his third year in the desert in the 'monotonous repetition of cooking water and hunting for "colours" which we never found'. On Christmas Day, there was a rare downpour, and he and his mates were able to celebrate by washing themselves and their clothes for the first time in six weeks:

> Even in the remote little mining camp Santa Claus did not forget us, and spread his presents, in the form of rain, on all alike. What a pleasant change to get thoroughly wet through! The storm had hardly lasted twenty minutes, but such was its violence that every little creek and watercourse was soon running, and water for weeks to come was secured and plentiful in all directions, but so local is a summer storm that five miles [eight kilometres] from the camp, no water or signs of rain were to be seen.[27]

Finally, in February 1895, Carnegie struck it rich when he walked into pieces of gold sticking out of the ground:

> It seems the simplest thing in the world to find a gold

mine . . . after you have found it. On Sunday 17 February, Paddy and I took a walk, and stepped on to an outcrop of quartz showing beautiful gold. Quite simple. Any fool can prospect.[28]

They had to wait until the next day, a Monday, to peg out their claim of about 18 acres (seven hectares), as pegging on a Sunday was still illegal. After three weeks of working the site, they decided to seek a government lease to continue mining, and it was decided that, while his mates would continue digging, Carnegie would go back to Coolgardie with the gold they had already found to buy a mining licence and more provisions.

But they were a long way from Coolgardie – almost 300 kilometres as the crow flies but more like 500 along the known tracks. Carnegie left on 4 March and decided to take the risk of trying a more direct route. On the way, he became seriously ill, not knowing at the time that he had come down with typhoid, which had become one of the biggest killers on the goldfields:

Every bone in my body ached and shot with pain. I could neither ride for more than a few minutes at a stretch; I was unable to eat, nor to drink the hot water in my canteen.[29]

Pressing on, he was saved when he came across a lone miner, who gave Carnegie a lift in exchange for helping 'with his loads'.

On reaching Coolgardie, Carnegie left the camels in the care of a local Afghan, Neel Bas, registered the mine with the gold warden and then admitted himself to the local hospital.

The concentration of a large number of men combined with the absence of water led very quickly to an unhealthy environment with no effective sewerage, and the first cases of typhoid were reported in December 1892, within three months of the discovery of gold. John Marshall described how the outside of the miners' settlement was 'one vast latrine' in which typhoid, 'that dreadful scourge of all new goldfields', became rampant and killed large numbers of men.[30] On Christmas Day 1896, when the epidemic was at its height, the *Menzies Miner* newspaper published a graphic description of the disease:

Typhoid is usually known by the patient being languid for a few days before the onset. He may first complain of a shiver, then he may vomit – often, he complains of violent headache, and usually has diarrhea. His skin is hot and dry, his tongue becomes white coated, the edges of his tongue and the tip being red, and the patient's eyes are usually bright and glassy. He often becomes deaf and stupid, raving at night . . . he has disgust for food, but often a great thirst. After a few days the abdomen becomes swollen, and is painful to the lower right side. Spots, like flea bites, often appear on the abdomen about the fifth day. He often complains of a sore throat and pains in his limbs . . . The lower half of the small bowel and the upper part of the large intestine are more or less covered with ulcers, and here is where death makes its onslaught. If one of these ulcers penetrates the bowel all is over in a few hours. Perforation or ulceration through the bowel usually occurs in the third week; it may occur at any time if the wrong food is given . . . Very few people understand this.[31]

After three weeks in the Coolgardie hospital, Carnegie went by coach to Southern Cross and then by train to Perth, where, at the home of the commandant, Colonel Flemming, he soon regained his health. Eventually, Carnegie sold his shares in his gold discovery and went home to England. A little over a year later, he returned to Australia and famously explored the inland of Western Australia from the Eastern Goldfields north to Halls Creek in the Kimberley.[32]

Carnegie was lucky to have survived his ordeal, as the death rate in the goldfields was high and was to remain so for a decade after the first discovery of gold at Coolgardie. According to the Scottish miner John Marshall, 'the number of deaths grew so great that funerals were often seen without mourners, the driver of the cart being the only one in attendance'.[33] Marshall also noticed that material from packing cases had to be used, as there was not enough wood and no one was ensuring the dead were properly buried:

> Everything was left to the undertakers, and sometimes through drink, sometimes with familiarity with death, they became callous. It was seldom that graves were sunk more than four feet [1.2 metres] deep; at times much less than that, and on occasions funeral parties had to wait till the graves were partly dug.[34]

The staff at the primitive little hospital in Coolgardie struggled, with few resources to tend to the growing number of sick and diseased men. According to Mrs Arthur Henry Garnsey, who was a nurse at the hospital, the medical staff were forced to use whisky for water and carpenters' tools for surgical instruments:

> The difficulties of hospital work were almost insurmountable for lack of water . . . the only water available was the strong salt water pumped up from the mines and put through the condensers . . . and in despair, when the water supply ran out, nurses often tried to cool burning bodies by damping the sponge in whisky or brandy; two liquids of which Coolgardie never ran short . . . The supply of surgical instruments was short, and carpenters' tools, sterilized (in a sort of a way), sometimes saved the situation. An ordinary brace and bit was in great demand for boring holes in bones, which had to be wired together. But, sad to say, in spite of our efforts and care, the death rate was very high . . .[35]

The hospital consisted of a number of long, corrugated wards built up on piles, some made solely of canvas. The nurses' quarters were two rows of hessian cloth hung from wooden-framed tents, which Garnsey complained 'gave us little protection from the dust storms, and the heat inside the camps was at times . . . suffocating'. The small hospital and the large demands on it meant there was no special treatment for anyone:

> There were no private wards. English aristocrats, Afghans, Italians, Australians, rough and tough miners, and Chinese, were side by side, in their beds.[36]

The congested hospital was made even busier by the need to care for patients with venereal diseases, which were rife in the legal brothels of the goldfields. Prostitution had come early to the goldfields, and prostitutes were among the first women to reach Coolgardie. Garnsey said that venereal disease was widespread among both the working women and their clients, and at the time it was difficult to treat:

> It hurts me to say that an entirely true picture of this wonderful mining centre must include a reference to one street on the outskirts of town . . . No description of this street is necessary . . . The keeping of a certain number of these 'houses' was allowed by law . . . The medical examinations did not keep a check on the awful disease which demands such a heavy toll. These women were frequently in hospital, brought in by their 'bosses'. A few of these unfortunates were Australians, but most were French and Japanese. The latter were such gentle things, with charming ways . . . However it was not women only who suffered, but also their 'visitors' . . . The special ward at the hospital for this kind of disease was always full, with special orderlies in attendance . . . There were several cases of suicide . . . for the cures we now use successfully were unknown then.[37]

Increasingly, as the goldfields spread across the desert, the use of camels became more common, and within a couple of years the 'ships of the desert' were widely regarded as indispensable:

> No one who has not visited it can realize the extreme aridity of Central Australia . . . Owing to the uncertain water supply . . . the camel . . . is largely taking the place of horses and bullocks for the transportation of supplies and provisions . . . The animals travel a week or more

without tasting water and thrive on bushes which sheep, horses and cattle will not touch.[38]

The camels had been brought into South Australia in the 1840s with their Afghan drivers and became a major source of transport in the development of inland Australia. The first were used to move supplies to inland farms and settlements in remote areas and for bringing back farming and mining produce to the coast for export. Then, from about the 1860s, they were increasingly used for the construction of the overland telegraph and later the building of railway lines.

Twenty-one-year-old New Zealander John Aspinal arrived on the goldfields from Dunedin in March 1895 and prospected for hundreds of kilometres around Coolgardie, Kalgoorlie, Mount Malcolm and Laverton before heading to Yerilla, some 200 kilometres north of Kalgoorlie, where he was tragically killed by lightning a year later. During his year on the goldfields, he kept a diary and provided a detailed description of the capability of the camel in that environment:

It is certainly surprising what you can pack on a camel . . . It is only necessary to see a camel loaded up with billies, buckets, picks, shovels, and other gear to recognize his general utility. There are corners and recesses all over for tying on small things and water bags are hung on his neck, giving him the appearance of a walking caravan . . . A camel is made to lie down by pulling the nose line and saying 'Hoo-ha-she-she-shah-h-h'. At this point, especially if a few Asian imprecations are added, he suddenly plumps down on his knees, and magnificently lowers the hind portion of his body. Making him get up does not require the knowledge of any barbarous language, a rousing kick in the ribs being the simplest method . . . Good camels can go about 10–12 miles [16–20 kilometres] an hour or say 100–120 miles [161–193 kilometres] a day and keep it up for several days at a stretch . . . At night the camels are turned loose [with] bells hung around their long necks.[39]

The first camel driver in Western Australia was believed to have been Mahomet Saleh, who travelled with the explorer Peter E. Warburton in 1872. Following the discovery of gold, Mahomet Saleh and his brother Tagh moved from South Australia to Western Australia and established a business carrying provisions to the Coolgardie goldfields using camels. Mahomet was a man of generous community spirit and donated money to local hospitals, fire-fighting and water-supply funds as well as making his camels and men available for search and rescue missions.

The Afghan camel drivers did not generally integrate with Europeans and tended to live in a separate part of the town, where they followed their Muslim religion and customs. Many Europeans looked down on them as 'negroes' who, by working for less pay, were holding down wage levels. The considerable discrimination against the Afghans led them eventually to protest to the governor general that they could not obtain gold-mining licences in Western Australia, were denied re-entry into the country if they visited their homeland and were unable to become naturalised Australians. Most that came to Australia were single or, if married, left their wives at home, where they hoped eventually to return, having become wealthier. Many remained single, some settled with Aboriginal women but only a few married white women.

Another of the great transport innovations of the Western Australian goldfields was the use of the bicycle. Perhaps nowhere else before or since has the bicycle been used so extensively, over such long distances and for such a variety of purposes.

The first bicycle had been introduced in Paris in the early nineteenth century, but the standard 'double diamond' frame, which became the prototype of the modern bike, was not invented until 1880. This is the design that became widely used in Western Australia.

Albert F. Calvert, author and gold-mine speculator whom the *New York Times* described as 'a West Australian millionaire . . . reputedly to be worth $2,500,000',[40] was amazed at the usefulness of the bicycle he witnessed on one of his many visits to the goldfields:

The bicycle plays an important role on the goldfields. Myriads of the two wheelers are met with, mounted by men of all ages and professions. In no part of the world is the machine more popular or more valuable, for the roads are flat, the horse feed is at an enormous premium. A bicycle, which needs neither food nor water, and which, and even with an indifferent rider in the saddle, is faster than the average hack, is of inestimable value. In its way it is as useful as a camel in the desert. The machines are all the latest pneumatic tyre patterns, which slide over the soft sandy tracks with comparatively easy pedalling . . . Until the telegraph wire was completed the bicycle did the work of the electric wire. Some of the best riders in the southern hemisphere . . . travelled regularly between

Coolgardie and Southern Cross. They were equipped with
the best machines and were trained to do the trip in the
shortest possible time.[41]

The bicycle could travel relatively smoothly over long
distances on the bush roads that had become hard and
flat from the heavy treading of the camels. In 1896,
gold was found at a site named British Flag, and Doctor
Charles Laverton rode almost 400 kilometres north from
Coolgardie in less than a week to the site that would later
take his name to invest in the new mine. On one trip, he is
said to have carried 600 ounces of gold back to Coolgardie
from Laverton on the handlebars of the bicycle.

Later the same year, Arthur Richardson, the son of a
doctor, rode from Coolgardie to Adelaide by following
the telegraph line across the Nullarbor Plain. Carrying
only a small kit and a water bag, he reached Adelaide on
Christmas Day, after 31 days of pedalling.

Because of the inhospitable living conditions in the
desert, fewer women and families joined the men on the
diggings of Western Australia than had been the case in
the earlier goldfields of the eastern colonies. One of the
first women to reach Coolgardie was Wilhelmina Sloss,
who came from Broken Hill in far western New South
Wales with her husband, Joseph, and her baby daughter,
Elizabeth.

They had arrived in early 1893 by boat at the port of
Albany on the south coast of Western Australia, which
was the most regular jumping-off point for people coming
from Australia's eastern states. A regular train service
ran from there to York and Perth, which were 300 and
400 kilometres to the north. From Perth to the diggings,

Wilhelmina and her daughter rode high on the top of a heavily loaded cart. It took them 15 sweltering hot days on the road, with nights spent camping by the roadside, to reach Coolgardie.

On the goldfields, the family lived in a wooden-framed canvas tent that typically would have been ten feet long and eight feet wide (3 x 2.5 metres), eight feet high in the middle and five feet (1.5 metres) high on the sides.[42]

Within two months of arriving, Joe Sloss left his wife and baby daughter to join the rush to Mount Youle, where gold had recently been discovered. On the way back, Joe came across Paddy Hannan and his mates, who had just found the abundant gold that started the great rush to Kalgoorlie. Joe immediately fetched his wife and baby daughter and joined the rush, with Wilhelmina becoming the first woman on the Kalgoorlie goldfields in July 1893.

By 1900, more than 600 local gold-mining companies had been floated on the London Stock Exchange, and more than 50 towns had been established across the hundreds of kilometres of the Eastern Goldfields, some of which lasted only a few years before becoming ghost towns.[43] In the last decade of the nineteenth century, more than a quarter of a million people passed through the Eastern Goldfields. Coolgardie's population grew to more than 25,000, and the town boasted more than 60 shops, 26 hotels, three breweries, seven newspapers, six banks, four schools, two theatres, two stock exchanges and 25 stockbrokers.

It was at Leonora, 270 kilometres north of Coolgardie, that a 22-year-old Herbert Hoover worked as a mine manager in 1897. Hoover, who would later become the president of the United States of America, was at the Sons of Gwalia mine, which was started when Swede

Jack Carlson and his mates found gold there in 1893. The Sons of Gwalia mine eventually became one of the largest of all Australian gold mines. Born in 1874, the son of a blacksmith Quaker, in a small village in Iowa and reared in Oregon, Hoover studied geology at Stanford University before working in mines in Nevada and Colorado. In 1896, he sailed to London, where he successfully applied for a mine manager's job at Berwick and Moreings gold mine, owned by the London and WA Exploration Company, based in Western Australia.

Arriving in Fremantle on the RMS *Victoria*, Hoover then took the train, which now ran as far as Coolgardie, before he started work in May 1897. Hoover found the country hard, commenting on the 'red dust, black flies and white heat'. He nevertheless established a reputation for hard work and hard-nosed decisions, making it clear he was prepared to make ruthless choices in the name of increased efficiency:

> The bad [ones] must go . . . They have been bought in the boom times when no attention was paid to the intrinsic value of the mine . . . Good engineers are called in as physicians to mend the lame ducks. This we do by killing the bad ones immediately. At least, that's what I do.[44]

Hoover was soon given a pay rise and made the manager of the mine at Leonora, where he increased the hours of work and set about hiring Italian labourers as they were thought to be more willing and less militant. He lived in a well-built house at Leonora, which survives as a museum and guest house.

After a little more than a year, and now a partner in the

mining company, Hoover was sent to China by his company's London headquarters. He and his wife arrived in Tientsin at the time of the Boxer Rebellion and spent their first month under fire, during which time he directed the construction of barricades and his wife, Lou, worked as a nurse. In only six years, Hoover became both successful and rich, with the *San Francisco Examiner* describing him in 1902 as the richest 28-year-old in the world.

¤

After more than a decade, the terrible water shortages of the Eastern Goldfields were finally overcome with the building of a huge water pipe from Perth. This remarkable engineering achievement involved the pumping of five million gallons of water a day from the Helena River on the western side of the Darling Range upwards by 400 metres, then using eight pumping stations[45] along a 600-kilometre, 762-millimetre pipe to the goldfields.

The colony's premier, Sir John Forrest, had first recommended the Goldfields Water Supply Scheme to the Western Australian Parliament in July 1896, but the project was not given parliamentary approval until 1897, and the contracts for the supply of the metal pipes were not signed with companies in Sydney and Melbourne until 1898.

The inspiration behind the pipeline and the man responsible for its design and construction was Charles Yelverton O'Connor, who had been appointed Western Australia's engineer-in-chief by Sir John Forrest in 1891. O'Connor was born in County Meath, Ireland, in 1843 to a well-to-do family and given an education that included training as an engineer. In 1865, aged 22, he migrated to New Zealand, where he worked as a surveyor and engineer for the next 25 years before being offered the job in Western Australia. With the responsibility for roads, railways and harbours, O'Connor successfully managed the expansion of the port of Fremantle.

The pipeline was built in the remarkably short period of only five years but was highly controversial. By early 1902, the year before the pipeline became fully operational, the Western Australian Parliament questioned O'Connor's competence, the value of the project, the time it was taking to complete and its very high cost.[46] The local newspapers did not hold back either, their attacks reaching a peak in February:

> And apart from any distinct charge of corruption this man has exhibited such gross blundering or something worse, in his management of great public works it is no exaggeration to say that he has robbed the taxpayer of this state of many millions of money ... This crocodile imposter has been backed up in all his reckless extravagant juggling with public funds, in all his nefarious machinations behind the scenes by the kindred-souled editor of the West Australian [newspaper].[47]

The pipeline was officially opened on 22 January 1903, and water first emerged from the other end of the pipe at Kalgoorlie two days later. The provision of a reliable water supply ensured the long-term viability of the goldfields, which remained among the world's largest gold mines into the twenty-first century.

Sadly, O'Connor did not live to see the completion

of his engineering marvel. On 10 March 1902, stung by the ferocity of the criticisms levelled against him, he rode his horse from his house along a deserted stretch of beach near Fremantle. He entered the water near Robbs Jetty and shot himself. In a suicide note, O'Connor explained:

> The position has become impossible . . . I fear that my brain is suffering and I am in great fear of what effect all the worry will have upon me . . . I have lost control of my thoughts. The . . . scheme is all right and I could finish it if I got the chance and protection from misrepresentation but there is no hope of that now and it is better that it should be given to some entirely new man to do who will be untrammelled by prior responsibility.[48]

¤

By the end of the nineteenth century, the population of the gold regions began to outstrip the population of the rest of Western Australia, and the miners would play a dominant role in the vote to create the nation of Australia.

In 1898 and 1899, New South Wales, Victoria, South Australia, Queensland and Tasmania had all voted in support of federation. Western Australia delayed putting the matter to the vote despite a petition of 23,000 signatures from the goldfields calling for the government to do so. The premier of Western Australia, John Forrest, was aware of the strong opposition to the idea, particularly among the pastoralists and those who saw little to gain from the union and feared the competition from the more populous eastern states that would follow the abolition of the colonial tariffs. On the other hand, the miners, many of whom had come to Western Australia for the gold but retained connections with the east, strongly supported federation.

In 1899, frustrated that the matter had not been put to the vote, the diggers on the goldfields began agitating for a separate colony to be called Auralia that would be 'a means towards the adoption of Federation'.[49] At a meeting in Coolgardie on 13 December 1899, a unanimous resolution was passed calling for the new colony, which would extend east to west from 118 degrees west to the South Australian border and from the south coast, including the ports of Albany and Esperance, to 26 degrees north, which is adjacent to the Northern Territory border:

> That this conference is of the opinion that other constitutional means having failed, the only course to redress the grievances of the eastern goldfields especially in the matter of Federation is to . . . petition Her Majesty the Queen for separation from the rest of the colony of Western Australia . . .[50]

At the prompting of the majority of the colonies, the British Parliament had passed The Commonwealth of Australia Constitution Act 1900. (The Act was given Royal Assent on 9 July 1900.) However, in the absence of support from the west, the original Australian constitution excluded any reference to Western Australia:

> Whereas the people of New South Wales, Victoria, South Australia, Queensland and Tasmania, humbly relying on Almighty God, have agreed to unite in one indissoluble

Federal Commonwealth under the Crown of the United Kingdom of Great Britain and Ireland, and under the constitution hereby established . . .

While there were some misgivings about the federation in Britain, there was also a widespread view that a united Australian nation would strengthen the British Empire, and it was hoped that Western Australia might join later.

The colony had already extracted a number of concessions that had been offered as inducements for it to join, including a continuation of intercolonial tariffs to continue for five years after federation.

Three weeks later, in the face of considerable opposition, Sir John Forrest recommended to parliament that a referendum be held, and the matter was finally put to the vote. As expected, most of the farming districts and a number of coastal towns, including Bunbury and Geraldton, voted against joining the federation. In Perth, the 'yes' vote was passed by barely 7000 votes, against nearly 5000 who voted 'no'.

However, it was the overwhelming vote from the goldfields that gave Western Australia the biggest majority vote of all the colonies. In the Coolgardie–Kalgoorlie region, more than 95 per cent of the 24,000 votes cast were in favour of federation, swamping all the results and securing an almost 60 per cent vote in favour of becoming part of the nation of Australia.

CHAPTER THIRTEEN

Lasseter's Lost Reef

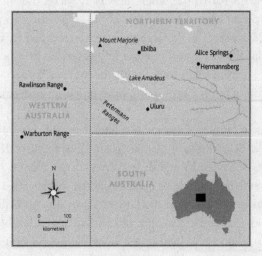

Central Australia

To my astonishment I could see fine flakes of gold . . .
Excitedly, I followed the outcrop – that's what it was – for
some distance. Then it disappeared. But soon I picked it
up again and, climbing a rise, I could see that it extended
for miles. Hastily I gathered a pile of samples, and filled an
empty oatmeal bag with them. I was determined to push
through with all speed now; this was an El Dorado.

No story of the Australian gold rushes would be complete without reference to Harold Lasseter and his claim to have found the world's biggest reef of gold in the remote heart of Australia.

Lasseter claims to have first found the reef in the desert country about 500 kilometres west of Alice Springs, deep in Central Australia, when he was 17 years old, in 1897. Thirty years later, he went with an expedition to locate the reef, and as he lay dying alone he recorded in a journal that he had found it again. However, no details of the reef's location were found with the journal, and scores of expeditions over many years have failed to find any trace of it.

Lewis Hubert Lasseter (he later changed his name to Harold Bell Lasseter) was born on 27 September 1880 at Bamganie, near Meredith in Victoria, the second son of John and Agnes (née Cruikshank). His mother died when he was an infant, and his father remarried. According to Harold Lasseter's son, his father had an older brother, Arthur, who was killed in the Boer War, a younger sister, Lillian, and a younger brother, Claude, who died of typhoid at the age of nine.[1]

His family says that Harold ran away from home at the age of 12 and lived and worked with a family on a farm in Colac in Victoria. There is little available information about his youth, but Lasseter later said that he served in the Royal Navy for four years until 1901.[2] This makes his claim to have first found the gold reef in the desert country west of Alice Springs in 1897 difficult to accept. Also, separate surviving records show that Lasseter spent more than a year from 7 October 1896 in the Boys Reformatory in Geelong, having been convicted of house-breaking and stealing.[3] He absconded from the institution on 10 October 1897, which makes it practically impossible for him to have been in Western Australia that year as he later claimed.

Around 1901, Lasseter travelled to England and then to the United States of America, where he got married for the first time, to Florence Scott of New York, in December 1903. Around 1908, he returned to Australia and became a farmer at Tabulam on the Clarence River in northern New South Wales.

Lasseter later said that, in 1913, he was the first person to submit a detailed plan for the erection of a single-arch bridge across Sydney Harbour, which was rejected as 'impossible to construct'. Over the next 20 years, Lasseter developed or invented a number of other radical schemes, including a proposal for a hydroelectric dam in Victoria's Gippsland and a variety of advanced military-weapons systems.[4]

In the First World War, Lasseter enlisted in the Australian Army, describing himself as a 'bridge engineer', in 1916 but was discharged in 1917 as 'mentally deficient'. His little-known military papers state that he had 'marked hallucinations' and record he had wanted to join the flying corps 'as a friend is coming to present him with an aeroplane' and that he had a 'peculiar manner and is constantly talking'.[5]

In 1924, at 44 years old and still married to Florence, he married Louise Irene Lilywhite, a nurse at Middle Park Hospital in Melbourne, whom he had met on a train at Tyabb on Victoria's Mornington Peninsula.[6] For his second marriage, he used his adopted name of Harold Bell Lasseter. Harold and Irene, whom he would refer to as Rene, would have three children together.

In 1926, Lasseter moved with the beginnings of his new family to the new capital city of Canberra and for the next two years worked on the construction of the national parliament building while living in a house built of flattened kerosene tins.[7]

In 1928, the family moved into a heavily mortgaged house in the Sydney suburb of Kogarah. It was two years later, while he was working on the construction of the Sydney Harbour Bridge, that Lasseter took his proposal for an expedition to rediscover his gold reef to John Bailey, the boss of the powerful Australian Workers Union.

The 59-year-old John, or 'Jack', Bailey was a rough and tumble union boss who had come up through the ranks. Born in 1871 in Manus Creek in New South Wales, he left school early to work with his labouring father before becoming a shearer. He was said to have been a brawling bruiser of the shearing sheds before becoming the president of the union's central committee for 18 years from 1915 till 1933. He was politically well connected and for five years, between 1920 and 1925, was a New South Wales member of parliament. Before the Lasseter expedition, he shunned the newspapers, rarely gave speeches and preferred to work behind the scenes.

Bailey said that Lasseter turned up in his office at McDonnell House, 321 Pitt Street, in June 1930 to explain how he had previously found the gold reef and how he wanted to go and relocate it.[8]

Errol Coote, who was to become the pilot of the gypsymoth plane on the Lasseter expedition, says he was in Bailey's office the day the 50-year-old, five-foot-two-inch (158 centimetre) Harold Lasseter came in to sell the idea of an expedition to search for his long-lost reef:

One day a small, bow legged individual, with a scraggy crop of black hair turning grey, walked into the sanctum of John Bailey. He told of a rich reef of gold in Central Australia – a reef of such length that it would be the largest gold-producer in the world . . . There were about four of us there at the time, including young Ernest Bailey, John Bailey's son.[9]

Initially, Coote said they all 'joined in a laugh at the little man's expense', but Lasseter persisted with his story, saying that he had started his quest 30 years before when he crossed Australia alone on a horse searching for rubies:

Away back in the late 1880s Lasseter said, I was doing a bit of seafaring, and was on a vessel going up the Queensland coast, when I heard of rich deposits of rubies in the MacDonnell Ranges in Central Australia. I left the ship in Cairns, secured a couple of horses, brought provisions, and set out for the MacDonnell. After many weary weeks I arrived at the supposed ruby field, and to my disgust found the gems were not rubies but garnets – ruby-coloured crystalline quartz . . . Thoroughly disappointed, I was determined to push on to the Western Australian coast and pick up a vessel at Fremantle or Carnarvon. According to the maps of those days the MacDonnell extended to the sea, so I thought I did not have much further to go.[10]

In recounting his story[11] to John Bailey and his colleagues in the Australian Workers Union offices, Lasseter said that when he reached the Western Australian border he found himself in the heart of the desert full of red sandhills and spiky spinifex. Changing direction and heading more to the south-west, his food was running out and the situation becoming 'desperate' when he stumbled on the gold reef:

> The queer colour of stones caught my attention. I picked up a couple and broke them. To my astonishment I could see fine flakes of gold . . . Excitedly, I followed the outcrop – that's what it was – for some distance. Then it disappeared. But soon I picked it up again and, climbing a rise, I could see that it extended for miles. Hastily I gathered a pile of samples, and filled an empty oatmeal bag with them. I was determined to push through with all speed now; this was an El Dorado.[12]

Almost immediately, the food for Lasseter's horses 'gave out':

> They died, and I was left alone in the sandy wastes, not knowing how far I was from the coast . . . Taking as much food and water as I could carry I tried to push ahead on foot. Water gave out when I was in the middle of sandhills, and the next thing I remember was an Afghan bending over me. He put me on his camel and took me to a camp.[13]

It was then that Lasseter said that he teamed up with the mysterious Harding, whom no one had since been able to trace:

> There I was nursed back to life by a surveyor and explorer, named Harding. He had examined the specimens. It appears that I still had them clutched in my hands when the Afghan found me, but everything else had gone.

Harding toyed with them and seemed fascinated by them. He declared it was the nicest looking stone he had ever seen and asked me to take him back and show him where they came from.[14]

Lasseter refused because he was still 'haunted by the nightmare of my experience' and said that he went on to Coolgardie and 'messed around on the goldfields' for the next three years. The two men kept in touch until around 1900, when Lasseter finally agreed to go with Harding to find the reef:

> We went up from Perth in a small coastal lugger, and from Carnarvon, with a string of camels, went practically due east. I remembered all the landmarks, and we found the reef again. All the horrors of the last trip had come vividly before me, but the relocation of the El Dorado completely compensated for that now. Together we traced the outcrop for about ten miles [16 kilometres].[15]

Lasseter said that he did not have an exact measure of the location of the reef and was not sure whether it was in the Northern Territory or in Western Australia. When he and Harding returned from the reef to Carnarvon on the Western Australian coast, they found their watches had lost time, which meant that their calculations of its location were inaccurate.

As Lasseter was giving his account, Coote said that the union boss, John Bailey, asked the obvious question: 'Why has it taken you so long to think about going after the reef again?' Lasseter gave the following explanation:

Harding tried to raise the capital for a company to go out there and develop the reef. But Kalgoorlie was booming. Gold was being easily won, and mining men turned a deaf ear to us. A proposition away out in the heart of the desert, even at three ounces to the ton, meant nothing to them. I went overseas . . . Harding died. Eventually the war broke out and I enlisted from here, but got my discharge in England. I then went to the USA, returning from there some years ago.[16]

He said that he had tried once more to locate the reef in 1911 from Oodnadatta in Central Australia but some of the men on the expedition came down with dysentery, while others found the going too difficult. After travelling only 300 kilometres, they abandoned the quest and turned for home.

Coote said that when Lasseter finished his long account, everyone in the room wanted to believe the tale:

Lasseter had finished his story, and everyone was silent. His obvious sincerity had impressed, and the prospect of 'ragging' him had vanished. We were now all quite serious. Each man in the room was developing the first symptoms of gold fever.[17]

John Bailey said that after interviewing Lasseter he was satisfied his story was genuine.[18] From then on, it seems that serious questions about Lasseter's claims were either glossed over or ignored. At a crowded meeting to discuss Lasseter's proposal in the Australian Workers Union offices a few days later, the famous aviator Charles Ulm[19] is said to have asked Lasseter about the bearings he took with the wrong time on his watch. Ulm pointed out that if Lasseter's watch was behind one hour, as Lasseter had claimed, and the earth completes a revolution every 24 hours, from a longitudinal point of view the reef must be somewhere in the Indian Ocean. But by now, as Errol Coote said, no one at the meeting was going to be swayed by the harshness of reality:

> The room veritably buzzed in the pause in proceedings that followed. Composed mostly of working men, who now rubbed shoulders with law clerks, business managers, a couple of doctors, journalists, and other professional men, the expression on their faces was the same. Everyone was talking gold. Eyes were bright; lips were being licked; workaday cares were forgotten. Everyone was gazing through the pearly gates of Prosperity, and each man was treading along streets of gold.[20]

Very quickly, amid considerable public excitement and government support, the union-backed Central Australian Gold Exploration Company raised its first £5000 in 24 hours.[21] Within days, they were fully subscribed at over £8000, plus another £10,000 loaned by John Bailey.[22] Harold Lasseter's wife Irene took out £25 of shares.[23]

The man chosen to lead the expedition to find the gold reef was 47-year-old miner Frederick Blakeley, whose chief qualification seems to have been that he was the younger brother of the well-connected Arthur Blakeley, the minister for Home Affairs in the recently elected James Scullin federal Labor government. Fred was born in Adelaide in 1882 to parents who had come to Australia from Yorkshire. He left school at 12 years of age and became a miner. At 14, he went by Cobb and Co. coach to White Cliffs, in north-western New South Wales, where he was said to have made a lot of money opal mining. He worked for about three years prospecting for gold in Western Australia and in various other jobs around the outback of New South Wales before bicycling through the Northern Territory in 1916 with two mates to Darwin, where they caught the boat back to Sydney. In the early 1920s, he went prospecting north of Alice Springs, but when he was appointed as leader of the Lasseter expedition he had never been to the west of the Northern Territory, where Lasseter's gold reef was thought to exist.[24] At the time of his appointment, he was working as a slaughter man in a Sydney abattoir.[25]

Blakeley explained how he heard about the job:

> I received a letter from my brother, Arthur Blakeley, who was Minister for Home Affairs in the Scullin Government . . . I went to see [John] Bailey who told me a chap had drifted in to his office with a very likely story of a gold reef he had found in central Australia.[26]

Blakeley became involved with the project at an early stage and said that after some 'plain talking' in Bailey's office he went for a walk with Lasseter in Sydney's Hyde Park, which was only 200 metres away. After spending the next four Saturday afternoons with him, Blakeley said he was satisfied with Lasseter's claims about the reef. He said that Lasseter had told him how, with the surveyor Harding, they had taken samples of gold from 'practically the whole length' of the reef, and while he was still suspicious about some of it, he said he would be prepared to go with a search expedition:

> I made my report. I told Bailey that I had taken a month
> to consider Lasseter's story. There were a lot of gaps in it
> but I felt there might be something in the yarn.[27]

Blakeley also noted that everyone associated with the venture was caught up in the widespread newspaper excitement about the prospect of new gold:

> Everyone was riding on a wave of enthusiasm, for here was
> something the country badly needed. Harry Lasseter the
> little nuggety man seemed to have shown a way to break
> the Depression. The Patriotic spirit was simply grand.[28]

There were a number of other expeditions being planned to search the centre of Australia at the time, but the Central Australian Exploration Company was the biggest, the best financed and the best equipped of them all. The plan involved sending out a ground party in trucks to prepare landing strips for a plane to land, which could then extensively reconnoitre from the air. The ground party was supplied with a big six-wheeled, two-and-a-half-ton Thorneycroft truck that had been donated to the expedition by the British Thorneycroft company to enable trackless desert exploration.

The plane chosen was a de Havilland biplane, named the *Golden Quest* for the expedition and fuelled by 600 gallons of petrol donated by the Atlantic Union Oil company. According to the pilot, Errol Coote, he had gone to Sydney's Mascot Airport and initially chosen a less suitable plane:

The first plane I saw in the hangar of de Havilland Aircraft Company was the Black Hawk, a super charged Gypsy Moth flown by Major de Havilland in the East–West Air Race. It had put up the fastest time in the race and would be the ideal bus for the job, I thought, especially if the reef were found. The price was £750 . . . I did not look any further but returned to Sydney and told the Baileys about the machine.[29]

However, the next day Coote was told by the aviator Charles Ulm that the wooden plane he had chosen was 'only fit for racing and stunting' and was persuaded to buy a gypsy moth made of metal instead.

Thirty-two-year-old Errol Coote was born in Sydney and brought up on the goldfields of Hill End and Gulgong. In the First World War, when he was 19 years old, he joined the army but served less than honourably. In 1918, he was imprisoned for stealing a motorbike and for repeatedly being absent without leave. He served out his sentence in France in 1919 after the war ended.[30] In the early 1920s, he became a journalist and worked on a number of newspapers, including the *Sydney Sun*, before taking up flying.

In a later account, the expedition team leader Fred Blakeley was highly critical of Coote:

He was a man of slight build and dark complexion, who packed short bursts of violent temper. His rig-out was laughable. He wore boots like girls wear to ride in at Shows . . . He did not possess the right temperament for such a trip since he was jerky and jumpy and a journalist with a vivid imagination who was always on the job.[31]

There does not appear to have been a great deal of expertise or experience in the design of the expedition, which was hurriedly cobbled together in a matter of weeks. The combined use of trucks and aeroplanes was untested on outback-exploration projects such as this and would prove to be a total failure.

Harold Lasseter was hired as the guide to the expedition for £10 a week and agreed to a contract that obliged him to give 'the exact location of the reef, or as near as possible' in exchange for ten per cent of the gold found.[32] (Interestingly, in the contract Lasseter stated that he had first found the reef in 1894, and not in 1897, as he had previously told the company. In 1894, Lasseter was only 13 or 14 years old.[33])

The oldest member of the team other than Lasseter was 48-year-old George Sutherland, 'a six foot [182 centimetre] slab of typical bushman' who was an experienced prospector and miner from New South Wales. Sutherland was sufficiently convinced of Lasseter's claim that in addition to joining the expedition he invested some of his own money in the company shares.

The youngest member of the team was the slightly built 21-year-old Englishman Philip Taylor, who became the expedition's mechanic. Taylor worked in Melbourne for the de Havilland Company and, as he was planning to marry, saw the expedition as the opportunity to make some extra money as well as to go on a great adventure.

For the first few weeks of the expedition, they also took with them 32-year-old Captain Blakiston-Houston, who was aide-de-camp to the governor general of Australia, Lord Stoneham. Blakiston-Houston was born in 1898 and attended Eton, then Sandhurst military college, before serving as an officer in the Hussars, then the new tank corps in France in the First World War. After the war, he served in Egypt and India before going to Australia. He served again in the Second World War in Egypt and East Africa. The English army officer was keen to experience something of Central Australia and used his annual leave entitlements to go. Fred Blakeley said he had some initial misgivings about the captain joining the mission but the Sydney office allowed him to go because 'it gave the personnel of the party a hoity-toity touch'.[34] Blakiston-Houston was the first to return to Sydney, and his view that there was a great deal of dissent in the expedition party did much to undermine the confidence of the directors in the expedition's leadership.

The team left Sydney in 'dribs and drabs'[35] for a trip of almost 3000 kilometres from Sydney to Alice Springs, where they would launch the expedition. Lasseter was the first to leave, on 7 July 1930, when he boarded a train with the Thorneycroft truck and headed for Broken Hill, on the western border of New South Wales.

In what may appear to have been an omen of the troubled times ahead, George Sutherland and the team leader, Fred Blakeley, missed their train from Sydney to Broken Hill. They finally caught up with Lasseter at Quorn, and went on together to Alice Springs, where they later met up with Captain Blakiston-Houston, who had made his own way there.[36]

On 19 July, Errol Coote took off from Sydney's Mascot Airport in the *Golden Quest* and headed 350 kilometres to Parkes in western New South Wales, where he picked up the mechanic Philip Taylor. Together, they flew on to Broken Hill, where a big crowd came out to the airport, then on to Oodnadatta and finally to Alice Springs on the afternoon of 22 July. The day Coote flew from Sydney, he was not qualified to fly the plane, as his pilot's licence had expired more than a year before. However, he had clearly made arrangements for it to be renewed, as a new one was issued the day before he landed in Alice Springs.[37]

In 1930, Alice Springs was only a small settlement that had a few houses for government officials, the Central Australian inland mission and a Catholic church. The Alice Springs telegraph office was opened when the Adelaide to Darwin telegraph line was built in 1872, and the nearby township of Stuart was only officially renamed Alice Springs in August 1933.

Blakeley said he became suspicious of Lasseter before they left Alice Springs when Lasseter claimed to recognise some buildings in the town from his visit there more than 30 years earlier – until the local postmaster pointed out they were no older than 20 years.[38]

The first stage of the expedition involved setting up a base camp at Ilbilba,[39] some 400 kilometres to the west of Alice Springs in the Ehrenberg Range, where they would clear an airstrip so Coote could then fly in with the *Golden Quest*. Ilbilba had been established as a camp a few years earlier by Donald McKay, who explored much of the south-west Northern Territory in 1926 and again in early 1930, when he had built an airstrip there for aerial surveying. Ilbilba was a 'soak', in that water could be found by digging even when the local creek dried up. It was an important site for a number of local Aboriginal groups, as it was a rare permanent source of water.

The team of six men – Fred Blakeley, Harold Lasseter, Philip Taylor, George Sutherland, Errol Coote and Captain

Blakiston-Houston – left Alice Springs on 21 July 1930, on what the expedition leader Fred Blakeley said was 'the best-equipped turn out that had ever been in this country'.[40] They also hired a local driver, Fred Colson, and his truck 'at £3 a day, providing him with petrol and tucker'[41] and a young local Aboriginal man named Mickey to help show them the way.[42]

The range of food taken by the team on their expedition from Alice Springs was probably the most extensive ever taken by prospectors to an Australian goldfield. It included pressed beef, bacon, pork, corned beef, tinned fish, oatmeal, cheese, sauces and pickles, canned peas and beans, pressed vegetables, dried fruit, vinegar and condensed milk. To cook and eat the food, they took a camp oven, four billycans, two fry pans and a box of cutlery. Their equipment included a five-gallon water condenser and two 20-gallon kegs, plus axes, picks, shovels, gold-panning dishes, shotguns, rifles, revolvers and 700 rounds of ammunition.[43] In a break with a convention that had been established on the Australian goldfields for almost 80 years, the team took no alcohol, other than some brandy in its medical kit.

The beginning of the trip was marred by the first of many disagreements between Lasseter and Fred Blakeley. Lasseter wanted to take a southerly route along the MacDonnell Ranges, but, as the expedition leader, Blakeley's preference for a more northerly route prevailed.

The first leg of the expedition west of Alice Springs was to prove difficult for the trucks, particularly the heavier Thorneycroft. For much of the journey, they needed to lay strips of coconut matting in front of its wheels to prevent the big truck becoming buried in the deep sand, but, even with the matting and several members of the team pushing from behind, it regularly became bogged and needed to be dug out. They were also forced to stop frequently to repair up to four punctured tyres a day.[44]

In addition to the problem of the sand, they had to use axes to cut a road through parts of the dense scrub wide enough for the trucks. At one stage, when they covered less than a kilometre in more than two and a half hours, Blakeley complained that it was the toughest country he had ever seen.[45]

Another early setback came with the failure of their radio, which they had brought to enable two-way communications with the directors of the Central Australian Gold Exploration Company in Sydney. They discovered that some of its valves were missing, so the radio could receive but not transmit signals. They were grateful, however, for being able to hear each night the 'news of the day' and the scores from a Test cricket match then being played between England and Australia in England.[46]

About two-thirds of the way to Ilbilba, they cleared an airstrip at a place they named Taylors Creek so the little plane could land and then sent Errol Coote the pilot back to Alice Springs in the truck driven by Fred Colson to fetch the *Golden Quest* and fly back out. Colson also took Captain Blakiston-Houston back to Alice Springs, as he was due to leave the expedition and go back to work for the governor general.

The rest of the team pressed on and, guided by compass and the help of the local Aboriginal boy Mickey, reached Ilbilba on 7 August, where they found the old McKay camp still in fairly good condition. Over the next few days, they established their camp and cleared a second landing strip of about 700 metres in readiness for the arrival of the plane.

The climate in Central Australia in the winter month of August is dry and mild, with temperatures reaching a maximum of around 25 degrees Celsius during the daytime but plunging to as low as three degrees at night. Very quickly, the team learned to stuff spinifex and bark under their camp stretchers for insulation against the cold when they slept.

Having arrived back in Alice Springs, Errol Coote flew the *Golden Quest* to the intermediate airstrip at Taylors Creek on 9 August, but when he was taking off to fly on to Ilbilba the plane failed to climb above some low trees and crashed. The plane ended up 'standing on its nose and upside down',[47] trapping Coote in the cockpit. Colson, who had driven back out to Taylors Creek, loaded the bleeding pilot into his truck and drove for the next 22 hours back to Alice Springs, where Coote was hospitalised with leg and head injuries. Colson then went back to Taylors Creek and loaded the stricken plane on his truck to bring it back to Alice Springs, from where it would be taken to Adelaide for repairs.

The crash of the *Golden Quest* was the first of many serious problems that would dog the Lasseter expedition, and it dashed any hope of an early discovery of the location of the gold reef.

Back in Sydney, concerned that the project would be seriously delayed, the directors of the Central Australian Gold Exploration Company ordered a new replacement plane and pilot on 14 August with instructions that it be sent as quickly as possible to join the expedition. The chairman of the company, John Bailey, later said 'there was great rejoicing' among the team when they received the news that a new plane was being sent.[48] However, Fred Blakeley didn't want another plane:

> I begged the Sydney crowd not to send another plane. If they wanted to help us a dozen fast-riding camels would get better results. But only extracts of my report were read out at the meeting and when I got back to Sydney I heard to my surprise people saying that it was I who had recommended another plane be sent out as quickly as possible.[49]

The team's mechanic, Philip Taylor, later claimed that he had also tried on a number of occasions to alert the directors of the company to the dangers of allowing an unaccompanied single-engine plane to fly in uncharted Central Australia.

Back at Ilbilba, Blakeley was becoming increasingly anxious about the approach of summer and decided to go on to look for the reef without waiting for the new plane to arrive:

> Once summer hits the country nothing can travel on it; not even motor trucks. A ground sun temperature of 175 degrees will stop any engine.[50]

It was a bright sunny day when, on 18 August, they finally left Ilbilba on what Fred Blakeley called the 'Big Push' to the west – and hopefully to the gold reef. But almost immediately after leaving Ilbilba, Blakeley complained to Lasseter that he was not pointing out the landmarks that would help them find the reef:

Harry had not complied with his contract to divulge this information to me. All I got out of him was on the day we left Ilbilba when I asked him for directions. He said, 'Keep, first of all, a point or two north of west,' showing me a position on the map of Lake Macdonald about 130 miles [209 kilometres] west of east.[51]

The going was again heavy and the progress slow. On a number of occasions, the giant spinifex dragged under the big truck and wrapped around the differential until it pulled the truck to a halt and had to be cut away before they could start again. Out in the distance, they could occasionally see Aboriginal people, who appeared to be keeping an eye on the newcomers but for most of the time preferred to stay out of sight.

On 24 August, they reached Mount Marjorie, which gave Fred Blakeley the chance to quiz Lasseter more closely as to where they were heading. During the afternoon, they spent several hours climbing to about 610 metres up the mountain together before coming down on the western side and walking around the southern end and back to their camp in the evening.

Blakeley said he was angry that Lasseter would give no clear directions other than to say that they were too far north and that he wanted the expedition to be 150 miles (240 kilometres) further to the south.[52]

Two days later, the expedition encountered steeper sand dunes and large boulders too big for the truck to pass, and Blakeley decided they should return to Ilbilba, replenish their stores from their base camp and then head in the more southerly direction suggested by Lasseter.

Lasseter argued that time, petrol, food and water were

all limited and they should go directly south and not return to Ilbilba. At first, Lasseter's view prevailed, but after another 30 kilometres of deep sand ridges that the truck could only slide down they turned and headed back. They reached Ilbilba on 27 August, meaning that the first serious expedition to find Lasseter's reef had lasted less than ten days.

Blakeley said they were surprised to find a well-built young German named Paul Johns at their camp, with five camels and two Aboriginal men. Johns told Blakeley he was a dingo hunter who made his living killing dingoes and selling their scalps back in Alice Springs, where he would buy more supplies and ammunition before heading off back into the bush:

> The white man called himself Paul Johns; he was a German of about twenty two years of age. He told us he had only been in Australia three years. I remarked that he spoke very good English and he replied that he did not know many words when he had come but the [Hermannsburg] Mission had taught him.[53]

Johns was born in Düsseldorf in 1906. Not much is known of his early life except that he appeared to be fairly well educated. In 1926, he travelled to Australia via England, where he had been refused entry, having been caught as a stowaway. Arriving in Adelaide, he worked his way up through South Australia in a variety of jobs before reaching Alice Springs in 1929. According to Pastor Albrecht of the Hermannsburg Mission, which is about 120 kilometres west of Alice Springs on the way to Ilbilba, Johns told him that he bought the camels when he heard Lasseter was coming, in the hope that he could hire them out to the expedition.[54]

When Blakeley met Johns at Ilbilba, he suggested that he hang around because the team might be able to use him.

On 30 August, Fred Colson arrived back at Ilbilba with his hired truck, bringing news that a new plane and its pilot, Pat Hall, were due to arrive. Hall turned up in the *Golden Quest II* a few days later, having picked up the now recovered pilot of the first plane, Errol Coote, in Alice Springs. After a two-and-a-half-hour flight, the plane had finally reached Ilbilba with no fuel left, and it was immediately obvious that it did not have a big-enough petrol tank to be effective in the aerial search for Lasseter's reef. After conferring with Blakeley, the two pilots agreed they should immediately fly the replacement plane back to Adelaide to be fitted with a larger engine and a bigger petrol tank that would almost double the range of the plane from 612 kilometres to over 1200.[55] In the meantime, the expedition would again be without a plane.

Before going back, Pat Hall took Lasseter up in the plane the following day using fuel that had been trucked in to Ilbilba. It was Lasseter's one and only flight, in which it was hoped he would be able to recognise landmarks from years before when he had first seen the gold reef.

There are varying accounts as to what Lasseter said when he landed two hours later. According to Blakeley, Lasseter would only say that from the air it still appeared to him that they were 240 kilometres too far to the north.[56] However, Errol Coote said that when he took Lasseter aside he was told they had flown within a few metres of the reef:

That afternoon, I led Lasseter aside. 'Did you pick up

your landmarks?' I asked without beating about the bush. 'Yes I did,' he said, 'and what's more I saw the reef. It's there as plain as a pike-staff. We flew at only 30 feet [nine metres] when we were near it. It is in the heart of mulga and timber country. It was impossible to land there.'[57]

At first, Lasseter would not give him any further information, but when reminded of his contract with the Central Australian Gold Exploration Company he was slightly more forthcoming. Lasseter was now arguing incessantly with Fred Blakeley and told Coote he was not ready to tell the expedition leader what he had seen:

Picking up a stick, Lasseter sat on the sand. He described the position of Lake Christopher as a radial point; then he indicated three hills which he said could not be mistaken – they look like three women in sun-bonnets talking to one another. About 35 miles [56 kilometres] to the south east was another hill shaped like a Quakers hat – tall, conical in shape with the top cut off. The reef lay about 10 miles [16 kilometres] east of the lake-let and, looking along the line of the reef in a north westerly direction, the Three Sisters (as he called them) appeared to be sitting at the far end of the reef. It was possible for a plane to land on the lake-let, he said, but close to the reef the country was thickly timbered; however it could be seen from the air, just peeping through the mulga.[58]

The next day, 4 September, Hall and Coote took the *Golden Quest II* back to Alice Springs and again ran out of fuel. However, according to Coote, they managed to glide down to the ground and land safely:

We ... came over the town about 2,000 feet [610 metres] up. Suddenly the engine gave a few asthmatic coughs and went dead. We were out of petrol; however, we were within gliding distance of the aerodrome and landed without mishap.[59]

Within 30 minutes of the plane's departure for Alice Springs, Blakeley and the team started out on their second attempt to find the reef overland by taking the more southerly route suggested by Lasseter. After several days, Blakeley said that they reached the point Lasseter had said he had wanted to get to:

We estimated we were about 150 miles [240 kilometres] from Mt Marjorie and were at the position Harry had asked me to go ... and the long range of hills we could see were the Petermann Ranges ... no more than 80 miles [129 kilometres] away.[60]

Blakeley said that he confronted Lasseter and pointed out that they were now almost 1300 miles (2092 kilometres) south of Carnarvon. '"In all your stories," I said, "you have never been more than six or seven hundred miles from Carnarvon."'[61]

In addition to having reached the point Lasseter said they needed to, they found that the road had again become impassable, and everyone – except Lasseter – agreed with Blakeley that they had no choice but to turn back:

I got up early and went to the top of the long sloping sandhill and saw the strangest sight of tumbled, tangled country . . . and the belief that if we could drive the truck into the valley we could never get back up out.[62]

Blakeley then said that he decided to abandon the search and return to Alice Springs to report to the directors of the Central Australian Exploration Company for fresh instructions. He also claims he then told Lasseter that when they got back to Ilbilba the German 'dogger' Paul Johns and his camels would be his 'one slender chance' to 'save yourself and your family from disgrace'.[63]

When they arrived back at Ilbilba for the second time, on 11 September, they found Paul Johns still there waiting and hoping to be hired by them. Rather than go back to Alice Springs with all the others, Lasseter agreed to go out again on the search with Johns and his camels.

Sitting around the camp, Blakeley wrote out a contract to hire Johns and his five camels for two months from 13 September 1930, 'to work with and under the direction of Harold B. Lasseter'. The contract was signed by Fred Blakeley and Paul Johns and witnessed by Lasseter and George Sutherland.[64]

According to Johns, the deal to hire his camels to the expedition came at a good time:

In August, 1930, I was out dogging near Lake MacDonnell when two Hermannsburg mission boys said white men were camped at Ilbilba. I found there Blakeley, Sutherland, Lasseter, Taylor and Coote, camped in the old Mackay Aerial Expedition shed. I had five camels with me. They had a Thorneycroft truck, and Moth plane. They were generous with rations. They engaged my camels at £5 a week to take Lasseter on, with tucker provided. Considering I was practically starving, I was very glad.[65]

Four days later, and for the third time in two months, Lasseter set out from Ilbilba to look for his gold reef. Paul Johns went with him while the rest of the team said goodbye and headed back to Alice Springs. Fred Blakeley described the last time he saw Lasseter:

> I packed all his personal effects on his riding camel; then I gave him my own prism compass, since the one he had was very unreliable. I also gave him my company's watch and revolver, so everything was set. I shook hands with him and wished him good luck . . . They moved off, Johns leading the string of camels with Harry walking wide near the last camel. We watched them out of sight; then I said, 'That's the end of my millions' for had the ten mile [16 kilometre] reef been found my cut would have been worth about seventeen million pounds.[66]

Little is known of the rest of the Harold Lasseter story other than from fragments of his journal that were found several months later near where he died, about 200 kilometres further to the south. However, Paul Johns provided a little-known account of their journey together after they left Ilbilba in an interview he gave 18 months later in Alice Springs. The interview, by the author and journalist Ernestine Hill, was not published until 1968[67] and then only in a small booklet of 100 copies:

> In 1932 in Alice Springs, I interviewed Paul Johns, then a tall stalwart young Englishman of Nordic fairness who came through the Heartree Gap with his string of seven camels from two to three years hunting dingoes

in the Musgrave, Main and Petermann Ranges and the wilderness between them out west. The following statement, here published for the first time, was taken by me verbatim from Paul Johns, his sojourn with Lasseter, eighteen months before, then recent and clear in his mind. His story is briefly and simply told, as a bushman tells it, without drama or ordeal.[68]

Most of Johns's account deals with his travels with Lasseter after the rest of the expedition returned to Alice Springs, and when he himself left Lasseter to his own devices and headed to the west and the south and across the Western Australian border:

We started the following morning, two of the camels carrying 32 gallons of water and stores for three months, with a dump of others in the bough shed. All the other men left for Alice Springs . . . We travelled east to Potati, then straight south. H. B. Lasseter was very reticent, a silent man, and would often ride for hours without speaking. We had no blackfellow. At Potati, by a small spring on the mountainside we discarded two drums of water and half of our rations to travel as light as possible. We went straight south from Potati, heading for Mt Olga, 60 miles [96.5 kilometres] beyond Mt Amadeus . . . It was 12½ days to Lake Amadeus, nine tenths of it over sandhills with no feed, no water. We could only average eight or ten miles [13 or 16 kilometres] a day up and down across the heavy sandhills. The camels were without water for nine days. They lived on parakelia and munyroo [desert grass]. We couldn't hobble them over night on account of poison bush . . . Fifty miles

[80 kilometres] from the lake you could see it, the water actually like a mirage. Amadeus is five or six miles [eight or nine kilometres] across. The lake has a white surface, a dazzling salt glare.[69]

About halfway across, the heavily laden camels crashed through the thick crust of the dried salt lake and into the soft salted mud underneath, which Johns said was similar to quicksand:

We got half way across when the camels bogged. They broke their nose lines and chucked their loads, and were too tired to extricate themselves. We fed them while freeing them and then chased them back.[70]

After finally crossing the lake, Johns said they began to run out of food and water:

We had two gallons left of not water but hot steaming smelly stuff – the heat and rough travelling had brought out the petrol from the seams of the drums. We were living on tinned beef and rice, but were mostly too weary and disheartened to eat – especially Lasseter. Millions of black ants crawled over us at night. There were plenty of emus but they were the only birds we saw.[71]

Johns said they finally made it to Mount Olga, about 30 kilometres west of Uluru, but the camels, despite their thirst, would not drink until sunset:

Before daylight we packed our camels and tried a couple of miles further down, and got across. Sandhills again, worse than ever. According to the map it was 35–40 miles [56–64 kilometres] to Mt Olga – it took us four days and must be about 60 [97 kilometres]. We had made our 16 gallons last over 10½ days . . . We came to Mt Olga at ten in the morning and hooshed down 100 yards [91 metres] from the spring. The camels slank down silently, and put their heads in the hot sand. When we took them to the spring they wouldn't drink. I dived my head into the water and nearly cried. I then drew bucketfuls of the water and gave each of the camels a few sips. At sundown, they filled themselves . . . We then went on to Mt Stephenson, a granite mountain with big reefs of crystalline quartz, also a little waterhole holding about 40 gallons.[72]

It was here that Johns said he doubted that Lasseter had ever visited the area before:

Lasseter knew all this, and yet he did not impress me as a man who knew the country, but rather one who had read about it.[73]

As they approached the Petermann Ranges, they met some friendly Aboriginal people and found a few 'colours' but no significant gold:

We had a spell of two days and then went on out towards the Petermanns. Before we got halfway we picked up some colours, just indications in flat ground of scattered quartz and reefs. It was 80 miles [129 kilometres] and five days to Winters Glen, a permanent waterhole. We struck heavy rain and were held up for about a week. Natives about here were very helpful and brought us wild figs – the tribe are Mialls, Pitchantara, Luritja. We could see their smoke signals 80 miles off . . . At Winters Glen I rode out on my riding camel and got bogged – three days digging him out, with no food. Working for hours at a time to mat him up on mulga bushes, at last I got him out, and after another day's wait we started. Our way had led us first south, then west, now it was northwest.[74]

According to Johns, they continued west over the border from the Northern Territory and deep into Western Australia, where he said he thought Lasseter was nearing his reef before the shortage of rations forced them to turn back to their base camp at Ilbilba:

The Petermanns are a wonderful country, best I have seen in Central Australia. Over the border to Sladen Waters, through the Rawlinson range, now we rode south west for 80 miles. I think Lasseter thought we were nearing the end of our journey. At any rate we were near the end of our rations. From Petadi, 70 miles [113 kilometres] south of Winters Glen, we turned back to Ilbilba for more rations. We travelled back in ten days.[75]

What Johns did not say was that he may have forced the issue to return to Ilbilba because his two-month contract with the Central Australian Gold Exploration Company was about to expire and he soon would be working without pay unless he was rehired.

They finally got back to Ilbilba on 29 October, having been away for more than six weeks. Johns said he and Lasseter agreed that Johns should go into Alice Springs for more supplies and fresh camels, and bring them back out to Lasseter. Johns also carried letters from Lasseter to the government resident in Alice Springs and the Central Australian Gold Exploration Company in Sydney. In his letter to the government resident, Lasseter outlined his plan to head for a watering hole almost a hundred kilometres south of Ilbilba, then to the Rawlinson Range, then Lake Christopher. He wanted Johns to follow with fresh supplies. In his letter to the company, he also gave the details of where he was heading but added that he had seen the reef.

Johns insists that he tried to persuade Lasseter not to venture out alone but to wait at Ilbilba – but Lasseter was determined to go back to peg his reef:

> At Ilbilba the camels were skin and bone. I told him his best plan was to wait at Ilbilba while I went in to Alice for fresh camels, to return in about three weeks.[76]

Johns said that when he left Ilbilba, he felt kindly towards Lasseter, who had made it clear he needed help and pleaded with Johns not to leave him stranded in the desert:

> He stood and watched me go. He was generous and likeable, and a good mate. When I was leaving, his last words to me were, 'Don't leave me alone too long . . .' I said, 'Look here Harry, I'll do my best. I'll be coming back as soon as I can.'[77]

Johns said that as soon as he reached the Hermannsburg Mission, which was a day short of Alice Springs, he cabled the government administrator, Vic Carrington, to alert him to Lasseter's precarious situation:

It was 4½ days to Hermannsburg, 290 miles [467 kilometres]. There I wired Administrator Carrington asking that he should wire the company regarding best thing to do. Reply came, 'Awaiting arrival aeroplane.' I told Carrington that Lasseter was in a grave position, and though he was a bushman he knew nothing about camels.[78]

When he finally reached Alice Springs, Johns discovered that in the six weeks he had been away the expedition team had been in disarray, and over the next few weeks a series of mishaps and blunders would render it dysfunctional.

In Alice Springs in late September, Fred Blakeley had reported the failure of the expedition to Sydney and his belief that Lasseter was a fraud. Sydney responded by sacking the team leader. '[They] informed me that I was to hand everything over to Coote as he was carrying on to help Lasseter,'[79] said Blakeley, who then returned to Sydney with his loyal colleague George Sutherland and would play no further role in the expedition.

Immediately on taking command, Coote made the fateful decision to move the base camp from Ilbilba to Uluru, about 200 kilometres to the south and closer to the Petermann Ranges, where Lasseter's reef might be located.

On 27 October, during a forced landing at Uluru, Coote crashed the plane. He says that he too was sacked and recalled to Sydney, to be replaced with a new plane flown by First World War ace captain William Leslie Pittendrigh:

At Sydney it appeared that my unfortunate experiences with the company's planes had unnerved the directors: they had already decided that another pilot, an Englishman with post war flying experience, would continue the search for Lasseter.[80]

Pittendrigh brought with him a geologist, Hambre, to replace George Sutherland.

The departure of Coote left the 21-year-old mechanic Philip Taylor as the only original member of the expedition team left in Central Australia to pick up the pieces and take charge of the expedition. Taylor was instructed to make contact with Lasseter, who was still the only hope of the company recouping their sizable investment.

However, the search for Lasseter was again delayed when the two new team members, Pittendrigh and Hambre, flew into Alice Springs on 19 December then the following day became lost, ran out of fuel and crash landed while heading on to Ilbilba. For the next two weeks, a frantic search, which was hampered by the onset of the wet season, was launched to find the two men.

It was only after they were found alive and safe – with the help of two Australian Air Force planes – on 2 January that the focus returned to finding Lasseter. By the time the mechanic Philip Taylor was ordered to rehire the German Paul Johns and his camels to start a search, Lasseter had been out in the desert by himself for more than two months.

Taylor and Johns left Ilbilba in mid-January on camels, but Taylor soon became ill and Johns said that after only three days he was forced to abandon the search in order to find medical help for Taylor:

[We] had instructions to follow Lasseter. We went south west to the sandstone reservoir where Taylor took ill with some kidney trouble. I never thought I would get him

411

back alive. I headed straight east for Hermannsburg, and they took him into hospital.[81]

With no members of the original expedition now available, Taylor sent an urgent message to the experienced bushman Bob Buck at Middleton Ponds station, who agreed to go out for the company and look for Lasseter.

Buck left in mid-January and spent several weeks following Lasseter's tracks – which were fairly distinguishable in the desert country – through Bowleys Range, across the Western Australian border to Lake Christopher via the Rawlinson Range. He then followed the trail back to the Petermanns, where he eventually found Lasseter's body three months later, on 25 April, at Shaws Creek, about 30 kilometres from Winters Glen and 80 kilometres west of Mount Olga.

Buck later told the coroner that he buried the decomposed body of Lasseter, along with one of his arms that 'the dogs had taken'. Buck said he saw no signs of violence and had been told by the local Aboriginal people that Lasseter died of starvation.[82]

Later on, Lasseter's notes were found close to where his body had been. Most of them were in a small, red, cloth-covered notebook that had a pencil holder on the side and a black ribbon to keep it tied together. Many of the pages remain intact, although some are very fragile and stained with dirt, water, food and possibly blood. On the cover, in hard-to-read dark capital letters, are the words 'TO MY WIFE', and many of the pages are addressed to his wife Rene and signed 'Harold' or 'Lasseter'. There were also some loose sheets and fragments of pages nearby, some of which are addressed to his wife too.

It is unlikely that the little red book was Lasseter's principal journal. Earlier in the expedition, Fred Blakeley observed that Lasseter had kept a separate diary, which has not been found:

> Every night since we started he had written in his diary, a nice looking volume about eight inches long, six inches wide and perhaps two inches thick [approximately 20 by 15 by 5 centimetres]. It was well bound, with a very fine black morocco cover and exceptionally good paper.[83]

The notes in Lasseter's red book are mostly undated and, apart from the first four pages, unnumbered. From the journal, it appears he may have continued west and southwest over the Western Australian border, where he wrote that he had found his reef. He would have been able to find some watering holes, which were more numerous in the wet summer months, when most of the annual desert rainfall of three inches (or 7.6 centimetres) occurs. At this time of the year, there is also more animal and bird life, though food is still scarce and difficult to procure.

In one of the few references to dates in the journal, he said that he found and pegged the reef shortly before Christmas but that his camels then ran off with most of his supplies:

> The reef is a bonanza . . . Darling, I've pegged the reef and marked the exact locality on the map which is buried in my kit on the sandhill where the camels bolted . . . on the East side . . . of the hill and I photographed . . . the date in . . . peg dated 23 December.

Lasseter probably camped at or near his reef over Christmas before starting the return journey in an easterly direction heading for the Petermann Ranges back across the Northern Territory border. He was too far from Ilbilba to be able to carry sufficient food to reach safety and had little choice but to try to survive until relief arrived. At first, he fell in with a group of local desert Aboriginal people who initially helped him but soon found they did not have enough food for him as well as their own families. Eventually, he ended up near Winters Creek, where some of the local Aboriginal people were friendly while others hostile:

> Later an old chap with a wart six inches by three inches on the back took pity on me . . . brought me some berries like Cape Gooseberries . . .
>
> I saw tracks this morning . . . it was the same family . . . which raided me that . . . scared the pigeons yesterday . . . they sneaked about the rocks above . . .
>
> Gave his lubra the checkered blanket as it was too heavy for me to carry and useless at this time of year . . . Blacks tried to kill me today while I was waiting . . . three spears were thrown but two shots drove them off one spear landed in a tree I had my back against within three inches of my neck the other two were on the side . . .
>
> The blacks seem . . . and gave me a rabbit that he . . . so I gave them my remaining blanket . . . one old fellow took a fancy to my hat, which was falling to pieces . . . so I gave it . . .

It is believed that Lasseter survived for about three months, leaving Ilbilba in early November and dying sometime in late January the following year, which suggests that an earlier attempt to reach him with fresh supplies may have saved his life.

Throughout his journal, Lasseter makes a number of references to the hope of being rescued. The notes indicate that he knew he was running out of time and was bewildered that no one had come:

> Darling, there is so . . . lot. I would like to say . . . to you but can't write . . . I've tried to make you happy.
>
> Rene Darling, Don't grieve me I've done my best and pegged the reef . . . take care of Bobby, Betty and Joy please, I want Bobby to be a Civil Engineer try and educate him for that. Darling I do love you so I'm sorry I can't be with you at the last but Gods will be done. Yours ever, x Harry xxxx
>
> . . . I can't understand . . . support or relief has not . . . afforded me.
>
> . . . If I could only know what the trouble is all about that no relief was sent or anything done at all. Oh it is awful indeed and the skeleton of me can scarce support the weight of my clothes.
>
> I loved you always as I love you now with all my heart and soul.
>
> I've brought this all on myself by going alone but I thought the blacks, tho' primitive, were fair dealing. Good Bye and God Bless you Rene darling wife of mine and may God Bless the children.

Lasseter calculated that the runaway camels would return home to Ilbilba and rescuers would know he was in trouble:

[I]t is now 25 days since the camels bolted – allowing
ten days to Ilbilba they should be near home by now,
then people will speculate a week as to where I am then
someone will be sent to Ilbilba . . . and a motor truck
could get me in two days if they . . .

. . . I'm just a skeleton now . . .

He was living in the hope that Blakeley and his colleagues
would eventually come back for him but did not know that
Blakeley and most of the team had been sacked the month
before and had already returned to Sydney:

Of course I was a fool to take on alone but relied on Paul
Johns to overtake me in 4 to 6 weeks at the outside. He
averred that he would overtake me in three weeks and
gave his word of honour not to let me . . . Also it was
agreed upon . . . Fred Blakeley when I . . .

. . . I am paying the penalty with my life . . . may this be
a lesson to others . . .

. . . DEAR RENE, I think I am near my finish I am
nearl . . . and crazy with sandy blig[84] . . . tormented with
flies and ants . . . I have shrunken from 35 inches to 29
inches [89 centimetres to 74 centimetres] and my waist
line has an even greater shrinkage . . .

Things became even more unbearable for Lasseter towards
the end:

. . . Darling I want you to remember me as when we first
met and the scarecrow I am now. Have shrunk still further
and the flies and ants have nearly eaten my face away. I
can do nothing against them . . .

... I don't know what happened to Paul Johns but I left him within reach of civilization ...

... I have watched and hoped for relief till I am about at the end of my tether ... with lots of water I can hold out for several days yet but agony of starvation may drive me to shoot myself ...

When Bob Buck's news of the discovery of Lasseter's body reached the outside world, it made the front pages:

LASSETER IS DEAD
Starvation ends his search for fabled gold reef
Body in shallow grave

ADELAIDE, Tuesday: Lewis Harold Bell Lasseter, the Sydney adventurer, explorer and prospector, is dead.

Lasseter died searching for the fabulously rich gold reef he claimed he once found. With his passing the mystery of the location of the reef remains unsolved.[85]

There has never been a satisfactory explanation for why it took several months to organise an expedition to rescue Lasseter, and even then only after the third mishap with the aeroplane made finding him imperative to recovering their investment. Paul Johns later said that the delay 'had tragic consequences for Lasseter'.[86] Years later, the chairman of the exploration company, John Bailey, blamed expedition leader Fred Blakeley for Lasseter's death:

The act of the Leader of the Expedition, Mr. Blakeley, on 13 September 1930 to relinquish his position of leader of the Expedition was a fatal mistake. He should never have let Lasseter get away from him . . . He is a very straight-forward, honourable person but he displayed a lamentable lack of ability as a leader . . . The sad ending of Lasseter must be placed upon Blakeley's shoulders.[87]

For his part, Blakeley says he did not relinquish his position but was sacked. In any event, he returned to Sydney in September 1930 and a serious search for Lasseter only began three months after he left the expedition.

After hearing of Lasseter's death, the directors of the Central Australian Gold Exploration Company remained committed to finding the reef and to salvaging what they could of the substantial investment they had made in the venture.

According to John Bailey, with Lasseter dead the company was entitled to a document Lasseter had prepared and deposited in a bank before the expedition left Sydney that indicated the location of the reef. Bailey said that, in his contract with the company, Lasseter had agreed to lodge the location of the reef in a sealed envelope that could be opened in the event of his death:

The agreement was drawn up and dated 14 June 1930 . . . it stated that Harold Bell Lasseter would write a statement giving the exact location of the reef . . . and that this statement should be deposited with the Bank . . . for safe custody, and should not be opened or otherwise dealt with except on the death of Harold Lasseter.[88]

Accompanied by his son Ernest, who was the secretary of the company, John Bailey went to the Bank of Australasia on the corner of Sydney's Martin Place and George Street, but the bank manager refused to hand over the envelope:

> [We] arranged an interview with the Bank Manager to see
> if he would hand over the particulars to the company. The
> Bank Manager said, 'Are you sure he is dead? If so, I want
> to see a death certificate from some qualified person.'[89]

But Bailey was unable to get the requisite certification:

> When Bob Buck reported that he found Lasseter's body,
> the Directors asked him to sign a declaration to this effect,
> but Buck refused to do this. He said he could not swear
> whether the skeleton was that of a white or black man.[90]

Unable to persuade the bank, Bailey and the Central
Australian Gold Exploration Company made an application
to the New South Wales Supreme Court, which ordered
that they be shown the contents of Lasseter's letter.

As it turned out, the letter still did not provide the
exact location of the reef, but the Central Australian Gold
Exploration Company organised a second expedition nevertheless. This time, no attempt was made to use an aeroplane and the principal mode of transport was the camel.
The expedition team of seven men was led by Bob Buck,
who was familiar with the country, and included two qualified geologists, a wireless operator and a photographer.

They left in September 1931, and after a fruitless
search that covered four different tracks in the south of
the Northern Territory and across the Western Australian
border, they returned on 10 December 1931 to report they
could find no trace of Lasseter's gold.

Lasseter has since become one of the great Australian

legends, prompting scores of expeditions in search of his lost reef in the parched deserts of Central Australia. Over the years, a number of people have claimed to know where it is, but no evidence has yet been made publicly available to prove the reef's existence.

Even if Lasseter had found the reef again before he died, it was to be of no value to him at the end. As he lay in the remote desert and made one of his last journal entries, he would have been speaking on behalf of many of the thousands who were smitten by gold fever over the previous 80 years of the Australian gold rushes: 'What good a reef worth millions. I would give it all for a loaf of bread.'

The night too quickly passes
And we are growing old,
So let us fill our glasses
And toast the Days of Gold;
When finds of wondrous treasure
Set all the South ablaze,
And you and I were faithful mates
All through the roaring days!

Then stately ships came sailing
From every harbour's mouth,
And sought the land of promise
That beaconed in the South;
Then southward streamed their streamers
And swelled their canvas full
To speed the wildest dreamers
E'er borne in vessel's hull.

Their shining Eldorado,
Beneath the southern skies,
Was day and night for ever
Before their eager eyes.
The brooding bush, awakened,
Was stirred in wild unrest,
And all the year a human stream
Went pouring to the West.

The rough bush roads re-echoed
The bar-room's noisy din,
When troops of stalwart horsemen
Dismounted at the inn.
And oft the hearty greetings
And hearty clasp of hands
Would tell of sudden meetings
Of friends from other lands;
When, puzzled long, the new-chum
Would recognise at last,
Behind a bronzed and bearded skin,
A comrade of the past.

And when the cheery camp-fire
Explored the bush with gleams,
The camping-grounds were crowded
With caravans of teams;
Then home the jests were driven,
And good old songs were sung,
And choruses were given
The strength of heart and lung.
Oh, they were lion-hearted
Who gave our country birth!

The Gold Rush

Oh, they were of the stoutest sons
From all the lands on earth!

Oft when the camps were dreaming,
And fires began to pale,
Through rugged ranges gleaming
Would come the Royal Mail.
Behind six foaming horses,
And lit by flashing lamps,
Old 'Cobb and Co.'s', in royal state,
Went dashing past the camps.

Oh, who would paint a goldfield,
And limn the picture right,
As we have often seen it
In early morning's light;
The yellow mounds of mullock
With spots of red and white,
The scattered quartz that glistened
Like diamonds in light;
The azure line of ridges,
The bush of darkest green,
The little homes of calico
That dotted all the scene.
The flat straw hats, with ribands,
That old engravings show
The dress that still reminds us
Of sailors long ago.

I hear the fall of timber
From distant flats and fells,
The pealing of the anvils

As clear as little bells,
The rattle of the cradle,
The clack of windlass-boles,
The flutter of the crimson flags
Above the golden holes.

. . . .

Ah, then our hearts were bolder,
And if Dame Fortune frowned
Our swags we'd lightly shoulder
And tramp to other ground.
But golden days are vanished,
And altered is the scene;
The diggings are deserted,
The camping-grounds are green;
The flaunting flag of progress
Is in the West unfurled,
The mighty bush with iron rails
Is tethered to the world.

'The Roaring Days', Henry Lawson

References

Chapter One: Hargraves

[1]   Hargraves, p. vii.

[2]   Ibid., p. viii.

[3]   Ibid., p. 73.

[4]   Bateson, p. 40.

[5]   Hargraves, p. 73.

[6]   Bateson, p. 46.

[7]   Hargraves, p. 72.

[8]   Bateson, p. 7.

[9]   Davison later wrote an account of his time in Australia and California (*The Discovery and Geognosy of Gold Deposits in Australia*), six years after Hargraves wrote his book. There are many strikingly similar passages in the two books, leading to the suggestion that Davison relied heavily on the contents of Hargraves's earlier work. It has also been suggested that Davison may have had a hand in the writing of Hargraves's book.

[10]   Davison, p. 3.

[11]   Ibid., p. 29.

[12]   Hargraves, p. 74.

[13]   Ibid., p. 75.

14 Ibid., p. 76.

15 Davison, p. 32.

16 Hargraves, p. 85.

17 Ibid., p. 82.

18 Ibid., p. 84.

19 Ibid., p. 87.

20 Letter from Hargraves to S. Peek, Hargraves, p. 90.

21 Hargraves, p. 90.

22 The gold reward was explained in a letter from Governor
    FitzRoy to Colonial Secretary Earl Grey on 11 June 1852.
    'About two years ago a Mr. Smith, who engaged in some iron
    works in the vicinity of Berrima, produced to the colonial
    secretary a lump of gold embedded in quartz, which he said
    that he picked up at a certain place, which he offered to make
    known to the government upon being previously rewarded
    for the intelligence by the payment to him of a large sum.
    The obvious reply to this offer was, that the government
    could enter into no blind bargain on such a subject, but
    that if Mr. Smith thought proper to trust the liberality of
    the Government he might rely upon being rewarded in
    proportion to the value of the alleged discovery, when that
    was ascertained.' British Parliamentary Papers 1852, Vol. 14.

23 Hargraves's evidence to the Select Committee, New South Wales
    Legislative Council, 23 October 1890, Mitchell Library, Q89 53.

24 Hargraves, p. 111.

25 Ibid., p. 113.

26 Ibid.

27 Ibid., p. 114.

28 Ibid.

29 Ibid., p. 115.

30 Ibid.

31 Ibid., p. 116.

32 Ibid.

33 Ibid.

34 Ibid., p. 117.

35 Tom and Lister, p. 3.

36 Hargraves, p. 118.

37 Ibid., p. 117.

38 John Rule, p. 26.

39 Hargraves, p. 119.

40 Ibid., p. 120.

41 Hargraves made no references to his family in the account he wrote of his adventures other than to say he married at 18 and first became a father at 19. However, according to his travelling companion in California Simpson Davison, Hargraves had a wife, Elizabeth (née Mackie), and five daughters waiting for him at East Gosford.

42 Hargraves, p. 120.

43 Letter from Thomson to Hargraves, 15 April 1851, library roll 7 1851–52, Mitchell Library, Ref 1 MAV/FM4 10867.

44 Hargraves, p. 122.

45 Letter from Thomson to Stutchbury, 5 May 1851, Papers Relative to Geological Surveyor, p. 252, Mitchell Library, Ref 1 MAV/FM4 10867.

46 Letter from FitzRoy to Earl Grey, 1 March 1849, Papers 252, Mitchell Library, Ref 1 MAV/FM4 10867.

47 Letter from Hargraves to Thomson, 30 April 1851, Papers Relative to Geological Surveyor, p. 252, Mitchell Library, Ref 1 MAV/FM4 10867.

48 Letter from Stutchbury to FitzRoy, undated but believed to be around 13 May 1851, Mitchell Library, Ref 1 MAV/FM4 10867.

49 Letter from Stutchbury to FitzRoy, 19 May 1851, Mitchell Library, Ref 1 MAV/FM4 10867.

50 McBrien, journal entry, 15 February 1823.

51 Evidence before the Select Committee on the Claims of Reverend W. B. Clarke, New South Wales Legislative Assembly, Votes and Proceedings, Vol. 2, 1861, p. 1186.

52 Davison, p. 53.

53 Ibid., p. 272.

54 Memo from Smith to Korff, 19 April 1850 and 30 May 1850, Papers of W. B. Clarke, Mitchell Library, State Library of New South Wales, ML MSS 139/57.

55 Letter from Thomson to Smith, 12 June 1851.

56 The letters to Thomson and FitzRoy were both republished in the *Bathurst Free Press* on 1 January 1852.

57 New South Wales Parliament, Records of Legislative Proceedings, 16 December 1852.

58 8 June 1853, reported by the *Sydney Morning Herald* on 9 June 1853.

59 Report of the Select Committee of the Legislative Council of New South Wales appointed to consider the Gold Fields Management Bill, 20 September 1853.

60 *Sydney Morning Herald*, 6 August 1875.

61 Ibid., 12 December 1891.

Chapter Two: Sydney – The First Rush

1 Capper, p. 20.

2 Ibid.

3 *Sydney Morning Herald*, 16 May 1851.

4 Letter from FitzRoy to Grey, 22 May 1851, Further Papers Relative to the Recent Discovery of Gold in Australia: in Continuation of Papers Presented to Parliament, 3 February 1852, Mitchell Library, State Library of New South Wales, ML DSM/Q553 41/G.

5 Ibid.

6   Mundy, p. 308.

7   Ibid., p. 309.

8   Rolls, p. 94.

9   Mundy, p. 316.

10 Ibid.

11 Godley, p. 356.

12 Erskine, p. 18.

13 *Sydney Morning Herald*, 21 June 1851.

14 In the month following 21 June 1851, more than 800 people came to the New South Wales goldfields from Melbourne, Adelaide and Hobart, including 710 men, 89 women, 45 boys and 41 girls (Erskine, p. 14).

15 Thomas Icely, New South Wales Parliament, 23 May 1851.

16 Mundy, p. 317.

17 It is believed that William Hall first arrived in Victoria in 1838, as he appears in the first Port Phillip census of that year.

18 Hall, p. 67.

19 Erskine, p. 12.

20 Ibid., p. 33.

21 Cannon, p. 182.

22 Mundy, p. 334.

23 Mitchell, *Diary*, 18 June 1851.

24 Mundy, p. 316.

25 Australian Journalist, p. 41.

26 Ibid.

27 Mitchell, *Diary*, 19 June 1851.

28 Ibid.

29 Erskine, p. 15.

30 Mundy, p. 313.

31 Letter from Hardy to Thomson, 5 June 1851, Further Papers Relative to the Recent Discovery of Gold in Australia: in

Continuation of Papers Presented to Parliament, 3 February 1852, Mitchell Library, State Library of New South Wales, ML DSM/Q553.41/G.

[32] Ibid.

[33] Ibid.

[34] Mundy, p. 372.

[35] A gunyah is constructed from the branches and bark of the eucalypt tree.

[36] Glasson, p. 5.

[37] Mundy, p. 333.

[38] Erskine, p. 19.

[39] Australian Journalist, p. 44.

[40] *Maitland Mercury*, 28 May 1851.

[41] *Sydney Morning Herald*, 2 June 1851.

[42] Australian Journalist, p. 40.

[43] Erskine, p. 30.

[44] Australian Journalist, p. 45.

[45] Erskine, p. 27.

[46] Letter from FitzRoy to Grey, 15 August 1851, Further Papers Relative to the Recent Discovery of Gold in Australia: in Continuation of Papers Presented to Parliament, 3 February 1852, Mitchell Library, State Library of New South Wales, ML DSM/Q553.41/G.

[47] Australian Journalist, p. 39.

[48] Mundy, p. 322.

[49] Ibid.

[50] *Empire* newspaper, 15 October 1851; *Maitland Mercury*, 22 October 1851.

[51] Richard Kennedy.

[52] McGowan, p. i.

[53] Richard Kennedy.

[54] Ibid.

55 *Maitland Mercury*, 15 October 1851.

56 *Bathurst Free Press*, 16 July 1851.

57 *Sydney Morning Herald*, 23 July 1851.

Chapter Three: A Bigger Rush in Victoria

1   The British Parliament legislation was given Royal Assent on 5 August 1850 to establish the separate colony of Victoria from 1 July 1851.

2   Census of 1851. New South Wales: 192,000. Victoria: 77,000. Tasmania: 70,000 (including 24,000 convicts). South Australia: 67,000. Western Australia: 5886. Queensland was then still part of the colony of New South Wales.

3   Blainey, *Our Side of the Country*, p. 16.

4   Van Diemen's Land was officially renamed Tasmania in 1856.

5   Blainey, *Our Side of the Country*, p. 32.

6   *The Alpenstock: Of Sketches of Swiss Scenery and Manners, 1829*, and *The Pedestrian: A Summer's Ramble in the Tyrol, 1832*.

7   *The Rambler in North America, 1832–1833*, and *The Rambler in Mexico, 1834*.

8   From 1851, La Trobe – and his successor, Sir Charles Hotham – held the title lieutenant governor of Victoria, until the title was changed to governor in May 1855 following the colony being granted a separate colonial government.

9   Blainey, *Our Side of the Country*, p. 35.

10 Howitt, p. 14.

11 *Argus*, 29 and 31 May 1851.

12 The 'neighbourhood of the Pyrenees' referred to was Clunes, and the precise spot where Esmond made the discovery was on the banks of Creswick Creek.

13 *Argus*, 3 October 1851.

14 Hall, p. 10.

15 Australian Journalist, p. 70, from a letter sent from Golden Point, 29 October 1851.

16 Ibid.

17 Ibid.

18 Letter from La Trobe to Grey, 25 August 1851, Further Papers Relative to the Recent Discovery of Gold in Australia: in Continuation of Papers Presented to Parliament, 3 February 1852, Mitchell Library, State Library of New South Wales, ML DSM/Q553.41/G.

19 Letter from La Trobe to Grey, 10 October 1851, Further Papers Relative to the Recent Discovery of Gold in Australia: in Continuation of Papers Presented to Parliament, 3 February 1852, Mitchell Library, State Library of New South Wales, ML DSM/Q553.41/G.

20 Letter from FitzRoy to Grey, 10 November 1852 (received in London on 5 February 1853), Further Papers Relative to the Recent Discovery of Gold in Australia: in Continuation of Papers Presented to Parliament, 3 February 1852, Mitchell Library, State Library of New South Wales, ML DSM Q553/41/G.

21 Clacy, p. 21.

22 Hall, p. 11.

23 Ibid., p. 12.

24 Ibid., p. 15.

25 Ibid., p. 16.

26 Ibid., p. 17.

27 Ibid., p. 19.

28 Ibid., p. 22.

29 There are 20 dwts, or pennyweights, to the ounce.

30 Hall, p. 27.

31 Ibid., p. 28.

[32]   Ibid., p. 29.

[33]   Ibid., p. 30.

[34]   Ibid.

[35]   Blainey, *A History of Victoria*, p. 30.

[36]   Ibid.

[37]   Thomas, Further Papers Relative to the Recent Discovery of Gold in Australia: in Continuation of Papers Presented to Parliament, 3 February 1852, Mitchell Library, State Library of New South Wales, ML DSM/Q553.41/G.

[38]   Australian Journalist, p. 56.

[39]   Ibid., p. 57.

[40]   Ibid.

[41]   Ibid.

[42]   Ibid., p. 58.

[43]   Letter from a 'gentleman', quoted in ibid., p. 59.

[44]   Letter from a Geelong farmer, quoted in ibid.

[45]   Diary of William Anderson Crawthorne, 1849–59, New South Wales State Library, MS B230.

[46]   Clacy, p. 25.

[47]   Charles Rule, 2 February 1852.

[48]   Ibid., 9 February 1852.

[49]   Ibid., 15 February 1852.

[50]   Ibid., 20 February 1852.

Chapter Four: The World Joins the Rush

[1]   The Marquess of Salisbury was prime minister from 1885–86, 1886–92 and 1895–1902. Lord Cecil inherited the title of the Marquess of Salisbury in 1868. (His older brother and most immediate heir to the title died in 1865.) His life traversed almost the entire Victorian age. He was born 11 years after Queen Victoria on 3 February 1830 and died two years later than her, in 1903.

2   Lord Robert Cecil, p. 8.
3   Ibid., p. 9.
4   Ibid., p. 10.
5   Ibid., p. 14.
6   Ibid., p 17.
7   Ibid., p. 21.
8   Ibid., p. 24.
9   Ibid., p. 32.
10 Ibid., p. 44.
11 Capper, pp. 8–10.
12 Ibid., p. 12.
13 Ibid., p. 62.
14 Ibid., p. 63.
15 Ibid., p. 68.
16 Ibid., p. 70.
17 Ibid., p. 71.
18 Ibid.
19 Ibid., p. 73.
20 Lubbock, p. 11.
21 *New York Times*, 12 January 1853.
22 Fayle, p. 246.
23 Hassam, p. 9.
24 Lubbock, p. 7.
25 Sherer, p. 1.
26 Ibid., p. 8.
27 Jupp, p. 765.
28 Sherer, p. 7.
29 Howitt, p. 19.
30 Ibid., p. 9.
31 Ibid., p. 15.
32 Ibid.
33 Ibid., p. 18.

References

34 Preshaw, p. 28.

35 'Census of Victoria: The Population of the Victorian Gold Field, March 1857, Covering the Warden's Districts of Ballarat, Castlemaine, Avoca, Sandhurst, Beechworth and Saint Andrews'. Total persons 166,550, of which 43,490 were females.

36 'Census of Victoria: The Population of the Victorian Gold Fields, April 1861, Covering the Warden's Districts of Ballarat, Castlemaine, Avoca, Sandhurst, Beechworth and Saint Andrews'. Total persons 228,181, of which 73,489 were females.

37 Skinner, p. 1.

38 Ibid., p. 24.

39 Ibid., p. 12.

40 Ibid., p. 15.

41 Ibid.

42 Ibid., p. 17.

43 Ibid., p. 18.

44 Ibid., p. 22.

45 Ibid.

46 Ibid., p. 23.

47 Ibid.

48 Ibid., p. 24.

49 Ibid.

50 Chen Ta, p. 16.

51 Jupp, p. 199, estimates that by the end of the early 1860s there were more than 25,000 Chinese in Victoria and nearly 13,000 in New South Wales. On the Palmer River diggings in Far North Queensland, there were over 10,000 in 1876 and 12,000 on the Hodgkinson in 1877. By the early 1880s, there were over 800 Chinese on the diggings in north-western Tasmania, and there were nearly 4000 in the Northern

Territory by the end of the 1880s. By the end of the 1890s, there were an estimated 5000 Chinese in Western Australia, even though Western Australian laws prohibited the Chinese from working on the goldfields.

[52] Rolls, p. 103.

[53] *Sydney Morning Herald*, 8 September 1852.

[54] *Maitland Mercury*, 5 February 1853; *Argus*, 7 February, 19 February, 18 March 1853.

[55] Rolls, p. 114.

[56] Ibid., p. 116.

[57] *Argus*, 28 August 1854.

[58] *Maitland Mercury*, 29 August 1854.

[59] Ibid., 21 February 1855.

[60] Rolls, p. 117.

[61] Hassam, p. 10.

[62] Fauchery, p. 4.

[63] Davison, p. 65.

[64] Handbill for the clipper *Isabella*, Australian National Maritime Museum.

[65] Davison, p. 66.

[66] Ibid., p. 67.

[67] Ibid.

[68] Ibid., p. 68.

[69] Ibid., p. 69.

[70] Lubbock, p. 23.

Chapter Five: Life on the Goldfields

[1] Clacy, p. 28.

[2] Ibid., p. 55.

[3] Ibid., p. 13.

[4] Ibid., p. 24.

[5] Ibid., p. 25.

References

6   Ibid., p. 22.

7   Ibid.

8   Ibid., p. 63.

9   Ibid., p. 69.

10   Ibid., p. 56.

11   Ibid., p. 136.

12   Ibid., p. 170.

13   Ibid., p. 175.

14   Emilsen, p. 50.

15   Clacy, p. 62.

16   Ibid., p. 56.

17   Ibid., p. 55.

18   Chandler, p. 67.

19   Ibid.

20   Clacy, p. 55.

21   Australian Journalist, p. 77.

22   Clacy, p. 58.

23   Advertisement reproduced in Bartlett, p. 48.

24   La Trobe Collection, State Library of Victoria.

25   Bradfield, p. 46.

26   Bruce Seymour, www.zpub.com/sf/history/lola/Lola-Seymourfiles.html.

27   *New York Times*, 28 April 1850.

28   *San Francisco Herald*, 22 May 1853.

29   *San Francisco Bulletin*, 2 November 1855.

30   *Adelaide Advertiser*, 1 December 1855.

31   *Geelong Advertiser*, 20 February 1856; *Sydney Morning Herald*, 25 February 1856; *Hobart Mercury*, 29 February 1856.

32   *Sydney Morning Herald*, 29 February 1856.

33   Ibid.

34   *Golden Era*, 3 August 1856.

35 Letter from a 'gentleman', quoted in Australian Journalist, p. 58.

36 Howitt, p. 16.

37 Fauchery, p. 84.

38 Pearl, p. 8.

39 Blainey, *Black Kettle and Full Moon*, pp. 283–6.

40 *Illustrated Sydney News*, 3 February 1853.

41 Pearl, p. 17.

42 *Sydney Morning Herald*, 19 November 1855.

43 Pearl, p. 18.

44 Ibid., p. 22.

45 Ibid., p. 24.

46 *Argus*, 20 November 1857.

47 *Argus,* 8 May 1857.

48 Australian Journalist, p. 61.

49 Hall, p. 11.

50 Pughe, reprinted in Pearl, p. 18.

51 Extracts from the journal 'A Visit to New South Wales', reprinted in *Fraser's Magazine*, November and December 1853.

52 Ibid.

53 Searle, p. 239.

54 Pearl, p. 4.

55 Jevons, p. 145.

56 Ibid., p. 147.

57 *Sydney Morning Herald*, 24 April 1860.

58 Sherer, p. 325.

Chapter Six: The Eureka Rebellion

1 *Geelong Advertiser*, 27 August 1851.

2 The licence fee became law in Victoria on 16 August 1851 and the first licences were issued on 20 September 1851.

3 'Report from the Commission appointed to Inquire into the

Conditions on the Gold Fields', Victorian Parliamentary
Papers, Legislative Council, Votes and Proceedings,
A 76/1854–55, Vol. II.

4   Moloney, p. 20.

5   Lord Robert Cecil, p. 25.

6   Howitt, p. 421.

7   Howitt used the pseudonym of 'Hermsprong' for Armstrong:
    'If I name him not exactly, there are ten thousand who can
    do it for me.'

8   Howitt, p. 424.

9   Ibid.

10 Carboni, p. 3.

11 It was claimed there were 23,000 signatories but the
    surviving petition in the Treasures section of the State
    Library of Victoria has between 5000 and 6000 signatories.

12 *Bathurst Free Press*, 21 August 1852.

13 Hotham to Bart, 18 September 1854, Dispatch no. 112,
    VPRS 1085/P unit 8.

14 Ibid.

15 Ibid.

16 Ibid.

17 Carboni, p. 13.

18 Hotham to Bart, 18 September 1854, Dispatch no. 112,
    VPRS 1085/P unit 8.

19 Ibid.

20 Hirst, p. 200.

21 *Argus*, 1 December 1854.

22 *Ballarat Times*, 12 November 1854.

23 Carboni, p. 26.

24 Hotham to Bart, 18 November 1854, Dispatch no. 148,
    VPRS 1085/P unit 8.

25 Ibid.

26 VPRS 937/P unit 10.

27 VPRS 1095 unit 3, bundle 1, number 16.

28 *Geelong Advertiser*, 2 December 1854.

29 Carboni, p. 35.

30 VPRS 1189/P unit 92, J54/14461.

31 Rede to Colonial Secretary, VPRS 1085/P unit 8, no. 4.

32 Lalor's account was published in the *Argus* newspaper
   several months later, on 10 April 1855, when he was still
   at large with a government reward posted for his capture.

33 *Argus*, 10 April 1855.

34 Ibid.

35 Ibid.

36 Ibid.

37 Ferguson, p. 59.

38 Ibid., p. 60.

39 Ibid., p. 61.

40 Ibid.

41 Ibid., pp. 61–2.

42 Ibid., p. 63.

43 The *Ballarat Times* articles appeared on 18 November,
   25 November and 2 December 1854.

44 Report of Captain J. W. Thomas to the major adjutant
   general, 3 December 1854, State Library of Victoria,
   VPRS 1805/P 162, enclosure N.7.

45 Ferguson, p. 66.

46 Letter signed by prominent landholders to Hotham,
   VPRS 4066/P unit 1, no. 50.

47 Letter from the Melbourne Council to Hotham,
   VPRS 1085/P unit 8, no. 17.

48 Resolution of the Victorian Legislative Council, 20 December
   1854, VPRS 1805/P unit 8, no. 16.

49 *Age*, 5 December 1852.

50   *Illustrated Australian News*, March 1855.

51   'Report from the Commission Appointed to Inquire into
     Conditions in the Goldfields', Victorian Parliamentary
     Papers, Legislative Council, Votes and Proceedings,
     A 76/1854-55, Vol. II.

52   Ibid.

53   *Age*, 3 April 1855.

Chapter Seven: The Chinese

1   *Argus*, 11 April 1855.

2   *Sydney Morning Herald*, 7 May 1855.

3   Young.

4   *Argus*, 23 May 1855.

5   Young.

6   Ibid.

7   Reverend William Young gave examples: 600 of the 1000
     Chinese men at Marlborough at the time of his report had
     wives in China, along with 450 of the 1000 at Daylesford
     and Hepburn, 150 of the 250 at Avoca, 3500 of the 7000
     at Beechworth, 300 of the 1000 at Castlemaine, Mopoke,
     Diamond Point and Golden Point, two-thirds of those
     at Sandhurst and 30 per cent at Ararat, Possums Gully,
     Beaufort, Commissioners Hill, Spring Hill and Canton Lead.

8   Lovejoy, p. 11, calculates that 38 per cent of Chinese miners
     on the Victorian goldfields were accompanied by relatives
     (18 per cent by brothers, 12 per cent by cousins and the
     remainder by their fathers, uncles, sons or nephews). A
     further 43 per cent were with friends, many they had known
     from childhood from the same villages in China. Seven per
     cent were with other people they knew and only nine per cent
     were alone and not part of a family or social network.

9   Young.

10. The Powerhouse Museum in Sydney has in its collection some of these tins, measuring about 100 x 90 x 90 millimetres.

11. Young.

12. Ibid.

13. Ibid.

14. From an article titled 'John Chinaman' by 'a Correspondent' published in the *Argus* newspaper, 23 May 1855.

15. *Argus*, 12 April 1855.

16. Ibid., 30 June 1855.

17. Jupp, p. 201.

18. Welsh, p. 6.

19. Young.

20. Ibid.

21. *Maitland Mercury*, 20 March 1852.

22. *Argus*, 24 March 1854.

23. Ibid., 12 August 1854.

24. *Maitland Mercury*, 2 September 1854.

25. *Argus*, 12 October 1854.

26. 'Report from the Commission appointed to Inquire into the Conditions on the Gold Fields', Victorian Parliamentary Papers, Legislative Council, Votes and Proceedings, A 76/1854-55 Vol. II.

27. *Argus*, 11 April 1855.

28. Ibid., 12 April 1855.

29. Ibid., 18 April 1855.

30. Ibid., 17 April 1855.

31. Ibid., 5 May 1855.

32. Ibid., 16 April 1855.

33. Colonial Secretary, Victorian Legislative Assembly, 23 May 1855.

34. Letter from Hotham to Grey, 2 April 1855, VPRS 1085/P unit 9.

References

[35] The town of Robe was named after Governor Frederick Holte Robe, who sailed into Guichen Bay in 1846. Guichen Bay had been named 40 years earlier by the French explorer Nicholas Baudin in honour of the French Admiral De Guichen.

[36] Melville, p. 108.

[37] Ibid., p. 109.

[38] Smeaton.

[39] Ibid.

[40] Ibid.

[41] *Adelaide Observer*, 19 July 1857.

[42] Ibid.

[43] Melville, p. 114.

[44] Welsh, p. 1.

[45] Ritchie, p. 31.

[46] Welsh, p. 1.

[47] Letter from Charles Dowling to the chief secretary of Victoria, 9 June 1857, Public Records Office, Victoria, 57/103 – A4381.

[48] Sadlier, p. 113.

[49] Young.

[50] Ibid.

[51] Curthoys, p. 109.

[52] Letter from the gold commissioner, Luisa Creek, 3 May 1858, New South Wales Archives Office, 58/1449.3578; Report of Gold Commissioner Griffin, 23 August 1858, *Journal of the New South Wales Legislative Committee*, 1858, Vol. 3, p. 130; Rocky River and Meroo petitions, Votes of Proceedings of New South Wales Legislative Assembly, 1858, Vol. 2, p. 947; Turon petition, *Journal of the New South Wales Legislative Committee*, 1858, Vol. 3, p. 303.

[53] *Bathurst Free Press*, 21 June 1857.

[54] Moye, p. 1.

55 *Sydney Morning Herald*, 25 February 1860.

56 Letter from Cloete to the undersecretary for lands,
15 February 1860, republished in Moye, p. 9.

57 *Sydney Morning Herald*, 22 July 1860.

58 *Goulburn Herald*, 4 April 1860.

59 Freeling, 'Report of the Surveyor General on the Apparent
Value of the River Diggings, and the Probable Success of
Those Who May Visit Them', 15 May 1860, republished in
full in the South Australian Advertiser, 17 May 1860.

60 Ibid.

61 Ibid.

62 Ibid.

63 *Argus*, 1 June 1860.

64 Freeling.

65 Preshaw, p. 45.

66 Ibid.

67 Ibid., p. 46.

68 Ibid., p. 48.

69 Ibid.

70 Ibid.

71 Ibid., p. 50.

72 Ibid., p. 51.

73 Ibid.

74 Ibid., p. 52.

75 Ibid., p. 54.

76 'Report from Gold Commissioner Cloete to Secretary Lands',
15 September 1860, New South Wales Legislative Assembly
Papers, 1860 (republished in Moye, p. 27).

77 Ibid.

78 Preshaw, p. 56.

79 Ibid., p. 61.

80 *Sydney Morning Herald*, 21 August 1860.

81 Ibid., 2 August 1860.

82 *Braidwood Observer and Miners Advocate*, 11 August 1860.

83 Ibid.

84 *Alpine Pioneer*, 31 August 1860.

85 Curthoys, p. 110.

86 Rolls, p. 165.

87 *Yass Courier*, 10 July 1860; *Morton Bay Courier*, 14 July 1860.

88 *Yass Courier*, 19 December 1860.

89 *Bathurst Free Press*, 2 February 1860.

90 *The Miner*, 2 February 1860.

91 *Moreton Bay Courier*, 21 February 1861.

92 The construction of the railway line reached Campbelltown in May 1858.

93 *Sydney Morning Herald*, 23 March 1861.

94 *Argus*, 21 March 1861.

95 Preshaw, p. 77.

96 *Sydney Morning Herald*, 3 July 1861; *Brisbane Courier*, 8 July 1861; *Argus*, 10 July 1861.

97 *Sydney Morning Herald*, 10 July 1861.

98 Ibid., 3 July 1861.

99 *Sydney Morning Herald*, 18 July 1861; Melbourne *Argus*, 22 July 1861.

100 Ibid.

101 Rolls, p. 170.

102 *Sydney Morning Herald*, 18 July 1861.

103 Ibid.

104 Ibid., 19 July 1861.

105 'Report of the superintendent of patrol to the minister of lands', republished in the Melbourne *Argus*, 22 July 1861.

Chapter Eight: The Gold Rush Spreads

1   Advertisement in the *Maitland Mercury*, 15 November 1851.

2   Blainey, *The Rush That Never Ended*, p. 74.

3   Ibid., p. 79.

4   David Kennedy, p. 90.

5   Higgins, p. 81.

6   Coates, p. 39.

7   Burke, p. 11.

8   Ibid., p. 15.

9   Ibid.

10 Ibid.

11 The collection was exhibited at the Philadelphia Centennial Exhibition in 1876 and the Paris Exposition Universelle Internationale in 1878.

12 Burke, p. 33.

13 Trollope, p. 284.

14 Ibid.

15 Ibid., p. 285.

16 Ibid., p. 288.

17 Ibid., p. 286.

18 Maxwell, p. 91.

19 Ibid.

20 Miller, p. 757.

21 *Wellington Advertiser*, 29 August 1861.

22 Ballarat *Star*, 2 September 1861.

23 Eldred-Grigg, p. 87.

24 *Otago Witness*, 30 November 1861.

25 *New Zealand Spectator and Cook Straits Guardian*, 23 April 1864.

26 *Hobart Colonial Times*, 14 October 1851.

27 Ibid., 24 October 1851.

28 *Hobart Courier*, 20 December 1851.

29 *Sydney Morning Herald*, 19 September 1871; *Western Australian Times*, 22 September 1871.

30 'Report of South Australian Government Resident in Darwin Captain Douglas to the South Australian Government', 21 August 1871, published in the *Brisbane Courier*, 27 October 1871.

31 Ernestine Hill, *The Territory*, p. 121.

32 'The Northern Territory and its Goldfields', Advertiser and Chronicle Office, Adelaide, 1875.

33 The Australian National Government became responsible for the administration of the Northern Territory in 1911.

34 *South Australian Register*, 20 March 1852.

Chapter Nine: Law and Disorder

1   *New York Times*, 24 August 1852.

2   *Victorian Government Gazette*, 21 April 1852.

3   The Orient Bank had £700 in notes and coins and 2067 ounces of gold in the escort, the Bank of New South Wales 521 ounces of gold and the Commercial Bank £3000 in notes and coins.

4   Thurgood, p. 24.

5   *Argus*, 2 July 1862.

6   *Hobart Mercury*, 5 August 1862.

7   White, Vol. 1, p. 264.

8   *Brisbane Courier*, 11 November 1862.

9   Thurgood, p. 13.

10 Ibid., p. 28.

11 Ibid., p. 30.

12 Ibid., p. 160.

13 Ibid., p. 161.

14 Ibid., p. 165.

15 Ibid., p. 178.

16 *Sydney Morning Herald*, 27 March 1863.

17   Queensland had become a separate colony from New South
     Wales in 1859.

18   *Brisbane Courier*, 14 March 1864.

19   Letter from Inspector of Police William Elyard to Pottinger,
     printed in the *Sydney Morning Herald*, 26 March 1865.

20   *Sydney Morning Herald*, 5 March 1865.

21   White, Vol. 1, p. 235.

22   *West Australian*, 30 April 1880.

23   *Maitland Mercury*, 29 August 1882.

Chapter Ten: Queensland Joins the Rush

1   Traill, p. 56.

2   Brown, p. 93.

3   Earlier finds of gold in and around Queensland included:
    Canoona, near Rockhampton, in 1858; Tooloom, in
    northern New South Wales, in 1859, which attracted diggers
    from Ipswich and other parts of southern Queensland;
    Clermont, 200 kilometres west of Rockhampton in central
    Queensland, in 1861; Calliope, 20 kilometres west of
    the port of Gladstone in central Queensland, in 1862;
    Warrick, 180 kilometres south-west of Brisbane, in 1863;
    Gavial Creek, Bouldercombe, in 1865; Rosewood, near
    Rockhampton, in 1866; Cloncurry, in 1867; Cape River,
    in 1867, which saw the first influx of Chinese onto the
    Queensland goldfields; and Nanango, 200 kilometres north-
    west of Brisbane in 1867.

4   *Morton Bay Courier*, 21 July 1858; *Sydney Morning Herald*,
    26 July 1858.

5   'A Retrospective Reverie', *Gympie Times*, 16 October 1917,
    republished in *Gympie's Jubilee*, The Gympie and District
    Historical Society, 1985, p. 19.

6   Ibid.

References

7   Nash, 'The Discoverer's Account', *Gympie Times*,
     15 October 1896, republished in *Gympie's Jubilee*,
     The Gympie and District Historical Society, 1985, p. 14.

8   Ibid.

9   Nash, 'Early Gympie Incidents', *Gympie Times*, 16 October
     1917, republished in *Gympie's Jubilee*, The Gympie and
     District Historical Society, 1985, p. 20.

10   'The Discoverer's Account', *Gympie Times*, 15 October
     1896, republished in *Gympie's Jubilee*, The Gympie and
     District Historical Society, 1985, p. 14.

11   Ibid.

12   *Brisbane Courier*, 17 October 1867.

13   *Maryborough Chronicle*, October 1867.

14   'Early Gympie Incidents', *Gympie Times*, 16 October 1917,
     republished in *Gympie's Jubilee*, The Gympie and District
     Historical Society, 1985, p. 20.

15   Ibid.

16   Edward Kennedy, p. 40.

17   Ibid., p. 3.

18   Ibid., p. 4.

19   Holthouse, *Gympie Gold*, p. 72.

20   Edward Kennedy, p. 51.

21   Ibid., p. 52.

22   *Maryborough Gazette*, 16 May 1868.

23   Edward Kennedy, p. 54.

24   Catherine Nash, p. 16.

25   Ibid.

26   Ibid.

27   Ibid.

28   Ibid.

29   Ibid.

30   Ibid.

[31] Ibid.

[32] Holthouse, *Gympie Gold*, p. 114.

[33] Letter from Nash to the Queensland commissioner for public lands, Archives Section, Public Library of Queensland, republished in Keesing, p. 258.

[34] Hooper, p. 4.

[35] Weitemeyer, p. 7.

[36] Ibid.

[37] Ibid.

[38] Ibid., p. 168.

[39] Ibid.

[40] Ibid.

[41] Ibid., p. 174.

[42] Ibid., p. 188.

[43] Ibid., p. 189.

[44] Ibid., p. 190.

[45] Ibid., p. 193.

[46] Ibid., p. 194.

[47] Ibid., p. 196.

[48] Loos, pp. 36–7.

[49] Hooper, p. 59.

Chapter Eleven: The Palmer River

[1] The prior explorers were Sir Thomas Mitchell and Ludwig Leichhardt in 1845, Edward Kennedy in 1848 and Hann's friend Richard Daintree in 1868.

[2] Holthouse, *River of Gold*, p. 7.

[3] Sir Arthur Hunter Palmer, 1819–98. Palmer was born in Dublin, the son of a navy lieutenant, and sailed to Australia as a 19-year-old in 1834. After many years working on farms in New South Wales, he became a successful pastoralist in Queensland. In 1866, he was elected to the Queensland

References

Legislative Assembly and was premier from May 1870 to
January 1874.

4   Hann, p. 7.

5   Ibid., p. 8.

6   Ibid., p. 13.

7   Holthouse, *River of Gold*, p. 7.

8   The other five were Albert Brandt, James Dodwell, David
Robinson, Peter Abelsen (also known as Peter Brown) and
Alexander Watson.

9   Gold was found on the Peel River and the Duncan, Nundle
and Dungowan Creeks about 45 kilometres south-south-east
of Tamworth in New South Wales in 1853.

10   Mulligan, p. 7.

11   Ibid.

12   Mulligan recorded in his diary, 'August 12th to 24th. We
remain in this our 13th camp on the Palmer. Here we got
payable gold,' p. 10.

13   Mulligan, p. 10.

14   Holthouse, *River of Gold*, p. 13.

15   *Queenslander*, 10 September 1873.

16   Ibid., 15 September 1873.

17   Holthouse, *River of Gold*, p. 15.

18   Ibid.

19   Ibid., p. 21.

20   Mulligan, p. 10.

21   Holthouse, *River of Gold*, p. 24.

22   Ibid., p. 19.

23   Dalrymple, p. 1.

24   Ibid., p. 3.

25   Cooktown was named after Captain James Cook, who had
been there a little over a hundred years earlier. In June 1770,
while he was sailing north along the east coast of Australia,

the *Endeavour* struck the Great Barrier Reef and was
seriously damaged below the waterline. He managed to sail
the stricken ship into the mouth of a nearby river, which he
named Endeavour after his ship. The ship was put on its side
for repairs, and Cook resumed his voyage on 4 August.

[26] Holthouse, *River of Gold*, p. 28.

[27] Ibid., p. 30.

[28] Mulligan, p. 21.

[29] Holthouse, *River of Gold*, p. 40.

[30] Ibid.

[31] Ibid., p. 49.

[32] Ibid., p. 40.

[33] Mulligan, p. 10.

[34] Weitemeyer, p. 211.

[35] Ibid., p. 213.

[36] Ibid., p. 276.

[37] Ibid., p. 277.

[38] Ibid., p. 222.

[39] Ibid., p. 223.

[40] Ibid., p. 278.

[41] Ibid.

[42] Ibid.

[43] Ibid.

[44] Ibid.

[45] Ibid.

[46] Holthouse, *River of Gold*, p. 50.

[47] Mulligan, p. 29.

[48] Holthouse, *River of Gold*, p. 55.

[49] Weitemeyer, p. 220.

[50] *Queenslander*, 4 December 1875.

[51] *Queenslander*, 8 January 1876.

[52] The *Queenslander*, 27 November 1875, reported that Sellheim

References

had said there were 6000 Chinese and only 1900 Europeans.

[53] Mulligan, p. 27.

[54] *Queenslander*, 18 June 1876.

[55] Ibid.

[56] Holthouse, *River of Gold*, p. 140.

[57] *Queenslander*, 27 November 1875.

[58] *Cooktown Herald*, March 1876.

[59] *Queenslander*, 27 November 1875.

[60] Ibid., 29 May 1878.

[61] Mulligan, p. 28.

[62] Holthouse, *River of Gold*, p. 80.

[63] William Hill, pp. 68–71.

[64] Holthouse, *River of Gold*, p. 88.

[65] *Cooktown Herald*, May 1876.

[66] Holthouse, *River of Gold*, p. 99.

[67] Corfield, p. 54.

[68] Queensland Parliamentary Debates, 1876, Vol. XX, pp. 376–7.

[69] May, p. 287.

[70] Hooper, p. 6.

[71] Holthouse, *River of Gold*, p. 196.

[72] Mulligan, p. 54.

[73] Ibid., p. 37.

[74] *Queenslander*, 1 January 1876.

[75] *Brisbane Courier*, 10 April 1876.

[76] Ibid., 19 April 1876.

[77] Holthouse, *River of Gold*, p. 132.

[78] May, p. 1.

[79] *Queenslander*, 10 June 1876.

[80] Mulligan, p. 59.

[81] Dempsey, p. 12.

Chapter Twelve: The Wild West

1   Named after the Earl of Kimberley (1826–1902), who was the secretary of state for the colonies.

2   In 1879, Alexander Forest explored the Fitzroy River and reported that gold might be found there. In 1883, a second government-sponsored expedition included a geologist, Edward Townley Hardman, who reported there was a 'great probability of payable gold being obtained on this part of the Kimberley'.

3   The township of Hall's Creek was not gazetted until 1897 and the apostrophe was not removed until 1914. In 1949, the town was officially shifted 12 kilometres, and the original settlement is now a ghost town of mud-brick buildings.

4   Perth Correspondent, *South Australian Register*, 7 May 1886.

5   Colonial Secretary's Office, State Records Office of Western Australia, 3223/86.

6   *Hobart Mercury*, 13 April 1886; *Northern Territory Times and Gazette*, 1 May 1886.

7   Perth Correspondent, *South Australian Register*, republished in the *Mercury Hobart*, 7 May 1886.

8   *Central Otago Newspaper*, 1 October 1886.

9   Kirwan, p. 33.

10 There is some dispute about when Bayley and Ford became partners. While it has long been accepted that the two met at Croydon in the Gulf of Carpentaria, Ford's daughter, Alice Kathleen Clemenson, wrote in the biography of her father, *William Ford and Coolgardie*, that the two men did not meet until January 1892 in Western Australia, only months before they found gold.

11 Carnegie, p. 2.

12 Ibid., p. 5.

References

13 Ibid., p. 7.

14 Ibid.

15 John Marshall, p. 21.

16 Ibid.

17 Ibid., p. 22.

18 Carnegie, p. 7.

19 Ibid., p. 8.

20 Ibid., pp. 7–8.

21 Ibid., p. 8.

22 Ibid., p. 12.

23 Ibid., p. 20.

24 Ibid., p. 21.

25 Ibid., p. 29.

26 Ibid., p. 32.

27 Ibid., p. 87.

28 Ibid., p. 107.

29 Ibid., p. 112.

30 John Marshall, p. 83.

31 *Menzies Miner*, 25 December 1896, republished in
    Strickland, p. 49.

32 Carnegie was interested in the potential of gold mining in
    the north of the state but also the possibility of an inland
    stock route from the cattle country in the Kimberley
    region of the north to the goldfields in the south. On
    9 July 1896, his party left on a remarkable expedition
    and walked 2000 kilometres through the Great Sandy
    Desert and the Gibson Desert, reaching Halls Creek on
    4 December. Three months later, they left to make the
    return journey and arrived back in Coolgardie in August
    1897, after a 13-month trip that covered almost 5000
    kilometres. Later in 1897, still only 26 years old, Carnegie
    returned to England, where he was honoured with a medal

from the Royal Geographical Society. Shortly after, his book was published and he headed to Nigeria, where he was killed by a poisoned arrow during a skirmish with a local native tribe at Kirifi on 21 November 1900. He was only 30 years old.

[33] John Marshall, p. 79.

[34] Ibid., p. 84.

[35] Keesing, p. 330.

[36] Ibid., p. 331.

[37] Ibid.

[38] *New York Times*, 29 July 1894.

[39] Aspinall, p. 90.

[40] *New York Times*, 24 January 1897.

[41] Calvert, p. 137.

[42] Letter from E. Cam Deland to his parents, 27 June 1895, published in Best, p. 33.

[43] Strickland, p. 7.

[44] Ibid., p. 85.

[45] Two of the original pumping stations were at Mundaring Weir; the others were along the route at Cundering, Merredin, Yerbillon, Ghouli, Gilgai and Dedari.

[46] Western Australian Legislative Assembly, 30 January and 3 February 1902.

[47] *Sunday Times*, 9 February 1902.

[48] Crown Law Department Inquest File, State Records Office of Western Australia, No. 997, Item 976, 1902, TLF Resource R5735.

[49] *West Australian*, 12 December 1899.

[50] Ibid., 14 December 1899.

Chapter Thirteen: Lasseter's Lost Reef

[1] Hubbard, pp. 28–9.

References

2   Lasseter's military records, National Library of Australia,
Series Number B2455, Barcode 3415152.

3   Victorian Public Records Office, ward register unit 9,
VPRS 4527/P.

4   Craig Wilson, The Legend of Lasseter, the Man, www.gold-net.com.au.

5   Lasseter's military records, National Library of Australia
Series Number B2455, Barcode 3415152.

6   Hubbard, p. 35.

7   Ibid.

8   Bailey Papers, Mitchell Library, ML A2753, p. 1. (Other
surviving files suggest Lasseter first saw Bailey in May 1930,
not June.)

9   Coote, p. 10.

10   Ibid., p. 11.

11   Lasseter gave a slightly different account of the story to the
Parkes Advertiser newspaper two years later, on 29 October
1932. According to the newspaper, Lasseter was interviewed
while passing through the town of Parkes in western New
South Wales on the way to Alice Springs to look for the reef.
In this account, Lasseter said that he landed at Townsville
and not Cairns in 1894 and not 1897, and caught the train to
Cloncurry, which was then the end of the railway line, where
he bought a horse, 'stocked up with food, rifle ammunition,
and, turning his face west-south-west, started on his long
trek'.

12   Coote, p. 12.

13   Ibid.

14   Ibid.

15   Ibid.

16   Ibid., p. 13.

17   Ibid., p. 14.

[18] Bailey Papers, Mitchell Library, ML A2753, p. 2.

[19] Charles Ulm and his flying partner Charles Kingsford Smith became popular heroes when they piloted the first flight from California to Australia in 1928. Ulm was born in Melbourne in 1898, enlisted in the army in the First World War and fought at Gallipoli and in France, where he was badly wounded. He died on a flight that disappeared over the Pacific Ocean in 1934.

[20] Coote, p. 18.

[21] Ibid., p. 22.

[22] Balance Sheet for the Central Australian Gold Exploration Company 1930, Bailey Papers, Mitchell Library, ML A2753.

[23] Ibid.

[24] *Canberra Times*, 2 July 1930.

[25] Coote, p. 17.

[26] Blakeley, p. 1.

[27] Ibid.

[28] Ibid., p. 4.

[29] Coote, p. 24.

[30] Coote Papers, National Library of Australia, Series Number B2455, Barcode 3415152.

[31] Blakeley, p. 12.

[32] Central Australian Gold Exploration Company, New South Wales State Records Office, 17/5745, p. 6.

[33] Ibid., p. 8.

[34] Blakeley, p. 12.

[35] Ibid., p. 6.

[36] Ibid.

[37] Coote Papers, New South Wales Library, ML MSLL 7777.

[38] Blakeley, p. 8.

[39] Ilbilba was also known as Ililla, Ililpa and Ilbilla.

[40] Blakeley, p. 9.

[41] Ibid., p. 8.

[42] Ibid., p. 3.

[43] Marshall-Stoneking, p. 26.

[44] Blakeley, p. 47.

[45] Ibid., p. 48.

[46] The fourth cricket Test match between Australia and England was played on 25–29 July 1930 at Old Trafford in Manchester, while the Lasseter expedition was en route from Alice Springs to Ilbilba. Nine days before they had left Alice Springs, on 12 July, Don Bradman had scored his record 334 in the third Test at Headingley in Leeds.

[47] Blakeley, p. 65.

[48] Bailey Papers, Mitchell Library, ML A2753, p. 5.

[49] Blakeley, p. 70.

[50] Ibid., p. 63.

[51] Ibid., p. 60.

[52] Ibid., p. 98.

[53] Ibid., p. 113.

[54] After the collapse of the Lasseter expedition, Johns became a naturalised Australian before returning to Germany, where he attended Nazi instruction school before becoming an active member of the SS. (Two of his brothers were officers in the Luftwaffe.) By 1940, he was in London, where he joined the Mosley fascist blackshirts and was looking at ways to be a saboteur, because he said he wanted to do all he could to help Hitler. He also told British intelligence officers during an interview that he had been active in the fascist movement while in Australia.

[55] They proposed to install a Gypsy Moth II engine to replace the Circus Mark II engine.

[56] Blakeley, p. 116.

[57] Coote, p. 85.

[58] Ibid., p. 86.

59 Ibid., p. 89.

60 Blakeley, p. 137.

61 Ibid.

62 Ibid., p. 136.

63 Ibid., p. 138.

64 Bailey Papers, Mitchell Library, ML A2753, p. 4.

65 Ernestine Hill, *Paul Johns's Statement*, p. 1.

66 Blakeley, p. 149.

67 A similar, though more dramatic, account of Johns's journey with Lasseter appeared in the *Sun* newspaper in Sydney more than two years later, on 9 December 1934, which was said to have been written by Johns. According to the article, 'This is an account of the last four months of Lasseter's life, of which no previous record exists, written by Paul Johns, the only man to see Lasseter during that time, and the last man to see him alive.' The newspaper story is unlikely to have been written by Johns, whose spoken English had only been recently acquired and command of the written language could not have been that developed. However, he may well have cooperated with a journalist in the preparation of the piece, which satisfies the tabloid nature of the story.

68 Ernestine Hill, *Paul Johns's Statement*, p. 6.

69 Ibid., p. 2.

70 Ibid.

71 Ibid.

72 Ibid., p. 3.

73 Ibid.

74 Ibid.

75 Ibid., p. 4.

76 Ibid.

77 Ibid., p. 6.

References

78   Ibid., p. 8.

79   Blakeley, p. 157.

80   Coote, p. 128.

81   Ernestine Hill, *Paul Johns's Statement*, p. 6.

82   CAGE Papers, National Library of Australia, Barcode 68988, p. 105.

83   Blakeley, p. 61.

84   Sandy blight is another name for trachoma, a chronic bacterial eye infection. The disease has been known since ancient Egyptian times and was thought to have been brought to Australia by European settlers. Its symptoms include swollen eyelids, inflammation and redness around the eyes, pain and weeping. Severe cases can lead to blindness. It is spread more widely in unhygienic, hot conditions and by flies.

85   *Sydney Mirror*, 29 April 1931.

86   *Sydney Sun*, 9 December 1934.

87   Bailey Papers, Mitchell Library, ML A2753, p. 6.

88   Ibid.

89   Ibid.

90   Ibid., p. 7.

Bibliography

Aspinall, John, *And Some Found Graves: The Goldfields Diaries of John Aspinall*, Hesperian Press, Carlisle, Western Australia, 1993

Austin, Kenneth Ashurst, *The Lights of Cobb and Co: The Story of the Frontier Coaches, 1854–1924*, Rigby, Adelaide, 1967

Australian Journalist, *The Emigrant in Australia or Gleaning from the Gold Fields*, Addey and Co., London, 1852

Barker, W. H., *The Goldfields of Western Australia*, Simpkin, Marshall, Hamilton, Kent, London, 1894

Bartlett, Robert, *First Gold: Ophir*, K. G. Printers, Orange, New South Wales, 1999

Bate, Weston, *Victorian Goldfields*, McPhee Gribble Penguin, Melbourne, 1988

Bateson, Charles, *Gold Fleet for California: Forty-Niners from Australia and New Zealand*, Urea Smith, Sydney, 1963

Best, Michael R. (ed.), *A Lost Glitter*, Wakefield Press, Adelaide, 1986

Blainey, Geoffrey, *Black Kettle and Fulll Moon: Daily Life in a Vanishing Australia*, Viking, Camberwell, Victoria, 2003

A History of Victoria, Cambridge University Press, Melbourne, 2008

Our Side of the Country: The Story of Victoria, Methuen, Sydney, 1984

The Rush That Never Ended: A History of Australian Mining, Melbourne University Press, Melbourne, 1969

Blake, Leslie James, *Gold Escorts in Australia*, Rigby, Adelaide, 1978

Blakeley, Frederick, *Dream Millions: New Light on Lasseter's Lost Reef*, Mary Mansfield (ed.), Angus & Robertson, Sydney, 1972

Bradfield, Raymond, *Lola Montez and Castlemaine: Some Early Theatrical History*, self-published, Vaughan, Victoria, 1980

Brown, Elaine and John Ferguson, *The Gympie Gold Field 1867–2008*, Gympie Regional Council, 2009

Burke, Keast, *Gold and Silver: Photographs of Australian Goldfields from the Holtermann Collection*, William Heinemann, Sydney, 1973

Butler, Richard, *The Eureka Stockade*, Angus & Robertson, London, 1983

Calvert, Alfred F., *My Fourth Tour in Western Australia*, William Heinemann, London, 1897

Cannon, Michael, *The Roaring Days*, Today's Australian Publishing Company, Mornington, Victoria, 1998

Capper, John, *The Emigrant's Guide to Australia: Containing the Fullest Particulars Relating to the Recently Discovered Gold Fields, the Government Regulations for Gold Seeking, &c.*, George Philip, Liverpool, 1852

Carboni, Raffaello, *The Eureka Stockade: The Consequence of Some Pirates Wanting on Quarter Deck a Rebellion*, J. P. Atkinson and Co., Melbourne, 1855

Carnegie, David, *Spinifex and Sand*, Pearson, London, 1898

Cecil, Lady Gwendolyn, *The Life of Robert, Marquis of Salisbury*, Hodder & Stoughton, London, 1921

Cecil, Lord Robert, *Lord Robert Cecil's Gold Field Diary*, Ernest Scott (ed.), Melbourne University Press, Melbourne, 1933

Bibliography

de Chabrillan, Celeste, *The French Consul's Wife: Memoirs of Celeste de Chabrillan in Gold Rush Australia*, Melbourne University Press, Melbourne, 1998

Chambers, William and Robert, *The Emigrants Manual: Australia and the Gold Diggings*, William and Robert Chambers, Edinburgh, 1852

Chandler, John, *Forty Years in the Wilderness*, Michael Cannon (ed.), Loch Haven Books, Main Ridge, Victoria, 1990

Chen Ta, *Chinese Migrations with Special Reference to Labour Conditions*, Washington, 1923

Clacy, Mrs Charles (Ellen), *A Lady's Visit to the Gold Diggings of Australia in 1852–53*, Hurst and Blackett, London, 1853

Clark, Charles Manning Hope, *A History of Australia*, Vols 1–5, Melbourne University Press, Melbourne, 1980
Selected Documents in Australian History, 1851–1890, Angus & Robertson, Sydney, 1962

Clemenson, Alice Kathleen, *William Ford and Coolgardie: The Biography of My Father, 1849–1932*, Gold Producers Association and Hesperian Press, Perth, 1988

Clement, Cathie, *Old Halls Creek: A Town Remembered*, Western Australia National Heritage, Mount Lawly, 2000

Coates, Loretto M., *The Spec*, self-published, 2001

Coote, Errol, *Hell's Airport and Lasseter's Lost Legacy*, Peterman Press, Sydney, 1934

Corfield, A. H., *Reminiscences of Queensland 1862–99*, A. H. Fater, Brisbane, 1921

Coupe, Robert, *Australia's Gold Rushes*, New Holland, Frenchs Forest, New South Wales, 2000

Crawthorne, William Anderson, *Diary of William Anderson Crawthorne 1849–59*, State Library of New South Wales, MS B230

Curthoys, Ann, 'Men of All Nations, Except Chinamen:

Europeans and Chinese on the Gold Fields of New South Wales', in Iain McCalman, Alexander Cook, Andrew Reeves (eds), *Gold: Forgotten Histories and Lost Objects of Australia*, Cambridge University Press, New York, 2002

Dalrymple, George Elphinstone, *Narrative and Reports of the Queensland North-East Coast Expedition 1874*, Queensland Parliament, 1874–1975, Mitchell Library, RAV FM 4 6 Roll Q 9

Davison, Simpson, *The Discovery and Geognosy of Gold Deposits in Australia*, Longman, London, 1860

Dempsey, Frank, *Old Mining Towns of North Queensland*, Rigby, Adelaide, 1980

Eldred-Grigg, Stevan, *Diggers, Hatters, and Whores: The Story of the New Zealand Gold Rushes*, Random House, New Zealand, 2008

Emilsen, William, *The Goldfield Diaries of William Diaper*, Hesperian Press, Carlisle, Western Australia, 1999

England, Kathryn, *Lasseter the Man, the Legend, the Gold*, Omnibus Books, Norwood, South Australia, 2003

Erskine, James Elphinstone, *A Short Account of the Late Discoveries of Gold in Australia*, T&W Boone, London, 1851

Fauchery, Antoine, *Letters from a Miner in Australia*, Georgian House, Melbourne, 1965

Fayle, Charles Ernest, *A Short History of the World's Shipping Industry*, Allen & Unwin, London, 1933

Ferguson, Charles, *The Experiences of a Forty-Niner, During Thirty Four Years' Residence in California and Australia*, William Publishing Co., Cleveland, Ohio, 1888

Garnsey, Mrs Arthur H., *Scarlet Pillows: An Australian Nurse's Story of Long Ago*, McKeller Press, Melbourne, 1950

Gittins, Jean, *The Diggers From China: The Story of Chinese on the Goldfields*, Quartet Books, Melbourne, 1981

Glasson, William, *The Romance of Ophir: The Discovery of*

Bibliography

Australia's First Payable Gold, Leader, Orange, New South Wales, 1935

Godley, John Robert, *Extracts from a Journal of a Visit to New South Wales in 1853*, reprinted in *Fraser's Magazine*, November and December, 1853

Golden Dragon Museum, *The Walk from Robe*, Golden Dragon Museum, Bendigo, Victoria, 2001

Gympie and District Historical Society, 'Gympie: A Retrospective Reverie', *Gympie Times*, 16 October 1917, republished in *Gympie's Jubilee*, Gympie and District Historical Society, 1985

Hall, William H., *Practical Experiences at the Diggings of the Gold Fields of Victoria*, Effingham Wilson, London, 1852

Hann, William, 'Copy of the Diary of the Northern Expedition Under the Leadership of Mr William Hann', Queensland Parliament, 1873–74, Mitchell Library, RAV FM4 6 Roll Q 8

Hargraves, Edward Hammond, *Australia and its Goldfields*, Ingram and Co., London, 1855

Hassam, Andrew, *Sailing to Australia: Shipboard Diaries by Nineteenth Century Migrants*, Manchester University Press, Manchester, 1994

Higgins, Matthew, *Gold and Water: A History of Sofala and the Turon Goldfields*, Robstar Publishers, Bathurst, 1990

Hill, Ernestine, *Paul Johns's Statement About Lasseter as Told to Ernestine Hill*, Scrivener Press, Adelaide, 1968
The Territory, Angus & Robertson, Sydney, 1951

Hill, William Richard Onslow, *Forty-Five Years' Experience in North Queensland, 1861 to 1905*, H. Pole & Co. Printers, Brisbane, 1907

Hirst, John Bradley, *The Strange Birth of Colonial Democracy: New South Wales 1848–1854*, Allen & Unwin, Sydney, 1988

Holthouse, Hector, *Gympie Gold*, Angus & Robertson, Sydney, 1999

River of Gold: The Story of the Palmer River Gold Rush, Angus & Robertson, Sydney, 1967

Hooper, Colin, *Angor to Zillmanton: Stories of North Queensland's Deserted Towns*, Bolton Print, Townsville, Queensland, 1993

Howitt, Alfred William, *Land, Labour and Gold; or Two years in Victoria*, Longmans, London, 1855

Hubbard, Murray, *The Search for Harold Lasseter: The True Story of the Man Behind the Myth*, Angus & Robertson, Sydney, 1993

Idriess, Ion, *Lasseter's Last Ride: An Epic in Central Australian Gold Discovery*, Sydney, Angus & Robertson, 1973

Jevons, William Stanley, *Letters and Journals of W. Stanley Jevons/Ed. By His Wife*, Macmillan, London, 1886

Jonnes, S. W., *Goldfield Reminiscences*, S. J. Tingay, Castlemaine, 1977

Jupp, James (ed.), *The Australian People: An Encyclopaedia of the Nation, its People and their Origins*, Cambridge University Press, Cambridge, 2001

Just, P., *Australia, or, Notes Taken During a Residence in the Colonies from the Gold Discovered in 1851 till 1857*, Durham and Thomson, Dundee, Scotland, 1859

Keesing, Nancy, *History of the Australian Gold Rushes; By Those Who Were There*, Angus & Robertson, Sydney, 1976

Kennedy, David, *Kennedy's Colonial Travel*, Edinburgh Publishing, Edinburgh, 1876

Kennedy, Edward B., *The Black Police of Queensland*, Murray, London, 1902

Kennedy, Richard, 'Braidwood and District Goldfield 1852', republished in Roslyn Helen Maddrell, 'Braidwood Goldfields 1850s, 1860s', *Tallanganda Times*, Braidwood, 1978

Kerr, John Hunter, *Glimpses of Life in Victoria/By a Resident;*

Bibliography

Introduced by Marguerite Hancock, Miegunyah Press,
Melbourne, 1996

Kirwan, John, *My Life's Adventure*, Eyre & Spottiswoode,
London, 1936

Lang, John Dunmore, *The Australian Immigrants Manual, or,
A Guide to the Gold Colonies of New South Wales and Port
Phillip*, Partridge and Oakley, London, 1852

Lasseter, *Harold Lasseter's Diary*, Mitchell Library, State
Library of New South Wales, N919 4291/4

Lhotsky, John, *A Journey from Sydney to the Australian Alps,
Undertaken in the Months of January, February and March
1834*, J. Innes, Sydney, 1835

Loos, Noel, *Invasion and Resistance: Aboriginal–European
Relations on the North Queensland Frontier 1861–1897*,
Australian National University Press, Canberra, 1982

Lovejoy, V., 'The Things That Unite: Inquests into Chinese
Deaths on the Bendigo Goldfields, 1854–1865', Public Record
Office Victoria, www.prov.vic.gov.au

Lubbock, Basil, *The Colonial Clippers*, James Brown, Glasgow,
1921

Marshall, John, *Battling for Gold*, Bruce and Davies, Melbourne,
1923

Marshall-Stoneking, Billy, *Lasseter: In Quest of the Gold*,
Hodder and Stoughton, Sydney, 1989

Matthews, Tony, *Graves, Gold and Gallows: Crime Calamities
and the Colonial Goldfields*, Central Queensland University
Press, Rockhampton, 2002

Maxwell, Eileen, *Written in Gold: The Story of Gulgong, the
Town on the 10 Dollar Note*, Gulgong Pioneer's Museum, 1970

May, Catherine Rosemary, *Topsawyers: The Chinese in Cairns,
1870–1920*, James Cook University, North Queensland, 1984

Mayne, Alan James, *Hill End: An Historic Australian Goldfields*

Landscape, Melbourne University Press, Melbourne, 2003

McBrien, James, *Traverse of Road from Emu Plains to Bathurst*, New South Wales State Records Office, 2/487 reel 2625

McCalman, Iain, Alexander Cook, Andrew Reves (eds.), *Gold: Forgotten Histories and Lost Objects of Australia*, Cambridge University Press, New York, 2002

McGowan, Barry, *The Golden South: A History of the Araluen, Bell's Creek and Majors Creek Gold Fields*, Capital Fine Print, Canberra, 2000

Melville, Henry Dudley, *Reminiscences of Henry D. Melville*, State Library of South Australia, D 6976 (L)

Menghetti, Diane, *Ravenswood: Five Heritage Trails*, James Cook University, North Queensland, 1992

Miller, Frederick William Gasgoyne, *Historic Central Otago*, Reed, Wellington, 1970

Mitchell, Sir Thomas, *Diary*, Mitchell Library, ML MSS C71, 1851

Geological Report on the Gold Fields in the Counties of Wellington and Bathurst, Sydney, W & B Ford, Sydney, 1852

Moloney, John, *Eureka*, Viking Press, Ringwood, Victoria, 1984

Mossman, Samuel, *The Gold Regions of Australia: A Descriptive Account of New South Wales, Victoria and South Australia, With Particulars of the Recent Gold Discoveries*, William S. Orr and Co., London, 1852

Moye, Daniel George (ed.), *Historic Kiandra: A Guide to the Historic District*, Cooma-Monra Historical Society, Cooma, New South Wales, 1959

Mulligan, James Venture, *From County Down to Down Under: Diary of James Venture Mulligan 1860*, transcribed by Lynette F. McClenaghan, Pat McClenaghan, Armidale, New South Wales, 1991

Bibliography

Mundy, Godfrey, *Our Antipodes, or Residence and Rambles in the Australian Colonies; with a Glimpse of the Goldfields*, Vol. III, Richard Bentley, London, 1852

Nash, Catherine, 'Recollections of the Rush', *Gympie Times*, 16 October 1917, republished in *Gympie's Jubilee*, The Gympie and District Historical Society, 1985

O'Grady, Desmond, *Stages of the Revolution: A Biography of Eureka Stockade's Raffaello Carboni*, Hardie Grant Books, Melbourne, 2004

Pearl, Cyril, *Sydney Revels of Bacchus, Cupid and Momus*, Ure Smith, Sydney, 1970

Preshaw, George O., *Banking Under Difficulties; or Life on the Gold Fields of Victoria, New South Wales and New Zealand*, Edward Dunlop and Co., Melbourne, 1888

Ritchie, Fiona, *Guichen Bay to Canton Lead: The Chinese Trek to Gold*, District Council of Robe, 2004

Rolls, Eric, *The Sojourners; The Epic Story of China's Centuries Old Relationship with Australia*, Queensland University Press, Brisbane, 1992

Rule, Charles Spandry, *From the Burra Mine to the Mount Alexander Diggings*, State Library of South Australia, D7486(L)

Rule, John, *Cradle of a Nation*, Yagoona, New South Wales, 1979

Sadlier, John, *Recollections of a Victorian Police Officer*, Penguin, Melbourne, 1973

Searle, Geoffrey, *The Golden Age: A History of the Colony of Victoria, 1851–1861*, Melbourne University Press, Melbourne, 1963

Sherer, John, *The Gold Finder in Australia: How He Went, How He Fared, and How He Made His Fortune*, Clarke Beeton, London, 1853

Silver, Lynette Ramsay, *Fool's Gold: Wiliam Tipple Smith's Challenge to the Hargraves Myth*, Jacaranda Press, Brisbane, 1986

Skinner, Emily, *A Woman in the Goldfields: Recollections of Emily Skinner, 1854–1878*, Edward Duyker (ed.), Melbourne University Press, Melbourne, 1995

Smeaton, Thomas D., *Our Invasion by the Chinese*, State Library of South Australia, D7477(T)

Stephens, S. E., *The Palmer Goldfields*, Palmer River Historical Preservation Society, New South Wales State Library, ML Q994.3631

Strickland, Barry, *Golden Quest Discovery Trail Guidebook*, Golden West Trails Association, Kalgoorlie, 2003

Testa, Angie, and Bill Decarli, *A Dead Man's Dream: Lasseter's Reef Found*, Hesperian Press, Carlisle, Western Australia, 2005

Thurgood, Noel, *The Gold Escort Robbery Trials*, Southwood Press, Sydney, 1988

Tom, William Jnr and James, John Lister, 'History of the Discovery of the First Payable Gold-field (Ophir) in Australia', *Western Examiner*, New South Wales, 1871, Mitchell Library, 991.6T

Traill, William Henry, *Historic Sketch of Queensland*, Landsdowne Press, Sydney, 1886

Trollope, Anthony, *Australia and New Zealand*, Chapman and Hall, London, 1873

Walshe, Robert Daniel, *The Great Australian Gold Rush and Eureka Stockade*, Literary Productions, Jannali, New South Wales, c.2005

Ward, Russell, *The Australian Legend*, Oxford University Press, Melbourne, 1965

Webber, Kimberley, *Daily Life on the Goldfields*, Macmillan Education, South Yarra, Victoria, 2001

Bibliography

Weitemeyer, Thorvald P., *Missing Friends and Adventures in North Queensland*, T. Fisher Unwin, London, 1892

Welsh, Lionel, *Vermillion and Gold*, Banyan Press, Melbourne, 1984

White, C., *History of Australian Bushranging*, Vols 1 and 2, Landsdowne Press, Sydney, 1975

Whittington, Vera, *Two Fevers, Gold and Typhoid: A Social History of Western Australia During the Decade 1891–1900 Under the Particular Influence of These and Other Related Factors, People and Events*, V. Whittington, Bentley, Western Australia, 1986

Young, Reverend William, 'Report of Conditions of the Chinese Population on the Goldfields', John Ferres, Government Printer, Melbourne, 1868

Index

Index

Index

Index

Index